The Family in Imperial Russia

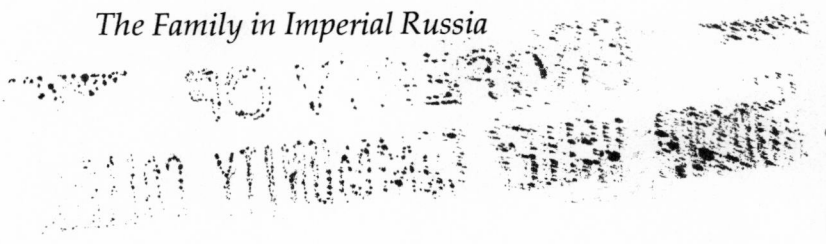

The Family
in Imperial Russia

NEW LINES OF HISTORICAL RESEARCH

Edited by

DAVID L. RANSEL

University of Illinois Press
URBANA CHICAGO LONDON

Bind

LIBRARY OF CONGRESS CATALOGING IN PUBLICATION DATA

Main entry under title:

The Family in Imperial Russia.

Papers presented at a symposium held at the
University of Illinois at Urbana-Champaign in
Oct. 1976.
Bibliography: p.
Includes index.
1.   Family—Russia—History—Congresses.
2.   Social classes—Russia—History—Congresses.
I.   Ransel, David L.
HQ637.F35   301.42'0947   78-17579
ISBN 0-252-00701-8

Baker

5.06

12.22.80

For Terry

Contents

Acknowledgments

Financial support for this project came principally from the National Endowment for the Humanities, with supplementary support and encouragement from the University of Illinois Russian and East European Center. In addition to the present contributors, a number of individuals assisted along the way with advice and commentary. The original symposium meetings in October, 1976, were greatly enlivened and enhanced by the participation and commentary of Barbara Anderson, Ethel Dunn, Ralph T. Fisher, Jr., Maurice Friedberg, Stuart Grover, Max Okenfuss, Demitri Shimkin, Mobin Shorish, and Benjamin Uroff. Special appreciation goes to Marc Raeff, who not only served as a chairman and commentator at the symposium but also gave helpful advice and guidance at several stages of the project. Gera Millar and Olga Aranovsky contributed their linguistic skills in the search for English equivalents of difficult terms in Antonina Martynova's article. Laurence Miller and his excellent staff at the Special Languages Division of the University of Illinois Library also cooperated at every stage of the work; their resources and knowledge greatly strengthened the overall effort. Kathy Forslund helped to photocopy the conference papers and guide the participants to the proper place at the proper time. Kate Michelson applied her bibliographic and editorial talents to the preparation of the manuscript, a task which otherwise would have required twice the time. Ann Lowry Weir of the University of Illinois Press greatly improved the accuracy and readability of several of the papers. To all these people, as well as to others too numerous to mention, the contributors and editor owe a great debt of appreciation.

—D. L. R.

DAVID L. RANSEL

Introduction

Family history, long the province of novelists and genealogists, has
recently attracted the attention of social historians interested in
influences shaping the domestic lives of ordinary people. This
interest has manifested itself in the study of numerous interrelated
problems: household and family structure, geographic and social
mobility, birth control, nutrition, health care, and the evolving
perceptions of various family members' and age groups' roles and
places in society. In exploring these questions, historians have
borrowed techniques from disciplines traditionally concerned with
the family, including demography, anthropology, sociology, psychology, folklore, and medicine. They have also made use of a variety of published and archival source materials (parish records,
household lists, health and sanitation surveys, and others) which
have been neglected in the consideration of more traditional historical problems. As a result, researchers have illuminated the family
from a number of novel perspectives, raised fresh questions, and
opened new lines of inquiry.

At present, most of this work focuses on western Europe and the
United States, with the largest efforts being concentrated on the
early modern era. In this area alone some cherished notions about
the family in past times have already undergone substantial revision. One of the first casualties was the view, frequently posited by
sociologists, of a direct evolution from the extended family of traditional society to the nuclear family of the modern industrial era.
Studies on historical demography by Peter Laslett, E. A. Wrigley,
J. Hajnal, and others have made clear that in America, England,
and many parts of western Europe the nuclear family prevailed
since early modern times and was not the product of industrializa-

tion and urbanization.[1] Moreover, the western demographic transition, signaled by general declines in fertility and mortality, appeared in England and some areas of the Continent well in advance of the modern machine age. A pattern of nuclear families, late marriage, and a large percentage of adults who never married sharply differentiated pre-modern English and western European society from its neighbors in eastern Europe and Russia (as well as from much of the rest of the world), where large joint and complex family households predominated and marriage was early and virtually universal. This has led to speculation that the small conjugal family in the West, far from being a consequence of urban industrial growth, may instead have established the preconditions for it.[2]

These findings have spurred investigations into methods of family limitation in the pre-industrial West and led to discoveries suggesting the widespread use of birth control as early as the seventeenth and eighteenth centuries.[3] Recent studies on infanticide, a method of population control thought to have been in check since late classical times, have shown that this drastic measure reached socially significant levels during much of the Christian era.[4] Indeed, Thomas McKeown argues that the abatement of infanticide in early modern times, along with substantial improvements in nutrition, may have played a central role in the rapid

1. Peter Laslett, *The World We Have Lost* (London, 1965); Peter Laslett and Richard Wall, eds., *Household and Family in Past Time* (Cambridge, England, 1972); E. A. Wrigley, *Population and History* (New York, 1969); J. Hajnal, "European Marriage Patterns in Perspective," in D. V. Glass and D. E. C. Eversley, eds., *Population in History* (London, 1965), pp. 101–146.

2. Recent summaries of the literature on this problem may be found in Tamara K. Hareven, "Modernization and Family History: Perspectives on Social Change," *Signs: Journal of Women in Culture and Society*, 2, no. 1 (1976): 190–206; E. A. Wrigley, "Reflections on the History of the Family," *Daedalus* (Spring, 1977): 71–85. Additional references to recent western works on the family may be found in the bibliography of the present volume.

3. Evidence for the seventeenth century is only scattered, but for the eighteenth century it is quite compelling. Jean-Louis Flandrin, "Contraception, Marriage, and Sexual Relations in the Christian West," in Robert Forster and Orest Ranum, eds., *Biology of Man in History* (Baltimore, 1975), pp. 23–47 (originally published in *Annales E. S. C.*, 1969); Orest and Patricia Ranum, eds., *Popular Attitudes toward Birth Control in Pre-Industrial France and England* (New York, 1972).

4. William L. Langer, "Infanticide: A Historical Survey," *History of Childhood Quarterly*, 1, no. 3 (Winter, 1974): 353–365; Barbara A. Kellum, "Infanticide in England in the Later Middle Ages," *ibid.*, 367–388; Richard C. Trexler, "Infanticide in Florence: New Sources and First Results," *ibid.*, 1, no. 1 (Summer, 1973): 98–116, and the many sources cited therein; Y.-B. Brissaud, "L'infanticide à la fin du moyen age, ses motivations psychologiques et sa répression," *Revue historique de droit francais et étranger*, 50 (1972): 229–256; Emily R. Coleman, "L'infanticide dans le Haut Moyen Age," *Annales E. S. C.*, 29, no. 2 (1974): 315–335.

population growth of that period and generated the social consequences with respect to family structure and industrialization that flowed from it.[5]

While these discoveries have effectively set aside previous sociological theories of family evolution, much still remains to be learned about the relationship of family structure to industrial growth and other social contingencies. Even the seemingly solid findings on the nuclear family in the pre-industrial West have not gone unchallenged. Subsequent research has revealed considerable regional and social variation, as might have been expected in view of the disparate conditions of life among peasants, artisans, merchants, and nobles, as well as in rural and urban settings, which obviously dictated different family and household structures at different times. In particular, recent inquiries employing family life-cycle techniques and household enumeration have called into question some of the earlier conclusions on the nuclear family which were based largely on cross-sectional demographic analysis. Lutz Berkner, for example, demonstrated the limitations of this kind of evidence in a study of an Austrian community through several generations. He found that cyclical configurations in family-building often allowed for the successive appearance of nuclear and extended (stem) forms in the same family.[6] Other scholars have shown that the nuclear family frequently yielded its privacy to lodgers or temporarily co-residing kin, and that the family, especially in the period of transition from village to urban industrial life, sometimes functioned as a unit of a wider kin network of mutual support. The western family may therefore have undergone a number of modifications, including what might be called a regression to certain extended forms, as it moved into the modern industrial era.[7] At any rate, the question seems to be much more complicated than was at first believed.

In addition to studying the directly measurable aspects of family relations, scholars have investigated the more elusive psychological structures or *mentalités*, the internalized rules that govern an

5. Thomas McKeown, *The Modern Rise of Population* (New York, 1976).

6. Lutz K. Berkner, "The Stem Family and the Developmental Cycle of the Peasant Household: An Eighteenth-Century Austrian Example," *American Historical Review*, 77 (April, 1972): 398–418.

7. Lutz K. Berkner, "Recent Research on the History of the Family in Western Europe," *Journal of Marriage and the Family*, 35, no. 3 (1973): 395–405; and the articles by Hareven and Wrigley cited in note 2.

individual's behavior in family and social life. Special attention has been given to sibling and parent-child interaction and to the economic and institutional imperatives of courtship, marriage, and in-law relations, as well as to the roles and behavior appropriate to different age groups at different times. Among other things, researchers have identified the concepts of childhood and youth—in fact, all the ages of man—as historical categories whose meanings have shifted over time. The best-known study is Philippe Ariès's provocative *Centuries of Childhood*, first published in 1960.[8] In arguing that the concept of childhood as a specific stage of development emerged only as late as the seventeenth century, Ariès opened up a new line of inquiry and placed the history of childhood in an entirely new light. More recently, Edward Shorter's *Making of the Modern Family* has asserted the importance of liberated sentiment in producing an early European sexual revolution that accompanied and spurred the urban industrial growth of the late eighteenth and early nineteenth centuries.[9] Although both works have drawn sharp criticism on documentary and methodological grounds, they have at the same time stimulated vigorous discussion and prompted a whole series of fresh inquiries. While a new generation of American and European historians is now putting these first syntheses to the test by plunging into the rich archival materials on western society, others have begun to branch out and establish the discipline in non-western fields.

This volume represents a first step in developing a social history of the family in the Russian area, an undertaking which should be of interest not only to Russian specialists but also to those working on western materials. Despite rapid advances in the study of the western family, the lack of comparative studies from other areas has hampered the articulation of theoretical and synthetic perspectives. Certainly the complex issues involving the relationship of the family to industrialization and urbanization cannot be understood without a knowledge of the process in Russia and eastern Europe, where the pre-modern context differed so radically from that of the West. Investigations in this area should be especially instructive, since the shift from the large co-resident groups typical of pre-

8. Originally in French, *L'Enfant et la vie familiale sous l'ancien régime* (Paris, 1960); trans. R. Baldick as *Centuries of Childhood: A Social History of Family Life* (New York, 1962).

9. *The Making of the Modern Family* (New York, 1975).

4

industrial Russia to the present-day conjugal family units of Soviet Russia was much more extreme than in the West. The Russian situation should, therefore, provide a good testing ground for the small body of theory now in gestation on the European family.

The present collection is predominantly the work of American scholars, a fact that underlines an important interdependence between Soviet and western scholarship on Russian history. Western specialists are to some extent dependent on Soviet research, in the sense that they rely upon documentary collections and monographs published in the USSR for source materials. Yet many have struck out on their own and have made independent contributions in areas that their Soviet colleagues are either unwilling or unable to tackle. This is particularly true in the field of social history, where in recent years pioneering studies by Marc Raeff, Walter Pintner, Michael Confino, and others have raised vital issues still unexplored in Soviet scholarship. In the process, such scholars have stimulated interest and involvement of Soviet researchers in the field.[10]

Family history has not been entirely neglected in the Soviet Union—witness the extensive literature on women's rights—yet it has usually been seen as a secondary, even incidental, problem. Such crucial issues as family structure, age at marriage, birth control, nurture, and child rearing, when mentioned at all, reflect a continuing reliance on impressionistic accounts. Another difficulty stems from the rigid division of labor that exists among Soviet academic disciplines: questions of family life have traditionally been the exclusive concern of ethnographers and have not come under the historian's purview. Ethnographers have produced some excellent historically oriented studies, but their work generally remains close to the present or, at best, goes back only far enough to draw sharp distinctions between pre- and post-revolutionary family relations. Futhermore, the ideological bias of Soviet ethnographers confines them to the conceptual framework of nineteenth-century

10. Marc Raeff, *Origins of the Russian Intelligentsia: The Eighteenth-Century Nobility* (New York, 1966); Walter Pintner, "The Social Characteristics of the Early Nineteenth-Century Russian Bureaucracy," *Slavic Review*, 29, no. 3 (September, 1970): 429–443; Michael Confino, *Domaines et seigneurs en Russie vers la fin du XVIIIᵉ siècle* (Paris, 1963). Important contributions to social history have also appeared in recent American doctoral theses. In addition to those produced by contributors to this volume, at least two others deserve special mention: Brenda Meehan, "The Russian Generalitet of 1730: Towards a Definition of Aristocracy" (University of Rochester, 1970), and Max Okenfuss, "Education in Russia in the First Half of the Eighteenth Century" (Harvard University, 1970).

evolutionary sociology.[11] Scholarship on the pre-revolutionary period would benefit from a broader perspective than that currently employed by ethnographers. Indeed, there is reason to hope that Soviet historians will soon turn their attention to this neglected field of research, as a recent article in a leading Soviet historical journal has pointed to the need for work on the social and psychological dimensions of the Russian family.[12]

In the meantime, American specialists in Russian studies have begun to utilize the perspectives and techniques of the new social history of the family. They are mining the rich collections of published materials on medicine, ethnography, folklore, local history, factory and housing inspection, public welfare and sanitation. Improved access to Soviet archives has made possible the first efforts at family and household reconstitution, promising new insights into the complicated problems of family structure, marriage, fertility, rural-urban migratory patterns, age-specific mortality, and many other little-explored aspects of Russian social development.

By 1976 it was possible to pull together these as yet scattered efforts and put them to the test of critical commentary in a conference setting. Scholars met in October at the University of Illinois in Urbana-Champaign, analyzed one another's work, and developed a basic bibliography on Russian family history. Afterward, they revised their papers for publication in this volume.

11. Lately the Soviets have been mounting a special effort to study working-class life. Among the best examples are the essays in *Etnograficheskoe izuchenie byta rabochikh* (Moscow, 1968), which includes discussions of method and bibliography, and a monograph by V. Iu. Krupianskaia and N. S. Polishchuk, *Kul'tura i byt rabochikh gornozavodskogo Urala (konets XIX—nachalo XX v.)* (Moscow, 1971), containing many tables and items of folklore in the appendices. Among numerous studies of village life, one should mention especially the collaborative work *Selo Viriatino v proshlom i nastoiashchem* (Moscow, 1958), which is available in an abridged English translation by Sula Benet, *The Village of Viriatino: An Ethnographic Study of a Russian Village from before the Revolution to the Present* (Garden City, N.Y., 1970). A recent summary of Soviet ethnography with extensive bibliographic notes may be found in Iu. V. Bromlei and K. V. Chistov, "Osnovnye napravleniia razvitiia sovetskoi entnografii," in *Etnografiia v strankakh sotsializma* (Moscow, 1975), pp. 7–51.

12. I. D. Koval'chenko and N. V. Sivachev, "Strukturalizm i strukturno-kolichestvennye metody v sovremennoi istoricheskoi nauke," *Istoriia SSSR*, no. 5 (September-October, 1976): 60–92. Siberian scholars seem to be leading the way in application of family history techniques, whose rich possibilities are demonstrated in a recent collection edited by M. M. Gromyko and N. A. Minenko, *Iz istorii sem'i i byta sibirskogo krest'ianstva v XVII—nachale XX vv.* (Novosibirsk, 1975), printed unfortunately in a press run of only 500 copies. Further references to Soviet work on historical quantification techniques are listed in the bibliography of the present volume. The participation of Antonina Martynova in this volume is a hopeful sign of the increasing cooperation in this area between American and Soviet scholars.

Good family history must first of all be good social history. Like the best models of western family studies, the essays in this collection are not merely concerned with the evolution of the family itself; rather, they treat the interactions of this basic social institution with the broader economic, political, and intellectual structures of Russian society. It is impossible to make sense out of Russian household and family relations without taking into account the impact of serfdom, the autocracy and its bureaucratic state system, the deep economic and psychological divisions between the poor and the privileged, and the social and intellectual ferment characteristic of nineteenth and early twentieth-century Russia. All the papers in this collection address these questions either implicitly or explicitly. Yet, as is unavoidable at this early stage of research, most of the essays yield only partial and tentative answers to the larger issues under investigation. We are still in the process of clearing the ground, formulating the key problems, and locating the proper sources for further study. Our objectives must therefore be limited. We seek first of all to show the present state of research in the field and to point out some of the directions for new inquiries. Beyond this, we hope that the essays and accompanying bibliography, by providing models and guidelines, will encourage others to undertake similar research. There has been an unfortunate reluctance on the part of Russian experts in the West to devote time and energy to problems of social and quantitative history, stemming no doubt from the difficulties of obtaining adequate source materials. If this collection does no more than allay those fears and demonstrate the opportunities for opening new vistas on Russian social history, it will have performed a valuable service.

A volume of this nature always poses organizational problems. Grouping the essays according to a single principle, be it chronology, methodology, or topic, seldom produces a satisfactory arrangement. Fortunately, in the present case the contributions fall rather neatly into five general categories, some methodological and others topical, which can be set in a broad chronological framework, beginning with the early nineteenth century and moving toward the 1917 Revolution.

The opening section demonstrates the application of psychohistorical techniques and treats the cultural and psychological dimensions of family relations among the nobility, intelligentsia, and imperial household. Since these studies rely heavily on literary sources (memoirs, diaries, child-rearing manuals, and belles-lettres), their subject matter is confined to the educated classes. Jessica Tovrov uses fictional writings to draw out the essential features of mother-child relations among the early nineteenth-century nobility. Barbara Alpern Engel, working in the same period, details the close affective bonds and resulting intellectual influence characteristic of mother-daughter relations among the intelligentsia. Richard Wortman focuses directly on the imperial family and traces the shift in the mothering role from the incorporation of stern masculine values in the early nineteenth century to a more affective, feminized imperial upbringing toward the end of the tsarist period. All three studies emphasize the strict division of male and female spheres in the traditional Russian household, as well as the impact of western models and influences in modifying traditional upper-class child-rearing patterns.

The remaining essays deal with the lower social orders. In the second section, on marriage and household, Andrejs Plakans explores the methodological problems of using household lists. In the process he identifies the phenomenon, apparently widespread in the Baltic province of Kurland, of placing children in non-parental households—a practice already known from some western European studies, and one that raises important questions about peasant household formation and community solidarity. In another pioneering study using both household lists and parish records, Peter Czap, Jr., follows the upward shift in age at first marriage on serf estates in central Russia during the first half of the nineteenth century; this change elucidates the joint family structure of the Russian peasant household and suggests a significant demographic transition in progress well before the emancipation of the serfs in 1861. Gregory L. Freeze likewise takes the mid-century reform era as a point of reference in discussing changes in the status of clerical families, the social stratum that most nearly approximated a caste group in pre-Reform Russia. He carefully delineates the various factors, from the internal dynamics of the clerical family to central government reform measures, that combined to open this caste and link it more firmly to the broader community.

Folklore and ethnography offer additional approaches to understanding the peasant household and are especially helpful in uncovering family relationship structures deeply imbedded in Russian culture and persistent over long periods of time. The essays by Stephen P. Dunn and Antonina Martynova reveal both the possibilities and the limitations of work in this area. In searching out the relationships characteristically expressed in folktales and epic songs, Dunn finds that these genres reflect a perhaps uniquely Russian system involving two separate sets of values—one female and the other male—which may relate to the strict division of the household sphere already noted in the psycho-historical essays. Antonina Martynova's study, based upon transcripts of 1,800 peasant lullabies, provides an intimate view of the daily life of the village and sketches certain characteristic features of the peasant mother's relationship to her child and to other family members, as well as analyzing the links between lullabies and primitive magical incantations.

Apart from statistical and ethnographic materials, the best sources on pre-revolutionary peasant life come from the field reports and diaries of physicians and welfare officials whose jobs regularly took them to peasant homes and villages. The essays in the fourth section draw on these long-neglected sources. My own article examines the rural-urban economic nexus underlying the care of abandoned and unwanted infants, showing how the children were used as commodities in a widespread traffic worked by poor village women to earn supplementary income. Samuel C. Ramer describes government efforts to train peasant midwives and analyzes the reasons for their failure and the resistance of villagers to modern obstetric care. Nancy M. Frieden investigates the efforts of physicians to improve child care practices through hygiene education and the establishment of rural nurseries. These studies are concerned with different methods used to check the unusually high infant mortality in Russia. Their findings illustrate the widely divergent attitudes of officials, intelligentsia, and peasants toward the value and nature of health care.

The two final papers feature the urban workforce and employ quantitative analysis in treating various behavioral correlates of labor migration, a central characteristic of the turn-of-the-century urban working class in Russia and elsewhere. Robert Eugene Johnson discusses the impact of labor migration on household formation in the migrants' home province and suggests its possible influence in reinforcing traditional family patterns and agricultural inefficiency. He also evaluates the possible effects of age- and sex-specific migration patterns in retarding the full assimilation of migrants into the urban workforce. Diane Koenker's study of urban working-class families and youth groups during the 1917 Revolution in Moscow points up the important role of youth socializing and romance in fostering political association.

There are many other issues that the contributors to this collection could not treat, or even begin to raise. We hope others will be encouraged to take them up. In particular, much more needs to be done on the basic demographic parameters of Russian social history, including such central questions as fertility, birth control, age-specific morbidity and mortality, sex ratios for different age groups, social classes, and geographic settings. We owe the beginnings of quantitative study on household and family structure to two of the authors represented in this volume, yet further investigations of households in various regions, time periods, and economic and social settings are required before useful comparisons and conclusions can be made. Questions of age role definition still remain to be posed, let alone resolved. Not only are such categories as childhood and youth poorly understood; except for scattered ethnographic materials, next to nothing is known about the role of the elderly in Russian families. While a good deal of impressionistic evidence exists on courtship and marriage—matters closely regulated by family and community in peasant society—attempts to analyze the content of these relations for comparative study or to set them in a quantitative framework with respect to age of menarche, age at first marriage, nuptial frequency, and fertility have scarcely begun. Bio-history, or the study of nutritional needs, diet, and their relation to morbidity, is now a recognized field in the West. If McKeown is right, it may be the key to explaining the "population explosion" of pre-industrial Europe, which affected not only the West but, with a slight lag, Russia as well. Sufficient data on Russian household budgets and on economic and medical statistics are available to give one hope that this field will undergo rapid development in the near future.

The bibliography in this volume, compiled by June Pachuta and Harold M. Leich, provides an introduction to basic reference sources and major monographs available for starting work in this field. We invite students and scholars specializing in Russian studies to take up these tools and embark upon this new and challenging field of historical research.

NOTE ON DATES AND TRANSLITERATION

Unless otherwise specified, all dates follow the Julian calendar, which in the nineteenth century ran twelve (and, in the twentieth century, thirteen) days behind the Gregorian. In some cases both dates are provided. The transliteration of Russian titles in the footnotes follows the modified Library of Congress system, with pre-1918 orthography updated in conformity with present-day Soviet practice. In the bibliography the original orthography of pre-1918 publications is retained, as is the full Library of Congress transliteration system (minus ligatures), in the interests of facilitating identification of materials in American library catalogs.

Archival citations in the footnotes employ the following standard Soviet abbreviations: f. = *fond*, op. = *opis'*, g. = *god*, otd. = *otdelenie*, st. = *stol*, k. = *karton*, razd. = *razdel*, d. = *delo*, ch. = *chast'*, l. and ll. = *list, listy*, ob. = *oborotnaia storona*.

Section One

Psychological Dimensions
of Family Relations

JESSICA TOVROV

Mother-Child Relationships among the Russian Nobility

From the opening sentence, Tolstoi's *Anna Karenina* concerned itself with the family and, more explicitly, with the problem of family happiness. The novel's immediate popularity, coupled with the controversy it provoked over women's place in society and the family, reflect the extent to which the problem of family roles was vital to Tolstoi's generation of the Russian nobility and educated classes. This paper will discuss and analyze the prominent features of mother-son and mother-daughter relationships within Russian noble families from the late eighteenth century to the era of the Great Reforms, when Tolstoi wrote. Attention will be given chiefly to the interaction between the social norms and the typical patterns of actual behavior in the mother-child relationships. During the time discussed here, changes took place both in actual behavior and in the norms themselves. Consequently, the individual had to cope not only with tensions arising from attempts to reconcile the ideal with the less than ideal, but also with tensions arising from the changing nature of the ideal itself.

Although this study is primarily concerned with maternal relationships, these clearly were only part of a larger family context. It will be well, therefore, to begin with a general discussion of the Russian noble family. The family in Russian noble society was a focus of intense loyalty and emotion.[1] Its members perceived it as

1. Sources for this study include household and child-rearing manuals, exhortations to children, pedagogical books and articles, memoirs, diaries, letters, fictional works for both children and adults, and travelers' commentaries. The pedagogical and child-rearing works and the exhortations to children are usually prescriptive. Memoirs, letters, diaries, and belletristic works provide particular conceptions of reality, of which normative standards are an important part. Norms in these descriptive works are presented no less powerfully for being implicit rather than explicit. Belletristic works (perhaps especially in Russian litera-

an organic whole whose sum was greater than a simple conglomeration of dyadic relationships. While they were important, dyadic relationships within the family were not expected to be complete in themselves or to stand alone. It was assumed that individuals in an extended or joint family (usually the preferred type) would find, in the family unit, the satisfactions and fulfillment lacking in any particular relationship.

A prominent feature of family and kinship structure throughout Russian society was its porosity and flexibility. Roles and relationships usually could be established or terminated by the performance or non-performance of appropriate behavior. If X was not a blood relative of Y but acted as if he were, Y would probably feel more closely related to X than to Z, a blood relative who acted as if he were not.[2] This flexibility of family roles and relationships has been well established for the pre-revolutionary peasantry. As Shimkin and Sanjuan point out, "The peasant household was above all a work unit so that non-contributing family members (e.g., drafted sons) might lose all rights while unrelated contributors could become exclusive heirs."[3] Referring to all nineteenth-century Russians, Friedrich writes that the familiar pronoun *ty* (thou) often indicated common experience—being classmates, revolutionary conspirators, etc. "At a more profound level, this usage was the felt extension of a kinship bond."[4] Writing in the middle of the last century, Baron von Haxthausen confirmed this view. "The Russian cannot live without a strong family tie. If he has none, he invents one; if he has no father he searches for and chooses one for himself and has the same veneration and affection for him as for a parent . . . if he has no children of his own he adopts some."[5] Among the peasantry, the most important criteria for establishing

ture) often choose as subject matter the difficulties involved in actualizing normative standards. When used in conjunction with the memoirs, diaries, and letters, these works can be quite informative about deviations from and attitudes toward norms.

2. For a thorough discussion of the concepts of behavioral definition and natural definition, see David M. Schneider, *American Kinship: A Cultural Account* (Englewood Cliffs, N.J., 1968).

3. D. Shimkin and P. Sanjuan, "Culture and World View: A Method Analysis Applied to Rural Russia," *American Anthropologist*, 55 (1953): 329.

4. Paul Friedrich, "Structural Implications of Russian Pronominal Usage," in *Sociolinguistics*, ed. William Bright (Los Angeles, 1966), p. 239.

5. Baron von Haxthausen, *The Russian Empire*, trans. Robert Farie (London, 1856), p. 103.

relationships were joint work and joint living arrangements. Among the nobility the important criteria included these considerations; in addition, other behavior defined as appropriate to a particular relationship was also involved.

This emphasis on behavioral definitions produced a certain flexibility and mobility in the family. On the other hand, a strict division between the sexes with clearly delineated spheres of competence for each provided counteracting rigidity. The depth of this sexual separation has again been well documented for the peasantry, whose eating arrangements, methods of inheritance, and rights to personal possessions were often governed by sex roles.[6] Although less marked than among the peasantry, significant outward manifestations of this sexual division also existed among the nobility. Sir Donald MacKenzie Wallace noted in 1877 that "the rigorous separation of the sexes, which formed a characteristic trait of old Russian society, has long since disappeared, but its influence may still be traced in houses built on the old model . . . having at the one end the male apartments, at the other the female apartments, and in the middle the neutral territory, comprising the dining room and the salon."[7] The division of the home into male and female quarters and the explicit transition of sons at age seven from the female to the male sphere (discussed below) were the most dramatic examples of the division between the sexes. Yet the more frequent use of the pronoun *ty* between persons of the same sex[8] and the occasionally observed practice of men and women eating different foods at the same meal reveals that the division extended into many areas of family life.

The emotional distance between men and women, the perception of the limited possibilities of cross-sexual communication and understanding, can be seen in many ways. During the 1770s a recently widowed woman sent her sons to live with a male friend but kept her daughter with her at home.[9] Almost a century later the writer Alexander Herzen kept his son with him after his wife's death

6. See esp. Friedrich, "Structural Implications"; *idem*, "An Evolutionary Sketch of Russian Kinship," *Proceedings, American Ethnographic Society*, 1962; *idem*, "Semantic Structure and Social Structure: An Instance from Russian," in *Explorations in Cultural Anthropology*, ed. Ward H. Goodenough (New York, 1964); Shimkin and Sanjuan, "Cultural and World View."
7. Donald MacKenzie Wallace, *Russia* (New York, 1961), p. 118.
8. Friedrich, "Structural Implications," p. 230.
9. Anna Evdokimovna Labzina, *Vospominaniia* (St. Petersburg, 1903), p. 20.

but entrusted the upbringing of his daughters to a female friend.[10] A children's story suggested that the epitome of disorganization in a particular home was manifested by the brothers fighting among themselves and the sisters fighting among themselves, with no reference to brother-sister fights.[11]

Time brought noticeable changes, however. As Wallace pointed out, by the mid-nineteenth century the strict physical division between the sexes diminished. Homes were less likely to be sexually divided; socializing with family and friends more frequently included both sexes. Even so, the division between the sexes continued to be an important part of the emotional atmosphere. In his 1843 child-rearing manual, Grum warned parents that girls and boys (even within the same family) should not have too much to do with each other, as girls might acquire masculine mannerisms and boys feminine ones.[12] Tolstoi, who understood women well, wrote in 1853, "Nothing can be more ludicrous than the feminine view of a man's life. . . . In the woman's sphere, on the contrary, a woman author has an enormous advantage over us."[13] The physical restructuring of a house obviously failed to eradicate the profound emotional separation of the sexes.

Another element that promoted rigidity within the family was the value placed on authority. This, too, was modified with time; by the mid-nineteenth century, a person in authority should have felt greater pressure to explain his/her decisions. In 1843, while explaining the considerable importance still attached to authority per se, Grum also stressed the responsibilities of an authority figure.

> The father should earn the love and respect of his children and servitors to such a degree that they both love and fear him, and so serve and obey him unquestioningly. The father can attain this only when the whole family is united, and every individual member is convinced that all the injunctions, instructions, and demands of the head of the family are inclined only to the good and well-being of the children and of the family as a whole.[14]

When considered along with the separation of the sexes, this con-

10. Alexander Herzen, *Byloe i dumy* (Moscow, 1967), II, 454.
11. "Dobraia doch' zameniaet mat'," *Drug detei* (Moscow), 1809, p. 409.
12. Konstantin Grum, *Rukovodstvo k vospitaniiu* (St. Petersburg, 1843–45), III, 385–386.
13. L. N. Tolstoi, *Dnevnik, Polnoe sobranie sochinenii* (Moscow and Leningrad, 1928–58), XLVI, 179–180.
14. Grum, *Rukovodstvo k vospitaniiu*, II, 363–364.

tinuing, albeit diminished, stress on authority reflected the family's larger division into two hierarchies, one male and one female. Each had its own sphere of competence and its own responsibilities, and these rarely overlapped.

Marriage was a central event in the culture of the Russian nobility, involving not just the marriage partners but many other people as well. A mother had an especially important role to play, together with a heavy emotional investment in both her son's and her daughter's marriages. An analysis of the impact of marriage on the mother-son and mother-daughter relationships therefore requires some preliminary comment on the general norms pertaining to marriage.

Marriages were sometimes arranged for interest *(raschet)*. While such marriages were not shameful, they also were not ideal. For some time love had been the ideal reason for marriage. In 1775 a husband, praising himself and defending his relations with his wife, emphasized that he had married her "only for love, entirely without a dowry."[15] Some fifty years later Tatiana Passek turned down a suitor of whom she was quite fond because, as she wrote in her memoirs, "I feel it is necessary to love other than I love [this suitor] in order to marry."[16] Later, when she was about to marry a man she loved deeply, she wrote, "He loves me—this is enough [for marriage]."[17] A father in Pisemskii's novel *The Simpleton* paid obeisance to the same ideal while defying it in practice. After browbeating his daughter into agreeing to marry a man she did not like, he piously declared to the suitor, "Your fate depends entirely upon our daughter's choice. We have no right to exercise force. . . . The voice of the heart is the one to be listened to in such matters."[18]

Although the ideal marriage throughout the nineteenth century was based on love, there was a shift over time in terms of practice. Literary sources suggest that, among the middle and lower levels of nobility, purely romantic considerations were playing a larger role by mid-century. In a story published in 1804, a father told his

15. *Arkhiv kniazia Vorontsova* (Moscow, 1895), XXXIV, 408.
16. Tatiana Passek, *Iz dal'nikh let; Vospominaniia* (Moscow, 1963), I, 378.
17. *Ibid.*, p. 379.
18. A. F. Pisemskii, *Tiufiak*, in *Sochineniia* (Moscow, 1956), I, 287–288. There were, of course, exceptions, and while most parents did not feel that they had a right to dismiss love considerations with absolute impunity, some did just that. One such person was the guardian aunt of Natalie Herzen. In 1839 she tried unsuccessfully to force Natalie into a loveless marriage, firm in the conviction that she was acting in Natalie's best interest. Passek, *Iz dal'nikh let*, II, 263–264.

daughter that she could not marry the man she loved because he was poor, without rank, and a social nobody *(neznaten)*. Early in the century this attitude did not define one as a bad father.[19] However, *Ol'ga*, a novel published in 1840, questioned the position of a father who forced his daughter to marry the man of his choice, rather than the man she loved. His wife felt compelled to apologize for him to their daughter; she explained that, contrary to appearances, the father truly had the daughter's happiness foremost in his mind.[20] But this change, while important, should not be overemphasized. In *The Family Chronicle* Sergei Aksakov gives us an example of the importance attached to love in the 1760s. A man of the middle nobility who sought to marry a girl for her money found it useful to impress her relatives with his great love for her.[21] After granting permission, the relatives justified their decision on the basis of the love between the couple.[22] The shifting emphasis on love meant that the attitudes of the marriage partners and their families toward various factors in the marriage decision may not have been in harmony. Such a situation undoubtedly added to the stress involved in the already delicate matter of arranging a marriage.

Along with the greater emphasis placed on love as a reason for marrying, marriage grew to be viewed as a bond uniting the husband and wife only, not their two families. While love had long been the nobility's ideal (if not their reality) in a marriage, the shift in emphasis from the extended family bond to the husband-wife bond involved a change in the ideal as well as in the reality. During the first half of the nineteenth century two norms of loyalty influenced the attitudes and behavior of the Russian nobility. One held that marriage did not so much create a new family as extend one or both of the already existing families, especially the husband's. In this definition of marriage, the parent-child (parent-son) tie took precedence over the husband-wife tie, and married children (sons) should continue to relate to their parents as obediently as they had during their childhood. An article on "Children's Duties to their Parents" exhorts married adults "not to undertake anything without first seeking the advice of your aging parents. . . ."[23]

19. "Neschastnyi Ma-v," *Zhurnal dlia milykh* (Moscow), 1804, p. 102.
20. Dmitrii M. Begichev, *Ol'ga* (St. Petersburg, 1840) part 2, p. 144.
21. Sergei Aksakov, *Semeinaia khronika* (Vienna, 1922), p. 105.
22. *Ibid.*, p. 112.
23. *Drug iunoshestva*, (Moscow, 1807), p. 110.

However, the second definition of marriage, which gradually developed in the nineteenth century, held that the husband and wife had established a new emotional unit consisting of themselves and their children, and that their ultimate loyalty should be to this unit. This definition carried with it the idea that the husband and wife were final authorities within this new emotional unit, responsible to no one but each other, God, and the tsar. Begichev's *Ol'ga* illustrates one aspect of this norm. One woman was advising another about her plan to move in with her daughter and son-in-law: ". . . you are taking upon yourself an important and difficult duty. Try to conduct yourself in such a manner that in no way will you be a burden to your son-in-law. Master patience, act with the greatest caution; in the smallest unpleasantness, inevitable in joint living arrangements, do not enter into any conflicts between husband and wife; support neither one side or the other; don't take upon yourself the role of arbiter or peacemaker."[24]

While increasing importance was given to the second definition of marriage, this remained a matter of emphasis only, not of the complete substitution of one for the other. Very few individuals were capable of discarding either one of these definitions of marriage.[25] The most common resolution involved a gradual shift in loyalty to the new family unit. The tempo of the shift depended on which definition was more meaningful to the people involved. Claims of loyalty from members of one's natal family could rarely be dismissed altogether, even if they seriously conflicted with claims from one's family of procreation. One writer exhorted his readers, "Brothers and sisters! There will come a time when one of your family will create another family. Such a separation, while it will weaken your ties somewhat, must never entirely break them."[26] This ambivalence was reinforced by the presence of many people with a vested interest in the marriage (a wife, a husband, and various relatives of each), and each individual had his/her own views and feelings about questions that arose. This complexity could—and frequently did—result in conflict, hurt feelings, and misunderstandings.

24. Begichev, *Ol'ga*, I, 193.
25. One fictional person who could make such a choice was Elena, heroine of Ivan Turgenev's *Nakanune* (Berlin, 1919), who left her parents to join her husband as a freedom fighter and said that her love for her husband had made her country and her family no longer her own (p. 412). Other Turgenev heroines take similar positions.
26. "Obiazannosti srodnikov odnikh k drugim," *Drug iunoshestva*, p. 124.

Jessica Tovrov

MOTHER-SON RELATIONSHIPS

Although Russian culture was permeated with hierarchical and authoritarian relationships, hierarchy and authority were not central to the mother-son relationship. A son, regardless of age, was expected to defer to his mother's wishes out of respect for her position and age; however, a mother seldom served as a real authority figure to her son after the earliest years of his childhood. Ideally, those who wielded effective power over the boy, who taught and punished him, who organized his life and decided his future, and certainly those who served as role models, were all men. The mother was peripheral to most activities in his life that were considered "important." Like most relationships between persons of opposite sex, the mother-son relationship was expected to be non-task oriented, relatively unstructured and non-authoritarian, and to allow more room for the expression of idiosyncratic personality traits than was the case with same-sex relationships.

The norm of the mother-son relationship called for the two to be loving and expressive; this norm was usually realized in actual behavior. The author of *Letter to One Mother on the Education of her Daughter* (1804) noted that mothers were more tender with and apt to spoil their sons, and fathers their daughters.[27] In general, judgment and criticism were out of place for both parties in the mother-son relationship, which should instead be characterized by tolerance and indulgence. Expressions and demonstrations of affection were prescribed, as were mutual confidences of a personal nature. Impersonal, serious discussions were not expected, and, while not wrong, would at least be considered odd. The attitude presented in a journal of pedagogically and morally instructive stories for children, *Friend of Youth*, is typical. Its 1807 edition included 15 stories in the form of conversations, all of which touched on serious subjects. Not a single conversation was between a mother and son.[28]

However, until the boy reached the age of seven or so, the ideal mother-son relationship was not the one of expressiveness and

27. *Pis'mo k odnoi materi o vospitanii docheri ee* (Moscow, 1804), p. 153.
28. *Drug iunoshestva.* Of the fifteen stories, four are between a father and son, four between a mother and daughter, two between a father and daughter, three between a male teacher and male pupil, one between an old man and a youth, and one between a mother and a governess.

indulgence just mentioned.[29] During this period the mother was, in fact, her son's legitimate authority and bore final responsibility for him. An 1807 article advised parents that "a mother must prepare her son for what he can learn from his father, and she must instill in him the beginnings of a feeling for justice, love of work, diligence, and charity."[30] Usually a noblewoman had a nurse or governess to help care for and train her children, but this did not diminish her responsibility. A mother should strictly oversee caretakers, as she alone was ultimately accountable for her son's training. "It is a mistake to think that being rich frees us from housekeeping duties. . . . It is imperative that tutors and governesses be supervised by the mother of the family herself," wrote one author.[31]

A mother's sense of responsibility for her son inhibited any tendency toward over-indulgence. Her desire to see him properly trained, her understanding of her role in this process, and the importance of stressing the seriousness of this training usually made a mother emphasize her position as her son's authority at the expense of an overtly affectionate relationship. Even if she felt less than the prescribed involvement with and responsibility for her son, a mother would still be aware that an overly indulgent relationship did not meet with social approval.[32]

29. It would be misleading to suggest that there was a specific age at which boys were always transferred to the male sphere, or even that there was one age that everyone agreed was proper for this transition. In *O vospitanii iunoshestva* (Moscow, 1807), Ivan Bogdanovich indicated that he thought the best time for this transition was when the boy was three (pp. 60–62). Pisemskii, in *Tiufiak*, ironically stated, "He had his own ideas about education which we find fairly correct: he believed that up to the age of ten a boy ought to live with his mother and receive a purely physical education, that is should sleep twenty hours a day, eat enormous quantities of potatoes, and play ball or ninepins half an hour a day for the development of his muscles. At the age of eleven he should be taken in hand by his father or tutor and made to learn by heart weighty tomes containing the grammar and vocabularies of ancient languages, besides a few dozen textbooks of various sorts" (I, 365). Tolstoi discussed his feelings at leaving the feminine sphere at the age of five, and the emotional difficulties involved ("Pervye vospominaniia," *Detstvo, otrochestvo, i iunost'* [Moscow, 1914], p. 259). I chose seven as a fairly typical age for this important break because it is the age most frequently mentioned in both prescriptive and descriptive sources. Grum, *Rukovodstvo k vospitaniiu*, II, 374, and Ekaterina Avdeeva, *Polnaia khoziaistvennaia kniga* (St. Petersburg, 1868), II 157, both mentioned seven as the optimal age for the boy's transition. The frequent mention of seven as the transitional age in belletristic works suggests that this was the expected and approved age for this move.

30. "Obiazannosti roditelei k detiam," *Drug iunoshestva*, pp. 122–123.

31. Ekaterina Avdeeva, *Ruchnaia kniga russkoi opytnoi khoziaiki* (St. Petersburg, 1845), p. ii.

32. Usually the nurse provided indulgence and overt affection for children of both sexes

This situation should (and usually did) change when, at about age seven, the boy made one of the most important transitions of his life—from the female to the male sphere. He was now supervised by men instead of women, and the transition frequently entailed a change in living quarters. Friedrich points out that at this age children, especially boys, switched from "thou" to "you" with their mothers, thus increasing the emotional distance between them, although some children of the upper aristocracy may have always used "you" with both parents. [33] In addition, the boy usually started his formal education around this time, so that his life became more organized and structured. Some of the poignancy involved in this transition is seen in an anonymous poem entitled "Greetings on the New Year from a son transferred to his father's guidance in the presence of his mother-teacher."

> Yesterday mama said to me
> That to daddy I was transferred
> She showed me the way to him
> And in him I will find mama.
> In his presence I will not be separated from you
> I will not forget your words
> You rule my soul
> With you is my *first love*
> All day and every moment
> I will repeat in my heart
> She gave me my first lessons
> My teacher and mother. [34]

With this reorganization of the boy's life, the cultural norm of expressive indulgence in the mother-son relationship emerged unfettered. The mother could now cease being an authority to her son. Sternness no longer had a place in the relationship; instead, she was expected to be indulgent and affectionate with him. Although the change of living quarters and the appearance of a male tutor were quick, if not easy, transitions in the boy's life, the mother's recession as authority figure usually took some time, perhaps years, to accomplish. If achieved by the time the son

---

at this point. The child's relationship with his or her nurse was an important and interesting one, too complex to receive a fair treatment in this short paper.

33. Friedrich, "Structural Implications," p. 234.

34. *Nezabudochka* (Moscow), 1826. Italics in text.

reached adolescence, it was acceptable. Occasionally, in opposition to the cultural norm, a woman would maintain an authoritarian role with her son until his adulthood or perhaps throughout her life. Saltykov-Shchedrin's mother for example, continued to run her sons' lives (and without the excuse of being a widow), but such a situation was neither normative nor typical.

After the boy was transferred to the male sphere, ideally, and usually in fact, the mother and son had few activities or concerns in common and encountered each other only in fairly limited contexts. They nevertheless remained important figures in each others' lives; consequently, projection and idealization tended to shape their attitudes toward one another. Projection and idealization were to some extent encouraged by the cultural norm calling for uncritical love between the two. The son in particular was encouraged to see his mother as the embodiment of virtue. Her basic virtue, in his eyes, was usually martyrdom; prototypically, the pain she had endured at his birth. Many elements in the son's emotional environment encouraged him to view his mother as having suffered for his sake. As Grum wrote in his handbook on child-rearing, "It is impossible to calculate all the physical and spiritual suffering which women must endure at the time or pregnancy, childbirth, and nursing."[35] Andrei Bolotov told how, as a boy of twelve, he received the admonition of his dying father to "love and honor [your mother] as long as she lives; she gave birth to you and reared you and shed many tears over you. . . ."[36] The tsarevich Konstantin Pavlovich also found the image of a man's mother suffering on his account to be a moving one. Addressing his officers in 1816 he said, "I love you . . . If I have made you unhappy, the weeping of your mothers will call to my heart."[37]

Shame and guilt often figured importantly in the mother-son relationship. Shame was commonly used in child-rearing from a very early age. S. L. Tolstoi depicted a typical scene in which a mother told her six-year-old son that she would be very ashamed of him if, when he read aloud in front of her friends, he read as poorly as some chidren did.[38] But shame as a method of control was not limited to the son's early years. After the boy's transfer to the male

35. Grum, *Rukovodstvo k vospitaniiu*, I, 57.
36. Andrei Bolotov, *Zapiski* (St. Petersburg, 1871), II, 119.
37. Nikolai Verigin, "Zapiski," *Russkaia Starina*, 1893, p. 417.
38. *Mat' i ded Tolstogo* (Moscow, 1958), p. 118.

sphere, the mother employed less explicit statements ("Wouldn't you be ashamed if. . .?" instead of "How stupid you are!") as an indirect but usually effective method of control.

Guilt, a corollary of the mother's "martyrdom," was rarely significant until the son had entered the male sphere, and it was usually an indirect (rather than direct) means of control. Ivan Turgenev's mother was expert at inculcating guilt feelings in her sons. When Ivan went abroad as a young man, she wrote him highly emotional letters telling him of her unhappiness in his absence and describing herself as "completely orphaned."[39] Although she failed to win his return home, she successfully instilled a heavy burden of guilt. As he later wrote, "It was so easy for her to force us to love her and take pity on her."[40]

The relative proportions of shame or guilt in any particular relationship are practically impossible to sort out;[41] each had a place in the Russian noble family. Whether shame, guilt, or some combination of the two predominated in a son's relationship with his mother, its role after the son had left the female sphere was much the same. Because a mother should not exert much authority over her son after his earliest years, she could influence him most effectively by manipulating these emotions. While child-rearing manuals do not mention these techniques, literary sources indicate that no stigma was attached to their use.

Another important aspect of the mother-son relationship was the son's use of his mother as intercessor after he had moved to the male sphere. In the Russian family, a common and often prescribed method of gaining the cooperation or consent of another person was through the intercession of a third person. Generally the most acceptable and most effective intercessor was someone with whom the pleader was not too closely identified. In other words, a sibling of the same sex and close in age would be a poor choice, while a person of another sex and another generation (preferably older, so as to add status) would make a good choice. Thus a boy would do well to choose his mother as intercessor and, if the request was at all reasonable, she would comply.

Like any other intercessor, a mother might fail to accomplish her

39. Nikolai Bogoslovskii, *Turgenev* (Moscow, 1959), p. 45.

40. *Ibid.*, p. 177.

41. Gerhard Piers and Milton Singer discuss the difficulty in distinguishing the two in *Shame and Guilt* (Springfield, 1953).

purpose, or the son's request might be so outlandish as to convince her that intercession was impossible or improper. When she could not successfully intercede for him, she could and should at least provide him with a refuge emotionally distant from demands of the male world that made him feel inadequate or confused. She should give her son solace and comfort and assure him that he was loved and approved of unconditionally. A mother's ideal role was to serve her son, in the poet Nekrasov's words, as a "guardian angel."[42] Memoirs and literary works like Tur's *Niece*,[43] in which the heroine consistently provided an emotional refuge for her son, suggest that mothers commonly played this role.

Some mothers found the role of guardian angel unappealing. Instead of adoration, they inspired awe and, although rarely admitted, sometimes even fear and hatred. Domination by a mother occurred most frequently when the father was either dead or continually absent and no other man was available to assume an adult male role. In these circumstances the mother usually felt obliged to abandon some aspects of her role as a mother in order to assume aspects of a household head.

Emotionally difficult as it was for a son (of any age) to rebel against his father in nineteenth-century Russia, rebellion against an authoritarian mother was perhaps even more difficult. Cultural norms strongly enjoined him to view his mother as a virtuous ideal who had suffered for his sake. Coming to terms with this conception of motherhood could, in itself, be hard. In addition, a son might feel that his mother was not living up to this ideal of motherhood, but at the same time he knew that he was not excused from relating to her as if she were. The situation would be exacerbated if the mother, instead of merely failing to act in the normative way, gave up the maternal role entirely and chose to take an authoritarian position. Saltykov-Shchedrin's ambivalent attitude toward Arina in his novel *The Golovlevs* suggests how difficult it was for a son who had an authoritarian mother to come to terms with her and with his situation.

A son who had seriously conflicting feelings about his mother, whether she was dictatorial or merely failed to actualize the norm of

---

42. Nikolai A. Nekrasov, "Mat'", in *Polnoe sobranie stikhotvorenii N. A. Nekrasova, 1842–1872* (St. Petersburg, 1899), p. 423.
43. Evgeniia Tur, *Plemiannitsa* (Moscow, 1851).

motherhood, could respond in several ways. Typically, he maintained a respectful demeanor toward her, while admitting to himself, if not to others, that his feelings were not the prescribed ones. Ritualized expressions of respect dominated his attentions to her. If the mother did not terrify her son into unquestioning obedience, the son might successfully combine overt deference with covert lack of respect. For instance, the adolescent Vladimir in Turgenev's *First Love* always kissed his mother's hands when he wanted to cut short a conversation with her.[44] In *Boyhood, Adolescence and Youth* Tolstoi described an adult son who considered it "a duty" to "respect" his mother. "In the drawing room he stammered and conducted himself in the most obsequious manner toward his mother, fulfilled all her wishes and scolded people if they did not do what [she] commanded, but in his own study and at the office" he countermanded his mother's orders.[45]

As a son approached adulthood, the mother's emotional distance increased. Characteristically, she projected more and more ideal qualities onto him. To some extent this unrealistic perception of her adult son was desirable, as it formed a positive expression of the separation of the sexes. In any case, it was common. Even the despotic Varvara Turgeneva, while not organizing her life around either one of her sons, idealized them once they reached adulthood. About Ivan she wrote in her diary, "Only Ivan is my sun; I see only him and when he is away, I don't see clearly, I don't know where I am."[46] In general, a mother felt unqualified to judge the behavior of her adult son; she merely assumed that it was beyond reproach. She deferred to her son's judgment more and more, perhaps even bypassing her husband's, although this could not be openly acknowledged.

It was only in the question of marriage that a mother should not and usually did not defer to her grown son's wisdom and common sense. Apart from financial aspects, the arranging of marriages was considered an area of feminine expertise. A mother was an authority in her son's marriage; this comes out clearly in a historical story about Tsar Mikhail which was published in 1817.[47] After the death of his first wife, the tsar wanted to remarry. He was fortunate

44. I. S. Turgenev, *Polnoe sobranie sochinenii* (St. Petersburg, 1898), VII, 40.
45. Tolstoi, *Detstvo*, p. 226.
46. V. N. Zhitova, *Vospominaniia o sem'e I. S. Turgeneva* (Tula, 1961), p. 32.
47. *Plutarkh dlia prekrasnogo pola* (Moscow, 1817), V, 97.

enough to have a good mother who sought her son's happiness and told him that she would give her blessing to any match he was pleased to make. While the author praised her for this attitude, it was nonetheless clearly implied that the mother, even of a tsar, had a right to veto the choice of a wife. Allowing him a free choice was an act of noteworthy graciousness on her part.

This norm specifying the mother's right to dictate her son's choice of a bride, coupled with the general norm enjoining a son to respect and defer to his mother, made a son's defiance of his mother's wishes a very serious matter, and usually quite a reprehensible one. A son might defy his mother in many ways and yet not risk marriage without her consent. Nikolai Turgenev lived with and supported his mistress and their illegitimate children for years, but he did not marry her until he finally obtained his mother's permission.

A son whose marriage intentions did not coincide with his mother's wishes would use a variety of techniques to gain her approval. In particular, reference to love or the absence of love could be a powerful method of persuasion. However, since arguments based on love did not invariably succeed, a son sometimes had to resort to rather desperate measures. In Dmitrii Lavrov's "Decisive Leap," a young man threatened to kill himself if his mother rejected the woman of his choice,[48] and in the late nineteenth century Aksakov's father presented his parents with a similar ultimatum.[49]

Problems did not necessarily end with the son's marriage, for there were conflicting norms about the proper allocation of loyalty after marriage. Not infrequently a mother (especially a widow) would feel that her married son, for whom she had sacrificed so much, was neglecting her. The son would be torn between his natal family and his new family, uncertain where his greater obligations lay.

Another, and usually the last, change in the mother-son relationship came when the mother's husband died. A middle-aged widow was fairly free to participate in activities outside the specifically feminine sphere of competence without risk of social censure. Frequently a widow with a strong aggressive personality chose to

48. *Zhurnal dlia milykh*, 1804, p. 218.
49. Aksakov, *Semeinaia khronika*, p. 137.

assume her husband's role in several areas. This created a difficult situation for the son, especially if he was a mature adult who expected to take over his father's roles.

Conflict between an adult son and his widowed mother over family headship was a predictable if not a necessary function of the family structure. There were two lines of authority, one male and one female. The emphasis on the division between the sexes made it proper for one male (the eldest son) to succeed another (the father). But another norm held that a husband and wife were a unit, and that upon his death it was proper for her to take over many of his roles, notably that of head of the family. In short, the rules were ambiguous. It was possible for a mother and son to find themselves battling (emotionally, not legally) for control of the estate and for the position of family head, each believing in the justice of his or her claim. Saltykov-Shchedrin's *Golovlevs* presents an example of the complex nature of such a situation.[50] In this case both mother and son, confused about where justice lay, tried to induce the other to accept the position that each wanted for him/herself. The son insisted that his mother sit at the head of the table as the mistress of the estate. She declined, saying bitterly that since the son had inherited the estate, he alone was the master. The son replied that she was the mistress on the estates of all her children. In this case the mother and son were arguing over the relationship between two aspects of the status of master/mistress *(khoziain/khoziaika)*—the legal ownership, and the more elusive concept of head of the household. The son, wanting his mother to assume the latter role, held that legal ownership did not determine the identity of the household head, and that his mother should fill this role because of her position in the family. The mother, angry at this turn of events, chose to play a martyr's role, insisting that the status of household head followed from legal ownership.

Typically, several factors prevented this situation from becoming an open power struggle. The son felt obligated not only to respect and defer to his mother, but also to view her as a moral and spiritual ideal. His mother, in turn, felt most virtuous when she was sacrificing for her son. Neither mother nor son felt comfortable openly seeking a position of authority over the other. Perhaps the usually veiled quality of this problem only added to the difficulty of resolv-

50. M. E. Saltykov-Shchedrin, *Gospoda Golovlevy* (Leningrad, 1970), p. 114.

ing it. The most common solution, and the one which most satisfactorily accommodated the different norms involved, was for the mother to be the titular head of the estate and the family, while the son exercised actual control in both areas. In the late eighteenth century, Labzina's first husband and his mother had such a relationship. The son nominally deferred to his mother's wishes and even asked her advice, while at the same time he continued to live his life exactly as he wanted.[51] Tolstoi fictionalized a similar situation in *War and Peace*.[52] The mother lived with her son and his family on the estate now legally belonging to the son. The son managed the estate and made all the decisions, but the mother was considered the head of the family. The complexity of the situation was succinctly expressed in a sentence which referred to a family member living "at her mother's; that is, at Nikolai's."

If such a compromise was achieved, it frequently happened that the mother, far from being merely a titular figure, maintained a position of real influence, becoming both a symbol of family solidarity and a focus of communication and interaction. Consequently, on her death, those persons who had defined themselves as one family by virtue of a common relationship to her, would cease to view themselves as one family, and the son would find himself with less to control.

Not all widows were in conflict with their sons. An ideal way for a woman to cope with widowhood was to emphasize the indulgent aspect of her relationship with her son and to completely orient her life around his. In return, she had a right to expect that her son would be grateful to her and keep her well-being foremost in his mind. Especially if the son was a bachelor willing to leave all the areas of feminine expertise to his mother, the arrangement could be mutually gratifying. This was the case with Herzen's bachelor cousin, "the chemist." According to Herzen, his cousin "touchingly surrounded [his mother's] lonely and infirm old age, as well as he could, with tranquility and attention."[53]

Unfortunately, the needs of mothers and sons did not always dovetail neatly. The mother might find that devotion to her son, though viewed as an excellent way for an aging woman to spend her

51. Labzina, *Vospominaniia.*
52. L. N. Tolstoi, *Voina i mir* (Moscow and Leningrad, 1936), II, 575.
53. Herzen, *Byloe i dumy*, I, 118.

Jessica Tovrov

declining years, was not wanted or needed by the son himself. It was not uncommon for a woman at this point to see her marriage, her home, her children as all having failed to,live up to the expectations that she had been encouraged to hold since girlhood. The fact that her son no longer needed her sacrifices would be one more example of life's failure to meet the normative definitions and rules.

MOTHER-DAUGHTER RELATIONSHIPS

The uncritical and effusive indulgence that was the norm in the mother-son relationship was a corollary of the emotional separation expected to exist between the two. In the normative mother-daughter relationship, stress fell on very different elements. The relationship should be characterized by a mutual identification so strong that the mother and daughter felt and acted as one person. One author wrote that "a daughter should never leave her mother's side without a real necessity to do so," and that she should confide everything in her.[54] Although hostile relations between all other family members could be envisioned without defining either of the parties as morally reprehensible, this was not true of the mother-daughter relationship. If a mother and daughter were in conflict, it almost always implied a condemnation of one of them, or perhaps both. Fictional writings reveal very few instances of hostile mother-daughter relationships. When a story required such a situation, it usually drew on a mother substitute—for instance, a stepmother or an aunt. This suggests that an antagonistic relationship between a mother and daughter, if not too threatening to contemplate, was at least more of a condemnation than the author wanted to attach to the characters.

Of course, the mother-daughter relationship did not occur in a vacuum. The pervasive division between the sexes, plus the characteristic emphasis on authority and hierarchy in the family as a whole, created a situation in which the mother had great power over her daughter, as well as complete responsibility for her until her marriage. Bogdanovich's work, *On the Education of Youth*, in discussing the proper upbringing of girls, addressed itself to mothers only, implying that this responsibility was the mother's

54. August Witzman, *Sokrashchenie glavneishikh dolzhnostei koi kazhdyi krist'ianin obiazan ispolniat' v tochnosti po svoemu zvaniiu i sostoianiiu* (St. Petersburg, 1799), p. 4.

alone.[55] This assumption was expressed even more clearly by a fictional father who, referring to his daughters, declared: "If their mother gave them a good upbringing, then of course, they would comprise my only pleasure and joy."[56]

One aspect of maternal control was the daughter's duty to confide completely in her mother. Countess Rostova in *War and Peace* optimistically believed that her relationship with her daughters was normative in this respect: "I know that I will always be the first confidante of my daughters."[57] The daughter should put unquestioning trust in her mother and internalize her mother's attitudes and opinions. In *The Niece*, a young woman expressed the subordinate posture that the ideal daughter would adopt vis-à-vis her mother. She announced that her only goal in life was to fulfill her mother's wishes for her, now with her mother's help, and, after her marriage, with the help of her husband. She added that fulfilling her mother's wishes was the only meaning that marriage had for her.[58]

The girl's subordination to her mother was not supposed to be eased by displays of affection on the mother's part. The relationship between a mother and daughter was similar to the one between a mother and son before the son was transferred to the male sphere. A mother's intense sense of responsibility for her daughter inhibited tenderness and spontaneity. Though it should be loving, the mother-daughter relationship was primarily task-oriented, devoted to the daughter's training. Expressed affection was potentially threatening to the normatively serious and formal approach of this training.

Thus the prescribed norm of the mother-daughter relationship had two aspects which often conflicted. While the relationship should be close, with the daughter completely open and confiding, it should also be strictly authoritarian. A fictional twelve-year-old girl who stated, "I feel that without the advice and without the permission of my mother I can do nothing," voiced an ideal that real daughters were expected to aspire to.[59] These two prescriptions

55. Bogdanovich, *O vospitanii.*
56. "Dobraia doch' zameniaet mat'," p. 409.
57. Tolstoi, *Voina i mir*, I, 54.
58. Tur, *Plemiannitsa*, II, 223.
59. "Koketochka," *Drug detei*, p. 3.

—unity and strict authority—combined to make the mother-daughter relationship a complex and conflicting one.

The normative rule specifying close identification between the two was mirrored in reality. Mothers and daughters usually felt inexorably tied together, identified more with each other than with anyone else, and tended to see themselves as a moral and emotional unit. A mother had the following advice for her daughter after the latter gave birth to a daughter of her own:

> Your daughter, for some time, will be part of yourself. Now she drinks your milk, soon she will begin to form herself according to your precepts, ideas, and convictions. For a long time you will be her only soul, support, and finally her guide in the world. Those who love you will love her, and people will be kind to her to please you and flatter her self-love to please you. Your daughter is your property. She is the work of your hands. . . .[60]

This intense identification could be confining and restrictive as well as supportive. It was an asymmetrical relationship, with the daughter totally subservient to her mother. Not only was she expected to obey her mother; she was also expected to confide in her. "I know that girls must hide nothing from their mothers,"[61] proclaimed one model child in a children's story. Yet a daughter was rarely so docile as not to feel resentment at the fact that the person in whom she must confide, to whom she must reveal herself, also wielded unquestionable power over her. For her own part, the mother bore responsibility for her daughter's behavior and often resented the girl's failure to comply with her standards. Rarely, however, did this resentment completely circumscribe the relationship. The lives of most women were colored by love-hate relationships with their mothers, which might be modified but were seldom entirely eliminated.

While a girl obviously went through numerous physical and emotional changes between her birth and her engagement, her mother viewed the entire period as largely of a piece. Throughout, the conscientious mother was concerned with preparing her daughter for adulthood—specifically, for marriage. Normatively, this preparation was central to their relationship, and a thorough involvement in it was the best expression of a mother's love. One

60. "O vospitanii devits," *Patriot* (Moscow), September, 1804, p. 293.
61. "Koketochka," p. 47.

writer expressed it thus: "The good behavior of girls, without which they cannot be happy, should be the first order of concern for their mothers."[62]

Russian child-rearing attitudes saw the good parent-child relationship as continually focused on direct instruction. This was especially true of the mother-daughter relationship; apparently it was difficult even to conceive of a positive interaction between a mother and daughter that was not moralistically or pedagogically inclined. Literature which touched at all on this relationship almost invariably depicted the mother as instructing her daughter.[63] A woman who seriously attempted to actualize the norms of motherhood might find that her need to train her daughter completely overshadowed her desire to play with or enjoy her. This was particularly likely if the woman had sons as well as daughters; in that case, if she wanted an indulgent, expressive relationship with a child, she could establish it with her son without having to endanger her position of teacher and authority figure to her daughter.

A mother's formality with her daughter was normative and should not be considered as demonstrating dislike or resentment. Occasionally, however, maternal resentment did become an element in the relationship. The identification between mother and daughter was so close that a failure on the daughter's part, even if no more than a failure to follow in her mother's footsteps, could cause resentment on the mother's part. This was especially likely if the mother herself was plagued by feelings of inadequacy and had turned to her daughter for compensation.

The daughter's sex occasionally added to a mother's resentment. Sons were deemed slightly more valuable than daughters, at least at birth, as Aksakov indicated in *The Family Chronicle:* "Of course, Sophia Nikolaevna, and still more Aleksei Stepanovich would have preferred a son."[64] This preference for sons seldom extended much past birth, but if for some reason a woman had particularly wanted a

62. Bogdanovich, *O vospitanii*, p. 214.
63. See, e.g., the stories in *Detskaia biblioteka* (St. Petersburg, 1820); *Detskie zabavy* (Moscow, 1792); *Patriot, zhurnal vospitaniia* (Moscow, 1804); *Drug iunoshestva* (Moscow, 1807); *Drug detei* (Moscow, 1809), *Nezabudochka* (Moscow, 1826); Mar'ia Rostovskaia, *Detskie zabavy* (St. Petersburg, 1909), written in the mid-nineteenth century; *Luchi, zhurnal dlia devits* (St. Petersburg, 1850). This pedagogical tone also dominated the mother-son relationship when the son was a child, and the father-son relationship, insofar as they interacted. It was less true of the father-daughter relationship.
64. Aksakov, *Semeinaia khronika*, pp. 255–256.

son, it might take her some time to forgive her daughter for this "accident" of birth.[65]

The daughter's response to her mother's attitude was usually ambivalent. She felt that everyone expected her to adore her mother, to look on her mother as her closest ally and omniscient protector. She heard from all sides that the best thing that could happen to her was to become like her mother. Characteristically, the girl did love, admire, and emulate her mother. Her mother embodied feminine beauty, graciousness, and wisdom; furthermore, she was married to her father, the ideal man. The daughter usually saw emulation as a way to win her mother's love. Labzina, for example, referring to herself at age ten, wrote, "My desires were only concerned with what would please my dear and honored mother."[66] Passek was encouraged by her nurse to adopt a similar attitude. "Be good so as to console your mother,"[67] her nurse would say when she misbehaved. "Pleasing mother" was the nurse's most powerful argument for good behavior.

Frequently a girl wanted to please her mother but would feel frustrated and confused, as in the following case related by Kovalevskaia.

> Sometimes I want to caress mama, to climb on her knee; but in one way or another, these attempts always end in my hurting mama through my awkwardness, or ripping her dress, and then I run away and hide myself in the corner with shame. For this reason I began to develop a sort of shyness toward mama, and this shyness was enhanced by the fact that I often heard nurse say that Anuita and Fedia were mama's favorites, and that mama disliked me.[68]

Since Kovalevskaia's mother exceeded the prescribed emotional remoteness, the statement should not be taken as an invariable attitude of daughters. Nonetheless, it clearly describes a daughter's adoration of her mother, coupled with an awkwardness and inability to be spontaneous in a mother's presence, so typical of girls. A mother's lack of overt affection for her daughter often produced stress. The spontaneity and indulgence she enjoyed with other

65. Sof ia Kovalevskaia, *Vospominaniia detstva* (Moscow, 1860), and Nadezhda Durova, *Kavalerist-devitsa* (St. Petersburg, 1912), are two examples of women whose lives were adversely affected by their mothers' desires for sons.
66. Labzina, *Vospominaniia*, p. 21.
67. Passek, *Iz dal'nikh let*, I, 104.
68. Kovalevskaia, *Vospominaniia detstva*, pp. 23–24.

adults could not fully compensate the girl for what she perceived as an inadequate relationship with her adored mother.

Many girls were forced to cope not only with their mothers' coldness, but also with the realization that it was impossible to live up to maternal expectations. The socially encouraged identification between mother and daughter, strengthened in some cases by personal maladjustments, made many mothers place unrelenting demands on their daughters. A girl might feel that, as far as her mother was concerned, no success was good enough.

The stresses were still greater if the girl had a brother approximately her age. She would see that her mother was affectionate and spontaneous with the boy, praising almost anything he did. Her mother would go to considerable trouble to convince the father or tutor to be less severe with her son, all the while treating her daughter severely. Whether or not a woman took seriously her role as her daughter's teacher and authority figure, the behavior deemed proper in her relationship with her daughter focused on mutual identification and authority, as distinguished from the indulgence central to her relationship with her son. Even if a woman did not actively participate in her daughter's training or feel the prescribed identification with her daughter, she would be inclined to treat her daughter and son differently. The daughter characteristically felt that she was treated not just differently, but worse.

The intense identification that usually characterized the mother-daughter relationship became especially problematic as the girl approached adolescence. Her feelings became more complex, and her need for privacy greater; at this point, a daughter might develop a virtual obsession with escaping from her mother. The only practical guise for escape was marriage. In Tur's *Niece* an adolescent girl, reacting to her mother's curtailment of her socializing, declared: "When I'm married I'll go to all the balls, all the parties, masquerades—I'll have many bouquets—and I'll try to have more lovers—in a word, I'll do whatever I want. I'll smoke cigarettes and ride horseback. I have thought about this for a long time. I'll do everything I can think of, and at that very minute."[69]

At around age sixteen a woman became defined as a *nevesta*. Usually translated as "bride" or "fiancée," the term was also used to denote a woman of marriageable age. Becoming a *nevesta* was an

69. Tur, *Plemiannitsa*, II, 134.

important definition of adulthood for a woman.[70] This was the watershed in her life, the time when all her mother's careful training would be put to the test, when the daughter (and, through her, the mother) would be judged either a success or a failure.

With the advent of the daughter's *nevesta* status, she was considered to have an even greater need for her mother. When Passek, whose mother had died when she was a small child, reached the age of fifteen, her father said for the first time that she needed a mother substitute. He connected this suddenly perceived need with the fact that it was time to think about Passek's marriage.[71] In *Ol'ga* it was regarded as particularly unfortunate that "an inexperienced young woman lacked, at her first entrance into society, the guidance of her mother."[72]

Perhaps the most important task a woman faced after actual childbirth was to see to it that her daughters were properly married. When the time came to find a husband for her daughter, a mother felt (often justly) that she had done all she could to insure her daughter's success. Perhaps she had even made considerable sacrifices herself. In order to get her daughters married, Saltykov-Shchedrin's mother overcame her remarkable miserliness and spent a large sum of money on properly outfitting them for a husband-hunting trip to Moscow.[73]

Regardless of the mother's good intentions and sacrifices, success or failure ultimately rested with the daughter. True, marriages were arranged in many ways; but a marriage in which the bride's attractiveness, disposition, and feelings were completely disregarded was very unusual. Consequently, this was a frustrating and anxiety-ridden situation for the mother: never before had so much been at stake, and her power of affecting the outcome so limited. The tension often caused the mother to treat her daughter with increased severity and stricter authority in an attempt finally to arrange her daughter's life the way she wanted it.[74]

The daughter, now actively engaged in what she had always known to be the most important activity of her life, usually felt that

70. The other important definitions of a woman's adult status were marriage and the birth of her first child.

71. Passek, *Iz dal'nikh let*, I, 220–221.

72. Begichev, *Ol'ga*, part 1, p. 87.

73. Saltykov-Shchedrin, *Poshekhonskaia starina*, p. 224.

74. Barbara Alpern Engel also discusses the increased involvement of a mother with her daughter at this point in her article, "Mothers and Daughters," in the present volume.

she and her mother had embarked together on a very important project. She remembered how, in her childhood, her mother had seen to it that she acquired the necessary skills. Now, on the husband hunt, her mother was her guide in society, telling her how to behave, with whom she ought to be ingratiating, and so on. Some mothers gave their daughters very specific help in finding and catching husbands. Saltykov-Shchedrin wrote, "A mother whose favorite daughter was marriageable must be convinced that under no conditions could a trip to Moscow in the winter months be overlooked."[75] A mother's help did not stop once she had maneuvered her daughter into the company of eligible men. Young women even relied on "their mothers for help in their evil conversations," as Bogdanovich disapprovingly put it.[76] If all else failed, the mother had recourse to an arranged marriage (with or without the use of formal matchmakers). Should the daughter not find an arranged marriage to her taste, the mother could force her into it simply by threatening to withdraw her help. Elizaveta Popova described such a case from 1807.[77] A noblewoman with a daughter twenty-two or twenty-three years old told the young woman that, if she did not marry the man she had picked for her, the mother would give her up as an old maid and concentrate on her younger daughters. This threat sufficed: the daughter capitulated and married a man she barely knew.

Despite her mother's help, it was typical for a daughter to resent her mother more strongly than ever. Seeing her goal of independence near and all the more desirable, the daughter found her mother trying more desperately than ever to impose her will on her. To make matters worse, the daughter's grandmother, nurse, governess—the older women who had played a part in her life and who had provided feminine companionship and alternative role models—were now definitely relegated to the background.[78] Just when the daughter's interactions with her mother were intensified, most of the other people to whom she had habitually turned for escape and support were no longer available.

75. Saltykov-Shchedrin, *Poshekhonskaia starina*, p. 226.
76. Bogdanovich, *O vospitanii*, p. 187.
77. Elizaveta Popova, *Dnevnik* (St. Petersburg, 1911), p. 61.
78. Zhitova, for example, described explicitly how her adopted mother's chambermaid was, in her eyes, a model wife and mother, and as such exerted a beneficial influence on Zhitova throughout her life. *Vospominaniia*, p. 40.

An unmarried woman saw marriage as freedom—specifically, freedom from her mother. At the end of the eighteenth century, Labzina's mother expressed this idea in a positive way when she told her daughter that, after her marriage, she would no longer be dependent on her (the mother).[79] A character in a Matiushkin play made a statement that reflects a more negative view of the mother-daughter relationship: "I promised to marry her and take her from her mother to a home of her own."[80] Tur also expressed what seems to have been a common sentiment: "It had nothing to do with love . . . if she wanted to be free, it was necessary to have her own home and to marry."[81] Women who married for love often fantasized about freedom as much as they did about the man they loved. A woman engaged to a man she did not love, perhaps a man she barely knew, would still joyfully anticipate the independence that went hand in hand with any marriage, no matter how dreadful. Like Julie in Pisemskii's *Simpleton*, forced by her parents to marry a man she disliked, she took comfort in the thought that "at least she would escape from her parents' rule, she would be a married woman and could go wherever she liked unchaperoned."[82]

Despite this joyful anticipation of independence, the daughter grew increasingly timid about leaving her parental home as her wedding day drew near. Usually the person she was the most reluctant to leave was her mother, although only a few months previously she had longed for nothing so much as to be free of her. In his memoirs Ivan Ostrozhskii-Lokhvitskii described a scene in which a bride was being taken "from her mother" in tears to enter a marriage she herself had wanted. Although her father was also present, Ostrozhskii-Lokhvitskii suggested that only the parting from her mother caused pain for the bride.[83]

As the *nevesta's* wedding day approached, her mother usually found herself beset by many emotions. In general, her attitude would match her attitude toward the daughter's other accomplishments. If the mother viewed the marriage as a good one, she would be proud of herself and grateful to her daughter for making them

79. Labzina, *Vospominaniia*, p. 31.
80. Aleksandr Matiushkin, *Nechaiannoe svidanie ili tri svad'by vdrug* (Moscow, 1810), p. 4.
81. Tur, *Plemiannitsa*, IV, 168.
82. Pisemskii, *Tiufiak*, p. 309.
83. *Zapiski novo-oskol'skogo dvorianina* (Kiev, 1886), p. 15.

both successful. If she did not like her son-in-law, she would feel disappointed, let down, and angry with herself, her daughter, or circumstances.

Many mothers worried about the kind of reception their daughters would receive from new in-laws; this was a matter of special concern if the daughter would be living with them. The ideal, of course, was for in-laws to view the bride as one of their own family and to love her accordingly. Some tried to actualize this ideal. When Vadim Passek announced his plans to marry Tatiana, his mother told the prospective daughter-in-law, "Now you are ours."[84] Generally, however, such an attitude was not expected.[85] On the contrary, her own female relatives often warned the bride that her husband's family would meet her with hostility; usually her mother stressed this point most forcefully. Tur told the story of a bride who wanted to "become a daughter" to her fiancé's parents and to "earn their love," while her mother tried to dissuade her from approaching her in-laws with such an unrealistic attitude.[86]

Jealousy was another common emotion that a mother might experience when her daughter married. Marriage reawakened the mother's own girlhood dreams of love and marriage and evoked the painful contrast between her expectations and her actual married life. Even in reference to Countess Rostova, who certainly loved her daughter Natasha, Tolstoi wrote of her "latent grudge which mothers always have in regard to their daughters' happiness in marriage."[87] When the actual wedding approached, a mother became beset by a deep sense of loss; all other emotions receded into the background. Although her relationship with her daughter had never been as expressive or as outwardly affectionate as her relationship with her son, her sense of identification with her daughter

84. Passek, *Iz dal'nikh let*, I, 381.

85. Linguistic as well as literary evidence points to the outsider status of the bride in her husband's family. Stankiewicz in "Slavic Kinship Terms and the Perils of the Soul," *Journal of American Folklore*, 71 (1958): 119, points out that derivatives of the word *nevestka* (woman marrying into the family) are often used for "weasel." Like a weasel, a *nevestka* was tolerated and treated like a relative but was not accorded family membership until she gave birth to a son. In "Semantic Structure," Friedrich discusses some linguistic phenomena of all of nineteenth-century Russian society, but with an emphasis on the peasantry. He agrees that the word *nevestka* carried the connotation of a transitional status. He further suggests that the *nevestka* was seen to be in danger from the house spirits, and was herself the bearer of unclean forces from without.

86. Evgeniia Tur, *Semeistvo Shalonskikh* (Moscow, 1891), p. 152.

87. Tolstoi, *Voina i mir*, I, 516.

was usually very strong, and the daughter's marriage meant a painful rupture.

Marriage was more important to the self-definition and social definition of a woman than of a man. Given the patrilineal nature of Russian kinship, a married man remained a more integral part of his natal family than did a married woman. He was more likely to inherit and run the family estate, more likely to live with his parents after his own marriage, and he had a legal right to a greater share of his father's estate on the latter's death. A married woman's natal family often referred to her as an "independent person" (*otrezannyi lomot'*). Not infrequently, however, in a less structured, less formal way, it was the daughter, not the son, who maintained the greatest emotional involvement with her natal family. Often this involvement was a function of her ties to her mother. A good example of this bond may be seen in Aksakov's *Family Chronicle*.[88] From the time his daughters were children, the father made it clear that he expected nothing from them because they would only leave home as soon as possible.[89] Nonetheless, after they had married and left home these same daughters kept up close ties with all members of their natal family, especially their mother. In this case the mother and married daughters formed a moral and emotional unit, closer in some ways than any other in the family.

Changes in the mother-daughter relationship did, of course, occur after the daughter's marriage. Physical distance and the daughter's involvement with her husband and a new life caused the ties with her mother to be restructured, if not weakened. On occasion, a mother resented her daughter's new emotional ties and felt abandoned. However, this was less likely than in the case of her married son, whose continuing participation in his natal family had been expected. Because a daughter's physical and emotional departure had been anticipated since her birth, the mother was more prepared to accept it. Typically, the diminished responsibility that the mother felt for the daughter, and the daughter's sense of greater independence from her mother, promoted a lessening of the mutual resentment that had been part of their close identification and strict hierarchical relationship. The daughter's marriage often provided the first opportunity for the emotional association be-

88. Aksakov, *Semeinaia khronika*.
89. *Ibid.*, p. 76.

tween a mother and daughter to become more a source of support and strength than of tension.

This paper has described two relationships in the Russian noble family. In both, certain values and types of interaction were stressed at the expense of others. The mother-son relationship emphasized expressed affection but little comradeship. The mother-daughter relationship stressed mutual identification and guidance but little overt affection. These relationships, like others in the family, offered only partial satisfaction of the emotional needs of the people involved.

In attempting to understand the affective meaning of these relationships, it is important to view them in the context of family life. Such an approach reveals two important points. First, the Russian noble family was held to be more than the sum of its parts; the sacrifices of individuals (or of relationships between individuals) for the sake of the family unit, while not ideal, at least were predictable and often were considered necessary. In sacrificing him/herself for the well-being of the family, the individual obtained the satisfaction of knowing that he/she had acted in accordance with the social norms and avoided the shame implied in acting otherwise. Second, each family member was, optimally, involved in many family relationships. Every relationship had a different emotional structure and satisfied different needs. As in all cultures, some needs generated within the family could not be satisfied therein. Nonetheless, any individual could reasonably expect some emotional gratification from relationships with other family members and from identification with the family as a whole.

BARBARA ALPERN ENGEL

Mothers and Daughters: Family Patterns and the Female Intelligentsia

One of the more unusual features of the radical female intelligentsia of the 1870s was the prevalence of strong mother-daughter ties among its members. A significant minority of them had mothers who sympathized with and even shared their unconventional aspirations.[1] Maternal support ranged from encouragement of educational goals to participation in revolutionary activities. Most of the women involved were of noble origin. Varvara Perovskaia, for example, was the wife of a former governor of St. Petersburg. In 1869, she helped her fifteen-year-old daughter Sof'ia attend the first advanced courses for women in Russia. Sof'ia Subbotina, another noblewoman, inherited a substantial estate upon her husband's death. She raised three revolutionary daughters and organized her own peasants to withhold taxes and recruits from the tsar. Such women maintained close intellectual and emotional ties with their radical daughters. To be sure, many radical women had to struggle fiercely with one or both parents to win their freedom; still, a significant minority managed somehow to avoid this debilitating conflict.

The sources of these unusual relationships can be found in family patterns of the educated nobility in the first half of the nineteenth century. These patterns, in turn, strongly affected the emerging female intelligentsia of mid-nineteenth-century Russia.

1. Among these women are to be found many of the most outstanding revolutionaries of the 1870s, including Sof'ia Bardina, Vera Figner, Sof'ia Perovskaia and the Olovennikova sisters. See Vera Figner, *Zapechatlennyi trud; vospominaniia* (Moscow, 1964); S. M. Stepniak-Kravchinskii, *Biographie de Sophie Bardina* (Geneva, 1900); A. V. Iakimova, "Pamiati E. N. Olovennikovoi," *Katorga i ssylka*, N. 98, 1933.

Well into the nineteenth century, particularly among the provincial nobility, traditional attitudes toward the family continued beneath a veneer of westernization. Both law and custom invested virtually absolute power in the head of the household, and most families remained hierarchical: the father was head; the wife, his assistant and executor; and children, like serfs, unconditionally submissive and obedient.[2] The family retained its economic, social, and political functions; as a result, considerations of property, connections, or lineage vied with personal inclination as reasons for marriage. Social norms did not include domestic felicity as a worthwhile end in itself.

Despite her subordination to her husband in the family hierarchy, the wife nevertheless occupied a position of considerable importance, both in her capacity as assistant to the head of the household and in her own right. She supervised household affairs and the production of food and clothing; if her husband was absent, as frequently happened, she might manage the estate as well. Motherhood occupied a relatively insignificant place among her various duties. Noblewomen bore their children and then turned their attention elsewhere, leaving them for others to rear. Due to the existence of serfdom, this did not mean that children were neglected. Serf women proved attentive, loving substitutes for the biological mother. First the wet nurse, then the nurse appear to have been utterly devoted to the child's needs. Socially inferior to their infant charges, serf women found it difficult to deny them anything. "The child was given the breast at his first cry, even if he had just been suckled. If the child did not quiet down and refused the breast, he was rocked in the cradle or carried to the point of stupefaction," writes one highly critical source.[3] Free from other chores and ordinarily without a husband to claim her attention, the peasant nurse offered a seemingly boundless source of love during a child's early years. Many memoirs portray the nurse with special warmth: "Nurse gave our family all her love and devotion. She had no life of her own: her joys and griefs were inseparable from ours."[4]

2. Parental power, absolute over both children, "does not cease, but is limited . . . when daughters marry, since it is impossible for a single individual to satisfy completely two authorities as absolute as parents and spouse." A. Kantorovich, *Zakony o zhenshchinakh* (St. Petersburg, 1899), p. 59.

3. E. Vodovozova, *Na zare zhizni* (Moscow, 1964), I, 124. She adds that children were not weaned until two or sometimes three years of age.

4. *Ibid.*, p. 59.

Dedicated to the interests of her charges, she provided a refuge and sometimes a counterbalance to the demands of the adult world. "For the first ten years of our lives, our nurse was the only person with whom we felt free and who did not try to break our wills," wrote Vera Figner, born in 1852 to a provincial noble family. "Only she could we love and caress without restraint."[5]

The first threat to the nurse's hegemony was often a governess, tutor, or school.[6] Representative of a higher social station, the governess (or tutor, or school) counterposed the world of rules and discipline to the nurse's world of love and gentle guidance. As one woman put it, "We were educated strictly and punished often."[7] Charged with the difficult task of civilizing the children, the governess might well appear a "monster" who would torment them.[8] The depiction of the arbitrary and punitive governess is as common as the portrait of the loving and protective nurse. Memoirs often describe open conflict between the two women, representatives of two almost irreconcilable worlds. The more the nurse had indulged the child, the more difficult became the task of the governess; the more punitive the governess, the more likely the child to take refuge with the nurse.[9]

Parents stood apart from these struggles. Fathers rarely became involved with children on a day-to-day basis, or so one must judge from their usual literary depiction as distant figures, less human beings than representatives of a rigidly hierarchical, authoritarian social order. Some, like the tyrant portrayed by Avdotia Panaeva in her semi-autobiographical *Tal'nykov Family*, actually beat their daughters.[10] Others did not need to resort to violence. "We feared him worse than fire," wrote Vera Figner of her father. "One glance, cold and penetrating, was enough to set us trembling."[11] From

5. Vera Figner, *Zapechatlennyi trud*, I, 57–58.

6. In the analysis to follow, I assume a sufficient level of wealth to maintain a governess or tutor in the home, but the analysis would also be relevant for girls sent to boarding school.

7. Nadezhda Belozerskaia, "Avtobiografiia," *Istoricheskii vestnik*, 34, no. 6 (1913):924. Belozerskaia was the child of a wealthy urban family.

8. So she seemed to one nurse, who had already over-indulged four of her charges. Ol'ga Bulanova-Trubnikova, *Tri pokoleniia* (Moscow-Leningrad, 1928), p. 145.

9. See, *e.g.*, Sof'ia Kovalevskaia, *Vospominaniia detstva* (Moscow, 1945); Avdot'ia Panaeva, *Semeistvo Tal'nykovykh* (Leningrad, 1928); A-va [A. N. Kazina], "Zhenskaia zhizn'," *Otechestvennye zapiski*, 219, no. 3 (March, 1875); Vera Figner, *Zapechatlennyi trud*, I.

10. Stepan Bagrov, the patriarch described in Sergei Aksakov, *A Family Chronicle* (New York, 1961), would be included in this category.

11. Figner, *Zapechatlennyi trud*, I, 58.

custom, law, the possession of serfs, and even from their own socialization, men gained a sense of mastery—if not in the political sphere, where most served the autocratic state in either a civil or a military capacity, then at least in the domestic one. [12] Most noblemen still received a military-style education, and they treated their children as if they were soliders, the only model they had for dealing with subordinates. "Unconditional obedience and crushing discipline was our father's motto," wrote Vera Figner. "We had to get up and go to bed at a definite time, we were always dressed in the same clothing as if it were a uniform, and we always combed our hair in the same way."[13] Society, moreover, expected men to behave as they did.

By mid-century, some children had grown aware of the conventions that bound their fathers. General Korvin-Krukovskii, retired from the army and living with his family in the provinces, kept his distance from his children. His daughter remembered him as "essentially good and loving, but he surrounded himself with an air of inaccessibility as a matter of principle."[14] Whatever the reasons, the result was the same: most daughters perceived their fathers as distant and forbidding. When men did not accept this role, it could upset the more conventionally minded. Aleksandra Tsevlovskaia, the traditional wife of a very westernized nobleman, accused her husband of over-indulging the children because of his concern for their education.[15]

Although less formidable, mothers often proved nearly as remote. Whatever the depth of maternal feeling, no one expected a noblewoman of means to nurture or socialize her small children.[16] One of the prerogatives of wealth, in fact, was freedom from the daily responsibilities of child care. The more conscientious mother

12. For an excellent discussion of the socialization of noblemen, see Marc Raeff, *Origins of the Russian Intelligentsia* (New York, 1966), esp. ch. 4.
13. Figner, *Zapechatlennyi trud*, I, 57–58.
14. Sophie Kovalevsky [Sof'ia Kovalevskaia], *Recollections of Childhood* (London, 1895), p. 123. Ekaterina Zhukovskaia, a contemporary, describes her father in almost identical terms. "He was good and honorable," she writes, but, like most people in the pre-reform era, he believed that "the head of the family must keep his children and chattels in a state of unconditional subjection." Ekaterina Zhukovskaia, *Zapiski* (Leningrad, 1930), p. 19.
15. Vodovozova, *Na zare zhizni*, I, 85.
16. Some mothers, although distant, were certainly loving. See, *e.g.*, Figner, *Zapechatlennyi trud*, I; A-va [Kazina], "Zhenskaia zhizn' "; Ekaterina Iunge, *Vospominaniia* (Moscow, 1933).

might assume a supervisory role, but most seemed satisfied to inspect their children in the morning and evening, and to receive reports from nurse, governess, or tutor. "Relations between parents and children were defined quite precisely," recalled the daughter of a noble family of relatively modest means. "Children kissed their parents' hands in the morning, thanked them for dinner and supper, and took leave of them before going to bed. Every governess spent most of her time trying to keep the children, as much as possible, from bothering the parents."[17]

There were a number of reasons for this distance between mother and child. The most obvious was the variety of other duties that a noblewoman performed, particularly in the provinces, where women often managed not only their households but other aspects of domestic economy as well. For example, immediately after their marriage in 1828, Nikolai Tsevlovskii, a provincial nobleman, assigned his wife her tasks: "I was to supervise the care of the children, to manage the household, the cattle yard and the house servants; he would supervise the serfs and the farming, and I had no right to interfere."[18] If husbands were absent, deceased, or simply lazy, the wife might also manage the estate herself.[19] Social duties absorbed the attention of noblewomen who could afford to live in the cities. "Mother was very kind, but we hardly ever saw her," reads a typical description. "She was usually out or receiving callers. We loved her, she held us, but we hardly ever spoke to her."[20] The frequency of pregnancy was another significant factor. Englishwomen in the mid-nineteenth century bore, on the average, six children.[21] Russian noblewomen probably conceived at least as often, since they had no contraception and (in contrast to Englishwomen) did not nurse their own children, thus losing even that unreliable means of birth control. Frequent child-bearing appears to be the predominant pattern. The mother of the anarchist Mikhail Bakunin bore eleven children during the first fourteen years of her marriage. Ekaterina Tsevlovskaia bore sixteen children in the first

17. Vodovozova, *Na zare zhizni*, I, 126.
18. *Ibid.*, p. 84.
19. Not infrequently, female memoirists (unusual women almost by definition) recall mothers who apparently preferred managing estates to rearing their offspring. See Vodovozova, *Na zare zhizni*; Zhukovskaia, *Zapiski*; and A-va [Kazina], "Zhenskaia zhizn'."
20. A-va [Kazina], "Zhenskaia zhizn'," p. 211. See also S. Streich, *Sestry Korvin-Krukovskie* (Moscow, 1934), p. 11, and Iunge, *Vospominaniia*, pp. 41–42.
21. E. A. Wrigley, *Population and History* (New York, 1969), p. 197.

twenty years of her marriage and justified her neglect of them by arguing that "a woman such as herself, who had carried a child beneath her heart every year, could not be a passionate mother."[22] Ekaterina Figner delivered eight babies in the first twelve years of her marriage. According to her daughter Vera, constant child-bearing deprived the children of their mother's company. High infant mortality rates undoubtedly discouraged emotional invest-ment in small children.

The lack of involvement between mother and daughter during a girl's early years eased her transition to maturity. If adolescent rebellion is, in part, an expression of the desire to end childish dependence on the parents, then such rebellions in Russian noble families may well have lacked the emotional intensity so common today. Most daughters of nobility did not develop great emotional dependence on either parent. While the mother remained central at every stage of development, her relationship with her daughter was mediated by other female figures. She left the care of her daughter to the wet nurse, then to the nurse, during the formative first five years; when the time came to impose society's rules on an unwilling youngster, the governess, tutor, or school usually served as the disciplining agent. These intervening figures attenuated both the primary attachment of infancy and the subsequent sense of loss in the daughter's feelings toward her mother. Equally important, a mother had nothing to gain from prolonging the infantile depen-dency of her daughter, since a woman's role had so little to do with child care.[23] Indeed, a mother's active role in relation to her daughter usually began when a girl became marriageable, at about the age of sixteen. She then entered her mother's world, the world of women, and the mother assumed full responsibility. In well-to-do families, she made sure that her daughter had the requisite social skills, and sometimes arranged marriages. In provincial families too poor to travel to the cities, a mother probably had more trouble finding a husband for her daughter, but the girl still re-

22. The sixteen children were by her own count. Neighbors, adding stillbirths and miscarriages, estimated that she had been pregnant nineteen times. Vodovozova, *Na zare zhizni*, I, 85.

23. Few psychologists have seen fit to treat the mother-daughter relationship. My own model is based primarily on Nancy Chodorow's excellent article, "Family Structure and Feminine Personality," in *Women, Culture and Society*, ed. Michelle Rosaldo and Louise Lamphere (Stanford, 1974).

Barbara Alpern Engel

mained her responsibility. For daughters whose families had access to society, a woman's world could appear compelling. "The doors to the parlor are open, and I can hear happy talk and laughter. Someone is playing a new polka in the hall. I sigh deeply and watch for a while. For me, this is heaven, the place I yearn for and for which they prepare me. But only at the age of sixteen can I be a full citizen there."[24] Not least among the pleasures of growing up was the possibility of unprecedented intimacy with the mother. "Mother drew me closer to her and talked with me. Our paths seemed to merge," wrote E. Iunge, the daughter of a successful society woman. "Mother's life was no longer separate from mine; we were always together. It seemed to me that before I had not understood her. I rejoiced in the change in our relations, and my love for her became a kind of idolatry."[25] As a daughter matured, she learned from her mother the dimensions of her destined sphere.

When mothers sought to control all aspects of their daughters' lives, a kind of cultural (as opposed to psychic) rebellion might occur. Tensions grew particularly acute during the 1860s, when the emancipation of the serfs brought a sharp break between generations. Radical critics of the period attacked the authoritarian family as well as serfdom and called for an end to all patriarchal relations. Young women heard their message eagerly. "Ask whatever noble family you would at that time, you always heard one and the same thing—the parents had quarreled with the children. An epidemic seemed to seize upon the children—especially the girls—an epidemic of fleeing from the parental roof."[26] In the face of insubordination, mothers reasserted their authority and tried to keep daughters in their place. One provincial noblewoman regarded books as the ostensible cause of another daughter's disastrous marriage and therefore forbade her younger daughter to read anything at all, fearing that the unmarried girl would also "get carried away."[27] Another young woman found that her relations with her mother deteriorated drastically when she became interested in "new ideas." "More and more often, mother found that I was behaving disobediently . . . 'What sort of disrespect is this!' she

24. A-va [Kazina], "Zhenskaia zhizn'," p. 221.
25. Iunge, Vospominaniia, p. 193.
26. Kovalevsky, Recollections, pp. 92–93.
27. Zhukovskaia, Zapiski, pp. 20–21.

would say angrily. 'Remember, you are in the presence of your elders!' "[28] Many mothers simply could not tolerate a daughter following a different path. "Where did you get desires and thoughts so unlike mine?" demanded a mother of her newly assertive eighteen-year-old daughter. "How can you express ideas without my permission?"[29] The feminist Mariia Tsebrikova explained this maternal behavior in terms of the overall powerlessness of women. "Your poor mother has never gotten her say," recalcitrant daughters would be told. "She served her relatives, she served her husband, and now you, too, refuse to give her what she wants."[30] While Tsebrikova correctly depicts the arbitrariness of maternal authority, she neglects the very real responsibility of mother for daughter. A woman discovering her niece with "nihilist" books, for example, automatically condemned the girl's mother. "To my mind, it is unforgivable that Liza allows her daughter to follow such a false and dangerous path, and that she does not immediately direct her to a different one."[31] Young women who defied convention risked poverty, spinsterhood, marital unhappiness—or worse. A daughter's lapse was her mother's failure.

By the early nineteenth century, Enlightenment ideas had begun to change conceptions of family life. To the most westernized members of the Russian nobility, the French Enlightenment, particularly the ideas of Rousseau, meant new emphasis on the individual, a re-evaluation of marriage and the family, and increased concern for children. Not surprisingly, educated men were the first to be affected. One of our earliest examples is Aleksandr Bakunin, the father of the anarchist Mikhail Bakunin. Twenty years of living abroad had imbued him with the liberal and humanist ideas of eighteenth-century Europe, and when he returned to Russia he married and established his family according to foreign conceptions of domesticity. The influence of Rousseau emerged clearly in the care Bakunin took in educating his children. Both he and his wife

28. E. I. Bervi, "Iz moikh vospominanii," *Golos minuvshego*, 3, no. 5 (May, 1915): 125.

29. A-va [Kazina], "Zhenskaia zhizn'," p. 172. By the mid-1870s, Kazina was addressing herself to pedagogical questions in the pages of *Otechestvennye zapiski*, 217, no. 12 (December, 1874): 193–229; 220, no. 6 (June, 1875): 337–366; 227, no. 8 (August, 1876): 383–410; 229, no. 12 (Dec., 1876): 281–322.

30. Mariia Tsebrikova, "Vospominaniia," *Zvezda*, 1935, no. 6, p. 191. Tsebrikova wrote extensively on women's issues during the 1870s.

31. Streich, *Sestry Korvin-Krukovskie*, p. 12.

instructed the children themselves, daughters as well as sons. In contrast to the untutored girls of earlier times, as well as to most noblewomen of their own generation, the Bakunin sisters received an excellent education, even if (true to Rousseau) it prepared them not for a worldly life but to embellish the domestic sphere. A woman was meant to be an angel in the home. Without relinquishing his position as head of the household, Bakunin placed new emphasis on domestic felicity, to which he devoted the rest of his life.[32]

Women were far less likely than men to be exposed to western ideas. Men, not women, traveled in Europe to complete their educations; men, not women, marched triumphantly into Paris with Alexander I's armies in 1814. A few educational institutions existed for women at the beginning of the nineteenth century, but they remained vastly inferior and far less numerous. During the first third of the century, most noblewomen received no education whatsoever, and those who did learned mainly French and deportment.[33] Education led to a son's advancement in service, but parents (fathers, mostly) had no such incentive to educate their daughters. Those who took the trouble to teach them were likely to be more progressive than their neighbors; hence girls received their first taste of western ideas within their own families.

Daughters of aristocratic families close to the court of Catherine the Great were among the first to be affected. The mother of Ekaterina Raevskaia, a woman "in advance of her times," had been born at the end of the eighteenth century and had acquired a love of learning from her father. To the disapproval of her friends, she taught her daughter not only reading and writing, but science as well.[34] The mother of the novelist Elena Gan', born into the Dolgorukii family, was equally well educated. She acquired an interest in botany, history, and archeology, and when she died she left volumes of sketches of local vegetation, which she had collected and identified herself.[35] Both women were fortunate to marry men who shared, or at least approved, their interests. Praskov'ia Ivanovna

32. A. A. Kornilov, *Molodye gody Mikhaila Bakunina* (Moscow, 1915), pp. 32, 33, 63, 72; E. H. Carr, *Michael Bakunin* (New York, 1937), p. 9.

33. Elena Likhacheva, *Materialy dlia istorii zhenskogo obrazovaniia v Rossii* (St. Petersburg, 1899–1901), II, 250–251.

34. "Vospominaniia Ekateriny Ivanovny Raevskoi," *Istoricheskii vestnik*, 19, no. 11 (November, 1898): 548; no. 12 (December, 1898): 947–948.

35. "Elena Andreevna Gan'," *Russkaia Starina*, 1886, no. 8, pp. 337–338.

Tatlina, born in 1808 to a traditional noble family of relatively modest means, was not so lucky.[36] Tatlina acquired an all-consuming love of learning at the home of a wealthy and westernized uncle. When a family quarrel kept her from her uncle's home, a good friend filched books for her to read. Enlightenment philosophers, Voltaire in particular, had an enormous impact on her thinking. But reading estranged her from her milieu. Her mother was deeply religious, Tatlina recalled, and old women who talked of nothing but the fear of God always filled her house. Tatlina had lost not only her religion but also her taste for feminine pursuits: "I wanted nothing to do with the kitchen or nursery." When she reached eighteen, her parents married her to a virtual stranger, a widower seventeen years her senior, a military man who utterly lacked her intellectual development and had thoroughly traditional views as to woman's place—"for him, a woman was an object." The two had nothing in common, and the marriage made her miserable. In addition, her love of learning was totally out of place in the barracks atmosphere in which they lived. Her only outlet became educating her children, especially her daughters.[37] "A person should be happy in this world," Tatlina reasoned. Her own experience had convinced her that marriage brings unhappiness and therefore that people should avoid it; hence a woman must be able to support herself. Over the opposition of husband, family, and friends, Tatlina provided her eldest daughter with musical training in the hope that teaching, the only calling possible for a noblewoman, could provide the girl with independence.[38]

By the 1830s and 1840s, western ideas had ceased to be the prerogative of an aristocratic few, due to increased educational opportunities and the proliferation of journals. Even in the provinces, noblewomen could stay abreast of the latest ideas. These had come to include a critique of women's role in the family and in society, under the influence of utopian socialism.[39] For women,

36. The rank or property holdings of her father are never stated. For a while he managed the enormous estates of Count Sheremetev; then, after the War of 1812, the family lived in a house her father had built in Moscow, where he evidently served in some civil capacity.
37. Her reading had cut her off from religious activity, and her husband owned no property for her to manage. Her social status barred her from the life of society, and presumably she lacked either the talent or the inclination to become a writer.
38. "Vospominaniia Praskov'i Nikolaevny Tatlinoi," *Russkii Arkhiv*, 37, no. 9 (1899): 190–224.
39. Likhacheva, *Materialy*, III, 220–230.

George Sand was the primary purveyor of western ideas. By putting abstract ideas into fictional form, Sand made them accessible even to the relatively unsophisticated.[40] But the impact was more emotional than theoretical. From Sand, women learned about "the truth of the heart" and the "great ideal of love." Soon it seemed that "all the scandals of our domestic existence, all the dissoluteness of women, the result of women's ignorance and men's depravity, were ascribed to George Sand."[41] It is true that Sand herself, as well as some of her Russian followers, used her ideas to justify resistance to society's limitations on emotional life. Mariia Ogareva, the wife of the poet Nikolai Ogarev and a follower of Sand, wrote in her diary: "I conceded nothing to society—not a single desire, not one of my beliefs, not a single impulse to love."[42] When two of Tatlina's daughters became enamored of Sand, their mother disapproved; while Sand provided an outlet for women, it was an unsavory one because her ideas awakened "the impulse to sensual love."[43] A few women discovered the feminist message in the ideas of utopians. Notable among these is Evgeniia Mikhailis, born in 1808, who published pseudonymously in a leading journal and, in the late 1830s, spoke of women's rights and women's need to work.[44]

Free love and feminism notwithstanding, the ideas of the 1830s and 1840s did not cause wholesale abandonment of domesticity. In fact, the result was precisely the opposite—a greater emotional investment in family life, to the occasional detriment of other aspects of women's role. Discussions tended to stress the companionate aspects of marriage: a woman needed education, for example, in order to "share her husband's thoughts and supervise the education of his children."[45] Moreover, in the absence of other options, the family remained the only area where women could implement their ideas. The freedom to love became the freedom to choose one's husband. The rights of the individual led to the demand for better treatment and respect from him, as well as the

40. "Zhorzh Zand," *Otechestvennye zapiski*, 232, no. 6 (June, 1877): 441. See also M. Gershenzon, "Russkaia zhenshchina 30–kh godov," *Russkaia mysl'*, 1911, no. 12, p. 54.

41. "Zhorzh Zand," p. 441; See also Gershenzon, "Russkaia zhenshchina," p. 55, and S. S. Shashkov, *Sobranie sochinenii*, (St. Petersburg, 1898), I, 653.

42. Gershenzon, "Russkaia zhenshchina," p. 55.

43. Tatlina, "Vospominaniia," p. 220.

44. N. V. Shelgunov, L. P. Shelgunova, and M. L. Mikhailov, *Vospominaniia v dvukh tomakh*, I, 17.

45. Likhacheva, *Materialy*, III, 220–230.

expectation of emotional gratification from the marriage itself. Marriage was no longer a relationship between master and servant; instead, it became a partnership, wherein the woman's role was equal to, although different from, the man's. In 1839 the influential novelist Elena Gan' wrote, "God has destined women to be at the heart of the household, the comforter of her chosen friend, the mother of his children." Women who fulfilled that role, she asserted, were just as useful as men.[46]

Unfortunately, the men whom such women married did not ordinarily share their wives' expectations of domestic bliss. Trained to serve the state, and as recipients of a military-style education, husbands lacked the refinement and sensitivity of their wives. Mariia Zhukova, born in 1805 and a popular novelist at the end of the 1830s, registered a typical complaint about men: "They have no time for emotions; the heart and its attachments are not their department. It's an entirely special item, not entered in their desk register or their regulations of bankruptcy."[47] As a result, education did not always bring a woman happiness, although it may have led her to expect it; since education raised expectations for love and companionship, it made the limitations of domesticity all the more disappointing and led to unhappy marriages. Denied one emotional outlet, women sought another in child-rearing, focusing especially on daughters, their traditional responsibility. Many, such as Tatlina, would undoubtedly have liked to spare their daughters a fate like their own, but before the 1850s there was little they could do. The lack of other options, emotional as well as vocational, left no real alternative to marriage.

By the late 1850s this situation had begun to change. The disastrous defeat in the Crimean War had called into question the very bases of society and challenged the legitimacy of all authority figures, including the patriarchal father. Emancipation of the serfs in 1861 undermined his role still further. At the same time, much of educated society welcomed the beginning of a new era. Radical writers called for a thoroughgoing regeneration of society and condemned the idleness and luxury associated with serf-holding. Educated women responded by reorganizing their domestic life accord-

46. Gershenzon, "Russkaia zhenshchina," pp. 59, 67.
47. M. S. Konopleva, "Mariia Semenovna Zhukova," *Golos minuvshego*, 1913, no. 7, p. 29. The quotation is drawn from her novel, *Provintsialka*.

ing to the latest ideas: they taught their children to be self-sufficient and they simplified their way of life, adopting an almost spartan austerity. Mariia Trubnikova was the daughter of a Decembrist rebel and was "almost a nihilist" in her views. Over her husband's protests, she renounced all unnecessáry luxury, taught her children to be simple in their dress, and made them do everything for themselves. Her daughter Ol'ga, born in the early 1850s, began to accompany her mother to lectures at the age of eight.[48] Sof'ia Subbotina, the daughter of a university professor, reared her three daughters in similar fashion. Her eldest, Evgeniia (born in 1853), later wrote: "We were not coddled. We slept at first on hay mattresses, and then we used Moroccan mattresses that were so hard that they were practically boards." Custom severely restricted the physical activities of noblewomen, but Subbotina (like Trubnikova) encouraged her children to exercise: "In our free time we did athletics; in the summer we swam in the pond, played giant steps in the garden, ran around and climbed trees as high as we liked."[49] A widow, Subbotina ran her estate and instructed her daughters in Russian, geography, arithmetic, religion, French, and music.

No longer able to change their own lives, the women could at least seek a brighter future for their daughters—a future that had become less remote because of expanding educational and employment opportunities. In 1856 the government permitted the opening of *gimnaziia* to girls of all estates. In 1866 pedagogical courses were opened to women, and in 1868 college preparatory courses were established in Moscow and St. Petersburg. In 1867 Nadezhda Suslova earned a medical degree in Zurich, and hundreds of women subsequently tried to follow her example. In 1872 a program for "learned obstetricians" opened at the Medical Academy in St. Petersburg. To be sure, education remained available primarily to the privileged. Nevertheless, new opportunities enabled women to participate in public life in unprecedented numbers, and educated mothers often encouraged their daughters to take advantage of such opportunities. Varvara Perovskaia first devised a special educational program for her daughter Sof'ia; then, when she could not carry it out, she helped Sof'ia and her older sister to attend college preparatory courses in Petersburg.

48. Bulanova-Trubnikova, *Tri pokoleniia*, pp. 136–137.
49. Evgeniia Subbotina, *Na revoliutsionnom puti* (Moscow, 1928), p. 12.

Ekaterina Figner, the wife of a forester, lent books to her daughter Vera and then helped her save money to go to Zurich to study medicine. Sof'ia Subbotina sought a good high school for her daughters and later paid for their medical studies in Zurich.

Educated mothers also tended to be more sympathetic than their husbands to radical ideas, probably because they derived less power and privilege from the existing order and therefore had less to lose from its demise. During the 1860s Varvara Perovskaia, the wife of a former governor, listened eagerly when her son Vasilii read the radical critics Pisarev, Dobroliubov, and others aloud during his summer visits to the countryside. "She would listen very attentively and raise questions at each step so as to absorb the material more thoroughly," Vasilii remembered.[50] During the height of the revolutionary movement of the 1870s, Mariia Trubnikova allowed her home to be used for meetings of radicals, for storing illegal literature, and even for visits of women such as Sof'ia Perovskaia, whose terrorist views she herself opposed and whose presence (after Perovskaia had become a fugitive) constituted an actual danger.[51] Ekaterina Figner helped her daughter Vera to smuggle funds to emigrés in Geneva, continued to see her after she had gone underground, and faithfully wrote to her in exile. Anna Vasil'evna Armfeld, another noblewoman, openly sympathized with her daughter Natasha's revolutionary goals, took pride in her activity, and assisted her as much as she could. When Natasha was imprisoned in 1878, Anna Vasil'evna obtained the plans of the prison and sought out people to dig a tunnel under her daughter's cell. The work was only half completed when all the prisoners were transferred to Perm. At that point, the mother grew so concerned for her daughter's welfare that she abandoned the capital to follow Natasha into exile.[52] Sof'ia Subbotina became a radical in her own right. During a visit to Zurich, where she had sent her daughters to study medicine, she participated enthusiastically in political discussions, attended meetings of the First International, and contributed money to strike funds and the radical emigré library. When she returned to Russia, she began to organize the peasants who worked her land, advising them to withhold taxes and recruits from

50. Vasilii Perovskii, "Moi vospominaniia," *Katorga i ssylka*, no. 15 (1925):98.
51. Bulanova-Trubnikova, *Tri pokoleniia*, pp. 146ff.
52. V. A. Anzimirov, *Kramol'niki* (Moscow, 1907), p. 96.

the tsar. After almost a year of such activity she was arrested, imprisoned, and subsequently tried in the enormous political trial of the 193. Among the other charges against her was the accusation of subverting her daughters and her ward, Varvara Shatilova.

In the first half of the nineteenth century, family patterns of the nobility placed a daughter firmly in her mother's sphere. When the child was young, however, the mother-daughter relationship was mediated by a series of female figures; only as a daughter began to mature did the mother become directly responsible for her. At that point, the exigencies of matchmaking necessitated careful supervision. Developmental stages were thus set off from each other as much by changes in personnel as by different experiences and expectations. Infantile dependency was thus attenuated, and "adolescence" became a prelude to the final stage of womanhood, a period not of rebellion but of entrance into the mother's world and acceptance of her values.

The western ideas which began to reach an educated minority of noblewomen in the 1830s and 1840s altered expectations of marriage and the family. Reading may not create feelings, but it can legitimize them, and women began to seek more emotional gratification from marriage and to take a greater interest in their children. Daughters, traditionally the mother's responsibility, probably received more of this attention than their brothers did. To the extent that the mothers were dissatisfied with their own lives, they encouraged their daughters to seek a different future. After 1861, acceptance of a mother's values could mean pursuit of an education, a career, or ideals that led eventually to revolutionary activism. Because of this connection with the mother, daughters who rebelled against society's definition of femininity did not necessarily risk the loss of their female self-image. The last letter of Sof'ia Perovskaia, who led the assassination of Alexander II, suggests the importance of this mother-daughter connection. "I have always regretted my inability to attain your level of moral perfection," she wrote to her mother on the eve of her execution, "but at every moment of doubt your image has sustained me."[53]

Investigation of family patterns in the second half of the nineteenth century has hardly begun. The number of articles de-

53. S. M. Stepniak-Kravchinskii, *Izbrannoe* (Moscow, 1972), pp. 470–471.

voted to motherhood and childcare increased greatly during the 1860s and 1870s, and progressive women read and responded to them.[54] "Mothers who had always loved their children now saw the light, and for the first time understood what it means to love and how to go about it," remembered Nikolai Shelgunov, an influential writer and critic of the 1850s and 1860s. "Children became the first members of the household and they were given the best, the brightest, and the most spacious rooms. No one had ever thought of physical development, and now it became a primary family concern."[55] If this new emphasis on motherhood came at the expense of other roles, and if the impact proved widespread, then it would be useful to compare mother-daughter relations during the second half of the century with those in the earlier period. Such a comparison could provide important insights into all aspects of the woman's role. In a society where sex roles are strictly defined, the mother-daughter relationship must be a crucial determinant of female personality. As is evident from the changes described in this paper, that relationship varies not only from individual to individual, but historically as well.

54. See "Ukazatel' literatury zhenskogo voprosa na russkom iazyke," *Severnyi vestnik*, July and August, 1887, entries 1641–1755.
55. Shelgunov, *Vospominaniia*, I, 137.

RICHARD WORTMAN

The Russian Empress as Mother

Like monarchs of all periods, the monarchs of nineteenth-century Europe strove to exemplify certain dominant values of their era. Prominent among these was a trust in the sanctity of the family and the high role of the parent. Queen Louise and King Frederick William III of Prussia, Emperor Franz-Joseph, and, of course, Queen Victoria became symbols of royalty's adoption of the familial values of the middle class. They created an aura of domestic respectability that enhanced claims to reverence and obedience that had been challenged by the French Revolution. The queen or empress, as first lady of the land, had to become the first mother as well, embodying the purity, wisdom, and selflessness associated with child-rearing. Her virtues would guarantee the sound moral development of her children and ensure the future of the dynasty.

The princesses who came from Germany (or, in one case, from Denmark) to wed the Russian heirs brought with them current European attitudes about the roles of the wife and the mother. Beginning with the reign of Nicholas I, the Russian royal house also adopted these attitudes, and family responsibility and loyalty became part of its ethos. Upon her arrival the future empress would take on a new name and a new faith and then become the subservient wife, devoted to the tasks the nineteenth-century mind as-

The empresses discussed in this paper are:
Mariia Fedorovna (1759–1828)—Sophie, daughter of the Duke of Würtemberg, wife of Paul I, mother of Alexander I and Nicholas I;
Aleksandra Fedorovna (1798–1860)—Princess Charlotte of Prussia, wife of Nicholas I, mother of Alexander II;
Mariia Aleksandrovna (1824–1880)—Princess Maximilien of Hesse-Darmstadt, wife of Alexander II, mother of Grand Duke Nicholas Aleksandrovich and Alexander III;
Mariia Fedorovna (2) (1847–1928)—Princess Dagmar of Denmark, wife of Alexander III, mother of Nicholas II.

signed to women—among them, motherhood. But the role of mother in the royal family would not be an easy one. There were problems inherent in the personal inclinations of the individual empresses, and maternal and royal obligations were in many ways mutually exclusive. In addition, the political and psychological circumstances of the Russian royal house often discouraged the mother's active participation in the lives of her children. This paper examines the evolution of the Russian empress's role as mother, particularly her relationship to the heir. My aim is to highlight several aspects of this relationship, in the hope that they may be explored more thoroughly in further research.

In Russia, as elsewhere, the emphasis on the family marked a rejection of the eighteenth century and its values. The reprehensible past was epitomized by Catherine the Great, who, possessed by ambition, flagrant in her inconstancy and indifference to the family, seemed threatening to the very notion of nineteenth-century legitimacy. Most important, she had been an accomplice in the murder of her husband. Catherine was a product of Peter the Great's succession law, which had eliminated the precedence of family and of men over women in the succession. The law had expressed a fear of the natural heir: the first-born son, as Absalom, was a potential threat to the strength and wisdom of the monarchy. Peter's succession law argued from the premise of utility: the successor had to be qualified to serve the best interests of the empire, regardless of his position in the family.[1]

In the eighteenth century, the heir's mother was suspect on two accounts. Not only could she use her influence over her son to further her own selfish political designs, but her closeness to the heir could also lead to personal attachment and dependency that would divert him from concern for the welfare of all. The qualities of the good monarch were strength, wisdom, and an ability to submit personal impulses to the voice of reason. The son was to be in the image of the father, or the present ruler, and to realize the hopes for a strong, enlightened monarch. After giving birth, the mother was accordingly banished from association with the heir. Eighteenth-century Russian monarchs followed practices of mother avoidance

---

1. *Polnoe sobranie zakonov rossiiskoi imperii*, Sobranie pervoe, 46 vols. (St. Petersburg, 1830–43), no. 3893, February 5, 1722. Hereafter cited as *PSZ*.

which were common in the absolutist states of Europe.[2] Peter the Great tried to keep his son Aleksei away from the tsarina Evdokiia Lopukhina; a generation later, Empress Elizabeth removed Grand Duke Paul from the care of his mother, Catherine, immediately after his birth, and Catherine, when empress, did the same, taking the Grand Duke Alexander away from his parents, the Grand Duke Paul Petrovich and the Grand Duchess Mariia Fedorovna.

The new attitude toward the family was heralded by the succession law of Paul I, promulgated in 1797. Issued in response to the power struggles and assassinations of the previous century, this law conceived the threat to the monarchy to be not the first-born son but the conniving empress who, devoid of family responsibility, pursued her own ambitions and disrupted the succession. The first words of the law ensured priority to the first-born son, and, following the "Austrian" principle of succession, gave preference to men before women. Proclaimed at the end of the coronation of Paul and Mariia Fedorovna and signed by both husband and wife, it took the form (extraordinary for Russia) of a familial act or collective testament.[3]

The 1797 succession law was a first, symbolic step toward transforming the empress from a political rival into a helpful member of the imperial family. It remained for the royal house to become a closely knit family and to fortify its power through kinship bonds. Tsar Alexander I, who came to the throne through the assassination of his father, cared little for his wife, and produced no heir, could not himself achieve this goal. But he held lofty ideals of family life which had been nurtured by the sentimental literature he had read. The emblematic event in this respect was a conversation with his younger brother Nicholas Pavlovich in 1819. Alexander pointed out that neither Konstantin (the second in line) nor he himself, both of whom had been brought up under Catherine's supervision, had enjoyed a happy family life or had provided an heir. Revealing that Nicholas was to be his successor, Alexander sadly confessed that he

2. See David Hunt, *Parents and Children in History* (New York, 1970), p. 17. Hunt writes of the upbringing of Louis XIII: "The dauphin was physically separated from his mother, discouraged from developing any kind of deep affective ties with her, reminded constantly that he belonged to papa; thus did absolutism attempt to sabotage the Oedipus complex."

3. *PSZ*, XVII, 910, April 5, 1797; B. Nol'de, "Zakony osnovnye v russkom prave," *Pravo*, 1913, no. 9, pp. 524–526; V. I. Zhmakin, "Koronatsii russkikh imperatorov i imperatrits, 1724–1856," *Russkaia starina*, 1884, no. 6, p. 636.

felt himself incapable of realizing his own ideal of family happiness.[4]

Nicholas Pavlovich, the first of Mariia Fedorovna's sons to be reared under her supervision, was also the first to see himself as a family man. While in Paris he had met the Duke of Orleans and had admired his close family life. "What enormous happiness it is to live that way, in a family," Nicholas exclaimed. "It is the only true and firm happiness," the Duke replied.[5] In 1819, the twenty-three-year-old Nicholas, though uncouth, unpopular, and poorly educated, could already boast a loving wife and a son. As Tsar Nicholas I, he would make fatherhood and paternal authority an important part of the image of manhood presented by the tsar. He personified the masculine virtues of potency, authority, and austere ruthlessness. The ability to win love, which his brother Alexander I had excelled in, would be relegated to the empress.

The nineteenth-century empress was to fit the new conceptions of the family and to act as cherishing mother to her child. Her principal sphere was to become the home, rather than the court or state. The official world came to represent alien and unpleasant obligations to her. "Both of us," Aleksandra Fedorovna wrote, "had a horror of everything that was *the court*."[6] She had to embody the purity and respectability of the regime, and, at the dynastic level, to act out the woman's nineteenth-century role as moral custodian of a society that otherwise could not afford morality. The model that she provided depended on her separation from the brutal and often gruesome demands of autocratic polity. She had to stand apart as a sentimental ideal, rewarded with admiration and even worship for her forbearance and passivity. No longer "mother of the fatherland," as Catherine II had been styled, she would become the mother of the family.

The empresses brought high notions about motherhood and the family with them when they came to Russia. As a girl, Mariia Fedorovna (1) had been taught that a mother's mission was to educate her children, an attitude reinforced by her own parents' long and close marriage. Aleksandra Fedorovna shared the familial values of her parents Queen Louise and King Frederick William

4. N. K. Shil'der, *Imperator Nikolai Pervyi: ego zhizn' i tsarstvovanie* (St. Petersburg, 1903), I, 122.

5. *Ibid.*, p. 46.

6. "Imperatritsa Aleksandra Fedorovna v svoikh vospominaniiakh," *Russkaia starina*, 1896, no. 10, p. 52.

III. Upon the death of her mother, her father told her that she had replaced the queen in his eyes. She always kept a bust of her mother on the desk in her study.[7] Mariia Fedorovna (2) came out of the strong patriarchal tradition of the Danish royal house. Of the nineteenth-century empresses, only Mariia Aleksandrovna lacked such a background, but she, too, brought to Russia feelings of the importance of a mother's role in the upbringing of her children.

Under Nicholas I, motherhood was extolled in verse, art, and architecture. Zhukovskii greeted the birth of the heir Alexander Nikolaevich with an epistle to Aleksandra Fedorovna that dwelled on the parents' joy and the feelings of the young mother.

> Your child, like a heavenly messenger,
> Told your soul of a better life,
> Lit the purest hopes within it.
> Now your wishes are not for you,
> Your joys not for yourself;
> Wrapped in diapers,
> Still without words, with unseeing eyes,
> He finds love in your eyes. . . .[8]

With the accession of Nicholas, a series of prints and paintings showing the royal family together were executed. These depictions appear to represent a departure from the eighteenth-century practices of separate portraiture or large court scenes. The English artist George Dawe completed a series of engravings of Nicholas's family; the most notable of these showed Aleksandra Fedorovna sitting, the seven-year-old Alexander Nikolaevich grasping her gown from the left, and the infant Ol'ga Nikolaevna resting in her right arm.[9] At Peterhof, Nicholas set off a small private estate, Alexandria, for the empress and built a "cottage" in English style where the family would create a rustic domestic life. There Aleksandra reigned as a kind of goddess-mother, indulging her whims and receiving ostentatious signs of love and respect.[10]

Yet if the symbols and gestures of family and motherhood became part of the new panoply of autocracy, the actual role of the empress

7. A. Th. Von Grimm, *Alexandra Feodorowna, Kaiserin von Russland*, (St. Petersburg, 1866), I, 58, 226.

8. V. A. Zhukovskii, *Polnoe sobranie sochinenii* (St. Petersburg, 1902), I, 124–126.

9. D. A. Rovinskii, *Podrobnyi slovar' russkikh gravirovannykh portretov* (St. Petersburg, 1886–89), I, 19–20.

10. See A. Shemanskii and S. Geichenko, *Krizis samoderzhaviia: Petergofskii Kottedzh Nikolaia I* (Moscow-Leningrad, 1932).

as mother was limited. The old suspicions of her lingered when it came to rearing and educating an heir. The callow and frightened princess who came to the court was not considered capable of rearing a future autocrat. In addition, the demands on her time for court ceremonial and charitable work were great, and current social mores did not allow an empress to participate in many of the more menial tasks of child-rearing. It was, above all, as child-bearers that the nineteenth-century empresses were exalted as mothers; beginning with Aleksandra Fedorovna, they acquitted this responsibility conscientiously. Aleksandra Fedorovna gave birth to five children in her first seven years of marriage; Mariia Aleksandrovna to her first four children in five years, and Mariia Fedorovna (2) to her first three in four years.

Other family members assumed the chief responsibility for directing and supervising the training and education of the heir. Mariia Fedorovna (1), who had seen her first children removed by Catherine, followed similar practices when she became a grandmother. While she could not separate mother and child, she did preside over the early upbringing of Alexander Nikolaevich and selected the staff that cared for him.[11] Though it may be true that Aleksandra Fedorovna chose Zhukovskii as Alexander's preceptor, her role in her son's education went no further. Nicholas I supervised the education of his children because the empress was burdened by so many other obligations that she could not attend to it.[12] Alexander II claimed to assign chief responsibility for his own children's education to his wife, Mariia Aleksandrovna: "she has more time for it." But in fact, her strong convictions and interest in state affairs aroused suspicions, and she was kept from exerting a significant influence on her sons' educations. Only the outcry of liberal public opinion in 1857 and 1858 about the careless education of the heir made it necessary for her to participate in the search for new preceptors.[13] Later in the century the misgivings about the heir's mother began to diminish. Mariia Fedorovna (2) played a

11. S. S. Tatishchev, *Imperator Aleksandr II: ego zhizn' i tsarstvovanie* (St. Petersburg, 1903), I, 6.

12. K. K. Merder, "Zapiski K. K. Merdera, vospitatelia Aleksandra Nikolaevicha," *Russkaia starina*, 1885, no. 7, p. 42; Grimm, *Alexandra Feodorowna*, II, 104, 112–114.

13. E. S. Kamenskii, "Ot detstva do prisiagi; iz zhizni avgusteishikh detei Imperatora Aleksandra II," *Istoricheskii vestnik*, 37, no. 1 (January, 1916): 102–103; F. A. Oom, "Vospominaniia," *Russkii arkhiv*, 34, nos. 5–8 (1896): 245.

significant role in Nicholas II's education, since it was not of great interest to Alexander III. She made every effort to keep tutors from gaining an influence over her son, perhaps distressed by the sway of her husband's tutor, Pobedonostev.[14]

It is clear that the grand duchess or empress had little contact with her children. From the moment of delivery, numerous servants saw to the care of the infant. Robust peasant women were brought in from their villages to feed him.[15] The nineteenth-century empresses could not or would not heed the dictum of the current child-rearing literature that breast feeding by the mother contributed to the child's well-being. Mariia Aleksandrovna, whose first-born son, Nicholas, had been given to a wet nurse, expressed the desire to breast feed her second, Alexander—but, like many of her wishes, this one was refused. Her father-in-law Nicholas I insisted that the child be fed by a wet nurse.[16] Fears for the empress's health, current expectations of how an empress should act, ceremonial demands, and the desire for more children all combined to discourage the empress from breast feeding.

Servants performed the early work of rearing. The heir spent his first years in the care of a staff of women, headed by a court lady of high standing and impeccable reputation. The children's nurses were foreigners, usually English, as were their governesses. It was common for the grand dukes to develop strong attachments to the women who cared for them in their early years and to remain fond of them throughout their lives. However, at about the age of seven they were abruptly removed to the care of men, who would seek to initiate them in the military ethos and practices that were important to autocracy and to provide them with the civil education necessary for governmental and diplomatic obligations. A hierarchy of officers and teachers saw to the "moral" and intellectual training of the heir, who was placed directly in the care of an avuncular officer enjoying the tsar's trust. The heir's mother would be invited, with his father to carefully prepared examinations where she could watch and approve of her son's performance.

14. E. Flourens, *Alexandre III, sa vie, son oeuvre* (Paris, 1894), pp. 77–78.
15. I have found direct mention of the use of wet nurses for Nicholas I, Nicholas Aleksandrovich, Alexander III, and Nicholas II. Aleksandra Fedorovna returned from Moscow to St. Petersburg separately from the heir, less than two months after the birth, suggesting that she was not nursing him.
16. A. I. Iakovleva, "Vospominaniia byvshei kamer-iungfery Imperatritsy Marii Aleksandrovny," *Istoricheskii vestnik*, 9, no. 2 (February, 1888): 410.

Descriptions of tsars' early childhoods are few and vague, making it difficult to reconstruct their daily lives. From available accounts, it appears that the children visited their mothers for one or perhaps two hours a day, rarely longer. When the empress was taking one of her frequent trips to Europe, for health reasons or to visit relatives, the children were deprived even of this contact. Aleksandra Fedorovna left in September, 1820, for a journey that lasted over a year, while the two-and one-half-year-old Alexander remained in St. Petersburg under the supervision of his grandmother Mariia Fedorovna. Mariia Aleksandrovna took a seven-week trip through Germany in the fall of 1843, only two months after the birth of her first son, Nicholas. She visited Darmstadt the next spring for six weeks while pregnant with her son Alexander. Among her subsequent travels was a lengthy trip to Europe in 1847, when Alexander Aleksandrovich was just two years old and Vladimir three months.[17] If one counts the time of confinement for births and convalescence, it is clear that there were long stretches when the young heir would be separated from his mother. Injunctions against reliance on servants and exhortations for the mother to take direct care of her child could lead only to fastidiousness in the selection of the nursery staff.

Yet, despite the obstacles to intimacy, Russian empresses appear to have exerted a significant influence on the development of the heirs' personalities. In their personal characteristics, mannerisms, and tastes the nineteenth-century tsars resembled their mothers far more than their fathers. Nicholas I's rigid self-righteousness and despotism, Alexander II's poise, flirtatiousness, and absorption with the frivolous and external, Alexander III's asociability and brooding religiosity, and Nicholas II's cold charm, suspiciousness, and secretiveness all appeared inherited from their mothers. The tsars emulated their fathers chiefly in their devotion to the principles of autocracy. The public image of the tsar, represented by the father, embodied demands that the heir found intimidating and beyond his powers. The heir saw his father as tsar, as a person rising to fulfill the demands and ceremonies of the office he was obliged to assume.[18] But the mother could act not only as empress but also as an individual with thoughts and feelings of her own. The heirs

17. Tatishchev, *Imperator Aleksandr II*, I, 116.

18. Richard Wortman, "Power and Responsibility in the Upbringing of the Nineteenth-Century Russian Tsars," Group for the Use of Psychology in History *Newsletter* (March, 1976), pp. 18–27.

seem to have received their notions of personal life from their mothers.

Although the empress continued to remain apart from the chief tasks of child-rearing, she was expected to·show affection and kindness to her children when she did see them. Barred from the formal tasks of socialization, she was allowed and encouraged to perform the role of emotional nurturer. In this sense the new conceptions of motherhood affected the ideas of how a mother should act and how a child should approach her, even if they did not greatly alter child-rearing practices in the imperial family. The heir may have spent little time with his mother, but this time was the high moment of the day. Since the quality and intensity of parental contact are often more important in shaping a relationship than the amount of time spent with a child, the empress could provide an emotional focus in the heir's life, and could serve as a highly praised model of virtue.

The importance of the empress to her children is evident from the feelings they expressed about her absence. Ol'ga Nikolaevna wrote that it was like "paradise" for the children to be near their mother, Aleksandra Fedorovna. They were desolate when she was gone: "If mother was away, we were like lost souls."[19] When Nicholas I and Aleksandra were in the south during the Russo-Turkish War of 1828, Alexander Nikolaevich, then ten years old, was inconsolable. He wandered through the palace at Tsarskoe Selo saying, "Here is where Papa and Mama have dinner. Here Papa sat, and there Mama. Where are they now?" He lost interest in play, and his usual cheerful manner disappeared. He wrote in his diary, "My nice Mama and Mary left for Odessa. I cried a lot."[20] Nicholas II, when about ten, lived for the two hours a day he could spend with his mother, whom he worshipped. It was a time of love and recreation in the midst of a general isolation and regimentation. "The children longed for their mother, enjoyed her warmth, did not want to be parted from her." When Mariia Fedorovna was giving birth to Mikhail Aleksandrovich, her sons could not see her, and they became forlorn. "The childrens' cheeks were sunken. They became pale and began to eat and sleep poorly."[21]

19. Ol'ga Nikolaevna, Grand Duchess, *Son iunosti* (Paris, 1963), p. 35.
20. Merder, "Zapiski," *Russkaia starina*, 1885, no. 2, pp. 355–356.
21. Il'ia Surguchev, *Detstvo Imperatora Nikolaia II* (Paris, 1953), pp. 88–90, 92–93.

Mariia Aleksandrovna was more reserved with her children, and her concern expressed itself in worry and strictness. She appeared sad in the presence of her children.[22] Yet the heir missed his parents when they were away in 1847. The four-year-old Nicholas exclaimed, "Papa went away. Mother went away. Lina went away. But what can we do?" Just before their return he said, "When Papa, Mama, and Lina come back I will be so happy that I will walk on my head."[23] The younger sons, including the future Alexander III, retained a sense of being deprived of parental warmth and attention, and they recalled these feelings bitterly later on.[24]

Loved, worshipped, regretted, the empress became one who was sought after and imitated by her children. She provided an example which, as Ol'ga Nikolaevna suggested, affected the children, even if she did not concern herself directly with them.[25] Her example was one of personal feeling and conduct, a model of emotional expression. The father had to contain or suppress his personal feelings and conform to the public image of tsar—a distant and awesome figure. The empress could provide an initial sense of comradeship and the first lessons in the ways that royalty could appear human.

The empress's treatment of the heir might conflict with the spirit of his formal education. She could shield him from the demands of strength and self-control impressed by his teachers; she could pamper him, and show understanding for his weaknesses. Or her refusal to provide such support could be viewed as rejection and lead to difficulties in expressing such feelings. The former pattern prevailed in the early lives of Alexander II and Nicholas II; in Aleksandra Fedorovna Alexander was able to find a way to avoid his studies and to go to the theater or for a walk. After a fall from a horse, which brought only rebukes from his father, he could spend a whole day in the company of his mother. Mariia Fedorovna's protective attitude toward Nicholas II was partly responsible for decreasing the rigor and seriousness of his education, resulting in a diminished importance being assigned to formal training. Mariia

22. A. F. Tiutcheva, *Pri dvore dvukh imperatorov, Vospominaniia, Dnevnik,* 1853–1882 (Cambridge, England, 1975), II, 65–66, 116–117.

23. S. A. Iur'evich, "Pis'ma ob avgusteishikh synov'iakh Aleksandra II," Unpublished manuscript, in New York Public Library, pp. 49, 131.

24. Oom, "Vospominaniia," p. 254; "Iz dnevnika A. A. Polovtsova," *Krasnyi arkhiv,* 33 (1929): 187.

25. Ol'ga Nikolaevna, *Son iunosti,* p. 35.

Aleksandrovna, on the other hand, did not provide such consolation for her children and was critical of their progress. Both Alexander III and Nicholas Aleksandrovich grew up without an alternative source of support in their mother, and both remained ill at ease in expressing their feelings.[26]

It was not only association and identification that fostered a bond between empress and heir, but also their common position as prominent but necessarily subservient members of the imperial family. Since both of them were potential rivals for authority, the tsar regarded them with suspicion when matters of state were at issue. They shared a common passive role, serving as parts of the ornamentation of autocracy; they were both gracious victims of the requirements of state. Aleksandra Fedorovna was to play the doll who displayed autocracy's conversion to domesticity and male dominance. In return for her effacement, she could count on the satisfaction of her caprices. For her amusement Nicholas I turned Peterhof into a playground where she could live in a world of make-believe. He treated her as a child, playing games by posing as a servant who brought her presents. She was called a little bird, *ptichka*, upon her arrival in Russia, and charmed all around her into obedience to her whims. She represents what Rieber has described as the "flirtatious" response to the dilemma of the woman's role in the nineteenth-century Russian court.[27] But the air of frivolity hid the isolation and condescension she felt as empress. Her public appearances alternated with increasingly frequent bouts of disease and nervous illness that made her the object of more serious attention.[28]

Her son, Alexander Nikolaevich, was paraded about as proof of the dynasty's persistence and fertility. On the day of the Decembrist revolt he was displayed, and at the coronation and the ensuing balls and festivities. His poise and charm won general admiration. Subordinating his own impulses, he, too, accepted a stage role. In his submission to the demands of the classroom, in his abandonment of his first real love, and in his participation in governmental matters, he struggled to accept this enforced denial. The letters of

26. Merder, "Zapiski," *Russkaia starina*, 1885, no. 8, pp. 224–225, no. 9, p. 433, no. 12, p. 504; Tiutcheva, *Pri dvore dvukh imperatorov, II*, 63–66; 102, 116–117, 191.

27. "Imperatritsa Aleksandra Fedorovna," p. 16; Alfred J. Rieber, introduction to Tiutcheva, *Pri dvore dvukh imperatorov*.

28. Grimm, *Alexandra Feodorowna*; Tiutcheva, *Pri dvore dvukh imperatorov*.

Aleksandra and Alexander to Zhukovskii at the time of the coronation express a common sympathy in the sharing of ritual excess.
Aleksandra, admiring the figure cut by her eight-year-old son,
sympathized with him for bursting into tears in the middle of the
ceremony. Alexander, in his turn, wrote Zhukovskii, "Thank God,
Mama stood that long ceremony."[29]

Both Alexander III and Mariia Aleksandrovna felt the effects of
Alexander II's suspicion of family members.[30] Mother and son were
treated as unwanted and insignificant. Mariia Aleksandrovna, a
melancholic woman of doubtful legitimacy and from a lesser German state, was alien to the demanding court milieu she was supposed to exemplify. After her arrival in Russia, she tried to share
her husband's interests, and she did enjoy discussions with him and
other important figures. Such eagerness, however, only revived
misgivings about her ambitions and stirred Alexander's insecu-
rities. At the moment of her husband's accession, Mariia was given
to know that her involvement in government could not be received
kindly, and she was removed from all possibility of influence. It was
said that these steps were prompted by rumors that the empress,
not the emperor, would rule. Mariia Aleksandrovna then retreated
into her own coterie. She found solace in mysticism and a
Slavophile absorption with Russia, becoming the model of what
Rieber describes as the "pietistic, sentimentalist, passive type." In
contrast to her frivolous predecessor, she attracted loyalty by her
sincerity and helplessness, evoking solicitude rather than delight.
Though not inclined to self-indulgence, she suffered from frequent
illness and nervous disorders, which made her well-being of concern to others.[31] Her son, Alexander Aleksandrovich, plodding and
dull, was regarded as something of an embarrassment and remained in the shadow of his older brother Nicholas until the latter's
death in 1865. Then he began to share his mother's mystical and
Russophile interests, encouraged by his tutor Pobedonostev. His
association with Pan-Slavism and attempts to meddle in government put him a virtual state of disgrace during the 1870s. Mean-

29. "Pis'ma Imperatritsy Aleksandry Fedorovny k V. A. Zhukovskomu, 1817–1842,"
Russkii arkhiv, 35, no. 4 (1897): 498–499.

30. I have omitted discussion of Grand Duke Nicholas Aleksandrovich here because of
the unusual circumstances of his education and the particular difficulties his life presents. I
hope to deal with him in a separate piece.

31. Tiutcheva, *Pri dvore dvukh imperatorov*, I, 79–81; II, 79, 117, 123; Rieber,
introduction to Tiutcheva, *Pri dvore dvukh imperatorov*; Oom, "Vospominaniia," p. 245.

while, the tsar's establishment of a second household with his mistress Dolgorukaia created a condition of open hostility between emperor and empress, and the tsarevich clearly sided with his mother.

In this context, we can see the tsarevich and empress sharing certain strategies in dealing with the overpowering figure of the tsar. In the face of Nicholas I's stern paternal sense of obligation and self-denial, Aleksandra Fedorovna and Alexander Nikolaevich strove to please by compliance, and conspicuous shows of joy and delight. Alexander II's distrust and contempt for members of the family led Mariia Aleksandrovna and Alexander Aleksandrovich to withdraw and find their own goals and interests—interests which were remote from, and often antithetical to, the tsar's. Alexander III, though a good family man, was intolerant of disagreement and grew violently angry when crossed; Mariia Fedorovna and Nicholas II used a combination of deceit and placation to cope with him. They used the same devices with others, particularly men, whom they regarded as outside of or threatening to their domestic alliance. Nicholas, who was unusually dependent on his mother, remained squeamish about befriending or trusting anyone outside the family. Wary of outsiders, mother and son propitiated them with superficial shows of civility. Writing to Nicholas when he was nineteen, during his first participation in military maneuvers, Mariia reminded him that everyone would be watching his first "independent" steps. She instructed him to behave courteously with his comrades but warned him to avoid "too much familiarity or intimacy," and to beware of flatterers. Nicholas replied, "I will always try to follow your advice, my dearest, darling Mama. One has to be cautious with everybody at the start." Contemporaries would remark on both his sociability and his extreme wariness of personal attachments.[32]

The foreign origin of nineteenth-century empresses created additional grounds for rapport. From the reign of Nicholas I, the imperial family began to stress its Russian character and to use Russian within the family and the court. The empresses had to endeavor to show their Russianness and to prove their fealty to their new nationality. They expressed their attachment to Russian culture in many ways, but most effectively in the piety of their orthodox faith. Their sense of national difference was shared by the

32. Edward J. Bing, ed., *The Secret Letters of the Last Tsar* (Toronto, 1938), pp. 33, 36.

heirs, who grew up with feelings of ambivalence about their own national identity. They usually spoke to their mothers in French or German, while Russian increasingly became the language of their everyday contacts outside the family. They were never quite sure what language was their own.[33] They, too, looked upon their Russian character as something assumed, external to themselves, to be discovered and displayed. They showed Russian tastes in dress and food and encouraged Russian art, music, and ballet. But devotion to the orthodox religion would be the chief expression of their national identity, just as their association with the church formed their most apparent bond with the Russian nation. The particular character of the piety of the last three tsars closely resembled that of their mothers.

In closing, we can say that the nineteenth-century Russian empresses exerted considerable influence on the characters, personal styles, and tastes of their sons, the heirs. The circumstances of autocracy gave the empress and the tsarevich similar roles to play in enhancing the image of the tsar-father. The empress's foreign origin made her something of an outsider, leading to uncertainties in the heir's own feeling of nationality. Initially, the sense of rapport between mother and son was discouraged by the fears of maternal influence that were intrinsic to eighteenth-century views of monarchy. As the royal house came to accept the middle-class values of childhood, motherhood, and the family, the barriers to mother-son closeness fell away and the stigmas were replaced by expectations of an affectionate relationship. The greater acceptance of the mother's role in emotional nurturing and the fear of the hostile world surrounding the imperial family made possible a more intimate relationship between mother and son. Nicholas II's closeness to his mother and dependence upon her were striking and characteristic of no previous heir.

While we can only speculate about the effects of this relationship, the example of Nicholas II would appear to confirm some of the old absolutist fears concerning close association of the heir with his mother. Mariia Fedorovna's influence over Nicholas's upbringing served to emphasize family ties at the expense of formal training and official obligations. Her protectiveness encouraged traits that

33. Alfred J. Rieber, "Commentary," *Group for the Use of Psychology in History Newsletter* (March, 1976), pp. 30–31.

contemporaries recognized as passive and infantile.[34] Yielding to affectionate feelings, whether toward his mother or his wife, Nicholas would sometimes allow emotional indulgence to take precedence over official obligations. Personal whim increasingly dominated his public personality as he seemingly assigned more importance to family life than to public office. The result was to jeopardize the separation between the tsar's public and private selves—a differentiation which had been intrinsic to the imagery of autocracy.[35] It became difficult for Nicholas to play the role of self-abnegating tsar who, in his devotion to office and nation, stood above personal attachments and sensitivities.

34. "Dnevnik V. N. Lamzdorfa," *Krasnyi arkhiv*, 46 (1931): 7–8; A. Mosolov, *Pri dvore imperatora* (Riga, n. d.), pp. 7–11; Elizabeth Narishkin-Kurakin, *Under Three Tsars* (New York, 1931), pp. 161–162; Charles Lowe, *Alexander III of Russia* (New York, 1895), pp. 369–370.

35. On the separation between the tsar's public image and personal life see Wortman, "Power and Responsibility," pp. 18, 26.

Section Two

Marriage and Household
among Peasants and Clergy:
Social and Quantitative Dimensions

ANDREJS PLAKANS

Parentless Children in the
Soul Revisions: A Study of Methodology
and Social Fact

Parentlessness in past European society had attracted the attention
of a number of historians, but not until recently has the phenomenon been investigated from the viewpoint of social structure. In
contrast to the earlier stress on institutions such as orphanages and
the laws that committed parentless children to them, the main
questions now appear to be who lived with whom and for how long,
and what happened when, in such microstructures as families
and households, mortality or other causes dissolved vertical family
links.[1] Such an emphasis is likely to continue for a time, at least
until we have a better idea of the quantitative dimensions and
structural significance of this and related social phenomena. As
recent studies of past English populations suggest, the problem
involves more than simply the proper understanding of the numbers under a census rubric such as, say, "orphans." In his analysis of
the mid-nineteenth century Lancashire town of Preston, Michael
Anderson surmises that parentless children were "present in a
sizeable proportion of households over most of rural and urban
England"; and Peter Laslett in his survey of the preindustrial
centuries of that country concludes, tentatively, that "a third or
considerably more of all married dependents could be parentally
deprived in traditional society, and . . . the figure seldom dropped

1. Compare, e.g., Ivy Pinchbeck and Margaret Hewitt, *Children in English Society*
(London, 1969), a traditional approach; and the structural approach in Michael Anderson,
"Household Structure and the Industrial Revolution: Mid-Nineteenth-Century Preston in
Comparative Perspective," in *Household and Family in Past Time*, ed. Peter Laslett and
Richard Wall (Cambridge, England, 1972); and Peter Laslett, *Family Life and Illicit Love in
Earlier Generations* (Cambridge, England, 1977), pp. 160–173.

77

below one-fifth even at times and in places with more favorable conditions."[2] It has been easier to make quantitative judgments, however, than to identify precisely who the parentally deprived actually were. Both Anderson and Laslett are forced to cope with ambiguous data that do not allow for precise distinctions between single-parent orphans and illegitimate children co-residing with a parent; between full orphans and children with living parents but in service in another household; indeed, between individuals whose family links have been broken through voluntary relocation and others for whom the break involved familial tragedy.[3] What we can learn from these excellent pioneering studies is that only the rare listing from the "proto-statistical" period of European record-keeping will allow us to distinguish "orphans" in the strict sense and analyze them as a clearly delineated subgroup of the total population.[4]

Geographically and culturally it is a long way from England to the Baltic province of Kurland on the northwest periphery of the Russian Empire. (See map.) In the pre-modern era, the resemblance between the Latvian-speaking peasantry of Kurland and the peasantries of Russia proper, in terms of domestic group structure, was far greater than between the Baltic peoples and the inhabitants of, for instance, the British Isles.[5] In the Baltic area, as in Russia, much of the population appears to have lived in domestic groups which were complex in terms of generations and co-resident relatives; in England, and perhaps in other western countries, the simple, two-generational domestic group (husband, wife, children, plus a few servants) seems to have been dominant throughout the

2. Anderson, "Household Structure and the Industrial Revolution," p. 227; Laslett, *Family Life and Illicit Love*, p. 170.

3. For further discussion of the data used by both authors, see Michael Anderson, *Family Structure in Nineteenth-Century Lancashire* (Cambridge, England, 1971), and Peter Laslett, *Family Life and Illicit Love*, pp. 162–165.

4. David S. Landes, "Statistics as a Source for the History of Economic Development in Western Europe: The Protostatistical Era," in *The Dimensions of the Past*, ed. Val R. Lorwin and Jacob M. Price (New Haven, 1972), pp. 53–91.

5. For domestic group structure in the Baltic area, see my "Peasant Farmsteads and Households in the Baltic Littoral, 1797," *Comparative Studies in Society and History*, 17 (1976): 2–32; and my "Seigneurial Authority and Peasant Family Life: The Baltic Area in the Eighteenth Century," *Journal of Interdisciplinary History*, 4 (1975): 629–654. For the Russian peasantry, see Peter Czap, colloquium presentation to the Cambridge Group for the History of Population and Social Structure, April, 1976. For England, see Peter Laslett, "Mean Household Size in England since the Sixteenth Century," in Laslett and Wall, eds., *Household and Family*, pp. 125–158.

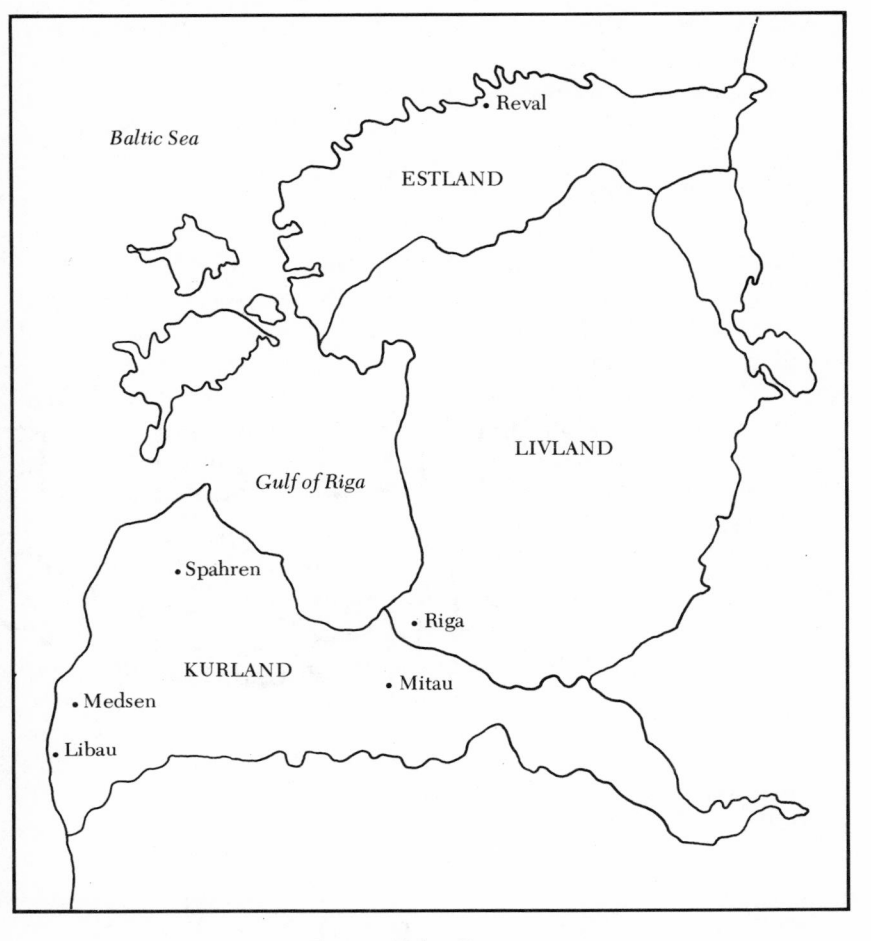

Russian Baltic Provinces

pre-industrial centuries. For the purpose of general comparisons, therefore, findings for the Baltic area would be of somewhat greater interest to Russianists than to Westernists.

There is another reason why investigations of the Baltic periphery should be of interest to students of Russian social history. The best enumerations available for the study of the Baltic peasantry during the eighteenth and nineteenth centuries are the soul revisions (*podushnye revizii*), which now stand ready to be exploited as sources for empirical knowledge of the peasant society of Russia proper. My research during the past two years has concerned the first Kurland revision of 1797. As is known from the work of the Russian scholar V. M. Kabuzan[6] and the Estonian historical demographer Sulev Vahtre,[7] these periodic tax censuses were introduced into imperial administrative practices by Peter the Great in 1719; they remained the only sources for aggregated population statistics concerning the Empire until 1897. To my knowledge, the revisions have not figured widely in other kinds of investigations, and when they have been used to investigate social structure, they have not been analyzed systematically or in terms of very large samples.[8]

Why study parentless children? From the viewpoint of the Baltic revisions, there are two answers to this question. The first has to do with methodology. We find that in numerous serf estates in 1797 a significant proportion of the total listed population (10–15 percent) consists of children without parents in the household. Some 20–30 percent of the population under fifteen years of age might be listed in this fashion, raising the question of what sorts of generalizations should be made about these children. In line with Anderson's observations, we might be witnessing the by-product of high adult mortality in the conjugal family unit, in which case such children would have to be treated as orphans proper. Or we might be in the presence of the practice (common elsewhere in Europe) of parents putting children out to work with others. The proportion might also be a combination of both types, which then have to be sorted out if

6. V. M. Kabuzan, *Izmeneniia v razmeshchenii naseleniia Rossii v XVII-pervoi polovine XIXv.* (Moscow, 1971).

7. Sulev Vahtre, *Estimaa talurahvas hingeloenduste andmeil, 1772–1858* (The Peasant Population of Estonia According to the Soul Revisions, 1782–1858) (Tallinn, 1973).

8. *E.G.*, L. S. Efremova, "Krest'ianskaia semia v Latgalii po dannym inventarei 1847–1849 gg.," *Latvijas PSR Zinatnu Akadēmijas Vēstis*, no. 10 (1971): 66–80.

the social structure is to be described accurately. Finally, we might be at the mercy of the enumerators' idiosyncrasies, as a result of which children and parents, even though co-residing in the same domestic group, would be described with status or occupational terms to the neglect of the familial relationship. In the Kurland revision, enumerators apparently received minimal instructions on how to prepare lists, and, in light of the differences of method, we must make sure that the peculiarities of individual listings are not treated as social facts. Throughout the German-language Baltic revisions the ambiguities inherent in such descriptive terms as *Aufzögling, Waisenkind, Pflegekind, adoptiertes Kind,* etc., require analytic care if the statistics based on them are to have any credibility.[9]

Beyond questions of method there stands the problem of describing the structural involvements of each new generation of peasant children as they passed through childhood and into adulthood. As William L. Langer has put it: "It seems clear that the history of childhood must be of major importance to any study of human society, for if, as it is said, the child is father to the man, it should be possible, with an understanding of any individual's or any group's past, to form a more intelligent judgement of their performance as adults."[10] In the Baltic area, the very few existing analyses of peasant childhood have featured "parentlessness" at center stage. The oral tradition—especially its Latvian variants—has highlighted the "parentless child" in countless songs, proverbs, stories, and legends. The Latvian ethnographer Klaustiņš sought to evaluate the significance of this element in the folk tradition by matching the results of content analysis of folk songs with the historical evidence in various kinds of population surveys (excluding the soul revisions), concluding that among the Latvian peasants the term "orphan" *(bārenis)* was generic and referred to any children (and some types of adults) living away from their parents.[11] The population surveys he used showed that in 1710, in the patrimonial estates of the city of Riga, some 11 percent of children were listed without

9. All cadasters and tax enumerations, as well as the Baltic regional censuses in the nineteenth century, were carried out in German. The first enumeration to use Russian was the imperial census of 1897.

10. William L. Langer, foreword, to *The History of Childhood,* ed. Lloyd de Mause (New York, 1974), p. vii.

11. R. Klaustiņš, "Der lettische Aufzögling und seine soziale Stellung," *Baltische Monatschrift* (1913): 373–397.

parents; in the Livlandic parish of Lude in 1763, approximately 5.9 percent of the population bore the label *Aufzögling*. In Lude, 21 percent of the total population lived as solitaries, i.e., without at least one other member of a conjugal family unit in the same household. Klaustiņš' researches were rather primitive, and his statistics questionable, but the problem itself is very real. If the folklore of this peasantry continued over many generations to devote attention to the travails of parentless children, and population surveys appear to corroborate the omnipresence of parentlessness, are we entitled to assume that significant proportions of the Baltic adult population grew up without the guidance and affection of natural parents?

Structural analyses of past populations will always be based on ambiguous data, since familial and quasi-familial status terms (such as "stepmother" or "foster child") are seldom used with absolute precision by enumerators. There are, in addition, two other problems: the simultaneous membership of an individual in several groups, including the familial, and the compositional changes of such groups over time. Full structural analysis of parentlessness in the Baltic area would need to consider all of these matters in turn; here we can only suggest the complexities that need to be resolved. Parentlessness in the first instance, resulted from the truncation of the conjugal family, a fundamental social unit of serf society. A widow or widower with children usually remarried, but this re-created family unit implied (for children as well as parents) involvement in step-relations which had not existed before. The totality of structural relationships in the community had thereby been altered. If both parents died, the child, now without support, became the charge of paternal and maternal kin—or of the estate, if such kin were lacking. Since special institutions for true orphans did not exist in the estate economies, kinless children frequently were assigned to live with peasants not related to them. The incorporation of such children into existing co-residential groups was accomplished through either fostering or adoption, but in both cases the totality of social relationships was again altered. Such truncation, dissolution, and re-creation of family units, and the absorption of solitary children into existing groups, were continually operating micro-processes within the estate population; the problem of parentlessness must be understood in this context. Co-residential groups were also undergoing changes. In the Baltic countryside several family units were normally joined together to comprise a farmstead, the basic residential group. The farmstead had its own developmental cycle which differed from that of its constituent family units. For one thing, labor obligations in the Kurland manorial economy were attached to farmsteads, not to individual families, making it imperative for a farmstead always to consist of approximately the same number of able-bodied people. The developments that expanded and diminished the family units of each farmstead must be kept analytically separated from those which affected the farmstead as a whole, even though the same persons were involved in both kinds of changes. When a farmstead head died, his demise altered not only his conjugal family, but also the future of the whole farmstead. And just as each conjugal family unit was involved in a farmstead, so each family and farmstead was involved in larger kinship groupings into which parentless children could be adopted if the necessity arose, or from which a family might gain adoptive or foster children. The oral tradition alludes to such kin groupings—descent groups, perhaps; or lineages, or kindreds—and suggests that they acted as corporate units on ceremonial occasions. Yet we have little hard social-structural data about how such groups operated among the Baltic peasants or among the European peasantry in general. Several of our detailed estate listings show the presence in the community of a sufficient number of the right kinds of kin but that is only the first step in the analysis of group activity. Nonetheless, because kin groups are an important aspect of human social organization, there is reason to suspect that they might also have been active in the Baltic area.

Ideally, then, parentlessness would have to be studied, first, as the result of a fundamental alteration in the conjugal family unit; second, in terms of the changes it brought to the membership of a farmstead and to that farmstead's developmental cycle; and, third, in reference to the alterations created in the living membership of a kin group. Of additional importance is the fact that, during the time when a parentless child was altering the groups into which he became reintegrated, his own status was changing. There is a personal life cycle involved here for parentless children; we can only guess at its successive phases and eventual outcome. We do not know, for instance, whether the life chances of children were restricted as a result of the loss of parents, or whether, after the child became reintegrated into another unit, the earlier parentless condition was of no consequence. We do know, however, that as a person grew older, the designations assigned to him by successive enumerations of the population changed. One must keep in mind that the various terms used to describe parentless children in the 1797 revision would change for those persons in the next. This suggests from the outset that, even though we can analyze parentless children as a group, they do not, therefore, constitute a class.

The potential of the soul revisions for dealing with some of these problems is considerable. Allowing for variations in how they were actually carried out, the soul revisions can be considered as household listings, describing the enumerated populations in a way that makes it possible for the analyst to use many of the methods suggested by the Cambridge Group for the History of Population and Social Structure.[12] The revision I have been working on—for Kurland in 1797—is, like many others, a voluminous document; approximately forty revision books cover upwards of 20,000 pages and contain disaggregated information on Kurland's rural and urban population during the last week of April of the census year. The Baltic provinces were enumerated late. The first revisions in Livland and Estland took place in 1782. In Kurland, which joined the Empire only in 1795, the first full revision (the fifth imperial revision) was carried out in 1797. Considering the documentary *Nachlass* of this first revision, the fact that it was to be followed by five more, and that these sources concerned only one small corner of the Empire, one can get some sense of the total bulk of materials for the whole Empire. If this material is to be used for wide-ranging structural analysis, the first order of business will have to be detailed source criticism of the kind which English scholars have carried out on, for example, English nineteenth-century censuses.[13] Reliability tests will have to be made to determine completeness of coverage, since even the 1797 enumeration in Kurland was erratic, according to a second count taken in some serf

12. See *An Introduction to English Historical Demography*, ed. E. A. Wrigley (New York, 1966); Peter Laslett, "Introduction," in Laslett and Wall, eds., *Household and Family*, pp. 1–89; E. A. Hammel and Peter Laslett, "Comparative Household Structure over Time and between Cultures," *Comparative Studies in Society and History*, 16 (1974): 73–109.

13. *E.g.*, P. M. Tillott, "Sources of Inaccuracy in the 1851 and 1861 Censuses," in *Nineteenth-Century Society: Essays in the Use of Quantitative Methods for the Study of Social Data*, ed. E. A. Wrigley (Cambridge, England, 1972), pp. 84–133.

estates in the following year. Some serfs had been left out of the enumeration; others had been attached to the wrong households. These tests for reliability can, however, be put aside temporarily if small enough samples are dealt with. My own work thus far has concerned individual estate lists which I could examine visually while computer analysis was being made of information coded from them. In the course of these examinations, it was possible to obtain what I believe to be very reliable statistics concerning household size and composition, size and composition of families within households, measures relating to age at first marriage, age differences between husbands and wives, and proportions of different kinds of relatives and non-relatives of household heads in the population. Some estates (one of which will be examined forthwith) were enumerated in enough detail for kinship information beyond the household to be recaptured; this made possible the linking of households to each other and the reconstruction of lineage segments.

Not surprisingly, Kurland's population at the turn of the century was overwhelmingly rural. P. E. von Keyserling, who appears to have used the 1797 revision as the basis of his calculations in 1805, put it at about 407,000 people, 94 percent of whom resided in rural districts (*Kreise*), and 6 percent in cities and towns.[14] Because we are interested in the rural population, Keyserling's tables are of further help for estimating the number of peasant residential units in each rural district, thus providing the opportunity to calculate their mean size in terms of inhabitants. Table 1 presents the results of this calculation.

TABLE 1. MEAN SIZE OF PEASANT DWELLING UNITS, KURLAND, 1797

District	No. serfs	No. peasant dwelling units (farmsteads)	Mean size of unit
Mitau	102,460	6,567	15.6 persons
Selburg	78,931[a]	5,116	15.4
Tuckum	56,251	3,779	14.8
Goldingen	76,595	5,556	13.8
Pilten	44,879	2,729	16.4

[a]Selburg district total includes 59,643 serfs and 19,288 free peasants.
SOURCE: Keyserling, *Beschreibung*, appendix I, "Tabelle über die Volksmenge . . . im Kurländischen Gouvernement."

14. Peter Ernst von Keyserling, *Beschreibung der Provinz Kurland* (Mitau, 1805), appendix I.

For brevity's sake, I shall refer to these dwelling units as households, although anyone familiar with the recent literature on the household will know the difficulties in classifying all European residential units according to a single definition of the term. The groups in which Kurlandic peasants lived were considerably larger than most households in other European populations, and parentless children were absorbed within these groups. The mean size of fourteen to sixteen persons appears to have prevailed throughout the province, though within each district, and within each parish within a district, the sizes could vary considerably.[15] These uncommonly large domestic groups were located on private and crown estates (*Güter*) which numbered 661 at this time, according to Keyserling's figures. The average estate had between two and three hundred serfs, a figure derived from the total rural population minus all the non-serf inhabitants, divided by the number of estates. Most Kurlandic estate owners thus could not rival the great Russian landowners in terms of owned "souls," and rare was the estate that had more than 2,000 serfs. The proportion of the total population of Kurland living in estates of moderate size appears to have grown during the eighteenth century. Whereas in the early 1700s approximately 29.9 percent of the population lived in estates with 201 to 800 people in them, by the end of the century that proportion had risen to half. The percentage of estates with populations over 1,500 had risen from 0.5 at the beginning of the century to 10.9 at the end.[16] The local social context of the parentless condition, therefore, involved increasing numbers of people as the century wore on, which meant more parentless children per estate, but also more families into which to absorb them.

The main purpose of the revision was to determine the number of males aged 14 to 60 who were subject to the head tax. Probably because Kurland had just become part of the Empire, the enumerators of 1797 listed the whole population of each rural estate and each town—men and women, and people outside (as well as within) the indicated ages. Fortunately for social history, the hundreds of enumerators involved in the project (usually estate

15. Andrejs Plakans, "Family Structure in the Russian Baltic Provinces: The Nineteenth Century," in *Sozialgeschichte der Familie in der Neuzeit Europas*, ed. Werner Conze (Stuttgart, 1976).

16. Edgars Dunsdorfs, *Latvijas vēsture 1710–1800* (History of Latvia, 1710–1800) (Sundbyberg, Sweden, 1973), p. 360.

scribes) treated the revision as an opportunity to go beyond the required minimal tax information. Their carefully prepared lists were, in a sense, property inventories, since serfs were a kind of property. Most estate listings provided information on the age and sex of each individual, his nationality and legal status, as well as on his position in the domestic group and on kin relation to the domestic group head. This kind of information is obtainable from almost all listings. The most detailed lists provide considerably more—in at least three estates, the most complete found so far, it is possible to discern how rural social structures were embedded in each other. In these estates one starts by noting the size and character of conjugal family units (CFU's) and how these are embedded in a group of co-residing kinfolk. It is not unusual to find CFU's which are part of a co-residing kin group of, say, two or three married brothers. These CFU's and groups of co-resident kin are, in turn, embedded in a larger farmstead population with a mean size of fourteen to sixteen people; in addition to the family and relatives of the farmstead head, it contained the families and relatives of landless farmworkers and retired people, and our "parentless" children. Then these farmsteads were part of still larger kinship groups involving non-co-residing siblings and their families —uncles, nephews, and the like. Ultimately, all the farmsteads and the people on the manor farm itself *(Hofleute)* were part of an estate, which either was a single, integrated population unit or consisted of a major *Hof* and *Beyhofe* (sub-estates apparently created for administrative purposes). The analytical possibilities of these kinds of data are considerable from the social-structural viewpoint, even though from Kabuzan's description of the revisions it is difficult to get the sense that such possibilities exist.

There are several ways to use these data for the study of the phenomenon of parentlessness. One might extract from a single-year data file all those young individuals who do not have parents co-residing with them, state their numbers as a proportion of the whole population, and link the results to similarly derived figures from subsequent enumerations. In this fashion one could obtain a time series showing the growth or diminution of the problem. This information could then be linked to socio-economic events, with the latter used to explain the former. In time, sufficient information may be obtained for such a procedure. At the moment, however, no such series of data exist, at least for the Baltic, and research in other parts of Europe has not yielded much more than generalizations about certain historical moments. Thus we do not know whether the problem of parentlessness grew worse in Europe's passage from the *ancien régime* to modernity; whether it was perceived as having worsened because methods for enumeration had improved; or whether in fact, as adult mortality rates decreased, all children regardless of social class lived longer in full conjugal family units. These facts presumably will emerge as research on these topics continues.

In the meantime, the structural approach to the revision of 1797 can be enlightening in other respects. It can introduce us to the difficulties of determining who parentless children were, how much of a problem they constituted, and how reliable a single-year enumeration is for an analysis of the problem. I propose to look at the problem of parentlessness in two estates of roughly comparable size; one has a maximum amount of social-structural information, and the other, what might be called a standard amount (for 1797). The first is Spahren in the parish of Talsen (Tuckum district), and the second, Medsen in the parish of Grobin (Goldingen district). Talsen parish lay in the very heartland of Kurland about equidistant from the Gulf of Riga on the east and the Baltic Sea on the west. Grobin, by contrast, was a seacoast parish, lying just north of the port city of Libau on the western coast of the Province. In April, 1797, Spahren had a population of 619 people, most of whom were Latvian-speaking serfs; Medsen's population was 532, with somewhat fewer serfs. In Spahren there were 259 children aged 1–14 (41.6 percent of the total population), whereas in Medsen the children numbered 183 (34.3 percent). Spahren claimed six children with both parents deceased (i.e., 2.3 percent of all children), while in Medsen 47 children (or 25.6 percent of all children) were listed in the revision as having no parents in the household. At first glance it would seem that Medsen had ten times as many parentless children, and a correspondingly greater problem of integrating these youngsters into the life of the community. But the nature of the enumerations in each estate tends to call this observation into question. In Spahren a maximum amount of information was provided for each individual on the list, including the names and locations of parents in cases of children who were living in farm-

steads other than those of their parents; in Medsen there was only a
standard amount of information provided, and children living away
from parents were not identified with respect to parentage.
Whereas in Spahren we can examine the revision in order to say
whether each child was truly parentless, in Medsen we are left with
a cluster of youngsters whose conjugal family membership remains
unclear. The fact that the Medsen listing was the format normally
used in estates in Kurland raises the important methodological
question of whether we are entitled to view the high parentless
population of Medsen (which approaches the levels Laslett posits
for pre-industrial England) as representative of the social conditions of the Kurland countryside, or whether we must revise the
Medsen figures (and other similarly high figures) downward in
terms of the Spahren conditions. One might also add that, had the
Spahren enumeration been carried out in the Medsen fashion, the
number of parentless children in Spahren would have been 32, or
13.9 percent.

In describing the social reality of serf life with respect to parentlessness, we are somewhat at the mercy of enumerators' techniques, unless there exist at least a handful of communities in
which information is maximal. The same point can be made by
looking at the status designations attributed to children, regardless of whether they had parents or not. For this, Table 2 is useful.

TABLE 2. FARMSTEAD STATUS OF CHILDREN UNDER 15 YEARS OLD

Status	Medsen	Spahren
Relatives of head of farmstead	95 (51.9%)	133 (51.3%)
Young farmhands (*Jungen*)	9 (4.9)	12 (4.6)
Children of *Knechte* (mature farmhands)	33 (18.0)	78 (30.1)
Children of lodgers	7 (3.8)	11 (4.2)
Herders (*Hütter, Hirte*)	38 (20.7)	0
Young female farmhands (*Mädchen*)	0	20 (7.7)
Others	1 (.05)	5 (1.9)
Total	183	259

The categories listed in Table 2 account for all farmstead statuses
of children in Kurland. The proportion of children who derived
their status directly from the head, either as his children or as his
co-residing relatives, was approximately the same in both estates.
About equal proportions of children of lodgers resided in each
estate, and about equal proportions of the young people were

Andrejs Plakans

Jungen. But several categories reveal considerable differences. Whereas there were no herders listed in Spahren, about one-fifth of all children in Medsen held that status; and whereas no *Mädchen* were listed for Medsen, 7.7 percent of the children in Spahren worked in that capacity. The larger number of children of *Knechte* can be explained by the somewhat greater number of *Knechte* in Spahren. Still, we are faced with discrepancies which seem to indicate different enumerating techniques.

Herders were apparently an indispensable part of the Baltic farmstead; they appear in almost all of the forty estates which I have prepared for machine analysis. It seems inconceivable that, on the one hand, Spahren had no youngsters watching the herds of livestock, geese, and ducks which were part of the farmstead economy; likewise, it is hard to believe that Medsen had no young girls serving on farmsteads as *Mädchen*, preparatory to the more demanding, responsible, and remunerative job of a full-fledged *Magd*. The junior statuses of *Junge*, *Mädchen*, and *Hütter* apparently did not have hard-and-fast criteria by which membership could be judged. These statuses pertained to jobs which were always held by young people, however, and there was a natural transition from them into more senior categories: *Hütter* became *Jungen* or *Mädchen*; *Jungen* became *Knechte*; *Mädchen* became *Mägde*. All of the herders listed in Medsen were over four years of age; twenty-three were between five and nine, and the other fifteen were ten to fourteen years old. The diminishing numbers in the last age category signaled the entry of some into the *Jungen* or *Mädchen* group. No *Jungen* listed in Spahren are in the youngest age group; only one is in the age group 5–9, and eleven are in the oldest group. In Medsen all *Jungen* appear in the top age group. The category *Mädchen* in Spahren has one person in the youngest age group, four in the next, and fully fifteen in the oldest. The patterns in these figures suggest the transitional nature of the statuses, and therefore (as we mentioned earlier) these status terms should not be viewed as descriptions of population classes. Underlying the formal 1797 terminology, processes of growth and maturation were at work for all children, regardless of whether they had parents. By correlating status designation and age, we can glimpse young people as they entered one status and left another. But when we are faced with the absence of necessary status terms, we enter the realm of educated

90

guesswork. There is a distinct likelihood that the enumerator of Spahren listed some children of the *Knechte* as such, rather than in terms of the jobs they were performing in the farmstead, including herding; likewise, some of the *Hütter* in Medsen were perhaps *Mädchen* who not only herded livestock but also did other tasks required of young female farmhands. For the youngsters in these listings, therefore, we cannot always deduce function from status, the jobs or chores the youngster actually performed in the farmstead economy from the categorical description the enumerator chose to use. This suggests that the familial condition of these youngsters is also very likely to be elusive, since the enumerators were probably more familiar with the economic than with the familial dimensions of estate life.

Let us now turn to a more detailed consideration of parentlessness, having been warned that the ground on which we have to tread is less than firm. In his analysis of the "parentless children" of Preston, Anderson presents a table which is reproduced here (in shortened form), together with information from our two estates for comparative purposes.[17]

TABLE 3. RELATIONSHIPS OF KIN OF HEAD TO HOUSEHOLD HEAD (% OF ALL KIN)

Relationships	Preston, 1851	Rural sample, 1851	Spahren, 1797	Medsen, 1797
"Stem family" members	46.1	30.9	18.9	86.3
Unmarried members of family of birth	14.1	17.0	17.1	4.5
Married siblings & families	9.4	6.2	36.9	0.0
"Parentless" children	28.3	42.1	0.01	0.0
Aunts, uncles, cousins	1.4	2.0	5.4	0.0
Wife's relatives	0.0	0.0	18.9	4.5
Others	.8	1.7	5.4	4.8
N	513	404	111	22

Anderson presents his tabulated information in order to discuss the structure of the rural (as compared to urban) household in mid-nineteenth-century England, whereas I have cited it in order to place in perspective the category of "parentless" children. Strictly speaking, the two sets of information (from 1851 and 1797) are not comparable as given, since to understand them fully one

17. Anderson, "Household Structure and the Industrial Revolution," pp. 217, 224.

would need to know more about what constituted the "household" in each area, how many conjugal family units were normally present in each household, and so forth. Leaving aside Medsen for the moment because of suspected imprecisions in its list, we can compare Spahren and Preston. Some important differences can be noted immediately in the general character of the groups that surrounded household heads in the two areas. Almost a fifth of the head's kinfolk in Spahren were related to him through his wife; this suggests, in contrast with Preston, that the dominant virilocal post-marital residence pattern had a pronounced subtheme of uxorilocality—of the husband, after marriage, joining the wife in *her* parent's farmstead. The Spahren figures also tend to be dominated by the high proportion of married siblings of the head and their families, which is a sign of the higher proportion of joint households than existed in Preston. But of special interest is the remarkable difference in the proportion of head's kinfolk allocated to the category of "parentless children" in the two areas. In both rural and urban Preston, this proportion is very high; in the Baltic estates it is negligible. It is obvious from the listings of both Spahren and Medsen that the parentless children referred to earlier (2.3 percent of all children in Spahren and 25.6 percent of all children in Medsen) did not enjoy the status of head's kinfolk most of the time and fell into the categories of the lower-status individuals who made up the rest of the farmstead population.

The identities of these parentless children in Spahren, where the information is relatively complete, are easy enough to determine. One was a thirteen-year-old girl from Geneva who lived with the family of the estate owner (*Erbherr*), presumably as a companion to his two young daughters. One twelve-year-old *Junge* resided in one of the estate's taverns. Neither of these individuals would have shown up as a relative of the head. One *Junge*, age twelve, resided in Esermuische farmstead; his parents were dead and he was listed not only as *Junge* but also as the farmstead head's brother's son. One two year old resided with her mother in Karkley Fritz farmstead; the mother is described as a *Magd* and as the daughter of the head's brother, so the child is the head's grandniece. The mother is not listed as a widow, and there is a likelihood that the two year old is an illegitimate daughter. Finally, there is a pair of parentless siblings living in Wirdang farmstead; they are described as a *Mädchen* and a

Junge and both are the children of the same deceased father. These six individuals (one with a mother) were the only "parentless" children in Spahren as of 1797, and only two of them had kin ties of second-degree nature to the head of their residential group. Young relatives of the head of the kind that Anderson found in such plentitude in England did not exist in Spahren. When nieces and nephews of the head were co-residing with their uncle, normally their parents were there also, since more than a third of the head's relatives in our Spahren table are listed as married siblings and their children.

In Medsen the information is somewhat more difficult to specify, since we are working with incomplete designations of relationships. The use of first-degree kinship terms as listing categories in Medsen allows us to be fairly certain that the forty-seven parentless children did not include the head's own children or grandchildren. Nearly all are designated as *Jungen,* or herders, but we do not know who their parents were (if they had living parents), or whether they were also indirectly related to the head of their residential group. Although we are entering the realm of speculation, we can narrow the range of possibilities by making comparisons with the Spahren data. First, let us look at the composition of conjugal family units (husbands, wives) which had no children listed with parents. (See Table 4.) The status of such units provides some clues concerning the kinds of parents who might have put their children out to work elsewhere. Of all married couples in Medsen, twenty-one had no children listed as living with them. Only one of these fell into the category of head or head's relative, which meant that most of the retired couples in those two statuses were living with children who had taken over their farmsteads or who were married to farmstead heads. In three cases the husband in an elderly childless couple still bore the designation of *Knecht;* in three other cases he bore the designation of *Walleniek* or no designation at all, which meant that he was landless and retired. Among couples where the wife was still

TABLE 4. CHILDLESS COUPLES IN MEDSEN

	Farmstead status of couple		
Type of couple	Head	Knecht	Others
Wife past child-bearing (50+ years)	0	3	3
Wife within child-bearing years (14–50)	1	12	2

in her child-bearing years (and thus potentially the mother of some of our young "parentless" children), only one was in the *Wirth* (head) category, and two were in the retired landless group. But the husbands in twelve such couples were *Knechte* and still productive members of the farmsteads, and their wives were young enough to have mothered the oldest "parentless" children. There is a considerable likelihood, therefore, that most of the forty-seven "parentless" children in Medsen came out of this last group of twelve couples. We can never tell the absolute number (lacking the parent-child tie), but the possibility appears great. The *Knechte* were landless, had incomes only from their status as farmstead employees, and would have benefited from having their children lodge and work elsewhere.

Another way of looking at this problem is in terms of the number of children whom each type of married couple did have with them in co-residence. Table 5 summarizes the data for Medsen on this point.

TABLE 5. NUMBER OF CHILDREN IN CONJUGAL FAMILY UNITS

Status of CFU	Number of children at home							Total children
	1	2	3	4	5	6	7	
Farmstead head ($N = 42$)	5	16	3	6	5	5	2	139 (78.9%)
Relative of head ($N = 2$)	2							2 (1.1)
Knecht ($N = 23$)	13	9	1					34 (19.3)
Artisan ($N = 1$)	1							1 (0.5)

There were sixty-eight conjugal family units that contained two parents and dependent children. Of these, 61 percent were the families of farmstead heads; another 33 percent were the families of *Knechte;* the rest were either the families of relatives of the heads, or other types. If we drop the relatives and lodgers as too few for comparative purposes, the contrast between the numbers and proportions of dependent children in the farmstead heads' and Knechte families is obvious. Almost 80 percent of all dependent children (listed with their parents) were children of farmstead heads, whereas only about 20 percent were children of *Knechte.* The largest listing of a head's family was nine people (two parents, seven children), whereas the largest ever achieved by the *Knechte* families was five. The great majority of *Knechte* families had either one or two children in immediate dependence, while nearly half of the heads' families had four to seven children present. Two other explanations of this phenomenon are possible: (1) landless persons had radically different attitudes toward child-bearing and practiced family limitation; (2) most of the *Knechte* tended to be younger than the heads and therefore would have had fewer children. While I do believe that some adjustment of the figures would be necessary in order to accommodate these possibilities, the more likely hypothesis is that the children of *Knechte* were being put out to work, whereas the children of heads were being kept at home. We can check the Medsen situation against the more complete information in Spahren to see whether the hypothesis is likely to hold.

In Spahren there is no doubt whatever concerning the parentage of the twelve *Jungen* and twenty *Mädchen* who were listed as being away from their parents. In all twelve cases the parents of the *Jungen* were landless: seven were *Knechte*, and five were retired and landless *(Walleniek)*. With respect to the *Mädchen*, twelve were the children of *Knechte*, one the child of a *Walleniek*, and seven the children of *Knechte* who were at the same time relatives (brothers, brothers-in-law, etc.) of the heads whose farmsteads they occupied. Had the enumerator in Spahren not been especially diligent, we would have had to identify these thirty-two youngsters as parentless. As it is, direct evidence confirms the inferences we have made about Medsen: namely, that most children who appear to be parentless in reality had living parents in the same community, and that in the vast majority of the cases these parents belonged to the landless group. The dimensions of the problem of parentlessness tend to diminish in light of these findings. There were some true orphans in each estate, and children who were living in step-relationships with their parents (these will be examined later), but by and large most children had parents in co-residence or elsewhere in the estate.

Michael Anderson has said that, in mid-nineteenth-century England, the placement of young children in other households for labor purposes was not done arbitrarily; rather, it followed kin lines.[18] Most of his "parentless" children are kin of the household head, and therefore it remains for us to investigate this problem in Spahren as well. In Medsen the links cannot be made, but in Spahren the superior documentation allows us to trace at least

18. *Ibid.*, p. 226.

first- and second-degree kin relations, if such exist, between a *Junge* or *Mädchen* and the other members of the farmstead on which they are residing. The results of this exploration are presented in Table 6.

TABLE 6. RELATION OF "PARENTLESS" CHILDREN TO OTHER RESIDENTS OF DOMESTIC GROUP, SPAHREN

Of 32 *Junge* and *Mädchen* under 15 years old:

Relation to other members of farmstead of residence unknown	10
Niece or nephew of head or head's wife	5
Relative of another older person in farmstead	10
Child of *Knecht* of head's relative in another farmstead	1
Parent residing elsewhere comes from farmstead where child presently resides	1
Parent is in farmstead from which an older co-resident of child comes	5

It should be pointed out that the age limitation placed on the definition of "children" reduces the number of cases available for examination. At the same time, the figures show that at least two-thirds of the "parentless" children were connected to someone else in the farmstead where they were residing. These connections were not by any means all of kinship, and only five of the twenty-two connected individuals were related to the head of the farmstead. But ten of the twenty-two were connected through kinship to a person other than the head, and the other seven were connected in a less direct fashion, usually through the child's parent. In any case, in Spahren there appears to have been a strong tendency to place children with people who either were kin, or were known; the proportion of such placements appears to be larger than could be accounted for by chance. Given the differing needs of the farmstead economies—the labor requirement attached to the farmstead, in addition to the labor needs of the farmstead's own lands—it would not be likely that a landless individual could always find his offspring a place with friends or relatives. But the figures point to this being an important consideration when youngsters were removed from their conjugal family units and placed elsewhere.

Judging by the figures reviewed thus far, the most frequent cases of "parentlessness" involved not orphans, but children who had been sent out to work by their parents. But what of true orphans? We have encountered some already amidst the quasi-parentless. There are no general statistics available for Kurland on this matter until the late nineteenth century; the empirical data for the earlier period are still in raw form. Assuming, however, that Kurland at the end of the eighteenth century had normal pre-industrial levels of adult mortality, we would expect a plenitude of orphans, and, correspondingly, a greater use of the term *Waisenkinder* in the historical enumerations. This designation is not to be encountered more frequently in the 1797 revision (and probably in other enumerations of this period) because orphans apparently were reabsorbed into existing groupings through rapid remarriage of the surviving parent, if there was one, or through adoption if both parents had died. Hence the relatively frequent use in the revision of such terms as *Pflegekind, Stiefkind, adoptiertes Kind, Aufzögling,* and the like, and the relatively infrequent use of *Waisenkind;* though in our two estates none of these terms is frequent. Behind all of these imprecise usages by the enumerator lay the social facts of adoption, fostering, and step-status, all of which have a wide variety of functions in other cultures.[19] Because Spahren and Medsen provide us with so few cases, we can only examine them individually and point to some practices that did exist in these serf communities.

In Medsen six conjugal family units included step-relationships or fostering; in three cases foster children *(Pflegekinder)* were involved. The estate owner had a seventeen-year-old foster son, though there were already three sons and one daughter (all teenagers) in the family. Another case involved a thirty-four-year-old tailor with an eighteen-year-old foster daughter and no other children; in the third case, a forty-five-year-old farmstead head who already had five children was the foster father to an eight-year-old-son. The events that led to inclusion of the children in these families are not known, but fostering obviously did not arise from childlessness of the foster parents. In addition, a sixty-three-year-old Medsen tavernkeeper and his fifty-five-year-old wife were taking care of two grandchildren (ages eight and four) who were thus co-residing with their young twenty-six-year-old aunt and one-year-old uncle, the other children of the older couple. There were also two remarriages which can be identified through the stated step-relationships *(Stiefkind, Stiefvater,* etc.). In one

19. Jack Goody, "Adoption in Cross-Cultural Perspective," *Comparative Studies in Society and History,* 11 (1969): 55–78.

case a fifty-five-year-old farmstead head had lost the wife by whom he had had four children who were still at home; his new wife, twenty-three years old, presented him with two more children. The resulting structure thus involved four children with a step-mother and six children who were step-siblings. In the other case, the remarriage had been between a sixty-five-year-old farmstead head and a forty-five-year-old woman. The personal relationships in this family group were rather complicated, since the man's children by his first marriage were still in the household and were them-selves married; furthermore, the new wife had brought into the marriage two children from her previous marriage. The situation was very likely to lead to disputes over inheritance rights, but at least in these cases children who had lost one parent did not have long to wait until a family unit was reconstituted—and, in the process, made more complex.

The better and more precise listings of Spahren provide us with eight case studies of remarriage. In three cases involving landless males, the mixed sibling group which the remarriages had brought together had already dispersed to other farmsteads when the revi-sion was taken, leaving as co-residents only the remarried parents. In one case, a forty-year-old tavernkeeper had taken a twenty-year-old bride and was starting another family in spite of the fact that five children from his previous marriage were still in the household. In another case a fifty-four-year-old farmstead head, remarried to a thirty-year-old woman, was living with his new wife and the children from the new marriage, though in other farm-steads he had seven children from his first marriage. In one farm-stead both the head and his *Knecht* were the second husbands of their respective wives; in another case a remarriage had created a sibling group in which the age gap between the only surviving child from the first marriage and the one that had resulted from the second was twenty-one years. Finally, also in Spahren, there was one case of a farmstead head who was childless but who had serving with him a *Knecht* who was designated as having been "adopted as the future head" *(adoptiert als künftiger Wirth)*.

Though the two estates provide us with a very small sample on which to base generalizations, these, and information from other segments of the revision, are nevertheless suggestive. True or-phanhood was not a condition which children experienced for a long time. There was a general dislike among landowners of "unincorporated" individuals: footloose paupers and youngsters who might become such, wandering beggar women with their (possibly) illegitimate or fatherless children—in short, people who were not ascribed to some existing residential group whose head could be made responsible for them. This general pressure was felt by the peasantry and no doubt added to any practical reasons for remarriage (to provide children with the missing parent), for adoption (so that a lineage could be continued in the office of the farmstead headship), and for fostering (which could add at least a small amount of labor to the labor pool). Woven into these instances of practicality there was probably what the anthropologist Meyer Fortes has called the axiom of amity in kinship relations: rendering a service to living or deceased kinfolk without expectation of reward.[20] As I have shown elsewhere in an examination of Spahren, few serfs in this estate were not affinally or consanguineally related to at least a handful of other estate serfs, due to a network of kinship relations that had been created over time because of restrictions on movement and corresponding endogamous marriages.[21] Few children in these estates could be orphaned and not have at least one uncle or aunt to take them in.

Our discussion of parentlessness in the under-fifteen age group in Baltic serf estates has led to the conclusion that the condition was quickly ameliorated. In a given year few children were true orphans in the full, compassion-provoking sense of the word: in Spahren there were only six such youngsters, or 2.3 percent of all children under fifteen. This is a remarkably low proportion, in contrast to the high minimum level (20–30 percent) postulated for pre-industrial England by Peter Laslett. The contrast between East and West may not be as sharp, however, because our calculations have used a very exclusive sample, whereas Laslett's samples are inclusive and look at the phenomenon among all unmarried people in dependent statuses regardless of age—that is, during a much longer period of their individual life-cycles than we have used. In Table 7 I have reviewed the Spahren evidence from the more inclusive viewpoint, with the intention of, first, underlining how much social statistics

20. Meyer Fortes, *Kinship and the Social Order: The Legacy of Lewis Henry Morgan* (London, 1969), pp. 219–249.
21. Andrejs Plakans, "Identifying Kinfolk beyond the Household," *Journal of Family History*, 1 (1977).

depend upon definitions of what is being measured, and second, creating the possibility of bringing the Spahren (Eastern) data into a comparative framework with Laslett's samples of English (Western) communities.[22]

TABLE 7. PARENTAL DEPRIVATION IN SPAHREN, 1797
(UNMARRIED DEPENDENTS)

Condition:	N	%
Both parents alive:		
1. Young people living with father and mother	282	67.3
2. Young people living in different farmstead from parents	68	16.2
3. Young people living in different estate from parents	13	3.2
One parent deceased:		
4. Orphans living with widowed parent	1	.2
5. Orphans living with father and stepmother	6	1.5
6. Orphans living with widowed mother and stepfather	4	.9
7. Orphans living with widowed parent and other relatives	15	3.5
Both parents deceased:		
8. Orphans living with grandparents	1	.2
9. Orphans not living with relatives but as members of farmsteads	29	6.9
TOTALS	419	99.9
Orphans as proportion of all unmarried and dependent young people (categories 4–9)	13.3%	
Parentally deprived as proportion of all unmarried and dependent young people (categories 2–9)	32.7%	

By using as the criteria of selection terms denoting dependent status *(Sohn, Tochter, Mädchen, Magd, Junge)* and disregarding ages, we have enlarged the Spahren sample from 259 (children under fifteen) to 419, the additional numbers being young people ranging in age to their late twenties. This larger sample probably includes all people for whom parentlessness would have been significant (and some for whom it would no longer have been so); it certainly includes all those who, on the basis of direct or indirect evidence, could be judged to fall in the "orphan" category in 1797. The most numerous group among orphans were those who by 1797 had lost both parents yet had acquired a status designation within a farmstead. Next in size stood a category (completely absent from

22. Table 7 is organized so as to be comparable to Table 4.2 in Laslett, *Family Life and Illicit Love*, p. 166.

English data) of orphans who were living with a widowed parent in a farmstead where the headship had been taken over by an older married brother of the orphan(s). As a subgroup, all orphans still do not amount to the proportions mentioned by Laslett. Yet if we expand the concept of parental deprivation to include those who were living *away* from parents, the proportion of the parentally deprived rises to the English levels. Over a fifth of the young people in Spahren did not experience on a daily basis personal interaction with both of their natural parents. The significance of such a familial condition for this enserfed population remains to be understood.

The re-creation of conjugal family units and the re-incorporation of orphans into existing full families frequently created problems of inheritance, which we can only note here without further discussion. In the estate regulations issued by the owner of the Kurland estate of Ugalen, for instance, it is said that when a farmstead head died and left a widow with underage children, the estate court had to see to it that the property of the father remained potentially heritable for these children when the widow remarried and became the mother of another sibling group.[23] In the estate of Stenden a similar regulation was promulgated, with the added provision that when the property of the deceased father was inventoried, two copies of the list were to be made and left with his relatives and the relatives of the surviving wife. In the estate of Linden, serf regulations stated that, when a farmstead head died and left a widow who was no longer of marriageable age, a "close relative" of the deceased head would be appointed to take care of the farmstead for the children of the deceased. These regulations suggest again that orphaned children of at least farmstead heads were not likely to become wandering, penniless beggars; that kinfolk were held accountable for their future at least during their minority; and that kinfolk were likely to resort to adoption (or at least to fostering) if it turned out that the farmstead was taken over by someone else. Correspondingly, we would expect to find few true orphans designated as such *(Waisenkinder)* in the ranks of at least those peasants with access to a holding.

The analysis must be brought to a halt here, even though we have not touched on some of the important matters raised earlier, such as

23. Arvēds Švābe, "Kurzemes muižas tiesības," *Izglītības Ministrijas Mēnešraksts* ("Estates Regulations in Kurland," *Monthly Journal of the Ministry of Education*), 2 (1922): 256–267.

the ways in which re-absorption of "parentless" children affected the developmental cycles of the host conjugal family unit and the host farmstead. Nonetheless, the revision segments examined show very clearly that we should not look for parentlessness or orphanhood as an unequivocal social datum in the Baltic countryside. On the one hand, children who were listed as parentless did have parents in the community living elsewhere; on the other, children who had been orphaned had been re-absorbed into existing domestic groups so quickly that enumerations carried out every fifteen years were likely to pick up only a few of them at a given moment. The children who had parents living elsewhere had been placed out to work, usually with other peasants who were kinfolk, or at least acquaintances, of the parents. For the landed, placing children out to work was apparently not a necessity, whereas for landless farmhands the enjoyment of a full conjugal family unit was apparently a relatively brief experience, when measured against the full developmental cycle of the family.

PETER   CZAP,   JR.

Marriage and the Peasant Joint Family in the Era of Serfdom

It will be allowed, that no country has hitherto been
known, where the manners were so pure and simple, and
the means of subsistence so abundant, that no check
whatever has existed to early marriage from the difficulty
of providing for a family.

— Malthus (1803)

"Oh come, come, Tanya! In those years we never heard
of love; elsewise my later mother-in-law would have
chased me right off the earth."
"But how, then, were you wedded, nurse?"
"It looks as if God willed it so, My Vanya was younger
than myself, my sweet, and I was thirteen."

— Pushkin, *Eugene Onegin*

Within the Greco-Roman Christian tradition from which Russian
marital law descended, marriage was held to be a voluntary but
controlled action reflecting commitment between the two contracting parties and between both of them and God. But in Russia, as
elsewhere in past times, marriage was a social and economic as well
as a personal and religious undertaking. Among peasants the
many-sided nature of the marital bond was clearly reflected in
customary law and in the prominent roles assigned to officials of the
peasant community, as well as to the church, in the practical and
ritual aspects of marriage. Marriage contracts—negotiated before
witnesses, including officials of the peasant commune (*obshchina*),

The author wishes to thank the International Research and Exchanges Board (IREX) and
the National Science Foundation (SOC 75–06555) for support and assistance. Grateful
acknowledgement is also due to the officers and staffs of the Central State Archive of Ancient
Acts (TsGADA) in Moscow and the State Archive of Riazan Oblast (GARO) for their
assistance in making available the documentation used in this work.

and dealing with such matters as dowry, wedding costs, gifts, provisions for wedding guests, and compensaton to be awarded should either party fail to honor the contract—reflected the property interests of the peasants. Among enserfed peasants in the eighteenth and nineteenth centuries, marriage vitally touched the property interests of the landlords *(pomeshchiki)* as well. A marriage, almost by definition, requires the establishment of an economic base for the newly married couple and their children. They must be attached in some way to an existing household or form an independent one—in either case, a step which required the landlord's direct or indirect participation.

Inasmuch as it influences the movement of individuals from one household to another, marriage affects the rate of formation of new households and disappearance of old ones. A marriage pattern thus becomes a central factor determining the structure and size of households. In a predominantly agrarian society where the household was the principal unit of economic production as well as consumption—and Russia in the era of serfdom was just such a society—the marriage pattern is intimately linked to the performance of the economy as a whole. As a calculated action, marriage is a more sensitive indicator than deaths or births of the effects of economic development and social and natural disasters. An inquiry into the origins of any society's marriage pattern and into the forces which sustain it will inevitably lead toward fundamental questions about its social structure, economy, and value system.

Before we can seek the origins and sources of strength of a marriage pattern, we must have a clear image of that pattern for a given time in history. Russian ethnology of the late nineteenth and early twentieth centuries devoted itself to compiling a record of peasant culture before it disintegrated under the impacts of emancipation and modernization. The effort resulted in collections of peasant traditions and minute documentations of everyday life in the peasant community and household.[1] From this qualitative approach to peasant life we learn that marriage provoked at least as much apprehension, sorrow, and lamentation as joy. Descriptions, songs, and proverbs portray young brides, bereft of their "maidenly

1. O. K. Agreneva-Slavianskaia, *Opisanie russkoi krest'ianskoi svad'by* (Moscow, 1887–89); A. Efimenko, *Issledovanie narodnoi zhizni* (Moscow, 1884), p. 2; A. V. Tereshchenko, *Byt russkogo naroda* (St. Petersburg, 1848); . A. Smirnov, *Ocherki semeinykh otnoshenii po obychnomu pravu russkogo naroda* (Moscow, 1878).

freedom," being led tearfully away from family and friends to the houses of "strangers" where they would thereafter make their homes. Not physical beauty, but submissiveness and the "endurance of a horse" were the qualities sought in a bride. Severe treatment by their mothers-in-law and occasional unwanted sexual advances from their fathers-in-law *(snokhochestvo)* were expected by young wives. Above all, peasant wives were expected to bear a large, vigorous posterity. Bitter words from the poet Nekrasov's "Red-Nose Frost" epitomized the harsh life of a Russian peasant woman in the serf era: "married, mated and subjugated to a slave."

This vivid but incomplete picture of peasant marriage and domestic life represents only part of the historical record of Russian domestic groups, their formation and development. A vast body of hard data in the form of demographic records, largely ignored by pre-revolutionary and Soviet investigators, holds out possibilities for firm empirical generalizations concerning marriage, child-bearing, and family organization which are at present completely absent from the study of pre-industrial Russian society. Historical demographic research of the kind pioneered by L'Institut National des Etudes Demographiques and the Cambridge Group for the History of Population and Social Structure currently has no parallel in Russian studies.[2] A holistic view of the peasantry, the bulwark of pre-industrial Russia, will emerge only from a successful synthesis of the older qualitative approach with newer methods based on the construction of numerous time-series of quantitative data. The object of this essay is to inaugurate steps toward such a synthesis by introducing a discussion—in quantitative terms—of peasant marriage behavior in the pre-emancipation era.

Thanks to the plodding toil of numberless zealous officials, there exist for eighteenth and nineteenth-century Russia sources for demographic history that are multifaceted, voluminous, and in some ways remarkable. The quality of these source materials naturally varies, but some can be shown to be highly accurate and reliable. The main sources fall into three categories: soul revisions *(revizskie skazki)*, enumerations of the taxable population conducted ten times between 1720 and 1858 by the central government; parish registers *(metricheskie knigi)* and parish confessional

2. *Family and Household in Past Time*, ed. Peter Laslett and Richard Wall (Cambridge, England, 1972).

lists *(ispovednye vedomosti)*, compiled continuously from the second half of the eighteenth century by Orthodox ecclesiastical authorities; and household lists *(podvornye opisi)*, private enumerations of agricultural serfs and household servants compiled more or less regularly by landlords beginning, as far as can be determined, in the late eighteenth century and continuing to the eve of emancipation. Data for this essay have been drawn from parish registers and estate household lists; they reflect the circumstances of proprietary serfs in two non-contiguous districts of Riazan Province for the period 1782–1850.

Regional variations in demographic behavior have been detected even in a country the size of Belgium. It goes almost without saying, therefore, that consideration for similar differences in Russia —even differences among estates of neighboring landlords in the same province—must, at this early stage of research, inhibit too facile generalizations about national patterns of demographic behavior or structure. I am concerned, therefore, to underscore the exploratory character of this essay's conclusions, rather than to assert the complete illumination of any problem it raises. The known data are promising, but only further study of them, and the completion of studies for other regions of the Russian Empire and categories of the peasantry, can provide a basis for sound generalizations about the questions discussed here.

Mikhailovskii and Sapozhkovskii districts were located in the southern half of Riazan Province, where the central black-earth belt begins to give way to the forests and the thinner soils of the north. Natural conditions were favorable for agriculture, which dominated the area's economy. Rye was the principal crop. In 1858 Riazan was the seventh most densely settled province of the Empire. The region was originally opened to settlement in the early seventeenth century as a buffer zone between Moscow and the Tatars, and its population was predominantly Great Russian. By the end of the eighteenth century in-migration was no longer a significant factor in the region's population growth. Nine-tenths of the population were peasants, approximately 56 percent of these proprietary serfs. The preponderance of peasants in Riazan was typical of the Russian provinces as a whole, although the proportions of state to proprietary peasants varied somewhat from region to region.

The availability of abundant source materials of extraordinarily high quality has led to the selection of the estates of Mishino in Mikhailovskii district and Pokrovskoe in Sapozhkovskii district for detailed study. Both estates belonged to the Gagarin family during the period under consideration in this essay. Mishino consisted of four villages with a total population of 1,173 agricultural serfs in 1814; the estate included two churches, one in the village of Mishino and another in Krasnoe. Pokrovskoe consisted of two villages and a portion of a third. The village of Pokrovskoe was a parish seat. In 1814 the total population of the estate was 1,789. Between 1814 and 1850 the populations of both estates grew, Mishino's to 1,423 and Pokrovskoe's to 2,086. At this stage of research it is premature to posit in what ways Mishino and Pokrovskoe may have typified agricultural settlements as regards the demographic behavior of their peasants. Both were larger than average, carefully managed proprietary estates whose prosperity was based upon the labor services *(barshchina)* of their enserfed peasants.[3] Whether state or proprietory serfs—living on smaller or larger estates, under different systems of exploitation, more or less conscientiously managed—developed markedly different marriage patterns from those of the Mishino and Pokrovskoe peasants remains to be demonstrated.

MARRIAGE SEASONALITY

Few data are now available reflecting marriage seasonality among the peasants of Riazan Province. However, those which are available show such a high degree of consistency that a tentative discussion of this interesting issue may be justified. Data for marriages throughout the entire population of Mikhailovskii district, including the district capital of Mikhailov, reveal three distinct seasons for marriage in 1782: a busy fall season beginning in September and ending in November; a winter season (January and February); and a less important spring season commencing with the end of Lent and continuing into the early summer. No marriages were celebrated in March or December, reflecting an effective ban on marriages by the Church during Lent and Advent. In nineteen parishes approximately 57 percent ($N = 102$) of all marriages were celebrated in the fall, 21 percent ($N = 38$) in the winter, and 17

3. I. D. Koval'chenko. *Krest'iane i krepostnoe khoziaistvo Riazanskoi i Tambovskoi gubernii v pervoi polovine XIX veka* (Moscow, 1959), pp. 127–136.

percent ($N=32$) in the spring. Eight marriages (4%) were celebrated in July, while none was celebrated in June or August.[4] In the rural parish of Mishino twelve marriages were celebrated in September and October and four in January. In 1850 Mikhailovskii district again saw no marriages in March or December. In eleven parishes 47 percent ($N=170$) of all marriages were celebrated in the fall, 32 percent ($N=117$) in the winter, and 10 percent ($N=38$) in the spring. A total of thirty-nine marriages, approximatey 10 percent occurred during June, July, and August. In the parish of Mishino, seven marriages occurred in October, three in January, two in May, and one in June.[5] In 1868 the ban on Lenten and Advent marriages still held throughout Mikhailovskii district, and the parish of Mishino still celebrated the preponderant number of its marriages in the fall, fourteen out of the annual total of seventeen. The other three occurred in January, April, and June.[6] The general pattern of large numbers of marriages in the fall, when the product of the harvest is plentiful, and small numbers during the busy spring and summer months, when the land must be prepared and the crops sown, is to be expected for an agricultural community. Without considerably more data it would be idle to speculate further about the significance of this pattern. Furthermore, only when change away from this pattern becomes noticeable—something that does not appear to have occurred in Riazan Province before 1868—does the problem become intriguing.

AGE AT MARRIAGE

Intrinsically and comparatively, the most salient features of a marriage pattern are the ages at which marriage occurs and the proportions of men and women ever marrying. My empirical findings on marriage for Mikhailovskii and Sapozhkovskii districts, based on information contained in parish registers, confirm the conventional wisdom that Russian peasants married early and in high proportions. These findings provide, however, the first precise definition of "early" for any sizable population of Russian peasants in the pre-industrial age.

4. *Gosudarstvennyi Arkhiv Riazanskoi Oblasti* (hereafter *GARO*), fond 627, g. 1782, op. 246, d. 19, Metricheskie knigi Mikhailovskogo uezda.

5. *Ibid.*, g. 1850, op. 246, d. 105.

6. *Ibid.*, g. 1868, op. 246, d. 147.

Tatiana's nurse in Alexander Pushkin's famous novel in verse, *Evgenii Onegin*, may have accurately reported her age at the time of her marriage (thirteen), and she could well have been correct about that of her groom, said to be still younger.[7] If she was correct about her husband, the marriage violated contemporary Russian Orthodox canon law regarding age at marriage: while thirteen was the lawful minimum for females, males were forbidden to marry before the age of fifteen. Parish registers for Mikhailovskii and Sapozhkovskii districts reflect almost total compliance with this rule.[8] Of course, it is unlikely that a parish priest would boldly inscribe a breach of canon law in his own parish records and subject himself to degradation and punishment. Nevertheless, evidence exists which strongly suggests that violations of the canon regarding age at marriage were not uncommon in the eighteenth century. Four edicts issued in the late 1700s refer to the recurrent problem of under-age marriages, especially unions of under-age males ("8 and 10 and 12 year old grooms") and females of "20 or more years."[9] The edicts repeatedly expressed concern that the marriage of pre-adolescent males to mature women led inevitably to "sin," "incest" between fathers and daughters-in-law, and even to parricide. The edicts do not indicate the magnitude of the problem with any numerical precision, and it is difficult to know whether the laws reflected a widespread practice or a statistically insignificant phenomenon whose sordid and taboo-violating consequences elicited an exaggerated emotional response.[10] At least in 1782, the latter was probably the case, given the relatively low proportion of males recorded as marrying at the lawful minimum age in Mikhailovskii district (23 out of 317); the most popular age for grooms was sixteen. (See Table 1.) The force of the edicts is clear, however—the reporting of ages at the time of marriage in some parish registers may be less than completely accurate, and as a

7. Alexander Pushkin, *Eugene Onegin*, trans. Vladimir Nabokov (New York, 1964), I, 162.

8. Examination of almost 4,000 marriage entries did reveal one, however, in which the groom's age was given as 14. *GARO*, fond 627, g. 1795, op. 246, d. 19, l. 24.

9. *Polnoe sobranie zakonov rossiiskoi imperii* (hereafter *PSZ*), 20, no. 14229 (1774); 20, no. 14367 (1775); 20, no. 14899 (1779); 21, no. 15295 (1781).

10. Gregory Freeze suggests that violations of canon law concerning minimum age for marriage in the eighteenth century were not uncommon, but he does not cite sources or speculate about numbers. See his "The Disintegration of Traditional Communities: The Parish in Eighteenth-Century Russia," *Journal of Modern History*, 48, no. 6 (March, 1976): 46.

consequence the average ages at marriage calculated from them, especially for males, may require some downward adjustment.

But any problems created by false reporting of ages at marriage need not be permanent. The generally high quality of parish registers for Riazan Province, which include the ages of the bride and groom as well as information about parents and places of residence, should make it possible to carry out population reconstitution studies on a parish-by-parish basis. Record linkage using soul revisions and household lists, which are likewise age specific, is also possible for some populations. When these studies can be done, the frequency of pre-adolescent marriage can be determined and the question of the accuracy of parish registers clarified. Until then, however, data from parish registers will be used as given.

The number of young people marrying at the canonical minima in the eighteenth century was relatively low. In Mikhailovskii district in 1782, of 333 women marrying for the first time, 1.5 percent ($N = 5$) had their ages recorded as thirteen. Among the men, 7.2 percent ($N = 23$) of 317 marrying for the first time were fifteen.[11] In Sapozhkovskii district in 1795 the proportions were smaller—0.3 percent ($N = 1$) of the young women, 5.9 percent ($N = 22$) of the young men.[12] A year later, proportions in the same district rose for women to 0.8 percent ($N = 3$), and declined for men to 5.4 percent ($N = 20$).[13]

By the mid-nineteenth century, recorded earliest ages at marriage for both males and females had risen by approximately two years. Parish registers for Mikhailovskii and Sapozhkovskii districts for 1850 show no brides below the age of sixteen, out of 1,070 marrying for the first time, and none of 1,002 grooms marrying below the age of eighteen. This apparent rise in earliest age at marriage was no doubt affected by an 1830 law which aimed to prevent the "harmful consequences" of premature marriage, and to improve morals among the young by increasing the minimum ages at marriage of males to eighteen and females to sixteen.[14] The law, however, only set a civil standard. Younger men and women would be lawfully joined in the eyes of the Church (so long as the canonical minima of fifteen and thirteen, respectively, were observed) but

11. *GARO*, fond 627, g. 1782, op. 246, d. 19.
12. *Ibid.*, g. 1795, op. 252, g. 19. Metricheskie knigi Sapozhkovskogo uezda.
13. *Ibid.*, op. 252, g. 20.
14. *PSZ*, Sobranie vtoroe, 5, no. 3807 (1830).

would open themselves, and others involved in the marriage, to fines at the hands of civil authorities. The regulation was later modified to allow ecclesiastical officials to lower the minimum ages in individual cases by six months.[15] Probably as a consequence, the parish registers of Mikhailovskii and Sapozhkovskii districts for 1868 and 1869 respectively reflect a corresponding decline in earliest ages at marriage. In the former district, of 492 women marrying for the first time, 1.8 percent ($N=9$) were recorded as fifteen; of 465 males, 5.4 percent ($N=25$) were recorded as seventeen.

TABLE 1. PROPORTIONS MARRYING FOR THE FIRST TIME, AGES 13–20, MIKHAILOVSKII DISTRICT (Percentages expressed as a proportion of the total number of first marriages)

	Females			Males		
Age	1782	1850	1868	1782	1850	1868
13	1.5	—	—	—	—	—
14	6.0	—	—	—	—	—
15	23.1	—	1.8	7.3	—	—
16	21.3	14.3	19.7	22.7	—	—
17	16.8	24.9	35.0	18.3	—	5.4
18	11.4	26.2	26.6	12.9	44.5	49.0
19	5.1	14.9	8.1	9.1	18.8	18.7
20	11.1	11.4	5.5	19.2	12.7	11.6

The increase of about two years in the *earliest* age was not fully paralleled by the rise in the *mean* age at marriage. While the mean did increase between 1782 and 1868, greater bunching of marriages in the 16–18 age group for women and 18–19 for men restrained its rise. Mechanisms which we do not yet fully understand impelled approximately 95 percent of all women marrying for the first time, over the entire period under review, to do so before their twenty-first birthday. The bunching effect was just as noticeable for men, although the proportion marrying for the first time before their twenty-first birthday was only about 85 percent. In the data now available, the mean age at first marriage for women rises from approximately 17.5 years in the late eighteenth century to approximately 18.2 years in the mid-nineteenth. The mean age at first marriage for men increased from approximately nineteen to twenty. With the slightly more rapid increase in mean age at first

15. I. C. Berdnikov, *Kratkii kurs tserkovnogo prava pravoslavnoi tserkvi*, 2nd ed. (Kazan', 1913), p. 328.

marriage for men, the difference in a couple's age at marriage also increased slightly, from 1.5 to 1.8 years. Between 1800 and 1850 the modal age at first marriage rose for both men and women—from 17 to 18 for men and 16 to 17.5 for women.

TABLE 2. AGES AT FIRST MARRIAGE—MEAN, MEDIAN, MODE—MIKHAILOVSKII AND SAPOZHKOVSKII DISTRICTS

Year	Number of Marriages		Mean Age		Median Age		Modal Age	
	Mikh	Sap	Mikh	Sap	Mikh	Sap	Mikh	Sap
Males								
1782	317		19.0		18		16	
1795		371		19.2		18		18
1796		372		18.9		18		17
1850	479	523	20.4	20.6	19	19	18	18
1868	465		20.0		18		18	
1869		364		20.3		18		18
Females								
1782	333		17.4		16		15	
1795		376		17.7		17		16
1796		379		17.4		17		17
1850	511	559	18.9	18.4	18	18	18	18
1868	492		18.0		17		17	
1869		365		18.3		18		18

Although they have not yet been systematically studied, the small proportion of first marriages occurring after the twenty-first birthday shows some noteworthy characteristics. Among men, especially those over twenty-five marrying for the first time, a substantial number are identified as "*dvorovyi*" (household serf), "*soldat*" (soldier), or "*pakhotnyi soldat*" (farming soldier). Older women are also frequently identified as "*dvorovaia*" (household serf). These people were serfs (or, in the case of soldiers, former serfs) who had been separated from families, communities, and the land. They lived apart (or at least distinct from agricultural serfs) as marginal members of rural peasant society. The soldiers, retired or no longer fit for service, returned to their homes with no automatic claim to land. The life cycle constructed around early marriage and integration into an existing economic/domestic unit was not typical for these non-agricultural serfs.

I will be the first to admit that final conclusions about age at marriage should not be based on the few points that have been plotted with the data used above. Yet the general tendency toward higher earliest and mean ages at marriage can be confirmed through additional data sources taken from the regions in which Mikhailovskii and Sapozhkovskii districts are located. In 1953, Hajnal presented a method for calculating mean age at marriage from census-type lists of inhabitants.[16] The virtue of this method for our immediate concerns is its dependence on a second, independently compiled set of data for the same category of population reflected in the parish registers. Hajnal's method has been applied to household lists of serfs from the estates of Mishino in Mikhailovskii district and Pokrovskoe in Sapozhkovskii district, with the following results. Singulate mean age at first marriage rises steadily for both men and women through three listings (1814, 1831, 1849) for the Mishino estate, confirming the trend apparent in the parish register data.[17]

TABLE 3. SINGULATE MEAN AGE AT FIRST MARRIAGE[a]

	Women	Men
1814	18.9	18.0
1831	19.4	18.7
1849	20.9	21.5

[a]Certain anomalies in the mean ages shown here—the higher mean for women than men in 1814 and 1831, and the generally higher singulate means than those calculated from parish register data—will be considered in the subsequent discussion.

A distribution of the population represented in these listings according to age, sex, and marital status shows the effect of additional tendencies displayed by data in the parish registers—the disappearance of marriages at 13–14 years of age for females and 15–16 for males, and considerable marriage bunching up to the ages of nineteen for women and twenty-one for men. In addition, the household lists for Mishino estate allow one to determine the

16. J. Hajnal, "Age at Marriage and Proportions Marrying," *Population Studies*, 7, no. 2 (1953): 111–136. Hajnal's method results in a figure called the "singulate" mean age at marriage, a simulation of the marriage experience of a single cohort of the population spread over all the years when marriage is likely to take place. This figure is different from the one obtained from parish registers, which reflects the mean age of everyone marrying in a given year. The latter figure is more prone to short-term fluctuation due to social and economic causes.

17. *Tsentral'nyi Gosudarstvennyi Arkhiv Drevnikh Aktov* (hereafter TsGADA), fond 1262, op. 2, Mishino imenie, d. 48, Podvornyi spisok g. 1814; d. 234, g. 1831; d. 400, g. 1849.

proportions of men and women ever marrying, information which parish registers cannot directly provide. The data reveal virtually universal marriage for both men and women. (See Table 4.) The thorough listings for Mishino estate do away with the need to speculate about the reasons for women over nineteen and men over twenty-four remaining single. In almost all cases they can be determined to be seriously handicapped—"hunchback," "halfwit," "blind," etc.

TABLE 4. PROPORTION EVER MARRIED, BY AGE, MISHINO ESTATE, 1831

			Males				
Age	15–19	20–24	25–29	30–34	35–39	40–44	45–49
Married	30.1	83.8	100	100	97.4	84.6	92.3
Widowed					2.6	11.6	
			Females				
Married	23.3	82.6	96.4	96.6	88.4	83.9	71.0
Widowed	—	1.4	1.8	1.8	9.3	12.9	25.8

DISCUSSION

One aspect of the marriage pattern reflected in the data from Mikhailovskii and Sapozhkovskii districts, early and nearly universal marriage for women, has been common throughout most of the world as far back as records go. Western Europe is the singular exception—for 250 years no nation therein has ever had mean age at first marriage for women as low as 20 years, at least for any sustained period of time.[18] In addition to high age at marriage, the "European pattern" is characterized by a small age gap between spouses and a high proportion of people who never marry.[19] The glimpse into Russian peasant marriage behavior which the data from Riazan Province afford us discloses an example of a robust non-European marriage pattern, but one with features and circumstances which warrant special attention.

In most societies studied by historical demographers to date, the groups of men and women had, within limits imposed by conventions and social and economic conditions, responded spontaneously

18. Peter Laslett, "Characteristics of the Western Family Considered over Time," in *Family Life and Illicit Love in Earlier Generations* (Cambridge, England, 1977), p. 29.

19. For a discussion of the uniqueness of the European pattern, see J. Hajnal, "European Marriage Patterns in Perspective," in *Population in History: Essays in Historical Demography*, ed. D. V. Glass and D. E. C. Eversley (London, 1965), pp. 101–143.

and flexibly to social and economic change. Russian serfs were less free to respond individually to external circumstances affecting their lives. The collective will of the community *(obshchina)* and the demands of the landlord could and did thwart the free play of variables which normally affect the timing and quantity of nuptiality—availability of mates, feasibility and desirability of marriage. A recent work by V. A. Aleksandrov demonstrates that the desire of landlords to increase the number of taxable units *(tiaglo*—a married couple) on their estates and guarantee the economic viability *(tiaglosposobnost')* of households frequently led them to interfere, either directly or through the peasant community, in the personal lives of their serfs. Each young couple brought a new *tiaglo* into existence. Aleksandrov cites the example of a Khar'kov landlord who established a schedule of fines to be levied annually on the fathers of unmarried females—6 rubles for young women eighteen and nineteen—and threatened to transfer to another landlord or give forcibly in marriage any young women reaching the age of twenty unmarried.[20] Other landlords instituted similar fines for females as young as fifteen and introduced fines on widows up to the age of forty.[21] Aleksandrov reports examples of similar regulations introduced as late as the 1820s, and he asserts that the landlord who did not directly set standards for the marriage of his serfs was the exception. Rules commonly required all young women to marry by the age of seventeen and young men by the age of twenty.[22]

Under pressure from landlords, village communities often took marital affairs into their own hands and arranged matches by lot. This method was used particularly for finding matches for widows and widowers.[23] Given the quantitative data for Riazan Province, Aleksandrov's case, based on selected material from scattered territories, could be somewhat overstated. While "bunching" was indeed a feature of the marriage pattern in Riazan, the gradual diminution in the number of marriages for women over seventeen suggests that draconian measures such as Aleksandrov describes may not have been as widely applied as he asserts. Yet evidence

20. V. A. Aleksandrov, *Sel'skaia obshchina v Rossii (XVII-nachalo XIX v.)* (Moscow, 1976), p. 304.
21. *Ibid.*
22. *Ibid.*, pp. 303–304.
23. *Ibid.*, p. 308.

that many peasants paid fines rather than marry off adolescent daughters who had begun to contribute to the household labor force indicates that peasants, as well as landlords, viewed marriage from an economic point of view; such evidence could be a measure of peasant resistance to landlord interference.[24] However that may be, some proportion of landlords intruded themselves into the domestic lives of their serfs, hurrying them into early marriages and rapid re-marriages after widowhood. This fact, taken with what can eventually be learned about marriage behavior among non-proprietary serfs, offers an empirical basis on which to study the contrast of peasant and landlord beliefs and behavior.

A considerable age gap between spouses in first marriages is a common feature of non-European patterns; sometimes the average difference is as great as nine years. In general, the younger the bride, the greater the age difference.[25] One exceptional feature of the marriage pattern displayed by the peasants of Riazan Province is the small age difference between spouses in first marriages. In the parish of Mishino in 1782, thirteen marriages occurred in which both partners were marrying for the first time; the men were an average of 2.0 years older than the women.[26] In the parish of Pokrovskoe in Sapozhkovskii district, twenty similar marriages took place in 1850; the men were 0.85 years older than the women.[27] Two men were younger than their brides. In the parish of Sarai, also in Sapozhkovskii district, twenty-eight first marriages occurred in 1850; the men were 0.96 years older than the women.[28] Although an examination of the 1814 household list for Mishino estate cannot yield directly the age at marriage of couples listed, men are shown to be an average of 1.7 years older than their wives.[29] In 43 percent of the married pairs, the wife was older than the husband. (In examining the list for this information, no attempt was made to identify first, second, or third marriages.)

The high proportion of wives older than their husbands in the

24. *Ibid.*, p. 305. The discussion of pressure of owners and resistance of serfs could profitably be compared with slaves in America in relation to their owners. See Herbert Gutman, *The Black Family in Slavery and Freedom, 1750–1925* (New York, 1976).

25. Ruth B. Dixon, "Explaining Cross-Cultural Variations in Age at Marriage and Proportions Never Marrying," *Population Studies*, 25, no. 2 (July, 1971); 215–216.

26. *GARO*, fond 627, g. 1782, op. 246, d. 19.

27. *Ibid.*, g. 1850. op. 252, d. 117, ll. 470–477.

28. *Ibid.*, op. 252, d. 117, ll. 427–438.

29. *TsGADA*, fond 1262, op. 2, d. 48, g. 1814.

1814 listing for Mishino estate, compiled toward the close of the Napoleonic invasion of Russia, was brought about in part by the higher than usual proportion of males 15–19 shown as married (54.7%) and the lower than usual proportion of females 15–19 shown as married (34.4%). Three-fourths of the married males aged 15–19 were married to older women, 10 percent to women the same age, and 15 percent to younger women. The wives of men in this age group were 1.4 years older than their husbands. Although the pool of marriageable males was diminished in 1814 by the need for recruits, forces within the community were apparently able to sustain pressure on single women (or, more realistically, their fathers) and on the remaining younger males to marry. This resulted in two fifteen-year-old males marrying women eighteen and nineteen, respectively, and two other teenaged males taking brides as much as six years older. This phenomenon, incidentally, underlies the singulate mean ages at marriage in Table 3, showing the bride's higher age in 1814. Since the population marrying in the years immediately preceding compilation of the 1814 household list has been included in the calculation of the singulate mean ages at marriage from the 1831 listing, that fact partly accounts for the persistence of a higher mean age at marriage for women in the latter year. Whether the circumstances which led to the high proportion of males marrying older wives in 1814—fewer males in the age cohort 15–19 (53) than females (90)—provide an insight into the eighteenth-century phenomenon of pre-adolescent male marriage remains to be determined.

Another characteristic of the singulate mean age at marriage should perhaps be mentioned here. Biases in the formula for calculating the singulate mean tend toward somewhat higher mean ages at marriage, compared with the same means calculated from parish registers. This phenomenon would help account for the consistently higher ages at marriage shown in Table 3 for the estate of Mishino, compared with figures derived from parish registers for the area surrounding that estate. However, local variation is probably more important in explaining the differences. Figures derived from the registers of Mikhailovskii and Sapozhkovskii districts reflect events taking place in over forty parishes in each district and more adequately represent the behavior of peasants in that region than behavior of the peasants of Mishino estate only. At this point we can only speculate on why the peasants of Prince Gagarin seemed to marry slightly later than peasants in the surrounding countryside.

The extreme situation which developed in Mishino during the French invasion of Russia brings into sharp focus a question already made pertinent by earlier observations that the overwhelming majority of young men and women experienced little or no adult life before marriage: How was a means of livelihood provided for newly married couples thrust into "adult" status while still in their teens? The answer is that such couples were incorporated into existing domestic economic units.

Detailed discussion of peasant household structure falls outside the purview of this essay, yet reference to certain of its features is necessary to an understanding of one important social force which sustained the marriage pattern being described here. The family or household *(dvor)* was the primary socio-economic unit in peasant society during the era of serfdom and for a considerable period afterward. As with nuptiality, very little of a quantitative nature has been adduced about its structural organization. Conventional wisdom asserts that, especially before the abolition of serfdom, most peasants lived in large joint families which were dominated by a *bol'shak* (head of household–patriarch) or, in some cases, *bol'shachikha* (female head of household), and which were closely linked with other larger social units such as the commune *(obshchina)*. My recent research into the structure of peasant households in the region of Riazan suggests that Russian social history has been reasonably well served by this conventional wisdom. The question that concerns us here is: Does a distribution of peasant households according to size and number of conjugal family units composing them justify the assertion that a system of large joint families was an essential element in sustaining the marriage pattern described here? The answer can be found in the household lists for the Mishino estates.

On the estate of Mishino in 1814, 78 percent of all households ($N=128$) consisted of two or more conjugal families (multiple family households). Almost 12 percent ($N=15$) were extended families and 8.6 percent ($N=11$) were single families (married couples alone or with children, and widows or widowers with children). The remaining 1 percent of the households consisted of solitaries.[30] Among the 11 single-family households, only one could be suspected of consisting of a recently married couple; however, a thirty-two-year-old man, his twenty-one-year-old wife, and their infant child did not constitute a typical newly married pair, by the standards of this community. In 1831 little change in this situation was apparent. Multiple family households were 76.3 percent of all households ($N = 152$), and 11 percent of the households were simple.[31] In 1849 the multiple family households had diminished to 65 percent of a total of 169 households, and the proportion of simple households had risen to 17 percent.[32] But, on analysis, the larger proportion of simple family households does not reflect greater opportunities for newly married couples to establish independent households. Instead, the larger percentage of simple family households seems to be accounted for by a modest increase in the rate of household division. By relieving young people approaching marriageable age of the need to establish the means for financial and residential independence, the Riazan peasant system of joint families facilitated the pattern of early and nearly universal marriage.

For the incorporation of newly married pairs into joint families to work as a device lowering the average age at marriage, several other obstacles relating to the availability of mates had to be overcome. Serfdom, which limited social and spacial mobility, limited the choice of spouses. The small size of settlements and pressure from landlords to confine marriages to their own peasants still further diminished the availability of mates. The usual constraints arising out of consanguinity, affinity, and godparenthood *(kumstvo)* further exacerbated the problem of marriage partners for peasants. Aleksandrov cites the case of a landlord who, in the 1740s, unsuccessfully attempted to eradicate the customs of godparenthood on his estate as they applied to marriage.[33] Other threats and pressures, however, including forced migration from one estate to another, were more often successful in removing impediments to a match. Young people were generally not left to search for and attract their

30. *Ibid.*
31. *Ibid.*, d. 234, g. 1831.
32. *Ibid.*, d. 400, g. 1849.
33. Aleksandrov, *Sel'skaia obshchina v Rossii*, p. 307.

own partners, but instead had the matter taken over by their elders, who assured not only that marriages occurred, but that they usually occurred sooner rather than later. A rigorous order of marriage according to age, clear from examination of successive listings of Mishino and Pokrovskoe households, was no doubt also a consequence of parental control over marriage.

A further factor affecting nuptiality—the desirability of marriage—requires little discussion. Neither social nor institutional alternatives to marriage existed in the peasant milieu. The desire to avoid fines or other penalties, and possibly even the loss of economic support, added further to the desirability of marriage.

We may never be able to weigh precisely the factors in the equation—the system of large joint families, an economy based on large landed estates, peasant traditions including inheritance, the interlocking of family and community, input of various sorts from the landlord, geography and patterns of settlement, etc.—that resulted in the marriage pattern described here. This should not deter us, however, from considering some of the consequences that immediately appear to flow from that pattern.

Age at marriage and the number of women who never marry are the most important regulators of population growth. The average Russian peasant woman spent a much greater part of her fertile period married (in many cases, virtually the entire fertile period) than any modern or early modern European woman we could compare her with. Women are more fecund in the earlier part of their fertile period, and there is historical evidence that women who produce their first children at age fourteen or fifteen could conceive another twenty children thereafter if no restraints are placed on fertility. The detailed demographic record available for late eighteenth and early nineteenth century Russia will make it feasible to study the role of marriage in the rapid population growth which occurred in the eighteenth century, and the still unexplained decline in the absolute numbers of serfs between the eighth (1834) and tenth (1858) revisions. A proposition of particular interest seems to be emerging from the data analyzed to date: the age at marriage, for women and men, apparently moved upward. Given the close links between age at marriage, population growth, and household structure, the period we are considering appears to be one of significant demographic transition—and, by implication, one of social and economic change as well.

One of the peculiar features associated with the western European pattern of marriage was, as Laslett has put it, that "children seem always to have been born to mature women, with an average age in the late twenties or the early thirties."[34] In Russia, children were produced by women in their early twenties or even their teens. In a society where both child mortality and general mortality were high, only if women marry early and produce children quickly would their parents (or, more likely, parents-in-law) be able to share the household with them and their children. And only if children are born when the mothers themselves are young enough would they be able to share a household with those children after the latter have married. From an examination of household lists, we know that these conditions were met by the majority of women. The average generational span of households on the Mishino estate between 1814 and 1849 is as follows: one generation, 2.2%; two generations, 31.3%; three generations, 59.0%; four generations, 7.45%. The high level of complex joint families implies the presence of grandparents, as well as numerous aunts and uncles, to fill the role of surrogate parents for children. This, together with the great authority of the patriarch, raises questions about the importance of the conjugal dyad as the primary social and emotional unit in Russian peasant society. Psychologists have yet to agree about how maturity in the mother affects the child, or how proximity and physical contact with the mother determine the development of a child's social behavior. Implications of the patriarchal joint family should raise additional related questions; one that should perhaps be contemplated by political sociologists and political scientists is the perennial junior status that was imposed upon a high proportion, possibly a majority, of males and females by the early marriage–joint family syndrome, which precluded them from ever succeeding to the statuses of household head and mistress of the house.

CONCLUSIONS

Data drawn from parish registers and serf household lists have made it possible, for the first time, to document a Russian marriage pattern. Source materials reflect identifiable individuals whose lives can be traced from beginning to end within a socio-economic

34. Laslett, "Characteristics of the Western Family Considered over Time," p. 42.

context which can also be reconstructed. The marriage pattern we have discerned shares only one feature with the well-documented European pattern of marriage—spouses were usually relatively close in age. Otherwise, the Russian pattern is distinctly non-European in its early age at marriage and negligible level of permanent celibacy. Because features of that marriage pattern have also been found widely distributed among people living under differing social and economic systems, hypotheses concerning links between this pattern and serfdom in general must be carefully approached. Can the serf marriage pattern described here be said to illuminate peasant beliefs or the norms of peasant culture? On the basis of evidence cited above from the work of Aleksandrov, evidently not. "Peasant culture" in the era of serfdom, with its own standards of correct behavior and cluster of beliefs, remains to be described, and the line of contact or competition between this culture and that of the landlords is still to be traced.

The generalizations made in this essay must remain subject to amendment as more data are examined and analyzed. Without new evidence, we can say nothing about the origins of this pattern or about changes it may have undergone as a result of the abolition of serfdom. The steady upward trend in the mean age at marriage over the time period examined in this essay suggests that a demographic transition was under way well before the emancipation of 1861—the act commonly held to be the great socio-economic watershed in modern Russian history. If these findings can be confirmed for other regions of the Russian Empire, they would only reinforce the views of Fernand Braudel and other social historians that wars, revolutions, and sudden institutional shifts are but "surface flashes of light" on a broad, deep continuum of change.[35] Petr Struve has written that the elements of slavery bound up with the institution of Russian serfdom had lost their legal/moral viability long before 1861, and that only the economic benefits associated with serfdom kept the institution alive until that date. Perhaps one manifestation of the gradual erosion of serfdom was the progressively reduced capacity of landlords to enforce their will in matters of peasant marriage and family organization.[36]

35. Fernand Braudel, "Time, History and the Social Sciences," in *The Varieties of History*, ed. Fritz Stern (New York, 1972), p. 420.
36. Petr Struve, *Krepostnoe khoziaistvo* (St. Petersburg, 1913), p. 154.

Throughout the life cycle of any group of people there is an essential tension among biological, social, and cultural forces. Value systems affect courtship, age at marriage and conception, and attitudes toward marriage and parenthood. Health and nutritional habits, which affect growth and reproductional efficiency, have largely social and economic origins, and these in turn are linked to value systems. Answers to many of the questions raised in this essay are not readily at hand. They will be found only through an interdisciplinary approach which diachronically examines the interaction of all these factors.

GREGORY L. FREEZE

Caste and Emancipation:
The Changing Status of Clerical Families in the Great Reforms

The reign of Alexander II generated far-reaching reforms, not only in secular society and government, but also in the Russian Orthodox Church. These "ecclesiastical Great Reforms," although virtually unexplored in the historical literature, brought fundamental changes in the traditional Church—its administration, clergy, educational institutions, and relationship to state and society.[1] Some reform plans, such as those in censorship and justice, were direct reactions to the secular reforms of the state, as the Church adjusted to new principles in parallel institutions of the government. But unique unto the Church was its primary, overarching problem—the "clerical question," a knot of complex issues involving the *dukhovnoe soslovie* or clerical estate.[2] The essential problem was the parish clergy's estate order, which had crystallized in

The present article is part of a broader study, "Emancipation of the Parish Clergy: Reform and Counter-Reform in the Russian Church," which has been supported by the International Research and Exchanges Board, the Fulbright Faculty Research Program, and the Russian Research Center of Harvard University.

1. For preliminary sketches of selected aspects of the ecclesiastical reforms, see N. Runovskii, *Tserkovno-grazhdanskoe zakonopolozhenie otnositel'no pravoslavnogo dukhovenstva v tsarstvovanie Aleksandra II* (Kazan', 1898); A. A. Papkov, *Tserkovno-obshchestvennye voprosy v epokhu tsaria-osvoboditelia (1855–1870 gg.)* (St. Petersburg, 1902); and Julia Oswalt, *Kirchliche Gemeinde und Bauernbefreiung; Soziales Reformdenken in der orthodoxen Gemeindegeistlichkeit Russlands in der Ära Alexanders II* (Gottingen, 1975).

2. The Russian *soslovie* represented something more than a European estate but less than a formal caste; here we shall follow the customary translation of "estate." Formally, the *dukhovnoe soslovie* included both the monastic (or black) and the parish (or white) clergy, for both belonged to the ecclesiastical domain (*dukhovnoe vedomstvo*). Only the parish clergy, however, composed a social estate, since they were not celibate and represented a large population of servicemen and their families. Consequently, throughout the Great Reforms authorities considered the problem of estate reform only with reference to the parish clergy.

the eighteenth century and remained rigid. It was directly responsible for a host of social and economic maladies and, in the view of
many, was the principal cause of the clergy's ineffective service and
low social status. Concern about these problems began to mount
after 1855, particularly after the publication in 1858 of a sensa-
tional exposé called "A Description of the Rural Clergy" *(Opisanie
sel'skogo dukhovenstva).*[3] In 1862 Alexander established a Special
Commission on the Affairs of the Orthodox Clergy to oversee
reform in the clerical estate, a change that many perceived as "an
emancipation of the clergy."[4]

To solve the clerical question and free the clergy from its rigid
estate order, it was essential to transform the clerical family, the
linchpin of the whole clerical estate. In contrast to the celibate
clergy of the Roman Catholic Church, the parish clergy of the
Orthodox Church by custom had to marry, and the clerical estate
consequently came to embrace not only priests and sacristans, but
also their wives and children. In the eighteenth century the family
played a primary role in forging the clergy into a separate estate; its
claims and interests determined the disposition of property, marriages, and even appointment to clerical positions.[5] Typically, a
cleric's son attended a church school and seminary, married the
daughter of another cleric, assumed the position of his father or
father-in-law, and directed his children along the same route. The
family thus steeled the walls around the estate; it rarely admitted
outsiders to its fold, and it reluctantly released its progeny to
lay careers. Although historians of the "state school"[6] conceived
of the estate as an unnatural artifact of autocracy, the clerical estate was in fact much more than a legal abstraction—it was *au fond*
a cohesive social group bound by economic interest, separate
subculture, and endogamous family ties.[7] By the mid-nineteenth

3. [I. S. Belliustin,] *Opisanie sel'skogo dukhovenstva* (Leipzig, 1858); see also my
"Revolt from Below: A Priest's Manifesto on the Crisis in Russian Orthodoxy," forthcoming
in *Russian Orthodoxy under the Old Regime*, ed. Theofanis G. Stavrou and Robert Nichols.
4. On the formation of the Special Commission *(Osoboe prisutstvie po delam pravoslavnogo dukhovenstva)*, see my "P. A. Valuyev and the Politics of Church Reform
(1861–1862)," *Slavonic and East European Review* 56, no. 1 (1978): 68–87.
5. See my *Russian Levites: Parish Clergy in the Eighteenth Century* (Cambridge,
Mass., 1977).
6. On the state school of historiography, see N. L. Rubinshtein, *Russkaia istoriografiia*
(Moscow, 1941), pp. 289–312.
7. See, *e.g.*, A. Gradovskii, *Nachala russkogo gosudarstvennogo prava*, (St. Petersburg,
1875–83), I, 210–211.

century the tenacious hereditary family order was so entrenched, so segregated from the rest of society that many contemporaries regarded the clergy as a "caste," something utterly unique in imperial Russia.

The term "caste" was no compliment—it was a deliberate pejorative, expressing alarm and dismay at the clergy's extraordinarily rigid estate order that seemed to be a fatal weakness, a primary reason for the Church's torpidity and waning influence. Abolition of caste required various reforms, such as the enrollment of outsiders in church schools, revision of the seminary curriculum, and an improvement of the clergy's economic condition to attract talented laymen to Church service. But most fundamental was reform of the clerical family, because it institutionalized the estate order, transmitting status, service, and culture to the clergy's progeny. Family reform consequently was a complex, over-arching task, one that raised profoundly important questions about traditional policy toward estate barriers, mobility, the legal status of women and children, the juridical unity of the family, and new forms of social welfare. Here we shall consider that reform of the clerical family —its motives, legislation, and impact upon the Church and clergy.

By the 1860s, as Russia embarked on its epoch of Great Reforms, there was broad agreement among educated contemporaries on the necessity of dissolving the clerical estate and transforming the clergy into an open social class. Not all shared that view, to be sure; some denied outright that the clergy represented a "caste," or averred that a separate estate was the surest way to protect the clergy from secular contamination and to ensure an abundance of candidates for the cloth in the future. For example, a diocesan committee in Kostroma declared in 1863 that "the estate order in the clergy should not only be left in full force, but should even be strengthened by still firmer, more prescriptive laws."[8] That view was rare, however; prevailing opinion was uncompromisingly hostile to the estate order and—quite wrongly—envisioned its abolition as a panacea for all the Church's failings. This reform consensus drew surprisingly broad support in educated society, claiming as adherents men of diverse ranks—bishops and governors,

8. Tsentral'nyi gosudarstvennyi istoricheskii arkhiv SSSR, fond 804 (Osoboe prisutstvie po delam pravoslavnogo dukhovenstva), op. 1, razd. 1, d. 54, l. 33.

priests and landowners, even members of the intelligentsia and ministers of interior.[9] The magnet that held this consensus together was the promise of numerous benefits—to Church, state, and society.

One major beneficiary was to be the Church. According to many critics, the clerical estate produced only a moribund, inert priesthood, and its transformation was a prerequisite for the development of a new class of effective, professional clergy. According to the common argument, one became a priest in Russia because of hereditary ties or family claims, not because of personal commitment or a "calling." As a result, Orthodox priests often tended to be merely hired artisans toiling at the altar, rather than dedicated pastors. Significantly, that view was expressed not merely by anticlerical laymen, but also by bishops and diocesan committees. For example, the bishop of Ekaterinoslav complained that the clergy, having had little chance of pursuing an alternative career, "of necessity remain in the clerical estate, without any inclination or calling for this [service], thereby increasing the number of people incapable and unfit for this office."[10] A diocesan committee in Nizhnii-Novgorod declared outright that the task was now "to give the Russian people pastors [chosen] more by calling than by circumstances or social origin."[11] Moreover, reformers blamed the estate for separating the clergy from their parishioners, thereby depriving the Church of its erstwhile influence upon society. As a diocesan committee in Novgorod argued, the clergy "has little influence upon the surrounding social environment: increasingly, it locks itself into its own special, narrow circle and, though placed to act everywhere in society, it stands apart."[12] That separateness also seemed at least partly responsible for anti-clericalism among the laity; one provincial official tersely observed that "as a consequence of the clergy's estate isolation, society began to feel hostile to people from the clerical estate."[13] In short, to produce better priests and

9. Suffice it to say that in 1858–59 N. Dobroliubov, P. A. Valuev, M. P. Pogodin, and Grand Duchess Elena Pavlovna took a keen interest in the "clerical question."

10. TsGIA, f. 804, op. 1, razd. 1, d. 74, l. 34. That kind of harshly critical view derived, at least in part, from the profound gulf separating the white (parish) and black (monastic) clergy. For references to contemporary literature on this problem, see Igor Smolitsch, *Geschichte der russischen Kirche* (Leiden, 1964), pp. 425–426.

11. TsGIA, f. 804, op. 1, razd. 1, d. 31, l. 25.

12. Ibid., d. 42, 1. 243.

13. Ibid., razd. 1, d. 104, ch. 1, ll. 12–12 ob.

renew public veneration for the clergy, abolition of the estate was essential.

Reform also promised tangible gain for the parish clergy themselves. In the first place, it would eradicate a problem that had long plagued the clergy—overpopulation, a plethora of sons unable to find positions. Once the state erected a rigid service structure *(shtat)* in the eighteenth century, demand for additional clergy remained minimal, and the clergy's natural demographic growth soon produced a superabundance of candidates. Overpopulation, though serious earlier, reached catastrophic proportions in many dioceses in the nineteenth century; even seminary graduates—not to mention the mass of dropouts—had difficulty finding clerical positions.[14] This imbalance between estate and service needs impelled the Church in 1849–51 to take drastic measures to reduce the number of seminarians in the most overpopulated dioceses, but the problem remained unsolved.[15] Although some outlying dioceses like Irkutsk still had difficulty filling vacant positions in the 1860s,[16] most bishops complained incessantly of a swarm of unplaced candidates. Typical was the report by the bishop of Vladimir in 1856 that "significant numbers of seminarians, who . . . have received no appointment because of the lack of vacancies, have continued to burden the diocesan administration."[17] The magnitude of alarm is suggested in the report of a clerical committee in Novgorod diocese in 1863: "The number of those now studying in ecclesiastical schools has risen to the point where they surpass Church needs and form a kind of proletariat in the clergy. Of this proletariat only a few leave the clerical estate to enter other positions (mainly in the bureaucracy); the rest seek refuge in monasteries, rural schools, and the homes of parents and relatives."[18]

14. *E.g.*, a secret synodal committee of 1849 found that there were 2,569 unplaced graduates of ecclesiastical academies and seminaries, and another 4,879 who were idle after attending a seminary or church school. (TsGIA, f. 796 [Kantseliariia Sv. Sinoda], op. 445, g. 1849, d. 354, ll. 1–10; f. 797[Kantseliariia Ober-Prokurora], op. 19, g. 1849, I otd., III st., d. 42644, ll. 1–44.)

15. For the decision to establish a "normal *shtat*" (limiting seminary enrollment to numbers commensurate with diocesan needs) and to allow the clergy to educate their children in secular schools, see TsGIA, f. 797, op. 19, g. 1849, I otd., II st., d. 42644, ll. 29–32 ob., and f. 802 [Uchebnyi komitet], op. 5, d. 12977, ll. 1–7.

16. "Prazdnye sviashchennicheskie mesta v Irkutskoi eparkhii," *Irkutskie eparkhial'nye vedomosti*, 1863, no. 4, pp. 37–38.

17. TsGIA, f. 796, op. 440, d. 1099, l. 16 ob.

18. TsGIA, f. 804, op. 1, razd. 1, d. 42, l. 272.

Such overpopulation wreaked havoc with clerical finances; families diverted scarce resources to educate their sons, yet they often realized no gain from the crucial investment. In the end many youths became sacristans, menial clerks, or fell victim to the draft *(razbor)* of "idle, excess clerical youths."[19']Overpopulation also caused the Church to spread thin the meager resources for ecclesiastical schools, as it attempted to provide education for the whole clerical estate. The result was grossly inadequate education that failed to provide proper training for the small number of priests actually needed by the Church.[20]

Abolition of the estate also promised to improve the clergy's status and rights. It would permit the clergy to intermarry with more prosperous strata and thus tap a vital resource that had saved many aristocratic families from ruin. The clergy also hoped to acquire new rights and privileges, for elimination of the peculiar clerical estate implied that the clergy would obtain a new legal status in secular law, especially for their families. Historically, the clergy's juridical separation as a group under Church (not state) jurisdiction had prevented the clergy from possessing a clearly defined status in formal state law. As a result, those who left the estate—widows and children—had no personally inalienable status and, depending upon the circumstances, could be inscribed into the poll-tax population of commoners. Acquisition of secular status also promised to enlarge the clergy's civil rights, especially in trade and business. The entire clerical family traditionally belonged to the ecclesiastical jurisdiction, and all were obliged to observe the ban against commercial activities by clergy, a rule that deprived the clerical family of potentially important revenues.[21]

Reform in the clergy also served the interests of the state. Most important for the emperor, it would produce clergy better fit to combat political and religious disaffection, particularly in the western provinces. The disenchantment of former Uniates with Orthodoxy, the rising influence of Catholicism, and the waxing bold-

19. For the policy and legislation on the *razbory*, see P. V. Znamenskii, *Prikhodskoe dukhovenstvo v Rossii so vremeni reformy Petra Velikogo* (Kazan', 1873), pp. 176–354.

20. Establishing an equilibrium between seminary enrollments and available means was a fundamental principle of the academy and seminary reforms of 1867–1869. See the explicit formulation in the report from Bishop Nektarii to the Synod (May 30, 1866) in TsGIA, f. 797, op. 87, d. 223, ll. 6–19 ob.

21. *Svod zakonov rossiiskoi imperii izdaniia 1857 g.* (St. Petersburg, 1857–60), IX, book 1, art. 289.

ness of the Polish nobility impelled Alexander and top government officials to seek improved clergy as an alternative to police repression.[22] The government could also hope to make better use of the clergy's sons, whose talent and education often went unwanted in the ecclesiastical domain. These youths were already an important source of personnel for the bureaucracy in the internal provinces before the 1850s; they were still uncommon, however, in the western borderlands, where they offered an attractive alternative to local elites that were neither Russian nor Orthodox.[23] Indeed, the government now had to find a solution to the overpopulation problem, for it had abandoned its traditional method of the *razbor* or conscription of excess youths into the army or poll-tax population. The government had not conducted a systematic conscription since 1831, and in 1856 it formally abandoned the policy because of its devastating effect upon the clergy's social status.[24]

To reap all these alluring benefits, reform in the clerical family had to be comprehensive, entailing three principal changes. The first was a redefinition of the status of clerical children, especially sons, enabling them to transfer freely to other social groups and simultaneously lowering barriers to the admission of outsiders. The second problem was to eliminate the custom of endogamous marriages, which flourished throughout the Empire even though they did not enjoy the sanction of law. The third task was to establish a secular status for the clergy's wives, or at least for widows desiring to leave the clerical estate. Although these reforms constituted but a part of the comprehensive Great Reforms in the Church, they claimed special importance and occupied much of the attention of the Special Commission.

At least in the view of authorities, the most urgent of the three tasks was the change in children's status. Formally, this included

22. That interest was paramount in 1858–60, when the tsar supported reform in a special synodal committee on the clergy in the western provinces. (For the journals of the committee, see TsGIA, f. 804, op. 1, razd. 1, d. 1.)

23. For selective data on the number of clerical offspring serving in central and provincial administration, see Walter Pintner, "The Social Characteristics of the Early Nineteenth-Century Bureaucracy," *Slavic Review*, 29, no. 3 (September, 1970): 429–443. While the clergy's sons constituted a sizable part of the administration, the absolute numbers were small and represented only a tiny proportion of the clerical estate.

24. See esp. the materials on the question of a *razbor* during the Crimean War in the archive of Metropolitan Filaret (Drozdov) of Moscow. (Gosudarstvennaia biblioteka im. V. I. Lenina, Rukopisnyi otdel, f. 316 [Filaret Drozdov], k. 65, d. 14, d. 16, d. 17, d. 18; hereafter GBL.)

daughters as well as sons, but in fact attention focused almost exclusively upon male progeny. Although there was some interest in the rights of daughters and especially in their education, authorities were mainly concerned about the boys, since they constituted the palpable problem of overpopulation as "unplaced seminarians." Reform was not a simple matter of "emancipation," however, for it had to ensure an adequate supply of future candidates for the clergy as well as to enable the excess to transfer freely to secular social groups. Still, the main task was to facilitate outward mobility; to determine why so few left the clerical estate, the Special Commission conducted a systematic survey of diocesan opinion in 1863, ordering each bishop (or, at his discretion, diocesan committee) to explain the failure to transfer and to recommend changes.[25]

The replies, as varied as they were prolix, almost unanimously confirmed that far too few left the estate, and that the backlog of unemployed seminarians constituted a critical problem.[26] A few ascribed the low mobility to a "natural" attachment to their estate and, especially, to the peculiar upbringing and way of life of the provincial clergy.[27] Family interests, according to some, also blocked freer movement: "Often, expecting aid and comfort from their [sons] alone, [families] try to keep them inside the clerical estate, correctly reckoning and knowing from experience that one can have little hope of aid from sons who have left this rank."[28]

25. The Commission collected opinions and information on four main problems: "(1) on the expansion of means of material support [for the parish clergy]; (2) on increasing the personal civil rights and privileges [of parish clergy]; (3) on opening to the clergy's children the pathway to useful work in all spheres of civil activity; and (4) on the opening of means for the close participation of the clergy in parish and village schools" (TsGIA, f. 804, op. 1, razd. 3, d. 470, ll. 11–12). The Commission decided to have the clergy in each parish church prepare answers for questions 1 and 4, and the bishop (or committee appointed by him) was to prepare comprehensive answers on all four problems. In the archive of the Special Commission (TsGIA, f. 804), the diocesan replies compose a significant part of razd. 1, and the voluminous replies by parish clergy are preserved in razd. 3.

26. A comprehensive summary of the diocesan replies was prepared by the Commission's staff (TsGIA, f. 804, op. 1, razd. 1, d. 104, ch. 1, ll. 117–207). Other background material (ll. 39–116) is also available in the Lenin Library under the title *Zapiska po voprosu ob otkrytii detiam sviashchenno-tserkovno-sluzhitelei putei dlia obespecheniia svoego sushchestvovaniia na vsekh poprishchakh grazhdanskoi deiatel'nosti.*

27. The Commission summary of reports lists 25 dioceses making such categories (TsGIA, f. 804, op. 1, razd. 1, d. 104, ll. 119 ob.–123). For particularly strong statements, see the reports from Kiev and Kaluga dioceses (d. 59, l. 62 and d. 36, l. 18).

28. Quoted from the report of the bishop of Ekaterinoslav (*ibid.*, d. 74, ll. 43 ob.–44). Similar comments were registered in the reports of Kaluga, Orel, and Tver' dioceses (d. 36, l. 18; d. 43, l. 22 ob.; d. 29, ll. 7 ob.–8).

Gregory L. Freeze

Some bishops argued that, however unsatisfactory the clergy's economic condition, it was better than available alternatives; every cleric, even if not prosperous, at least had something to eat and a place to sleep.[29] Although virtually all denied any kind of "estate prejudice" or belief that the clergy was superior to other groups, many admitted the obvious truth that few youths were willing to volunteer for a lower status in the poll-tax population. In the words of the bishop of Kursk, seminarians "consider it a disgrace to enter the poll-tax population."[30]

The reports placed most of the blame on other barriers to transfer. One was the hostility of lay society, where resentment ran deep against the clergy's offspring as ambitious parvenus in the bureaucracy. The governor-general of Kiev noted that society opposed the entry of clerical children to "government service, just as they feel hostile to admitting Jews into state service"; he decried the anomaly of a Christian society where the priests' sons had to conceal their family background as if their fathers "were criminals."[31] The Church lodged similar complaints. The bishop of Ekaterinoslav, for example, wrote that "society shows no inclination at all of admitting the youths of clerical origin into [secular] offices and professions."[32] Another barrier was the clergy's education: the seminary provided no trade or business training, and the seminary experience—divorced from worldly ways, inculcating humility and submissiveness—hardly prepared youths for a secular career.[33] In most dioceses the clergy did not even have the right to enroll their sons in secular schools; nor could most clergy afford the luxury of tuition in government schools.[34] The university also lay beyond the grasp of most clergy's sons; in the words of the bishop of Riazan,

29. Eight diocesan reports made this point (*ibid.*, d. 104, ch. 1, ll. 126–128). See esp. statements by authorities in Kursk and Orel (d. 34, ll. 43–44; d. 43, l. 23).
30. *Ibid.*, d. 32, l. 45. For a synopsis of the nineteen reports making that kind of statement, see d. 104, ch. 1, ll. 157 ob.–158.
31. *Ibid.*, razd. I, d. 104, ch. 1, ll. 12–12 ob. Similar complaints about Polish repression of clerical youths were made by the bishops of Kiev and Minsk (d. 59, 1. 63 ob.; d. 83, l. 16).
32. *Ibid.*, d. 74, ll. 47 ob.–48; see similar statements in the reports from Nizhnii-Novgorod and Novgorod (d. 31, l. 18; d. 42, l. 98 ob.). A total of eleven dioceses expressed this opinion (d. 104. ch. 1, ll. 134–135 ob.).
33. Typical of such statements were the views expressed in the reports from Kiev and Ekaterinoslav (*ibid.*, d. 59, ll. 62–62 ob.; d. 74, l. 47 ob.).
34. Twenty-six dioceses expressed this opinion (*ibid.*, d. 104, ch. 1, ll. 125–126 ob.). Particularly forceful were those from Astrakhan, St. Petersburg, Viatka, and Nizhnii-Novgorod (d. 35, 1. 44 ob.; d. 49, ll. 17–17 ob.; d. 28, ch. 2, ll. 158–158 ob.; d. 31, ll. 19–20).

"seminary graduates, although capable, cannot enter higher lay schools because of their parents' poverty."[35] But, according to many reports, the most important barrier was legal discrimination—laws that discouraged the clergy's sons from entering state service. These laws applied most harshly to sacristans' sons, who, unless they graduated in the first division *(pervyi razriad)* of the seminary, were categorically excluded from entering state service. Even those who qualified (including the priests' sons) faced formidable hurdles: should they fail to find a position within one year or subsequently lose their positions, they could not return to the clerical estate but were "to be inscribed in the poll-tax population."[36] As the clergy noted with considerable vexation, the sons of Lutheran pastors in the Russian Empire enjoyed greater privilege, possessing all the rights of personal nobles.[37]

To facilitate mobility, the diocesan reports recommended several important changes. One was to redefine completely the status of the clergy's children by giving them a secular status and excluding them from ecclesiastical jurisdiction. Most bishops and committees wanted the priests' sons to have the rank of nobleman (either hereditary or personal) and sacristans' sons to be honored citizens (either hereditary or personal). That proposal was profoundly revolutionary, implying a break with the estate and family system that ascribed a father's status to his children; it aspired directly to transform the clergy from an estate to a rank of servitors. The new status automatically solved the problem of "excess candidates," for the clergy's sons would hold a lay rank and be admitted to the clergy only in sufficient numbers to satisfy Church needs. The reform also would tear down the various legal barriers that thwarted entry into state service, for the youths would enjoy all rights attendant to their secular status, be it noble or honored citizen. Furthermore, several reports advocated educational reform so that the clergy's sons could make full use of their new rights. In particular, youths should have a right to matriculate in state schools, should receive special aid or tuition exemptions, and should be able to return and serve the Church if they wished. Some committees and bishops also advo-

35. *Ibid.*, d. 46, l. 10 ob.
36. *Svod zakonov*, IX, book 1, art. 291–294. For a detailed analysis of all pertinent state laws, see TsGIA, f. 804, op. 1, razd. 1, d. 104, ch. 1, ll. 136 ob.–150 ob.
37. See, *e.g.*, the complaint by an archpriest in Astrakhan (TsGIA, f. 804, op. 1, razd. 1, d. 35, ll. 51 ob.–52 ob.)

cated changes to facilitate the transfer of youths to a military career, primarily by reducing the period for promotion from the ranks to the officer corps and by giving special financial aid to those interested in such a career.[38]

An important additional impetus to reform was a report to the emperor in 1867 from the governor-general of Kiev, A. P. Bezak. In the past the emperor had proved especially responsive to ecclesiastical reform as a means of reinforcing the Church—and therefore state—authority in the western provinces, and this case proved to be no exception. Bezak argued that the bureaucracy there remained largely composed of Catholic Polish nobility, despite government intentions to Russify local administration. The reason lay in the peculiar social system of the region: the nobility consisted almost entirely of Poles, the middle class was Jewish, and the peasantry was unfit for government service. But, he pointed out, there was one resource still untapped: the children of the Russian Orthodox clergy, who were both Russian and qualified. Unfortunately, however, the clergy's children were locked inside the clerical estate, rarely matriculating in state schools or entering state service. More generally, he noted that, whereas in Germany and England the pastor's sons entered "all forms of state service and culture," it was different in Russia: "In our country (with a few exceptions due to special circumstances) seminarians who do not receive priests' positions can only become *d'iachki* or *ponomari* [sacristan ranks], or become the victims of need and poverty, and from time to time because of their excess, are dispatched *en masse* to military service along with peasants and vagrants." In order to redirect this wasted talent to state service, Bezak proposed to separate the seminarians from the clerical estate and confer on them a secular legal status, to eliminate legal impediments (such as vulnerability to inscription in the poll-tax population) to civil service careers, and to offer free education in state schools, especially wherever Catholics now constituted a majority. Alongside a passage in Bezak's memorandum citing the aim of Russification, Alexander made a marginal note that this is "an idea with which I am in complete sympathy." The emperor sent the report to the Committee of Ministers, which endorsed Bezak's recommendations and

38. *Ibid.*, d. 104, ch. 1, ll. 159 ob.–207 ob.

transmitted his report to the Special Commission for immediate consideration.[39]

The commission reviewed these reports closely and by December, 1868, had adopted its final recommendations, generally heeding the advice of the diocesan committees and Bezak.[40] It agreed that youths remained in the clerical estate primarily because of legal barriers and the fear of consignment to the lowly poll-tax population: "Instead of transferring from the ecclesiastical rank to the poll-tax statuses, they regard it as preferable to wait a few years for a position in the ecclesiastical domain *(dukhovnoe vedomstvo)* than to deprive themselves and their children of the right to exemption from the recruitment and poll-tax obligations." The commission concluded that the clergy's children must be separated from the clerical estate and should be listed in church records only as an "administrative formality." Instead, youths should legally hold a status most approximate to that of their fathers—hereditary honored citizen for priest's sons, personal honored citizen for sacristans' sons.[41] Those statuses by definition conferred the right to enter service or engage in any business without risk of falling into the poll-tax population. The commission saw no need for special laws allowing the clergy's sons to matriculate in secular schools, since the *gimnaziia* statute of 1864 had already removed any obstacles there. But it did admit the need for special economic aid to enable youths to study in state schools, and urged the ministry of education to provide special tuition exemptions for the clergy's children, particularly in the southwest. That proposal had the firm support of Count Dmitrii Tolstoi, the chief procurator *(Ober-Prokuror)* of the Synod and real director of the Special Commission, who was simultaneously the minister of education.[42]

39. *Ibid.*, ll. 3–22; another copy *ibid.*, razd. 3, d. 472, ll. 110–126 ob. For the resolution of the Council of Ministers, see the extract *ibid.*, d. 104, ch. 1, ll. 25–26 ob.

40. *Zhurnal Osobogo prisutstviia*, no. 30 (December 18, 1868–January 9, 1869) (ibid., razd. 3, d. 472, ll. 82–108 ob.)

41. Metropolitan Isidor of St. Petersburg, formal chairman of the Special Commission, insisted that the priest's sons receive the rank of personal noble. The administrative secretary of the Commission, I. Tersinskii, opposed the suggestion, arguing that one cannot inherit personal nobility—that, in fact, was the very meaning of the status. Tersinskii to Chief Procurator Tolstoi, December 29, 1868, *ibid.*, razd. 1, d. 104, ch. 1, ll. 211–212 ob.

42. In May, 1868 (before completing its final proposals), the Commission inquired at the Ministry of Education about the possibility of aid to the clergy's children. In his reply the deputy minister opposed blanket tuition exemptions for clerical youths, arguing that some clergy could afford to pay tuition, that excessive exemptions would upset ministry finances,

Somewhat more troublesome and complicated were the reforms in the legal status of the clergy's children. These changes required the approval of the State Council, which raised two objections. The council first objected to the proposal that priests' sons receive the rank of "hereditary honored citizen," noting that its department of laws had already received numerous complaints about the "undue proliferation" of this rank.[43] To avoid that controversy, the council proposed to confer on the youths the rank of "personal nobility," a higher status and one that in any event bequeathed to their children the rank of hereditary honored citizen. In addition, the council expressed concern about making transfer *too* easy, and questioned "whether the abolition of laws attaching the clergy's children to the ecclesiastical rank will not cause some difficulties in staffing clerical positions." Chief Procurator Tolstoi, representing the Special Commission, denied any risks or dangers. He argued that most clergy would still prevail upon their sons to remain in the clergy, that many youths would still prefer a free seminary education, and that "no doubt in time, especially after the material condition of the clergy has been improved, forces [from other *sosloviia*] will not be slow to appear" and seek entry to the clergy.[44] With that assurance, the State Council approved the reform, and Alexander signed it into law on May 26, 1869.[45] Journals and newspapers acclaimed the reform as a major step toward curing the ills of the parish clergy.[46]

Thus the government made a significant change in the traditional estate order: it detached the clergy's children from the "juridical family" and gave them an entirely different status. It tacitly violated the traditional principle that a man transmitted his status to his wife and children, a rule that underlay the integrity of the family in the

---

and that it was "morally" bad to undermine the principle of parental responsibility. However, he admitted the possibility of some exemptions and suggested a special fund for the western provinces (*ibid.*, d. 104, ch. 1, ll. 27–32). In the Commission itself, Tolstoi later proposed a substantial increase in tuition exemptions, and the Commission resolved to leave further action to the discretion of the Ministry of Education. Isidor to Tolstoi, January 15, 1869 (*ibid.*, ll. 289–291 ob.).

43. *Ibid.*, ll. 325–326 ob.
44. *Ibid.*, ll. 319–322.
45. *Ibid.*, ll. 315–318.
46. E.g., see "Proekt reform v dukhovnom vedomstve," *Sovremennyi listok*, 15 January, 1869, pp. 1–2; "Otmena dukhovnogo zvaniia dlia detei dukhovnykh lits," *ibid.*, 7 June, 1869, p. 1; "Novaia reforma v dukhovenstve," *Pravoslavnoe obozrenie*, 1869, no. 6, pp. 895–902.

estate system. The reform could have cited some vague precedents: children did not acquire the full rights of their estate until they reached maturity, and in some cases children did hold a status different from their fathers.[47] Nevertheless, the reform marked a systematic break in policy, one that caused many observers to regard the new law as equivalent to the elimination of the juridical estate in the clergy.[48]

The second major reform was the abolition of the hereditary order: the endogamous marriages and family disposition of clerical positions that wove a tight mesh around the clergy. This marital order had firm roots; though based only on custom, it "has become virtually a law," as one cleric pointed out.[49] It derived in part from a requirement that the priest's wife be as morally irreproachable as her husband. To guarantee such purity, especially in an age of pervasive secularization, bishops preferred that the priest marry the daughter of another clergyman, since a fellow cleric was more likely to give the girl a proper upbringing than the townsman, peasant, or even nobleman. But real strength of the custom derived from more worldly concerns. Ecclesiastical endogamy performed several important social and economic functions: it guaranteed pensions to retiring clergy, provided welfare for orphans, and permitted the dispensation of clerical positions as dowry. The backbone of the system was the right of *sdacha mest*, family control over positions: a cleric's position went to a qualified seminarian who agreed to marry the former priest's daughter and thereafter to support the retiring priest and his family. Clergy desiring to marry outside the clerical estate encountered stiff opposition from the bishop, who defended the interests of clerical families and the "honor" of the estate. For example, in the 1840s Bishop Iakov of Saratov rejected the request of one cleric to marry outside the estate ("the petitioner is ordered to marry a girl in the clerical estate"), and in a second case even ordered the local ecclesiastical superintendent "to find for the petitioner a girl in the clerical estate." When one youth demurred marrying a girl from the clerical estate, the bishop thundered that "the petitioner is slandering the clergy: there is nothing on earth better in richness of means and

47. *E.g.*, children born to a man in a poll-tax status who subsequently became priests, retained their father's original poll-tax status. *Svod zakonov*, IX, book 1, art. 4, 273, 294.
48. Znamenskii, *Prikhodskoe dukhovenstvo*, p. 354.
49. TsGIA, f. 804, op. 1, razd. 1, d. 60, l. 8 ob.

incentives for a virtuous spiritual life," and ordered the town archpriest to point out local beauties still available.[50] The result was a clerical version of *mariage de convenance*, which aroused widespread criticism yet persisted tenaciously up to the Great Reforms.[51] Even a liberal critic like Ioann Belliustin, who had vehemently condemned the practice in his "Description of the Rural Clergy," obtained his own position in this manner—and in 1859 (the year *after* his book was published) he tried to provide for his family in the same way.[52]

Diocesan reports of 1863 sharply condemned clerical endogamy on several grounds. They pointed out that the custom lacked foundation in canon law or government statute and—unknown to the Early Church and appearing only belatedly in Russia—could not even raise the shield of historical legitimacy. More important, such endogamy caused serious disorders. It mechanically joined people through bargains, not through assurances of compatibility, and the consequence all too often was marital conflict that scandalized the parishioners. As a diocesan committee in Novgorod emphasized, "those who marry do so purely out of calculation and without feelings of mutual attraction, [have] completely different personalities and interests, [and] often are of quite different ages."[53] Besides causing marital problems between priest and wife, such marriages also generated conflict between the priest and the swarm of unwanted in-laws he was now bound to support. Furthermore, marital connections prevented the bishop from selecting the best seminarians to fill vacancies, which were disposed not according to merit but through the private bargains between families. The haggling over positions, the occasional newspaper advertisements, the spectacle of footloose seminarians bargaining with a priest for his position and daughter—all this demeaned the

50. A. Pravdin, "Rezoliutsii Saratovskogo Preosv. Ioakova," *Saratovskie eparkhial'nye vedomosti*, 1878, no. 4 (pribavlenie), pp. 78–79.

51. See, *e.g.*, Nikitinskii, "O tom, kakim obrazom zameshchaiutsia sviashchenno-tserkovno-sluzhitel'skikh mest," *Den'*, April 9, 1864, pp. 1–4, and May 16, 1864, pp. 1–12; P. Oraztsov, "Neskol'ko slov o domashnem byte sel'skikh sviashchennikov," *Sovremennyi listok*, April 18, 1864, p. 1; A. Tachalov, "K voprosu ob uluchshenii byta sel'skogo dukhovenstva," *Dukh khristianina*, 1863, February, otd. 3:105–123; A. Sokolovskii, "O zachislenii vakantnykh sviashchenno-tserkovno-sluzhitel'skikh mest za sirotstvuiushchimi devitsami dukhovenstva," *Dukhovnyi vestnik*, 1864, no. 8, pp. 268–274.

52. I. S. Belliustin to M. P. Pogodin, August 10, 1859 (GBL, f. 231/2 [M. P. Pogodin], k. 3, d. 50/2, l. 23).

53. TsGIA, f. 804, op. 1, razd. 1, d. 42, ll. 85 ob.–86.

clerical rank, eroding any claim to spiritual authority. Some money-wise bishops also pointed out that endogamy deprived the clergy of a chance "to improve their material position through marriage to a well-to-do fiancée."[54] But most important, warned the critics, endogamy drove a wedge between the priest and his flock. An archpriest in Astrakhan, for instance, wrote that endogamy "serves as one cause of the estrangement of the clerical estate from other [estates],"[55] and a priest in Kursk diocese spelled out the full consequences of that social distance: "Through the loss of this right [to choose freely a spouse from any estate], other estates—seeing that the clergy shuns any kinship ties with them —become estranged from the clergy as a special caste locked inside itself, and such a split produces a coldness between the clergy and other estates and one may even say a certain disdain for [the clergy]."[56] The bishop of Riazan presented a similar argument, declaring that exclusive marriages within the estate made the clergy "into a caste" and caused "what we now see—the split between the clergy and other estates."[57]

Some did defend endogamy, however. Most adamant was the diocesan committee of Kostroma, which vindicated the clergy's estate order and admitted the need for few changes. It admonished reformers not to anticipate a sudden wave of profitable marriages between priests and rich heiresses; free choice would not lead to advantageous matches as long as aristocrats disparage the clergy, a problem not to be overcome by mere law.[58] The bishop of Kaluga rejected a proposal by his diocesan committee for free choice of spouses and warned that exogamous marriages would expose the clergy to the corrupting influences of lay society, which is "alien in spirit, way of life, concepts, and in all respects to the clergy." He added that this was especially likely since "the influence would not be from the upper strata of society, but from the lower."[59] Although the rank-and-file clergy had no chance to comment on this question in 1863, reports in the late 1860s suggest that they regarded hereditary control of positions as essential to their families'

54. *Ibid.*, d. 150, ch. 1, l. 18.
55. *Ibid.*, d. 35, l. 50 ob.
56. *Ibid.*, d. 34, l. 70 ob.
57. *Ibid.*, d. 46, ll. 21–21 ob.
58. *Ibid.*, d. 54, ll. 12 ob.–18 ob.
59. *Ibid.*, d. 36, ll. 17–17 ob.

well-being.[60] A priest from Tula, for example, argued that the clergy were too poor to entice rich fiancées, that endogamy assured the selection of girls familiar with the traditions and rigors of clerical life, and that control over positions was the only dowry available to the impoverished clergy.[61] Among Church and state authorities, however, the prevailing spirit of the 1860s was one of staunch opposition to hereditary claims.[62]

The legal moorings for intra-clerical marriage—the right of *sdacha mest*—were sundered in 1867. Acting upon a proposal from the chief procurator, the State Council approved a revision of an earlier law that authorized the disposition of clerical positions to provide welfare for aged clerics and their families. The decree itemized the serious disorders that ensued from family control of positions: candidates with family claims had precedence over candidates of quality, positions remained vacant until family claimants reached legal or marriageable age, parish clergy had to share their small incomes with numerous in-laws, and diocesan administration was overburdened with lawsuits over the contracts and deals. The State Council therefore ruled that clerical positions could no longer be used for the sake of social welfare: "As a form of charity for aged clergy and [after their death] their families—the appointment of relatives and children to their positions is hereby abolished, and in staffing vacancies which appear upon the death or release of clergy from service, [in choosing] among those candidates under the jurisdiction of the diocese, do not consider kinship with the deceased or released [clergy] as a circumstance giving them precedence before other persons." The Council also outlawed the practice of reserving positions for daughters, "with a right of appointment to these positions those candidates who marry such girls." To eradicate the custom of bargaining altogether, the State Council forbade authorities to enforce any legal contracts between priests and former families which would oblige the new clerics to share their income. Although this decree did not

60. "Obozrenie 1867 g. po dukhovnomu vedomstvu," *Sovremennyi listok*, January 6, 1868, p. 1.

61. See, *e.g.*, "Pis'mo sel'skogo sviashchennika k bratu po sluchaiu sostoiavshchegosia ukaza o zapreshchenii dukhovenstva zakrepliat' svoi mesta za det'mi," *ibid.*, January 10, 1868, pp. 5–7.

62. For a synopsis of diocesan views on the right to select a wife from any *soslovie*, see the *zapiska* of the Special Commission in TsGIA, f. 804, *op.* 1, razd. 1, d. 150, ch. 1, ll. 18–19.

authorize the clergy to marry outside the estate, it freed appointment from family claims and diocesan welfare.[63]

The Special Commission considered the problem of endogamy in 1870–71, as it planned changes in the legal status of clergy and their families. It summarized the findings of the diocesan reports, reiterating the many arguments against a closed marital order, and expressed general agreement with the need to permit clergy to marry outside the clerical estate. It noted that there was now no legal basis for the bishop to require that candidates marry within the clerical estate, for the reform of May 26, 1869, placed the clergy's children outside the ecclesiastical domain—and thus beyond the bishop's authority. Since custom alone was at stake, the commission ruled that no changes were required in the Digest of Laws, and that it would suffice for the Synod to distribute an appropriate circular to provincial bishops.[64]

The third and final reform concerned the status of clerical wives. The diocesan reports of 1863 had shown considerable concern about the inferior status of the clergy's wives, who nominally shared their husbands' status insofar as they remained in the clerical estate. If her husband was defrocked and expelled from the clergy, the cleric's wife also suffered: however innocent, she had followed her husband into the lowly status of the poll-tax population. More frequent and more onerous was the hardship of the clerical widow. Since the Church had virtually no funds for pensions, the widow needed a new source of income, which ordinarily meant remarriage. But that was fraught with risk: a widow who married a man from the poll-tax population lost her privileged status and acquired that of her new husband.[65] The diocesan committees and bishops complained partly about the evident hardships involved, but they were also sensitive to the implicit discrimination: women of other privileged statuses could lose their rank only for the commission of a crime.[66] Loss of privilege was so important that some widows

63. *Ibid.*, f. 1149 (Gosudarstvennyi sovet), op. 7, g. 1867, d. 72, ll. 2–7 ob., 11–14; *Polnoe sobranie zakonov rossiiskoi imperii*, Vtoroe sobranie (St. Petersburg, 1830–84), 42, no. 44610 (May 22, 1867); hereafter *PSZ*.

64. Zhurnal Osobogo prisutstviia, no. 40 (March 1, 1871) in TsGIA, f. 804, op. 1, razd. 3, d. 472, ll. 242 ob.–244 ob.

65. *Svod zakonov*, IX, book 1, arts. 272, 283.

66. For a general summary of diocesan opinion, see the Commission's synopsis ("O pravakh dukhovenstva soslovnykh, semeinykh i po imushchestvu i o sushchestvuiushchikh

preferred to form unions out of wedlock rather than lose their status; the sad lot of Kliuchevskii's mother (who did not remarry and bore several illegitimate children) poignantly illustrates the problem.[67]

The diocesan reports urged a number of significant changes. One was to confer upon the clergy's wives an inalienable privileged status, independent of the clerical estate, which they should retain even if, as widows, they remarried into a lower-status group. According to most proposals, a priest's wife should hold the status of personal noble, a sacristan's wife that of personal honored citizen.[68] Many recommended extending the rights of women and children to engage in trade and commerce; especially if given a secular status outside the ecclesiastical domain, they should be free from traditional restrictions and have an opportunity to supplement the family income in "seemly" businesses.[69] A few committees and bishops also proposed revisions of the general inheritance laws to give larger shares to mothers and daughters, and less to the sons (who received the lion's share of inheritances).[70]

The Special Commission finally considered the problem of wives' status in 1870–71. It had prepared its preliminary report as early as 1869 but deferred action at Tolstoi's command until the State Council approved the proposals on the clergy's children. In his view, the reform meant "the elimination of the clergy's organization as a caste" and opened the door for similarly far-reaching changes in the status of clerical wives.[71] In its proposals of March, 1871, the commission suggested that clerical wives, like their children, be severed from the clerical estate and "be listed in their husbands' service records only for the sake of information," not as a sign of juridical status. Unless the woman had held the status of nobility prior to marriage (which was inalienable in any event), the commis-

v zakonakh ogranicheniiakh v obshchestvennoi deiatel'nosti dukhovenstva") in TsGIA, f. 804, op. 1, razd. 1, d. 150, ch. 1, ll. 15–15 ob.

67. See M. N. Nechkina, *Vasilii Osipovich Kliuchevskii* (Moscow, 1974), p. 58.

68. TsGIA, f. 804, op. 1, razd. 1, d. 150, ch. 1, ll. 24 ob.–25.

69. For an overview, see the *zapiska* synopsis *ibid.*, 11. 22 ob.–23 ob. For particularly strong support for such a change, see the reports from Kiev and Viatka (*ibid.*, d. 59, 1. 46; d. 28, ch. 2, ll. 148 ob.–152 ob.)

70. A summary of diocesan opinion is *ibid.*, d. 150, ch. 1, ll. 19 ob.–20. See esp. the recommendations of the Astrakhan and Nizhnii-Novgorod committees (*ibid.*, d. 35, ll. 40 ob.–41; d. 31, ll. 9–10).

71. D. A. Tolstoi to I. Tersinkii, February 16, 1869 (*ibid.*, d. 150, ch. 1, l. 1).

sion chose to confer the status of personal noble on priests' wives, and personal honored citizen on churchmen's wives—in other words, the same status as had recently been given to their children. The new statuses were permanent; a widow who remarried in a lower-status group did not forfeit her rights and privileges. The commission declined, however, to act upon proposals that the inheritance laws be revised in order to assure a fair share to widows and daughters, declaring that such a change was superfluous since sons "voluntarily" gave support due to mothers and sisters. The commission apparently was not excessively concerned about the plight of clerical women, though it may also have been deterred by the prospects of tampering with the whole maze of inheritance law. Finally, the Commission ruled that no special laws were needed to enlarge the commercial rights of clerical families, and that a synodal or episcopal resolution would suffice.[72]

The proposal to redefine the status of wives encountered stiff opposition in the State Council, which admitted the need for changes but objected to the specific proposals of the commission. The council's department of laws, which reviewed the proposals first, argued that under Russian law all legal rights were determined by ascription to one of four estates and insisted that this general order must be upheld. Admittedly, declared the department, "because of important reforms of late in the present reign, there have been considerable changes in the mutual relations between estates and in the rights conferred upon each of them, but the [system of] estates remains in all its former force."[73] When the State Council took up the matter at a plenary session, it concurred. While admitting that the law of May 26, 1869, constituted a significant exception to the principles of an estate order, it firmly resisted further deviations: "The proposal to annul the attachment of clerical wives to the clerical estate and to assign them to other estates represents an exceedingly important change in the whole system of distributing people among estates." This decision marked a striking change in government social policy, a return to the traditional system of estates. The State Council justified its decision by arguing that the commission's proposal would create a status contradiction

72. *Ibid.*, ll. 24–27; Zhurnal Osobogo prisutstviia, no. 40 (March 1, 1871), *ibid.*, razd. 3, d. 472, ll. 242 ob.–244 ob.

73. *Ibid.*, razd. 1, d. 150, ch. 1, ll. 74 ob.–75.

within marriage: whereas Russian law ascribed a husband's status to his wife so that the union would be "equal," the commission planned to assign the wife to an entirely different social estate. The council added, with transparent sophistry, that the "law" knows no ranking of statuses and estates, thus rejecting the commission's complaint that a widow's ascription to the poll-tax population was a humiliation.[74] The council did recognize the serious problem of clerical widows, however, even if it might deny that "to belong to one or another estate is humiliating." To ease the lot of widows, it proposed that only their status, not that of wives, be redefined; such a step would avoid the problem of marital inequality while solving the chief social problem—the plight of clerical widows. The council then returned the whole matter to the Special Commission for further deliberation.[75]

The Special Commission considered the State Council's proposal later in 1873, and its staff prepared a memorandum that reviewed the whole problem. It noted that the question could be solved in three ways: by redefining the status of widows only (as the State Council proposed), of all wives (as the commission had proposed), or of both clergy and wives. It objected to the State Council's suggestion of a special status for widows by pointing out that a woman would thereby achieve a desirable secular status through her husband's death—an unseemly idea, to say the least, and one that implied that clerical status was inferior. To redefine only the status of wives also raised problems, since it seemed to introduce a status difference between man and wife. The memorandum for the first time considered the idea of conferring a secular status upon both clergy and wives, thereby avoiding the discrepancy of an "unequal marriage." Yet that solution, too, had its drawbacks; most important, it threatened to turn the clergy into a bureaucratic rank *(chin)*, to confuse the grace of priesthood with secular privilege.[76]

For another opinion on the problem, the commission's secretary submitted the memorandum to the head of the Second Section, Prince S. N. Urusov. A legal authority and member of the Special Commission from its inception, Urusov objected vehemently to the proposal that the clergy receive a secular status: "[Such a change] would pervert the very meaning of the clerical rank, arousing in the

74. *Ibid.*, ll. 74–84.
75. *Ibid.*, ll. 68–73.
76. For the memorandum ("Izlozhenie dela"), see *ibid.*, ll. 89–110.

popular mind a confusion of the blessing of priesthood with promotion into a lay rank and would change the very essence of the priest's relationship to society, which consists in the fact that the priest—in general respect for his position as one of divine origin—is a person equally close to all strata of society, from the lowliest to the highest." While criticizing the State Council's sophistry that demotion to the poll-tax status was no humiliation, Urusov agreed that it would be wrong to violate the basic principle that a man and wife share the same status. Consequently, as the least of all evils, he endorsed the suggestion of the State Council—to redefine the status of widows only. However unseemly, it would achieve the main objective of easing the plight of widows and enabling them to remarry freely.[77]

In a final review of the problem, the Special Commission —before bowing to the inevitable—issued a sharp rebuff to the council's main arguments. It pointed out that the Russian social system was no simple set of four estates, and that the Digest of Laws, rife with ambiguities of terminology and definition, created a far more complex system of order and status. In any event, it declared, the clergy did not constitute a typical estate: present law deprived an individual of his status and rights upon leaving the clerical estate, implying that the occupation (*not* the estate) conferred privilege that was only temporary. Noting that no other estate had such a rule, the commission concluded that the clerical estate was "peculiar," and that revisions here would not be that extraordinary. Indeed, the very uniqueness of the clerical estate was responsible for the plight of the clergy's widows, who, if not born to the nobility or honored citizenry, "are converted into the general mass of people of the lower status and subjected to inscription into the poll-tax estates." That policy was a severe blow to clerical honor, since the common people—regardless of the neutrality of the Digest of Laws—perceived the poll-tax status as a lower rank and thus viewed the widows' reassignment as a humiliation. The commission also denied that redefining a wife's status would violate the marital union, since different statuses would have no practical consequences. Nevertheless, aware that opposition to its proposal was overwhelming, the commission agreed to redefine the status of clerical widows only, not wives. The new proposal re-

77. *Ibid.*, ll. 115–117 ob.

ceived approval from the State Council and, apart from minor adjustments and clarifications in the ensuing years, the family reform drew to a close.[78]

Reform in the clerical family thus wrought fundamental changes: sons could transfer easily, widows had a secure status, and clerics could freely marry outside the clerical estate. Even though they were not as comprehensive as some reformers of the 1860s had hoped, such changes yielded important benefits. Overpopulation, for example, ceased to be a bane of the clergy; hereafter diocesan annual reports no longer complained of hordes of unneeded seminarians. The reform had, moreover, virtually expunged the clerical estate from imperial law. Although the Digest of Laws still listed the clergy as one of the four estates, legal historians like Korkunov concluded that the clergy—once the very model of an estate—now least approximated that order.[79] More important, the iron-clad "casteness" rapidly began to decompose, and from the 1870s on it no longer figured as a theme in the secular or church press.

The reform caused new problems for the Church and clergy, however. One was a sudden paucity of clerical candidates in many dioceses as the Church, after decades of supernumerary candidates, suddenly discovered that its pool of seminarians was insufficient, that the "best seminarians" fled in droves from the clerical estate, and that in some dioceses bishops could not even staff the churches.[80] In 1875 the bishop of Orenburg, for example, complained that "in this diocese there is a shortage of priests, and many parishes remain without priests and earnestly request that these be appointed, but there are none available."[81] The new legal rights of clerical sons, the privileged exemption from university

78. Zhurnal Osobogo prisutstviia, no. 59 (February 6–March 6, 1875), ibid., razd. 3, d. 473, ll. 88–108; razd. 1, d. 156, ch. 1, ll. 88–89 ob.

79. N. M. Korkunov, Russkoe gosudarstvennoe pravo, 8th ed. (St. Petersburg, 1914), I, 275–276.

80. For examples of public alarm at the problem, see G. Z. Eliseev, Begstvo seminaristov (St. Petersburg, 1876); P. Postnikov, "Ot chego vospitanniki dukhovnykh uchebnykh zavedenii ukhodiat v svetskie zavedeniia?" Tul'skie eparkhial'nye vedomosti, 1879, no. 8 (pribavlenie), p. 236.

81. TsGIA, f. 796, op. 442, d. 642, l. 21 ob. See similar complaints from bishops in Olonets (d. 641, ll. 30 ob.–31), Samara (d. 652, ll. 17–17 ob.), Ufa (d. 661, ll. 14–14 ob.), Tomsk (d. 659, l. 7 ob.), Tobol'sk (d. 658, ll. 18 ob.–19), Astrakhan (d. 616, ll. 24–25), Kazan' (d. 630, ll. 21 ob.–22 ob.), Chernigov (d. 648, ll. 9 ob.–10), and Vladimir (d. 618, ll. 25 ob.–26). A few bishops, however, still complained of excess candidates, as in Iaroslavl' (d. 666, ll. 9 ob.–10) and Voronezh (d. 621, l. 13 ob.)

examinations,[82] the gloomy prospects for appointment to desirable positions in the Church[83]—all these factors coalesced to drive off the clergy's children. The bishop of Samara complained in 1875 that "many fathers, especially among the urban clergy . . . more and more frequently are preferring to send their children from the very start of their education not to ecclesiastical but to secular schools."[84] In 1880 Archbishop Savva of Tver observed that "recently almost all the more capable and gifted students left the seminary before graduation (at least until 1879), [and] those who complete the seminary are the weaker, less capable students who then make the main contingent of candidates for the clergy."[85] Significantly, other estates failed to fill the gap, and data on the 1870s and 1880s show that few outsiders enrolled and finished the church schools and seminaries.[86]

Reform also worked severe hardships on the clergy and their families, for abolition of the hereditary order deprived the group of

82. For the policy of the Ministry of Education on the admission of clerical sons to the university, see *Sbornik postanovlenii po Ministerstvu narodnogo prosveshcheniia* (St. Petersburg, 1871–93), vol. 4, no. 453 and vol. 7, no. 343; *Sbornik rasporiazhenii po Ministerstvu narodnogo prosveshcheniia* (St. Petersburg, 1866–1901), vol. 5, no. 271. The result was a sudden flood of clerical offspring into the universities; in 1875 they represented 35 percent of all university students (G. I. Shchetinina, "Universitety i obshchestvennoe dvizhenie v Rossii v poreformennyi period," *Istoricheskie zapiski*, 84 [Moscow, 1969]: 166). For more detailed statistics, see V. R. Leikina-Svirskaia, *Intelligentsiia v Rossii vo vtoroi polovine XIX v.* (Moscow, 1971).

83. The parish reform of April 16, 1869, systematically reordered the structure of parishes and clerical service and had a decisive effect on encouraging youths to leave the clerical estate. It sharply reduced the number of positions and parishes and forbade the ordination of any new candidates until excess clerics had been relocated. More important still, it required all new candidates to serve first as sacristans, whose legal and economic position was intolerably low for most seminary graduates. For the reform itself, see *PSZ*, vol. 44, no. 46974; for statistics on its implementation, see I. V. Preobrazhenskii, *Otechestvennaia tserkov' po statisticheskim dannym s 1840–1 po 1890–1 gg*, 2nd. ed. (St. Petersburg, 1901).

84. TsGIA, f. 796, op. 442, g. 652, l. 17 ob. See a similar complaint from Kiev diocese in "Deti dukhovenstva v Kievskikh gimnaziiakh," *Kievskie eparkhial'nye vedomosti*, 1879, no. 9 (pribavleniia), pp. 7–8.

85. TsGIA, f. 797, op. 50, g. 1880, 3 otd., 5 st., d. 182, ch. 2, ll. 59 ob.–60. Similar complaints were expressed by the bishops of Kishinev, Nizhnii-Novgorod, Orenburg, Olonetsk, Khar'kov, Chernigov, Tomsk, Poltava, and Saratov (*ibid.*, ch. 1, ll. 4–5; ch. 2, ll. 2 ob., 5–6, 8–8 ob., 29–29 ob., 82 ob.–83, 158 ob., 234 ob.–235, 294 ob.–302).

86. For example, even by 1880 diocesan reports show only a few outsiders at church schools and seminaries. Seminary reports for 1880–81 reported the number of outsiders enrolling in that year to represent much less than 10%: 4% in Saratov (2 of 54), 6% in Kiev (6 of 99), none in Viatka, 8% in Novgorod (9 of 112), 9% in Riazan (13 of 140), 8% in Ekaterinoslav (19 of 228), and 8% in Vladimir (11 of 123). The figures for total enrollment in the lower church schools *(dukhovnye uchilishcha)* were roughly similar: 5% in Novgorod (22 of 417), 4% in Viatka (31 of 850), 14% in Riazan (174 of 1,259), 5% in Kiev (42 of 874), 15% in Ekaterinoslav (68 of 461), and 9% in Vladimir (85 of 990). (TsGIA, f. 802, op. 9,

its traditional and only form of social welfare. The authorities hoped to compensate for that loss through special pension funds and parish councils, but neither yielded much benefit to the clergy.[87] The clergy's daughters suffered most from the reform, which abolished *mariages de convenance* but provided no compensation, economic or cultural, for the loss. The bishop of Simbirsk, though a firm supporter of the ecclesiastical Great Reforms, wrote in 1880 that candidates for the clergy "often marry the daughters of peasants, soliders, townspeople and petty officials, while the clergy's daughters are ignored by them, especially if they do not possess a substantial dowry."[88] As one disillusioned priest complained, "the law [abolishing *sdacha mest*] in itself is marvelous, but what are the consequences? The priest is now obliged to give his daughter to the worst peasant."[89] Schools for clerical daughters expanded, but slowly; by 1880 they existed in only half of the dioceses, their enrollments were still small, and their facilities were so limited that further growth was impossible.[90]

Significantly, precisely because the Church failed to provide alternative forms of social security, bishops felt obliged to recognize family needs and interests, the new reforms notwithstanding. Ambitious seminarians complained that local authorities still made appointments according to the petitions of orphans and widows, rather than on the abilities of candidates.[91] But the reforms created a loophole for episcopal compassion, as the 1869 resolution of the bishop of Viatka bears witness. The prelate admonished widows not

---

razd. 1, d. 4, ll. 177 ob., 188, 216, 216 ob., 229, 268, 276, 298 ob.; razd. 2, d. 2, ll. 25 ob., 110 ob., 129, 164 ob., 171 ob., 194; d. 4, ll. 224, 273, 291, 306–306 ob.; d. 8, ll. 71 ob., 124, 158, 196 ob., 206 ob., 254; d. 15, ll. 344, 363, 382, 296 ob., 406 ob., 417 ob.; d. 25, l. 189 ob.; d. 41, ll. 161–161 ob., 194 ob., 204, 229 ob., 261, 282, 320).

87. On the failure of parish councils, see the assessment of their work in 1885 in "Eparkhial'nye otgoloski (nashi prikhodskie popechitel'stva)," *Tserkovno-obshchestvennyi vestnik*, 1885, no. 5, p. 1. Annual statistical reports bear out that assessment: the numbers of councils declined in many areas, and the councils devoted little of their resources to aiding the clergy. See, *e.g.*, the report for 1882 in TsGIA, f. 796, op. 164, g. 1883, d. 2519.

88. TsGIA, f. 797, op. 50, g. 1880, 3 otd., 5 st., d. 182, ch. 2, l. 71.

89. Ferapont Vinogradov, "Delo uluchsheniia byta dukhovenstva," *Sovremennyi listok*, February 18, 1870, pp. 3–4; see also P. Kutepov, "O nedokonchennoi reforme dukhovenstva," *Tul'skie eparkhial'nye vedomosti*, 1874, no. 14 (pribavleniia), p. 62.

90. See the assessment for 1879 in "Zhurnal Uchebnogo komiteta," TsGIA, f. 796, op. 161, g. 1880, d. 379, ll. 3–6.

91. "K voprosu o reformakh v dukhovenstve," *Sovremennyi listok*, September 13, 1869, p. 1.

to request the bishop to find candidates to marry their daughters, but added that "it is a different matter if a worthy candidate for the clergy himself wishes to marry the daughter of the petitioner."[92] In 1880 the bishop of Ekaterinoslav candidly wrote the chief procurator, "I have always permitted and now permit the transfer of positions of priests, deacons and sacristans to children and sons-in-law to support families and household finances where circumstances permit and the candidate is worthy."[93] A survey of bishops showed that, while most condemned the maladies of the former rigidly hereditary order, some admitted recognizing family interests and others agreed with the need for a partial restoration of family rights and claims.[94]

What caused these problems in the family reform? For one thing, the incompleteness of the reform: although the legal order of the estate had been dismantled, the accompanying economic reform of the clergy failed. Whereas the commission expected a more prosperous clergy that could provide adequately for daughters and entice laymen to enter church service, that prosperity never came to pass. The much-heralded "improvement in the material condition of the clergy" stalled and, when the commission was abolished in 1885, the whole question was deferred to some future date. Reform was also warped by insufficient attention to women's status. Not only were authorities unwilling to modify the traditional status of wives, but they also failed to take strong interest in the needs of clerical daughters. Even the efforts to establish special schools for clerical daughters sprang from a desire to mold better wives and mothers, not to prepare women for professional careers. Finally, the empire's complexity defied simple, centralized solutions; social and economic patterns varied so greatly from region to region that any sweeping change was certain to cause considerable disorder and strain.

Thus in many respects the family reform proved a great disappointment. In order to dissolve the "caste order" that seemed responsible for the clergy's problems and maladies, the reform

92. *Viatskie eparkhial'nye vedomosti*, 1869, no. 14 (ofitsial'naia chast'), p. 269.
93. TsGIA, f. 797, op. 50, g. 1880, 3 otd., 5 st., d. 182, ch. 1, ll. 44–44 ob.
94. Among those willing to permit restricted observance of family rights were the prelates in Iaroslavl', Tver', Simbirsk, Don, Chernigov, Polotsk, Tambov, Ufa, Poltava, Tula, and Kher'son dioceses (*ibid.*, ch. 2, ll. 17–17 ob., 59–59 ob., 71–71 ob., 79–79 ob., 84 ob., 113–113 ob., 132–133, 182–183 ob., 231–232, 269–270 ob., 321–322 ob.)

separated the clergy from the estate, freeing their children from the clerical estate and facilitating new relationships between the clergy and other social groups. But if the reform solved some problems, it also created others for the Church and clergy. Dissatisfaction with the family reform and other parts of the ecclesiastical Great Reforms mounted steadily in the 1870s, a vital backdrop to the counter-reforms that K. P. Pobedonostsev would pursue in the 1880s.

Section Three

Family Relations in Folklore

STEPHEN P. DUNN

The Family as Reflected
in Russian Folklore

The aims of this paper are quite modest and, to a certain degree, preliminary; its scope is subject to a number of important limitations, both philosophical and formal. First, the sources do not permit the reconstruction of anything like a complete "working model" of the family, even for the period to which they relate. This is not so much because the sources themselves are incomplete, or corrupt, or present difficulties in interpretation (although all of these things are no doubt true to some extent) as because the folk, in their capacity as verbal artists, have omitted or generalized many of the data which the modern social scientist would need for such a reconstruction. Second, only narrative genres of folklore will be considered—and not all of these. Omitted from consideration are historical songs, which generally record actual events, as well as lyrical songs, *chastushki,* and proverbs. Third and finally, I will not attempt the kind of formal analysis which a professional folklorist might undertake, in which different versions and regional variants of the same theme would be compared in order to draw geographical or historical conclusions. Instead, I intend to treat my texts in a basically literary way.

Accordingly, my material consists of *byliny* (epic songs), folktales, and ballads. Each of these types of work has certain distinctive features which determine, among other things, the kind and amount of social information one can expect to glean from them, as well as the nature of the limitations to which this information is subject. Since this paper is primarily a historical investigation, I shall take the three forms according to the periods which they reflect.

Stephen P. Dunn

Folktales

Although this paper deals with the family as reflected in Russian folklore, one should not necessarily conclude that the structure being reflected is always that of the Russian family. The point about folktales proper *(skazki)*—as distinct from historical legends or prose renderings of epic poems, which also find their way into a great many collections of folktales—is that, for the most part, they reflect an extremely archaic period. There are exceptions: for example, animal stories or fables can hardly be said to reflect any particular period, and certain humorous stories or tall tales, called *Schwänke* in German, sometimes carry satirical references to the feudal nobility or to particular events.

Many folktales contain royal personages and poor peasants, and one might think that the background was a pre-capitalist type of stratified society. In a few very well-known cases, such as the story of Cinderella, this is really the case, or at least the tale has been modified to reflect this kind of society. For the most part, however, the royalty is of an extremely archaic kind: the queen does the cooking, the princess helps with the laundry, and so forth.

It is also important to remember that many folktales are international. The stories, or at least their elements, are found over extremely broad areas in various combinations. As a result, they often fail to reflect Russian or German or Italian conditions specifically. In contrast, *byliny*, or epic songs, being of later origin, are more specific.

Within the broader category of folktales, there is one type which we conventionally call the fairy tale. As far as the Russian material is concerned, this is a misnomer, because there are no fairies in them: the Russian technical term is *volshebnye skazki*, or magical folktales. In Russian folklore studies, this category is rather sharply defined. Here, for example, is the way Propp describes it.

> The designation "fairy tale" [or "magical folktale"] should be applied to . . . the type of folktale which begins with a mistreatment or an injury done to someone (kidnapping, expulsion from home, etc.), or else with the desire to possess something (the king sends his son to seek the firebird), and then develops through the protagonist's departure from the home, the meeting with a benefactor who offers him a magical means or an assistant, with the help of which he will find the object of his search. Further on, the folktale presents a duel with the adversary (the principal form being the duel

with the serpent), the return, and the pursuit. This composition frequently presents certain complications. When the protagonist has already returned home, his brothers throw him over a cliff. Later he reappears, submits himself to a trial by completing dangerous tasks, ascends the throne, and gets married, either in his own realm or in that of his father-in-law.[1]

Although somewhat rigid, this formula probably works better for the Russian magical folktales than for those in Grimm's collection, for example. The formula needs, nevertheless, to be modified to take account of the very frequent cases in which the protagonist is a woman. It is obvious from what Propp says here that the folktale —at least the magical variety—has a great many conventions and is very far removed from any kind of immediate reality, although, as Propp points out, it does contain elements which can be connected with various primitive religious rites and ideas, such as the taboos to which kings and high priests were subject and which are developed in great detail in Fraser's *Golden Bough*. But, in addition to these changes, there is one very significant point to be made: namely, that the danger or misfortune which starts the action of the magical folktale according to Propp's formula, in those cases where it does not arise merely from poverty or bad luck, comes from within the family. Either the protagonist brings it on himself or herself by violating a taboo, or the person responsible is another family member. In this connection it is significant also that the responsible person is very frequently a stepmother and that the victim in the Russian folktales is always (as far as I have been able to discern) a stepdaughter, never a stepson. In the western European folktales, particularly those in Grimm's collection, one sometimes finds a son and daughter sharing the position of victims, as in the story of Hansel and Gretel; this is not the case in the Russian folk literature, as far as I know.

The cruel stepmother is almost a cliché in the European folktale generally. This is scarcely an accident, because the introduction of a stepmother violated the integrity of the family as a unit, and she is therefore a disturbing or dangerous element. However, in the Russian folktale the stepmother is treated differently, at least in some cases. The following paraphrase of one of the folktales in Afanas'ev's collection illustrates the point. (No attempt is made here to render into English some of the formulaic phrases that mark

1. V. Ia. Propp, *I radici storici dei racconti di fate* (Milan, 1949), pp. 28–29.

the Russian folktale, as they would sound rather odd in English.)
The story is called "Starukha-Govorukha," which means, roughly,
"The Talkative Old Woman."

> Day and night the old woman grumbles. Why doesn't her tongue
> hurt? And always it's about her stepdaughter, who isn't bright and
> doesn't behave properly! Whether she goes or comes, or stands or
> sits down, nothing is right! From morning to evening she goes on like
> a well-tuned fiddle. Her husband is tired of her, everyone is tired of
> her, enough to run out of the courtyard! The old man harnessed the
> horses, intending to go to town carrying millet, and the old woman
> called out: "Take the stepdaughter too, take her even into the dark
> woods where there is no road, only get her off my neck."
>
> The old man took her. The road was long and hard, all woods and
> swamps. Where should he leave the girl? He looks: there stands a
> little house on chicken legs, with a dumpling for a door and a pancake
> for a roof; it stands and turns around. "Better leave the daughter in
> the house," he thought; he set her down, gave her millet to make
> porridge, slapped the horses, and drove out of sight.
>
> The girl remained alone; she ground the millet and cooked a big
> pot of porridge, but there was no one to eat it. A long, miserable
> night came: if you lay down your side got sore, and if you looked up
> your eyes got tired with looking. There was no one to talk to, it was
> boring and terrible! She stood on the threshold, opened the door to
> the forest, and called out: "If there is anyone in the dark forest, come
> and be my guest!" The wood demon replied; he came in the form of a
> young man, a Novgorod merchant; he came running and brought
> presents. Today he comes and talks, and tomorrow he brings gifts; he
> brought so much that there was nowhere to put it.
>
> And the talkative old woman was bored without her stepdaughter.
> It was quiet in the house, her stomach was heavy, and her tongue
> dried up. "Go, husband, and fetch the stepdaughter; fetch her from
> the bottom of the sea, or take her out of the fire. I am old and sick, and
> there is no one else to go for her." The husband did as he was told: the
> stepdaughter came riding in, and when she opened the trunk and
> hung the goods on the line stretching from the cottage to the gate,
> the old woman was about to open her mouth and greet her in her old
> way, but when she saw it she set her lips together, seated the guest
> under the icons, and began to make much of her and to say: "And
> what does your ladyship desire?"[2]

There are a couple of things worth noting about this story. First,

2. A. N. Afanas'ev, ed., *Narodnye russkie skazki* (Moscow, 1957–58), III, 145 (#97).

there are no supernatural elements, except the description of the little house where the girl stayed, with the pancake for a roof and the dumpling for a door, and this is obviously a convention which appears in many Russian and German folktales. The wood demon might also be considered a supernatural element, strictly speaking. In fact, Propp equates him or her with a witch who often appears in these stories, and who lives in the little house. But on the whole the story is naturalistic. The stepmother is not a witch, and not even particularly evil; she is just an ordinary pain in the neck and a compulsive scold. There is an important distinction to be drawn here between the *form* of a particular folktale and its social *content*, as presumably perceived and interpreted by the people who originally told and listened to the tale. For example, "The Talkative Old Woman" could be interpreted as a recasting of the Persephone-Koré myth—that is to say, an allegory of the seasons —in which the stepdaughter's stay in the little woodland house corresponds to Koré's sojourn in the underworld, and the stepdaughter's return parallels the advent of spring and the revival of vegetation.[3] However, I doubt that the original tellers of the tale or their audiences paid much attention to this aspect. To them, the stepmother probably represented not Persephone or any other classical deity or personification of natural phenomena, but merely some quite specific chatterbox whom they knew personally. In other words, they were telling (or listening to) a tale, not a myth. In this respect, "The Talkative Old Woman" contrasts with other folktales (including some Russian ones, such as "The Fire Bird" and "The Snow Maiden") from which the magical and miraculous elements jump out at us, and whose essentially mythic nature cannot be disregarded.

"The Talkative Old Woman" no doubt reflects the actual situation in many peasant families, and with a minimum of conventionalization. In addition, the handling of the supernatural elements in this story resembles the handling of the same kind of elements in certain of the stories collected by the Brothers Grimm, for instance, "The Man Who Travelled to Learn What Fear Was" or "The Brave Tailor." In the former case, the hero is challenged to spend three nights in a haunted house; although various queer

3. I owe this suggestion to Olga Aranovsky, whom I thank for this and several other useful comments on the present paper.

things happen to him, he is too stupid or unimaginative to be scared by them. In the latter, the little tailor sets out to seek his fortune and has various adventures with giants, etc. In both cases the supernatural elements are treated humorously. The same is probably true in "The Talkative Old Woman."

The Russian tale is one of a group which might be called the stepmother cycle; some of them do have magical elements which are more central, where the stepmother is in fact a witch or a monster. I chose "The Talkative Old Woman" because it presents the stepmother-stepdaughter conflict in pure form, so to speak. Other cases, where the conflict is between the step-daughter and the stepmother's own daughter, illustrate a different kind of cleavage within the family, and a different kind of danger.

In one of his books Propp interprets the little house in the forest—and, in fact, the entire sequence of events outlined in the quotation given above—as being derived from the custom of male initiation at puberty. He interprets the stepmother in her hostile role as a substitute for the father; the father originally took his sons out into the woods to be initiated, an act which was regarded by the sons (and by the other people) as hostile, because they were afraid of what might happen. Later, because people did not understand this, the stepmother was substituted for the father. However, there are two things wrong with this theory. First, it is difficult to explain the vitality and wide distribution of these stories by interpreting them as a kind of religious allegory, which is essentially what Propp and others try to do. Second, in the story paraphrased earlier, it actually *was* the father who took his own daughter into the woods and left her, albeit at the urging of the stepmother. From what is known about the Russian peasant attitude toward women, at least as reflected in proverbs, this seems somewhat incongruous and suggests that the real position of women among the Russian peasantry was not necessarily what the male ideology would have one believe.

The very next story in Afanas'ev's collection, "The Daughter and the Stepdaughter," is obviously a variation on the same theme. The stepdaughter is sent out into the woods, stays in a little house, is helped by animals of the forest, and comes back after a while, bringing all kinds of goodies. But in this case the stepmother says to her husband, "Aha, if your daughter can do that, so can mine," and she sends her own daughter out. However, her own daughter has the wrong attitude toward the animals, and they fail to help her. As a result, she comes to a bad end, and only bones return from the forest sojourn. The conclusion of this story is interesting because it contains mention of a specifically Russian peasant institution in the folktale proper (as distinct from the kind of story which is intended to be taken as true). While the stepmother dies of grief and meanness because of the death of her daughter, the story closes with these words: "The old man lived happily ever after with his daughter and took a distinguished son-in-law into his house."[4] This is precisely what a Russian peasant would try to do, if he had an only daughter and needed someone to carry on the farm; from this we can conclude that at least the ending of the story is a fairly recent addition, even though the body of it is archaic.

Another matter relating to the family appears very clearly in folktales; the relation between older and younger brothers in particular, and siblings generally. It is nearly always the youngest brother who succeeds and gets the brass ring, after the other brothers fail. (Incidentally, Propp's idea that the hero is thrown off a cliff or otherwise assaulted by his brothers at the end of the story cannot be supported by examples from the Russian folk literature, although there are some elsewhere.) One can interpret the primacy of the younger brother in various ways. For instance, the Soviet folklorist E. M. Meletinskii, who made a study of this theme, regards it as evidence of a custom whereby the younger son inherited the father's property or position.[5] The problem with this theory is that this custom existed in the Russian context only in a very special sense, and as a very late phenomenon. Basically, it was a social security device for the old folks. The younger son inherited the farm, or part of it, on condition that he provide a home for the parents when they became too old to work. In other words, he was inheriting a responsibility, rather than a privilege; at least this was the way most people thought of it. It makes more sense, therefore, to look upon the success of the younger son in the folktale as a kind of compensatory device—that is, to interpret it in psychological terms as one would interpret the Cinderella theme. The folk seem always to feel that the last shall be the first, either in terms of the

4. Afanas'ev, *Narodnye russkie skazki*, I, 147 (#98).
5. E. M. Meletinskii, *Geroi volshebnoi skazki* (Moscow, 1958).

historical process (as in regard to various millenarian ideas) or in stories. The brother who succeeds where the others fail is not only the youngest, but also lazy or impractical; in some cases he is actually retarded, or considered so by other people. If we accept this interpretation, then it turns out that the theme of the lazy or stupid but successful younger brother is the expression of a very elementary kind of social protest transferred from the general level of society to the specific level of the family. I think this is a legitimate interpretation because certain other stories (particularly some of the stories in Grimm) contain people of very low social position such as grooms, plowmen, tailors, or broommakers who make their fortunes and become kings or marry princesses. In such cases, the element of social retribution is very obvious.

One folktale in Afanas'ev's collection illustrates the theme of the younger brother in a very curious way. It is a highly archaic tale and presents the family explicitly as a microcosm of society; furthermore, it contains many of the themes or devices common to Russian folktales. Since it is much too long to paraphrase, discussion will be restricted to a few elements. The story is called "Baba-yaga and Zamoryshek." The title requires explanation: Baba-yaga is the witch of the Russian folktale and, according to some interpretations, she is also the ancient Slavic goddess of death. "Zamoryshek" means "the weakling." In another version of the story he is also called "Posledyshek" which means "the latecomer." The beginning of the story is quite significant:

> There was an old man with an old woman: they had no children. No matter what they did or how they prayed, the old woman could not bear. One day the old man went to the woods for mushrooms; on the road he met an old grandfather.[6] "I know," he said, "what is in your thoughts; you are always thinking of children. Now go to the village, and gather one fresh egg from each household, and set hens on all of these eggs; you will see what happens!" The old man went to the village; in that village there were forty-one households; he went around to all forty-one and gathered an egg from each and put hens on forty-one eggs. Two weeks went by, the old man and old woman

6. I should explain here that the first man who was mentioned in the first sentence isn't necessarily old. In peasant language *starik* (literally, old man) merely means husband, just as it does in certain circles now. On the other hand, when the text says "grandfather," or *ded*, this definitely means an old man with a long beard who usually has something special to say, as in this case.

looked—and from those eggs there were born boys; forty of them were strong and healthy, and one didn't come out so well—he was sickly and weak.[7]

This is obviously a representation of the primeval community in which everyone is equal, because the eggs out of which the boys hatched were provided by all forty-one households in the village. In the case of the one weakling, physical weakness is compensated for by occult powers.

The story goes on to tell how the boys grow up very fast, in a matter of hours, and turn out to be very good workers. The weakling helps with the housework, taking on a female role. One day the other boys are cutting hay in the field; they make forty haystacks, but overnight one of the haystacks disappears. The weakling says he is going to find out what happened, and he goes to the blacksmith and asks him to make a chain long enough to bind a man by wrapping him from head to toe. The weakling keeps watch; it turns out that a supernatural horse has come out of the ocean and eaten the haystack. When the weakling throws the chain over the horse and tames her, she says to him: "Well, since you've been able to ride me, I'll give you my colt." Forty horses then come out of the ocean, and the forty-one sons of the old man become, in effect, a mounted army. "In the morning, the old man heard neighing and trampling of hooves in the courtyard; 'What's this?' and here his son the weakling drove a whole herd of horses in. 'Hello, there, brothers,' said he. 'Now we all have a horse; let's go to look for brides.' . . .

"They rode around for a long time in the wide world, but where would they find so many brides? They didn't want to get married separately, so that no one would be offended; and what mother can boast that she has borne forty daughters?"[8] Again we see the primeval community which is supposed to do everything as a unit. The story goes on to tell how they came to the Baba-yaga's palace, and she tells them that yes, she has forty daughters. They arrange a marriage, again collectively, but on the wedding night the supernatural horse tells the weakling to have his brothers exchange clothes with their wives. As a result, the Baba-yaga's servants cut off the heads of her own daughters. The story ends with the motif

7. Afanas'ev, *Narodnye russkie skazki*, I, 166 (#105).
8. *Ibid.*, p. 167.

known in folklore as magical pursuit and escape: a magical object is waved or put behind oneself to create an obstacle over which the pursuing forces cannot pass.

On the basis of what has been said, the following hypothesis may be advanced. Because of its extremely archaic character, the Russian folktale proper does not usually reflect the peasant family in any literal way or as belonging to any identifiable historical period. Rather, it uses the family and family relationships as a metaphor for the community or society at large, in the sense of either the primeval community of equals or the stratified society where privilege and perceived injustice exist.

EPIC SONGS

Byliny, or epic songs, differ from folktales in a number of significant ways, even though prose renderings of *byliny* are sometimes found along with other kinds of material in collections. The most important differences, for our purposes, are these: first, the *byliny* are directed to an audience different from that of the "fairy tales," an audience of adults. Consequently, *byliny* are much more serious in tone, even to the point of being tragic—although some of them, as we will see later, do contain "fairy tale" motifs. Second, they represent a different historical milieu. In place of the essentially timeless world of the folktale, we find a world marked by early feudal relationships and presided over by a perfectly real historical personage—namely, Prince Vladimir of Kiev. Of course, this is not meant to imply that the *bylina* is historically accurate or based on fact—on the contrary, in some cases older themes (particularly fairy tale themes) were merely inserted mechanically into this context. In addition, there are other *byliny* besides those of the Kievan cycle; for example, some reflect the conditions in Novgorod during a slightly later period. One of the most famous *byliny,* "Sadko," belongs to this group.

The *bylina* typically deals with a struggle between a Russian champion and a foreign enemy or invader. The latter may be either an identifiable historical personage, such as one of the Tatar or Mongol military leaders, or a non-human monster. Monsters are particularly common in the early *byliny*. As Propp says; "Epic poetry shows whom the folk consider to be a hero, and for what services."⁹ The struggle has an adversary aspect which is not typical in the folktale except where it has been influenced by *byliny* themes. Certain features of the *byliny* distinguish them from the *Iliad*, the Germanic epics, and the medieval, semi-literary epic poetry of western Europe. It is striking that the heroes of *byliny* are not noblemen or kings or princes, as the heroes of other epics tend to be. Rather, they are independent peasants, or their children, who have taken service as Prince Vladimir's personal bodyguards and are sent out by him on various missions, perhaps to collect tribute or to suppress a bandit. These peasant soldiers have various adventures, either while on these missions or when they are on their way to Vladimir's court in order to take service. In any case, the values and world-view reflected in the *byliny* are not aristocratic, even in the sense that the Homeric poems are, although they do show certain resemblances.

The perspective in the *byliny* is always and unmistakably male, which is not true in all folktales or in the ballads which come later. Some *byliny* deal with courtship and wooing, and women of course play a part in these; however, the women are almost always passive figures who wait for the men to fight for the opportunity to marry them. There exist stories of various foreign potentates, some of whom are presented as monsters, who come to Kiev desiring a match with Vladimir's daughter or with some other noblewoman; they lay siege to the city and have to be defeated militarily. In cases where the hero himself does the wooing, the picture is different. Usually the hero hears about a very beautiful princess in some distant place and goes off to find her, or else, on his way to perform some errand for Vladimir, he chances upon a lady in the woods or by the river and she, in effect, seduces him. It nearly always turns out badly. One of the most typical *byliny* of this type, an extremely interesting one from many points of view, is the one called "Mikhailo Potyk," after its main character. Mikhailo is sent out by Vladimir to collect tribute in one of the outlying regions. On his way he sees a white swan in the river; as he lifts his bow to shoot it, the swan calls out to him—"Hey, don't do that"—and turns into a beautiful girl who asks him to marry her. He takes her back to Kiev with him, apparently without having carried out his original assignment for Vladimir. (Incidentally, a *bylina* with this kind of

9. V. Ia. Propp, *Narodnyi geroicheskii epos* (Moscow, 1958), p. 5.

opening was probably not originally part of what is called the Kiev Cycle but was later inserted.) Before the marriage, the bride lays down the condition that, if she should die first, Mikhailo has to be buried alive in the grave with her. Of course, since this is a *bylina*, and therefore tragic both in the principle of its construction and in its view of life, the girl does die first and Mikhailo is buried in her grave. But as he sits there more or less waiting to die, one of two things happens, depending on what version of the *bylina* is presented: either a snake crawls toward the body of the girl, or the girl herself turns into a snake and comes after Mikhailo. In the second case, this action reveals that the girl was a witch in the first place (or an evil spirit; in any case, a non-human entity of some kind), and in these versions Mikhailo simply hacks her to pieces and then escapes from the vault. In other versions, the snake appears and Mikhailo grabs it, kills it with a pair of tongs, and rubs its blood on the body of his bride so that she revives. Versions where the story takes this turn continue by saying that Mikhailo is again sent off from Kiev by Vladimir on business, and that during his absence his wife is abducted. (It is not always clear how or by whom.) When Mikhailo hears about this, he naturally goes in search of her and calls on his friends Ilya Muromets and Dobrynia Nikitich to help him. In reply to this request, Mikhailo's two friends say the following:

"It will not be an honor to us, or win the praise of heroes,
To ride in pursuit of a woman.
But it will be a shame and expose us to ridicule;
Therefore you, brave young man, you go alone."

In analyzing the story, Propp has this to say:

The *bogatyr* who is conquered by the emotion of love cannot be depicted as a hero in the real sense of this word. The real heroes of this part are no longer Potyk but Ilya Muromets and Dobrynia Nikitich. . . . These are new heroes no longer connected with the traditions created by the course of Russian life and Russian history. We have already seen that they are to some degree counterpoised to Potyk. They are heroes of another type and character. They bring the action to a happy ending, and thanks to them Potyk is saved, returns to his senses, and is avenged on his wife, the witch. . . .

The search for his wife is not a heroic feat[10] but expresses the flaw

10. The Russian word here is *podvig*, which always refers to heroic adventures in the real sense.

of Potyk—a flaw which brings him to shame and from which he is saved by Ilya and Dobrynia.[11]

In the last phase of the story, Mikhailo finally comes to the place where his wife is hidden. She has him imprisoned in an underground chamber where he is chained to the wall. From this unenviable situation he is rescued by his two friends.

There are two ways to regard this denouement. Propp makes the point—and is backed up by other Soviet folklorists—that, in falling in love and marrying or going after the wife who has disappeared, the epic hero goes outside his proper role. *Bogatyrs* are soldiers, basically, and in this instance they have become distracted by something else and have broken regulations. On the other hand, one could look at the tale as an expression of a frankly male-chauvinist viewpoint that women do not matter and are not worth taking seriously. Get involved with them and you get into trouble.

Finally, other folklorists who have written on this theme appear to have overlooked one aspect of it. The opening of this particular *bylina*, with the swan turning into a girl, seems like a fairy tale. In fact, the first part of the story of Mikhailo Potyk is based on a fairly widespread folktale motif which turns up in Grimm under the title "Die Drei Schlangenblätter" or "The Three Snake Leaves."[12] The story, very briefly, is this: The son of a poor peasant takes service in the king's army and acquits himself well. As a reward he is offered a match with the king's daughter, but she sets him the same condition that the swan girl sets for Mikhailo. While he is in the vault with her, a snake comes; he kills it, but then another snake comes and revives the first one by means of some leaves from a plant. The soldier uses the same leaves to revive his dead wife and afterward gives them to a trusted retainer, saying: "Look after these carefully. We never know when we might need them." After this point, the story is quite different. When the soldier is sent overseas on a mission by the king, he takes his wife along. She falls in love with the captain of the ship on which they are sailing; together they plot to throw the soldier overboard. They succeed, but he is revived by his retainer with the help of the three leaves. After they return to shore and expose the unfaithful wife, she is condemned to death. Signifi-

11. Propp, *Narodnyi geroicheskii epos*, p. 143.

12. Jakob Ludwig Karl Grimm, *Kinder- und Hausmärchen gesammelt durch die Brüder Grimm*, ed. Carl Helbling (Zurich, n.d.), I, 132–137 (#16).

cantly, there is no suggestion that the wife is a witch or evil spirit: she is merely an unfaithful woman. More important is the fidelity of the retainer who saves his master. The authors of the main commentary on Grimm seem to have missed this particular parallel with the *byliny*, although they do mention parallels with other Russian folktales.[13] In interpreting "Mikhailo Potyk" there is considerable temptation to treat it psychologically and to say that this *bylina* expresses the typical Russian distrust of foreigners, particularly foreign women or women who take matters into their own hands, because Mikhailo loses his heroic status by falling in love and marrying, and he regains it by cutting up his wife into little pieces. Although the same message is implicit in the Grimm story, it never comes to the surface, even though there is contrast between the faithful retainer and the unfaithful wife.

Several other *byliny* make the same general point in different ways. However, before leaving the subject of *byliny*, I want to mention two other cases which seem to qualify this point. First is the *bylina* called "Dunai," after its protagonist. This is one of the classic epic songs about wooing or courtship, which are found more frequently in the south Slavic tradition than in the Russian one. The story opens with Vladimir at a meeting or a feast, at which he tells his warriors that he has decided he needs a bride. In order to find a bride of adequate status, he must journey to a foreign country—a venture which always involves great risk, as well as the chance of what might almost be called ritual pollution because of the peculiar quality of Russian patriotism. Dunai was not one of the original Russian *bogatyrs;* in fact, some versions say that for a long time he served the king of Lithuania, rather than serving Vladimir, and in some versions he is also depicted as living outside the city of Kiev in a luxuriously furnished black tent. On both counts he appears to be non-Russian, because a proper Russian would not live in a tent, let alone a black one. In one of the earlier *byliny* of the same cycle, Dunai is supposed to have served in the court of Lithuania and the king's elder daughter is alleged to have fallen in love with him. Because he brags of this at a feast, the king has him put in irons and handed over to the executioner; he is saved by the king's daughter, who gives him clothes and weapons and sends him off to Kiev. The

13. J. Bolte and G. Polivka, *Anmerkungen zu den Kinder- und Hausmärchen der Gebrüder Grimm* (Leipzig, 1913–32), I, 126–131.

main part of the cycle tells how Vladimir commissions Dunai to go and make a match with the younger daughter of the King of Lithuania. The king refuses the match, on the ground that Vladimir is not of sufficient status. Dunai finally forces him to acquiesce.

The next episode consists of a battle between Dunai and his former sweetheart Nastasia, who is presented as an Amazon. (This particular part of the story shows that not all *byliny* deal with passive female figures, yet the story ends on a different note.) The battle ends with Dunai's victory, but just as he is about to raise his knife and dispatch her, Nastasia recalls their old times together. He changes his mind and takes her to Kiev, along with her sister. What Propp, says at this point in his analysis of the *bylina* is very interesting and symptomatic of his attitude.

> In calling Nastasia to Kiev and offering her marriage, Dunai expiates his guilt in relation to her. It would seem that he was carrying out an entirely noble act. The possibility of a happy outcome is given in the development of the theme, and some of the weaker singers take advantage of this: Evpraksiia is brought for Vladimir and Nastasia for Dunai, and the song ends with a double wedding. . . . But this ending is entirely alien to the spirit of Russian epic poetry; it would have been appropriate in a fairy tale, but in epic poetry the hero's marriage to a foreigner is, as a rule, impossible, and if it takes place, it always ends tragically.[14]

The denouement begins with a feast in Vladimir's court, at which Dunai brags of his various heroic feats. His wife replies frankly that he cannot be compared with the other *bogatyrs*, and that as far as archery is concerned she can outshoot him anytime. He becomes angry and challenges her to a contest. She does outshoot him, whereupon he shoots her in the breast, despite the fact that she is pregnant with his child. At the end of the song he is gripped by remorse and commits suicide after ascertaining that she was pregnant, a fact of which he had apparently been ignorant. Although Nastasia is not a passive female in the usual sense, and not a source of trouble like some of the other women in *byliny*, she is placed in the position of victim and therefore she is ultimately passive. For his part, Dunai loses his heroic status not by marrying, but by showing himself to be an ordinary, ignoble killer.

14. Propp, *Narodnyi geroicheskii epos*, p. 115.

Stephen P. Dunn

BALLADS

The Russian ballads reflect a historical reality different from what we find in the folktale or the *bylina* (if, in fact, we can speak of historical reality in the folktale at all) and are also governed by a quite different aesthetic.[15] In order to make clear the influence of this aesthetic on the treatment of family relationships, I quote here a passage from the introduction to a fairly recent Soviet collection of ballads, and then apply to my main topic the points made therein.

The ballad focuses its attention on the fate of an individual human being. Events of significance to the people as a whole, and ethical, social and philosophical questions, are refracted in ballads through the prism of personal relationships and destinies. Thus, the tragedy of thousands of people taken prisoner by the Tatars is reflected in a ballad about one woman who meets her daughter in Tatar captivity, and the conflict between wealth and poverty in feudal society is visible in the ballad about the two Lazaruses, one of whom refuses a piece of bread to the other, who is a beggar. The problem of the vanity of human ambition is set forth in the ballad of Anika, the warrior who encounters death. What is especially important is that in ballads there are no generalizing conclusions which throw a bridge from individual fate to that of mankind as a whole. Generalization is present in the ballad only as an artistic result.

The epic character of the ballad is reflected in the fact that, as in epic poetry generally, its narrative is conducted "in the author's voice," in the tone of an objective and consecutive account of events. Ballads do not contain lyrical digressions, emotional explanations, moralizing asides—or, in a word, any active intervention by the "author" in the plot.

The specific artistic character of the ballad is determined by its dramatic emphasis. The composition, the means of depicting human beings, and the very principle according to which the phenomena of life are described and classified—all are subordinated to the requirements of dramatic expressiveness. The most characteristic compositional features of the ballad are its limitation to a simple conflict, its compression, the intermittent quality of the exposition, the large amount of dialogue, and the increasingly dramatic repetitions. The ballad is more concentrated than the *bylina*. Its action is

15. This form of folklore is designated in Russian by a western loan word *(ballada)*, which may indicate that it is not entirely a native Russian form. The *skazka* (folktale) and the *bylina* definitely are native forms, despite their similarities in terms of subject matter and social function to folklore genres found elsewhere.

reduced to a single conflict, to one central episode, and all events preceding the conflict either are set forth with extreme brevity . . . or are completely lacking, so that the ballad begins directly with dramatic action. . . .

The events following upon the basic conflict are likewise discarded. A daughter finds out that her father has killed her mother. A son discovers that his mother has killed his wife. What happened after that the ballad does not say.[16]

The narrow focus and particularity of viewpoint which characterize the ballad prevent it from abstracting from family relationships, or treating them in a purely symbolic way, as is usually done in folktales and *byliny*. For this reason, among others, a full analysis of family and sexual relationships as reflected in the Russian ballad would require a small book, with an elaborate critical apparatus. However, some important points can be made very briefly. First, the reflection of social reality (including family relationships) in the Russian ballad is relatively objective and multifaceted (insofar as the aesthetic of the ballad permits), though of course not complete or exhaustive. Secondly, the point of view is not exclusively male but, on the contrary, more often female or neutral; in fact, many of the titles given to Russian ballads sound like newspaper headlines, such as "The Queen Dies in Childbirth" or "A Cossack's Wife Dies in Childbirth." Both of these deal with a situation which would never come up in epic poetry.

Third, Russian ballads often present an implied critique of the feudal social order, particularly as it makes itself felt within the family. This is not the case in the *byliny*, whose heroes are presented (insofar as they remain faithful to their heroic mission) as defending the interests of the people as a whole embodied in the Old Russian state. This critical attitude toward the feudal social order[17] is related to another aspect of the aesthetic of the ballad —namely, its complete lack of heroic dimensions or of any attribution of super-human qualities or abilities to its characters. In this

16. *Narodnye ballady*, ed. A. M. Astakhova and V. Balashov (Moscow, 1963), pp. 7–8.
17. Two caveats are in order with regard to the use of the concept of feudalism here. First, Russian feudalism during the post-Mongol period showed marked differences from the feudalism of medieval western Europe. Second, the concept of feudalism as used by Soviet historians and folklorists is both broader and narrower than that common in western historical scholarship, since it refers primarily to an economic system and does not necessarily imply the fragmentation of political power and the elaborate hierarchical organization characteristic of medieval Europe in general.

respect the Russian ballad resembles the western European one, in approach and viewpoint, although not in form.

To summarize, in the folktales *(skazki)* one finds the family presented as an abstract model for the community or the society as a whole, with certain specific relationships (e.g., between mother and stepdaughter) emphasized and elaborated on. In epic poetry, the depiction of relationships between sexes and generations is subordinated to political considerations and to very definite masculine value-systems. Finally, in the ballads there emerges a fairly balanced and realistic reflection of the family as it actually existed in feudal Russia, with both masculine and feminine values represented, and with a particular concentration on critical and tragic periods and events. This differential emphasis gives one the impression that in Russian folklore two separate value systems—a masculine one and a feminine one—are represented in the various folklore items, and I would hazard a guess that this sets the Russian apart from other European folklore traditions. This matter requires further research, on which knowledgeable historians, sociologists, and folklorists ought to collaborate, because no single specialty is equipped to handle it alone.

ANTONINA MARTYNOVA

Life of the Pre-Revolutionary Village as Reflected in Popular Lullabies

Lullabies serve a definite practical purpose—putting a child to sleep. They also serve a socialization function by accustoming a child to human speech, acquainting it with the people and objects which surround it, and conveying elementary moral lessons. As an artistic phenomenon, lullabies express women's thoughts and feelings, and in this respect they resemble lyrical song.

The way in which lullabies are sung is conditioned by their basic function: the rocking of the cradle is accompanied by singing, which continues until the child falls asleep. There is no clear demarcation among separate pieces, which directly follow one another or are linked only by a refrain consisting of special "lullabying" words. One can distinguish four types of these combinations (spevy): 1) traditional lullabies (more than thirty of these have been identified), with their variants; 2) improvised songs which are somehow associated with the traditional songs; 3) compositions of other genres performed as lullabies; and 4) works having literary origins.[1] This article will deal with works of the first group, traditional lullabies. The source material consists of approximately 1,800 texts transcribed during the past 150 years in the northern, northwestern, central, and eastern regions of Russia, primarily as sung by peasants. Relatively few of these transcriptions have been published; most repose in various state archival collections.

Arising out of the everyday life of the village, popular lullabies mirror that way of life. Despite their own harsh living conditions in

This article has been translated from the Russian by David L. Ransel and Benjamin Uroff.
1. On the classification of the songs, see A. N. Martynova, "Opyt klassifikatsii russkikh kolybel'nykh pesen," *Sovetskaia etnografiia*, no. 4 (1974), pp. 101–115.

pre-revolutionary Russia, peasants looked upon children as a blessing, as a source of happiness and meaning in their lives. A. A. Titov has reported that "peasants . . . view the birth of children as a sign of God's blessing on the parents, whereas not having children is considered a misfortune."[2] The noted ethnographer A. A. Makarenko wrote at the end of the last century: "Barrenness for the peasant woman is a most painful situation . . . it often constitutes a source of moral humiliation . . . deprives her finally of the joy of having children through whom alone a mother can firmly implant herself in the family of her husband and can be guaranteed consolation and comfort in her old age."[3]

Lullabies clearly express this feeling of love toward children by wishing sleep, good health, and a good life.

> Sleep by night,
> And grow by the hour.[4]
>
> Sleep well,
> Arise happy.[5]

Not infrequently they contain an appeal to God to grant more children.

> Grant God to give seven.
> Don't take from the five [I have],
> But increase them to ten.[6]

In the songs a mother speaks the most tender words to her child: darling, goodness, dear, desired, comely, God-given, desired one, and so forth.

> Slumber, Vasen'ka,
> Slumber, beloved,
> Go to sleep, precious.[7]
>
> Sleep, dear child,
> Precious, golden child.[8]

2. A. A. Titov, *Iuridicheskie obychai sela Nikola-Perevoz Sulostskoi volosti, Rostovskogo uezda* (Iaroslavl' 1888), pp. 51–52.

3. A. A. Makarenko, "Materialy po narodnoi meditsine, Uzhurskoi volosti, Achinskogo okruga, Eniseiskoi gubernii," *Zhivaia starina*, 7, parts 1–4 (1897):241.

4. D. I. Uspenskii, "Rodny i krestiny, ukhod za rozhenitsei i novorozhdennym," *Etnograficheskoe obozrenie*, 7, no. 4 (1895):91.

5. *Rukopisnyi otdel Instituta russkoi literatury* (Pushkinskii Dom), Akademiia Nauk SSSR. raz. 5, k. 3, pap. 7, no. 39 [hereafter *IRLI*].

6. *Ibid.*, k. 80, pap. 1, no. 1, l. 3.

7. *Ibid.*, k. 69, pap. 6, no. 14, l. 3.

8. N. Popov, "Narodnye predaniia zhitelei Vologodskoi gubernii, Kadnikovskogo uezda," *Zhivaia starina*, 13, parts 1–2 (1903):204.

Generally the techniques of artistic invention are applied sparingly—except in songs addressing the child directly, where one finds the most varied tropes, including metaphors, similes, and paraphrases.

> Sleep, my little sun,
> Sleep, little grain of wheat. [9]
>
> Sleep, my own one,
> Little goldfish. [10]
>
> You cozy warmer,
> Grow, little helper
> You'll surely be my little envoy,
> And go whither I send you. [11]

Although sleep and nourishment are the primary necessities for a young infant, the plight of the pre-revolutionary peasantry forced a mother to dream of giving her children enough to eat. In one song, doves discuss what to feed an infant. The many variants of the lullaby provide a listing of foods: porridge, white bread with milk, pastries, *tiuria* (a bread-and-water soup), honey-cake, etc. The realistic description of the nursing infant's food corresponds to actual living conditions. In the pre-revolutionary village a newborn was given a pacifier or *soska*, i.e., a linen cloth tied with string into a bag containing chewed rye bread, porridge, or cakes. In 1897 A. A. Makarenko, who knew a great deal about the living conditions of peasant children, wrote: "How can one reproach a mother for failing to follow the best methods of feeding an infant when it is evident that she is totally ignorant of them, because no one has told her anything about them? Even if she should learn some things, as a result of circumstances beyond her control she often cannot put them into practice amid a life full of constant toil, care, and deprivation." [12]

Another no less popular theme of lullabies is the description of the cradle.

> He shall have a cradle
> In the high castle chamber,
> On a supple chain,
> And fastened by rings of silver.

9. *IRLI*, k. 117, pap. 4, no. 2, l. 1.
10. *Ibid.*, k. 69, pap. 6, no. 14, l. 3.
11. *Ibid.*, k. 117, pap. 4, no. 2, l. 2.
12. Makarenko, "Materialy," p. 232.

The whole cradle is gilded,
Lined in golden damask.
Marten at his head,
Sable at his feet,
And covers of black beaver. [13]

This lullaby probably reflected the imagination of the peasant mother as she poetically transformed her child's rather rude hammock-crib into a luxurious cradle. Such idealization of objects and persons is typical in many genres of popular poetic creativity. [14]

Texts also contain realistic depictions of peasant cribs and cradles.

For our little Mashen'ka
There is an oaken crib,
With wooden chains,
And tin rings,
A rocking loop of woven fibers. [15]

I lay your head on the pillows,
Tattered clothing under your side
And a bundle of straw,
Sleep soundly, little angel. [16]

Rocking was a customary and indispensable method of calming infants. A. A. Makarenko recorded that "even as they enter this world peasant children already suffer from internal disorders (*gryz' na nutre*), day and night set up incredible crying fits as a result of umbilical hernia (*gryz' pupka*) . . . . develop thrush and are seized by 'infantile' convulsions . . . . Growing weak from an inadequate

13. *IRLI*, k. 12, pap. 4, no. 25, l. 18.
14. At the same time, one might cautiously suggest that these songs contain a description of real-life cradles, if only of those very far removed from peasant life. A. E. Pokrovskii gives the following description of the cradle used by the seventeenth-century grand duke Ivan Mikhailovich: "The cradle is upholstered in golden satin on a red field with small fans in hues of azure and white silk . . . . Attached to the cradle on long wooden rods are four rings with a hallmark and hinges of gilded silver." In "Fizicheskoe vospitanie detei u raznykh narodov, preimushchestvenno v Rossii," *Izvestiia obshchestva Liubitelei estestvoznaniia, antropologii i etnografii*, 19, no. 1, *Trudy antropologicheskogo otdela*, 7, nos. 1–3 (Moscow, 1884): 175. See also I. Zabelin, *Domashnii byt russkikh tsarei* (Moscow, 1872), pp. 211, 215. Rich *boiar* families probably possessed similar cradles for their infants. These luxury cradles were, it must be assumed, fashioned by common artisans, who embodied in them their esthetic conceptions and ideals. Nannies and wet nurses may have reflected the observations on the descriptions of the luxury cradles in their songs, for in rich and famous families these women were usually peasants who not only nourished their charges but also accustomed them to the sounds of their native songs.
15. *IRLI*, k. 3, pap. 7, no. 30.
16. *Ibid.*, k. 2, pap. 9, no. 4.

diet, babies begin to waste away, stop growing, and suffer from premature senility ["*sobach'ia starost'*"; literally, "a dog's old age"] until an ever-watchful death relieves them of their sufferings."[17] Makarenko likewise pointed out that peasant women, overburdened with work and deprived of the opportunity to acquire even an elementary understanding of medicine and hygiene, found cradle-rocking almost the only available means of calming a sick and crying infant.

A. E. Pokrovskii assembled an enormous quantity of material on child care practices in various sections of the country, and his book paints a grim picture of the unhygienic living conditions which were the cause of many illnesses for peasant children. He further writes that "if a child cries hard from the discomforts just described, the nannies and grannies decide that he is crying because he needs to be fed and try to stuff him full of milk, porridge, chewed breads and the like, or else they try to calm him by rocking his cradle as much as its suspension allows, so that from the excessive rocking the child is frightened half to death and thereby sinks into sleep."[18]

Naturally, rocking an infant demanded a great deal of time, and not without reason does the mother complain in some songs:

> These aching arms come
> Not from lugging firewood—
> But from rocking Shurochka.[19]

> Sleep, child, more soundly,
> I've no time to fuss with you:
> We need to sow and reap,
> And not to wag our arms.[20]

Lullabies reflect parents' desire to gladden the child with presents and treats. True, the gifts are very modest, and the songs do not speak of toys or sweets. In one song a child is promised a white bread roll, which his father will bring. In another he is promised felt boots, an indispensable item for the cold winter. This song is filled with loving concern:

> We shall buy our boy felt boots,
> To cover his little legs,

17. Makarenko, "Materialy," p. 230.
18. Pokrovskii, "Fizicheskoe vospitanie," p. 181.
19. *IRLI*, k. 69, pap. 9, no. 44.
20. *Ibid.*, k. 69, pap. 9, no. 42.

And let him go down the path;
My little son will walk along,
Wearing his new felt boots. [21]

A peasant woman could imagine no future for her son or daughter except one of toil. Lullabies list nearly all the types of peasant labor that would await the child: "catching fish," "working," "going out into the world," "plowing the land," "felling trees," etc. [22] One text forecasts a hard future for the child:

You'll do much walking barefoot,
And have your fill of hunger. [23]

Another motif often found in lullabies is the child as a replacement for its mother and father:

I rock my son,
In hopes he will replace me,
I rock my daughter,
In hopes of a son-in-law. [24]

But the songs also reflected a sober understanding of the circumstances of peasant life. Things were not going to change even after the child had grown up, at least not for the parents.

I have rocked my babe,
And willed to it that things be different,
There'll be some changes,
There'll be some bread.
But for me there'll be no change,
I'll see nothing different,
I'll eat no bread and salt. [25]

However, there exist some songs which echo a peasant mother's dreams of future wealth for her child.

You'll grow up great—
And walk in gold,
Clothed in purest silver. [26]

21. G. K. Zavoiko, "Kolybel'nye pesni i detskie igry u krest'ian Vladimirskoi gubernii," *Etnograficheskoe obozrenie*, 27, no. 1 (1915):124.
22. Only one transcription known to us reflects a mother's desire that her son become a clerk.
23. *IRLI*, k. 117, pap. 4, no. 12.
24. *Ibid.*, k. 69, pap. 9, no. 74.
25. *Ibid.*, k. 17, pap. 34, no. 17, l. 21.
26. *Arkhiv Geograficheskogo obshchestva SSSR* (hereafter *AGO*), raz. 36, op. 1, no. 56, l. 18. Possibly this song also reflected the actual living conditions of the wealthy classes,

The reality of peasant life with its constant toil is mirrored in lullabies. One of these could be called a melodic depiction of everyday life.

> Father went afishing,
> While mother hews the wood,
> And grandma cooks the fish soup.[27]

Numerous variants list the family's daily tasks—mother goes off to milk the cows, grandma carries in the firewood, nanny washes the baby's diapers, sister waters the calf, grandpa carts manure. The song is still widespread in our own day.

Another popular song describes presents given to relatives. To some extent, the song conveys the attitude of the mother toward various members of the family. The most typical text runs as follows.

> Lull, lullaby,
> For mother silk cloth,
> For sister mittens,
> For grandma bast shoes,
> For father red calico,
> For brother fancy sleeves,
> For grandpa felt boots.[28]

In this song the present for the mother scarcely varies. In the father's case, however, one encounters not only the promise of red calico for his shirt but also of a knout or whip (*pogonial'ka*) for his shoulders. The brothers (usually referred to as "brave lads," but sometimes as "rascals") receive boots, sheepskin jackets, silver watches, horses, kaftans, and sometimes the promise of a sound thrashing. Many variants of the gifts intended for sisters range from clothing to modest peasant adornments such as muslin sleeves and pearl earrings. A somewhat ironic attitude toward the grandfather

---

as does the following one, which mentions "mammies," "nannies," and "serving girls" (*matushki, nianiushki, sennye devushki*):

> Nannies, mammies,
> Rockabye the baby.
> Serving girls,
> Lullaby it.

(*IRLI*, k. 69, pap. 9, no. 249.)

27. P. V. Shein, *Velikoruss v svoikh pesniakh, obriadakh, obychaiakh, verovaniiakh, skazkakh, legendakh i t. p.*, vol. 1, part 1 (St. Petersburg 1898), p. 4.

28. *IRLI*, k. 69, pap. 9, no. 123.

is evident in the character of his gifts. For him there were not only boots of felt and leather, but also one hundred pounds of tobacco: "Do whatever you like—sniff it or smoke it, or make soup out of it." The grandmother, on the other hand, is promised a fur hat, felt boots, bast shoes, and red shoes. The songs also mention the godmother and the nanny.

Lullabies often mention animals, particularly the cat. As an animal that sleeps during the day, it was apparently perceived as a kind of sleep-bringer. In some parts of Russia people put a cat in the empty cradle before laying the infant down, in hopes that the child might sleep more soundly. Perhaps the earliest songs about cats were those in which a cat is asked to bring sleep:

> Cats, kittens,
> Scurry up the crib,
> Bring Volodia sleep. [29]
>
> Grey cats,
> Bring drowsiness. [30]

In most of the texts, however, the cat is asked to rock the infant, to lull the child to sleep.

> Come, cat, stay the night,
> Come and rock the little babe.

Various transcriptions of this song mention different payments to the cat. Besides the traditional "piece of pie" and "pitcher of milk," they promise bread, meat, a bowl of porridge, cabbage soup, lumps of sugar, etc.

In addition to the cat, other domestic animals mentioned include dogs, sheep, and cows; among the non-domesticated, hares, martens, and sables.

Finally, although the great mass of lullabies directly express a mother's love for her child, certain songs contain a wish for the child's death. Of the roughly 1,800 lullaby transcriptions we have studied, only 80 exhibit this motif. Yet the geographical distribution and times of their transcription indicate that these works existed in a variety of provinces over a century. This group of lullabies no doubt owed something to the notion of an equivalence between death and sleep. Furthermore, wishing death upon weak,

29. *Ibid.*, no. 224.
30. *Ibid.*, k. 165, pap. 33, no. 155.

crippled, or hopelessly sick and starving infants (in years of crop failure or natural calamity) also had a basis in the harsh economic conditions of life. In these cases, the songs were dictated by a humane wish that the child might escape the torments of hunger and disease. Such songs may also have been associated with a belief in the exchange of children by an unclean power, which had substituted its own mentally defective or deformed child for the real infant. In addition, some texts express a desire for the death of a child born out of wedlock. As a rule, the attitude toward an illegitimate child and its mother was scornful and severe. Realizing that her child faced a very difficult future, a mother might have regarded its death as a blessing. Because of the changing social conditions in the Russian village, songs of this type have been gradually disappearing from the active lullaby repertory.[31]

Being one of the oldest genres of folklore, lullabies may at one time also have functioned as charms and incantations. Birth and early childhood were accompanied from very earliest times by rituals having magical significance. As late as the end of the nineteenth century a variety of charms and taboos surrounded a Russian peasant woman during pregnancy. She was not supposed to behold any frightening omens or occurrences, glimpse grotesque animals, or listen to the cries of certain birds. Many signs could foretell a child's sex and whether it would be born living or dead, good-natured or malicious. N. Sumtsov has written about the diverse superstitions connected with a newborn child and its mother: "The infant is menaced by a great many dangers from evil spirits. The newborn child, which is regarded as unclean, and its mother, likewise unclean until the time of her ritual purification, are easy prey to forces hostile to mankind."[32] Prohibitions, charms, and rituals therefore accompanied the most significant stages of early childhood: the first ablution, choice of name, selection of godparents, baptism, first cutting of hair, first steps, etc.

Rocking of the cradle could have the significance of a magic ritual. Among many people, Russians included, the belief existed that one

---

31. For a detailed treatment of these songs, see A. N. Martynova, "Otrazhenie deistvitel'nosti v krest'ianskoi kolybel'noi pesne," *Russkii fol'klor*, 15 (Leningrad, 1975), pp. 145–155.

32. N. F. Sumtsov, "O slavianskikh narodnykh vozzreniiakh na novorozhdennogo rebenka," *Zhurnal Ministerstva Narodnogo Prosveshcheniia*, 212 (1880): 80.

must not rock an empty cradle lest the child lose its repose or even die. According to Russian belief, furthermore, two people were not supposed to rock the cradle together, or leave it uncovered; otherwise such unclean powers as the "midday spirit," "day-spirit," or "cradle spirit" *(poludennik, dennik, zybochnik)* might be able to steal into it. Nor was it permissible to place an unbaptized infant in the cradle. In some places people attempted to guard the child's health, life, or slumber by placing various articles in the crib; for example, a knife, a special fishbone signifying sleep, and special herbs. These acts and charms were intended to ward off evil spirits. Similar survivals strongly suggest that at one time lullabies themselves may have served as incantations and charms.

Desire-incantations and appeal-incantations bear the closest resemblance to lullabies.[33] Appeal incantations are based on the primordial notion that every occurrence, article, element, or state is a being with which one can communicate, upon which one can act, to which one can appeal. In lullabies one finds Sleep, Drowsiness, Rest, and Quiet *(Son, Drema, Pokoi, Ugomon)*, which aid in maintaining the child's repose. Rest and Quiet are apparently encountered solely in lullabies and incantations (primarily those read over a sick child suffering from "sleeplessness"). Often lullabies contain appeals addressed specifically to Sleep and Drowsiness.

> Sleep and Drowsiness,
> Come into Vania's head.[34]

The formula for conjuring up mythical beings can also be found in spells and incantations directed against insomnia, as in the following report. "If a baby is unable to sleep, they carry it to the henhouse at dawn for three days and while holding it in their arms they say the following words three times: 'Hen, take the insomnia from this child (calling it by name), grant it sleep, let slumber and drowsiness come into its head.' "[35] Appeals to Quiet are common in lullabies. "Slumber, go to sleep . . . May Quiet claim you." Sleep-Quiet is also asked for at dawn in incantations. "Dawn—

33. See N. Krushevskii, *Zagovory kak vid russkoi narodnoi poezii* (Warsaw, 1876); N. Poznanskii, *Zagovory* (Petrograd, 1917).
34. *IRLI*, k. 78, pap. 9, no. 56.
35. *AGO*, r. 36, op. 1, no. 56.

little dawn! take the sleepless one, the restless one, and grant us sleep-quiet."[36]

Wishes that the child sleep, grow, and be healthy are common in charms and incantations. At the time of the first ritual ablution in the bathhouse, a charm is uttered in accompaniment to all the actions of the woman who washes, steams, and swaddles the baby. It could include the following motifs:

> Don't expect to be rocked,
> Don't expect to be held,
> There are some whose nights are long,
> But for you they will be short.[37]

Such motifs are altogether consonant with those occurring in lullabies; for example, the following:

> Sleep without lullabying,
> Sleep without cradling,
> Without rockabyeing.[38]

Incantations, as well as lullabies, may contain the wish that the newborn child be clever and have a happy future.

> May colorful clothes bedeck your shoulders!
> And good thoughts fill your mind![39]

Among the lullabies that wish the infant sleep and growth, there are texts which express these wishes in set formulas: "Sleep healthy and arise happy," or "Sleep by night and grow by the hour." The latter refrain corresponds textually with the wish for sleep found in the following incantation: "I am not the one steaming [you]; it is the old woman Solomonida, who washed and steamed the true Christ Jesus himself into sleep, into quiet, to God's mercy; *sleep by night and grow by the hour*, don't listen where the dogs bark, but listen where people talk."[40]

Only a few lullabies mention charms for warding off evil spirits. Among them is the well-known text included by N. V. Shein in his

36. P. S. Efimenko, *Materialy po etnografii russkogo naseleniia Arkhangel'skoi gubernii* (Moscow, 1878), part 2, p. 199.
37. *IRLI*, k. 1, pap. 40, no. 4.
38. *Ibid.*, k. 5, pap. 13, no. 2, l. 28.
39. *Ibid.*, k. 66, pap. 1, no. 69.
40. Makarenko, "Materialy," p. 390.

collection *Velikoruss*, in which, under the influence of Christian ideas, an appeal is made to an angel for protection of the infant.

> From all sorrow,
> From all misfortune,
> From distress,
> From bloodshed,
> From the evil
> Of hostile men.[41]

N. Poznanskii, who shed new light on the important role of rhythm in magical rituals and pointed out the genetic kinship of incantation-songs and charms, remarked on the possibility that Russian charms were at one time chanted. Along with this, it is worth noting the relationship between the word *baika*—one of the popular designations for lullabies—and the verbs *baiat'* and *bait'*, which as recently as the 1860s in some areas of Russia still retained their archaic meanings of "to whisper," "to engage in sorcery," and "to cast spells."[42]

All this evidence gives grounds for assuming that in early times lullabies could have possessed magical significance. Certainly the texts known to us from nineteenth- and twentieth-century transcriptions retain traces of ancient magic. The images of the mythological Sleep and Drowsiness, which figure prominently in lullabies, are unquestionably of great interest. Often they are drawn rather vaguely, as undefined forces that should "weigh down upon" or "roll down upon" the infant and close its eyes. In a few songs these images emerge more clearly. One text, for example, pictures them as very small creatures that can move around on a spider's web.

> Sleep walked on a thread,
> Drowsiness on a spider's web.[43]

Occasionally these beings walk, converse, quarrel, and are clothed as people.

> Sleep walks upon one bench,
> Drowsiness upon another.
> Sleep wears a white shirt,
> While drowsiness is in a blue one.[44]

41. Shein, *Velikoruss*, p. 91.
42. V. Dal', *Tolkovyi slovar zhivogo velikorusskogo iazyka* (Moscow, 1935), I, 35.
43. *IRLI*, k. 66, pap. 2, l. 58.
44. *Ibid.*, k. 78, pap. 9, no. 65.

These creatures are blind, and they do not so often walk as "wander" about in the streets, entryways, and inside the peasant hut. Having difficulty locating the cradle, they go about inquiring where it may be found. It seems to have been an indispensable condition for lulling a child to sleep that it come into actual contact with beings of this type.

> Sleep-Drowsiness came
> Wandering about the benches,
> And laid down in Alesha's crib.
> Sleep went to his head,
> Drowsiness to his feet. [45]

With time, people evidently began to forget the functions of these images. Sleep and Drowsiness would walk, keep watch, and put the child down to rest as if fulfilling the duties of a nanny. Like an ordinary peasant nanny, Drowsiness came to receive its wages in the following song.

> Little Miss Drowsiness
> Went to Semen in the courtyard.
> Semen's wife
> Gave her a little dress.
> —Well, thank you, Mar'iushka!
> —To your health, Miss Drowsiness. [46]

As time went on, songs appeared that contained appeals to Christian figures. Despite the apparently wide circulation of these motifs, we have been unable to find them in a fixed form. The most popular were probably the one addressed to the Blessed Virgin to lull the child to sleep:

> Blessed Virgin, mother of God,
> Lay the child down to sleep. [47]

and the one addressed to the child as the gift of God:

> God granted you life,
> As a gift from Christ. [48]

Yet even these songs have many variants. Invoking the name of God, the saints, the Blessed Virgin, the apostles, and the angels

---

45. G. Dobriakov, "O kolybel'nykh pesniakh," *Vestnik vospitaniia*, 25, no. 8 (1914), p. 153.

46. Uspenskii, "Rodny i krestiny," p. 91.

47. *IRLI*, k. 69, pap. 9, no. 34.

48. Shein, *Velikoruss*, p. 3.

apparently had the aim of protecting the infant from unclean powers, which, according to existing notions, were especially dangerous in the period preceding baptism.

The foregoing textual analysis and comparison of variants transcribed during the past 150 years lead to the conclusion that the content of lullabies and their system of images underwent only gradual changes in the pre-revolutionary period. However, internal developments in the traditional repertory increased their tempo during the Soviet period, for reasons which are natural and altogether obvious. The historical fate of lullabies is closely tied to the everyday life of the peasants, and the psychology and worldview of the peasantry bears directly on the content of the songs. The fundamental changes in the outlook and in the social and living conditions of the peasantry that took place in the Soviet period could not help being reflected in lullabies. Certain traditional topics and motifs are passing into oblivion, while others are being retained. It is probably accurate to say that songs describing a golden cradle have passed into oblivion. Songs about Sleep and Drowsiness and about gifts to relatives, as well as lullabies wishing the death of a child, also appear to be gradually disappearing.

The question of the contemporary status of the genre is difficult to resolve without on-the-spot investigations of the lullaby repertory in individual villages and regions. Of interest in this connection is the research carried out under M. N. Mel'nikov's direction in the city of Novosibirsk and one of its provincial villages; it included the study of the lullaby repertory of a large number of women.[49] This investigation showed that, as a rule, only elderly women still remembered the traditional poetry. Very few young mothers, especially urban ones, could recall any lullabies. Of eighty women surveyed who were residents of the city of Novosibirsk and under fifty years of age, nearly half did not know any lullabies. These observations correspond to our own. Analysis of materials transcribed in recent years likewise suggests that the genre is on its way to extinction. The particular configuration of economic and cultural conditions, together with the local oral tradition in poetry, may accelerate or retard this process in different regions of the country. Nonetheless, the gradual disappearance of former customs, including the use of the hammock-cradle and the practice of rocking it

49. M. N. Mel'nikov, *Russkii detskii fol'klor Sibiri* (Novosibirsk, 1970), pp. 62–63.

to lull an infant to sleep, is linked to the general rise in the cultural level of village life. This, in turn, is leading to the disappearance of lullabies themselves.

Section Four

Welfare and Medical
Intervention in Peasant Birth
and Child Care

DAVID L. RANSEL

Abandonment and Fosterage of Unwanted Children: The Women of the Foundling System

The first systematic effort to deal with Russia's unwanted children came in the reign of Catherine II, with the establishment of large foundling homes at Moscow and St. Petersburg. Designed by the enlightenment educationist I. I. Betskoi, the two homes were to provide foundlings with advanced moral and technical training and turn them into a new class of free urban citizens or, as Betskoi liked to say, the "third estate" that Russia so sorely lacked. But almost as soon as it was launched, this ambitious scheme collapsed under the weight of the steadily rising numbers of children entering the homes. Within four years the overcrowded Moscow home had to forgo the original plan of rearing the children in the central institution, instead sending them out to peasant villages for care and feeding. Although intended as a temporary measure, the policy remained in force, and by the nineteenth century what evolved was quite contrary to Betskoi's hopes and expectations. Instead of central educational institutions for the production of enlightened urban dwellers, the homes served as processing points for an ever increasing stream of unwanted children. Rural as well as urban women delivered their babies to the homes, and the children who survived the first few weeks were handed over to peasant wet-nurses who carried them out to populate villages in the districts surrounding the two capital cities. This movement of children into the central

Financial support for research on this topic was provided in part by the American Council of Learned Societies, and by the University of Illinois Russian and East European Center and Center for Comparative International Studies. I also want to express my thanks to Antonina Martynova, Rodney Bohac, and Barbara and Peter Maggs, who provided supplementary data for some of the tables and graphs.

homes and out to the countryside constituted a vast human traffic with significant (if not entirely understood) economic, social, and demographic consequences. At the height of the traffic in the 1880s the Moscow home alone was receiving upwards of 17,000 infants annually and dispatching more than 10,000 to outlying district villages. In 1882 there were 41,720 foundlings in 32,002 foster families scattered throughout 4,418 villages.[1] The St. Petersburg home administered a similar program, admitting over 9,000 children per year.

Many aspects of the foundling homes need to be studied, including their administrative history, their policy development, and the social and economic impact of their programs. This paper illuminates the role of the women who availed themselves of the homes' services: those who gave up their children to the homes, and those who took them under their care in the villages as wet-nurse foster mothers. These women were central to the functioning of the homes, and yet very little is known about their social and occupational status or about the motivations that induced them to abandon their own children or to foster those of others. This type of inquiry helps to assess the economic and demographic consequences of the foundling traffic by providing a view of the nexus that formed between the urban child-welfare institutions and the women who used them, either as a dumping ground for unwanted children or as a source of income as foster mothers. The study also sheds light on the greater question of Russia's evolving social conditions as it advanced along the road to industrialization and urbanization.

WOMEN ABANDONING CHILDREN TO THE HOMES

It would be most instructive if one could establish the social and occupational status of the women who gave up their babies, and then explore the connections between their status and their motives for abandonment. Unfortunately, Betskoi's system intentionally shielded the women's identities, thus leaving contemporaries and historians in the dark about these crucial issues. Eager to stem what he perceived as a rising number of infanticides, Betskoi wanted to make delivery of children to the homes as painless as

1. N. F. Mikhailov, "K voprosu o vliianii pitomnicheskogo promysla na krest'ianskoe naselenie," *Trudy vos'mogo gubernskogo s"ezda vrachei moskovskogo zemstva* (Moscow, 1886), pp. 136–137.

possible. Hence, a half-century ahead of the "advanced" Paris foundling hospital, his institutions adopted the *tour*, or secret reception system, by which children could be left at the homes with no questions asked other than the baby's name and whether it had been properly baptized.[2] Any employee bold enough to inquire further ran the risk of losing his job. Of course, officials made impressionistic judgments based upon a mother's appearance or notes and clothing sometimes left with a child.[3] But these were of little help, inasmuch as children often came not with their mothers but in the arms of midwives and other couriers. There were even instances of whole cartloads being brought in by *kommissionerki*. For a fee, these enterprising women collected unwanted children in the villages and district towns, cared for them temporarily, and, when enough babies had been gathered to make the journey profitable, packed them into a wagon and hauled them to the metropolitan home.[4] Under these conditions, home officials could not possibly form a reliable picture of the foundling's family or social position.

There was one exception to this rule. From 1810 to 1815 the St. Petersburg home introduced an experimental ban on secret reception and kept more detailed records on the children. Unfortunately, these listed only the mother's estate *(soslovie)*, with no indication of her occupation and living conditions. Except for the interesting discovery that a substantial number of serf children entered the home (an illegal practice unless sanctioned by the serf owner), the records yielded only the unenlightening information that the largest categories of mothers were peasants and "people of various ranks."[5]

The absence of reliable data did not inhibit officials and social

2. Scarcely anyone questioned Betskoi's assertions about the need for the homes, although I have seen little evidence that the streets of Russia were cluttered with unwanted children in the eighteenth century. The suspicion thus exists that Betskoi erected the institutions merely to ape the enlightened behavior of rulers abroad. One critic argued that this premature establishment, if such it was, unduly stimulated abandonments. See discussion in *Issledovaniia o vospitatel'nykh domakh* (St. Petersburg, 1868), p. 20.

3. A. Piatkovskii, "Nachalo vospitatel'nykh domov v Rossii," *Vestnik Evropy*, 5 no. 6 (1875): 295–296, 298; M. G. ***, "O vospitatel'nykh domakh v Rossii," *Arkhiv sudebnoi meditsiny* (1869), no. 3, p. 57.

4. *Russkie vedomosti* (May 31, 1887), no. 147; *Detskaia pomoshch'* (1887), no. 23, p. 754. Tolstoi gave a very accurate description of the commerce in his novel *Resurrection*, as might be expected, since he used many contemporary news items in composing the work. He noted the *kommissionerka's* fee as 25 rubles.

5. The Moscow home was scheduled to run the same experiment, but the war conditions made it impossible to set the system up on a proper basis. For a breakdown of the data from

critics from making policy recommendations based upon the sparse materials available. They interpreted these variously, depending upon their attitude toward reform. The issue that most agitated them was whether a large number of legitimate children were entering the homes under cover of the secret reception. Although Betskoi had made no distinction between legitimate and illegitimate children, by the nineteenth century officials came to view the institutions as solely for those born out of wedlock. As they saw it, the only justification for secret reception was its function of concealing the shame of the unwed mother, who otherwise might prefer murdering her infant to exposing her sin. While officials suspected violations of this policy and occasionally took minor preventive measures, their fear of provoking a rash of infanticides caused them to shrink from outright abolition of the secret reception right up to the 1890s, when the unmanageable number of foundlings finally compelled a major overhaul.[6]

Despite official hesitation, reformers continued through much of the century to push for abolition of the *tour*. Among other things, they marshaled statistics to prove that the homes were overburdened with legitimate children who could only be weeded out by a system requiring identification of the mother *(iavnyi priem)*. The analyses offered by the reformers, while none too sophisticated, raised some interesting questions. They showed that, as early as the 1790s, the number of children given up to the St. Petersburg home was roughly equivalent to one-fifth of all new births in the city, whereas the rate of illegitimacy was only about 4 percent.[7] By the mid-nineteenth century the picture was even more startling. As the figures in Table 1 indicate, the number of entries at the St. Petersburg home was running between one-third and half the number of children born in the city. Even assuming that most of the children entering the home went unrecorded in the birth registers (the

---

the St. Petersburg home, see *Issledovaniia o vospitatel'nykh domakh*, p. 55, and O. A. Tarapygin, *Materialy dlia istorii S.-Peterburgskogo vospitatel'nogo doma* (St. Petersburg, 1878), part 2, p. 49.

6. S. E. Termen, *Prizrenie neschastnorozhdennykh v Rossii* (St. Petersburg, 1912), pp. 28, 60–64, 165–168. On Nicholas I's fear that parents of legitimate children were using the homes as vehicles for lifting their offspring out of the bonded state and his measures against this, see N. V. Iablokov, "Prizrenie detei v vospitatel'nykh domakh," *Trudovaia pomoshch'*, 1901, no. 4, pp. 423–424.

7. *Issledovaniia o vospitatel'nykh domakh*, pp. 21–23, 69; M. G. ***, "O vospitatel'nykh domakh," p. 81.

TABLE 1. HOME ENTRIES, POPULATION, AND BIRTHS IN ST. PETERSBURG, 1830–45

Year	No. of entries to SPb home	Population of SPb	No. of births in SPb
1830	4,091	435,500	9,661
1831	4,182	437,700	9,779
1832	4,323	439,900	9,912
1833	4,515	442,890	9,094
1834	5,183	449,100	10,335
1835	5,226	451,974	10,313
1836	5,360	461,700	9,928
1837	5,371	468,625	12,422
1838	5,273	470,100	12,511
1839	5,474	471,400	13,161
1840	4,604	472,800	13,339
1841	4,615	474,300	12,343
1842	5,156	475,500	13,557
1843	5,032	477,100	11,297
1844	5,277	478,500	14,865
1845	5,808	480,000	19,276

SOURCE: *Imperatorskii Petrogradskii vospitatel'nyi dom, otchet za 1914 god* (Petrograd, 1915), appendices, p. 2.

statistics are unclear on this point), in some years entries to the home exceeded one third of the number of new births.

Obviously, some children were coming from outside the city. For some years (1845 is the clearest example), if the foundlings are counted exclusively among the urban born, the resultant birth rate exceeds 50 per 1,000, an altogether incredible figure for a population with a male-female ratio of 1000:514.[8] One must certainly look to the countryside. In the case of Moscow, fairly reliable calculations indicate that perhaps 45 percent of the children brought to the home came from outside the city.[9] The percentage for St. Petersburg was undoubtedly smaller, since, unlike Moscow, it had a thinly populated hinterland and did not serve as a national transportation hub. Therefore, the reformers may have had a point about the number of legitimate children entering the home under cover of the secret reception. Unless the city was experiencing with a vengeance what Edward Shorter has called the nineteenth-century explosion of illegitimacy, or an unlikely number of rural women were reaching the city with their illegitimate progeny, a large portion of the children coming to the St. Petersburg home must

8. From an 1843 survey by the Ministry of Internal Affairs, published in A. G. Rashin, *Naselenie Rossii za 100 let* (Moscow, 1956), pp. 277–278.
9. Mikhailov, "K voprosu o vliianii," pp. 136–137; Peshch-v, "Moskovskii vospitatel'nyi dom v sovremennom ego polozhenii," *Vestnik blagotvoritel'nosti*, 2, no. 12 (1898):70–71.

have been legitimate.[10] Statistical analyses of the Moscow situation are even less helpful, in view of the large area from which the Moscow home drew its foundling population. Nevertheless, on the bases of rather crude reckonings of date of entry and number of children baptized, observers speculated that in Moscow, too, legitimate children comprised a sizable share of the infants placed in the home.[11]

These analyses were probably more notable for their propagandistic than for their scientific value. Yet they had enough substance to strike a blow at the theory that the chief motivation for abandonment was the shame of illegitimacy. Poverty was also an important cause, self-evident in the case of legitimate children. Even for women with illegitimate children, poverty may have played as big a role as shame in prompting them to deliver their infants to the homes.

Long before accurate statistics on the social and occupational background of abandoning mothers became available, officials had reason to suspect that the broad categories designated simply as peasants and "from various ranks" concealed a high percentage of women employed in domestic service. This hypothesis had been demonstrated in surveys of western European foundling homes. Toward the end of the century there was similar evidence closer to home: the Prague lying-in hospital registered roughly 85 percent of its patients as domestics. In Russia itself, at least one of the *zemstvo* foundling shelters established after the 1864 reforms kept records on the mothers and showed nearly the same proportion of domestic servants.[12] Indeed, this figure might have been guessed by a look at the composition of the female workforce of Russian cities. As late as 1900, when women were entering the ranks of industrial labor in substantial numbers, female domestics constituted a large majority of working women in the towns. In St. Petersburg over 92,000 women worked in domestic service, as compared to 57,848 in

10. For what it is worth, the *Statisticheskii vremennik* for 1866 put the illegitimacy rate in St. Petersburg at only 11.89 percent. Cited in S. S. Shashkov, *Istoricheskie sud'by zhenshchiny* (St. Petersburg, 1871), pp. 427–428.

11. *Issledovaniia o vospitatel'nykh domakh*, pp. 38–40.

12. N. N. Ginzburg, "Prizrenie podkidyshei v Rossii," *Trudovaia pomoshch'*, 1904, no. 4, pp. 491–493. See also the case studies of female infanticides in P. N. Tarnovskaia, *Zhenshchiny ubiitsy* (St. Petersburg, 1902), pp. 320–342, concerning women who were probably in much the same situation as the abandoning mothers but who took a riskier way out of their dilemma. All 16 were peasants: 11 menials, 1 a bookkeeper, the rest unemployed.

industry.[13] In Moscow as late as 1912 domestic servants still represented the largest single component of the female workforce, amounting to 25 percent of all independently employed women.[14]

TABLE 2. FEMALE DOMESTIC SERVANTS AS A PERCENTAGE OF WORKING
WOMEN IN ST. PETERSBURG AND MOSCOW

	1881	1882	1890	1897	1900	1912
St. Petersburg	37.3	—	32.8	33.6	32	—
Moscow	—	34.4	—	32.1	—	25.2

SOURCE: *S.-Peterburg po perepisi 15 dekabria 1881 goda*, II, part 2, pp. 302–309; *S.-Peterburg po perepisi 15 dekabria 1890 goda*, part I, sec. 2, pp. 50–55; *S.-Peterburg po perepisi 15 dekabria 1900 goda*, sec. 2, pp. 90–105; *Perepis' Moskvy 1882 goda*, sec. 2, pp. 131–134; Rashin, *Naselenie Rossii*, p. 333; *Pervaia vseobshchaia perepis'*, *1897 g.*, XXIV, XXXVII.

The situations of female domestics made them likely candidates for roles as abandoning mothers. Predominantly rural-born and peasant by estate, they came to the cities illiterate and unskilled and could seldom find positions as factory or shop workers. Having few qualifications and little family life in the cities, they were easy targets for economic and sexual exploitation. Unlike some categories of industrial workers who enjoyed at least minimal wage and vacation guarantees, the female domestic lived in a kind of personal bondage. With a good family, she may have had a more desirable situation than the factory worker, one that shielded her against the shock of urban life. But often her position was far from secure and subject to great abuse. If she refused to fulfill her master's whims or fell ill, she could be thrown into the street.[15] Having left the tightly controlled atmosphere of village life, these women must have experienced considerable trauma on entering an alien urban society that treated them as commodities and subjected them to economic deprivation and personal humiliation. When they sought relief from these conditions in a sexual union—tempted perhaps by the expectation of matrimony or, in some cases, forced by unscrupulous masters—and became pregnant, the practical course was to deliver the child to the foundling home. A mother

13. *S.-Peterburg po perepisi 15 dekabria 1900 goda* (St. Petersburg, 1903), part 2, pp. 42–105. The number of women in industry does not include those in commerce, hotels, or restaurants.

14. There were nearly 100,000 servants, 93 percent of whom were women. Rashin, *Naselenie Rossii*, p. 333.

15. Ginzburg, "Prizrenie podkidyshei," p. 492.

could not, as a rule, retain her employment while caring for a small child. Nor was the situation necessarily better for the minority of female domestics who were married. Since husbands and wives often worked in different homes, these women were in no better position than their unwed counterparts to keep their children.[16]

This speculation about the social and occupational background of abandoning mothers was dramatically confirmed by the detailed statistical picture that emerged after the abolition of secret reception in the 1890s. Under the new rules, which permitted entrance of illegitimate children only, women had to reveal their identities upon delivering babies to the homes (with certain exceptions, noted below) and then stay on at the institution to nurse their infants through the difficult early weeks of life. For the first time officials were in a position to conduct an accurate survey of the mothers—if only those mothers who could still use the home, as the new rules produced a drop of roughly one-third in the number of entries.

The most thorough statistics concern the abandoning mothers' social estate. However, these merely reveal that, as at the beginning of the nineteenth century, the mothers still fell into two broad undifferentiated categories, this time peasants and lesser townswomen *(meshchanki)*.[17] Much more significant were the data on occupation. Unfortunately, the published records of the homes gave a full occupational breakdown on all abandoning mothers only for the years 1910–14. Yet the figures for the St. Petersburg home indicate that even at this late date, when the number of female domestics relative to the total female workforce had long been in decline, domestic servants clearly predominated, representing a percentage far in excess of their numbers in the total urban population. Fragmentary data for the preceding nineteen years suggest that the over-representation of female domestics among abandoning mothers was even greater in that period. From 1891 to 1909 the St. Petersburg home recorded the occupation only of mothers who, after delivering infants to the foundling home, agreed to accept a subsidy to care for the children in their own homes or at their place of work. Although the percentage of women receiving

---

16. *Issledovaniia o vospitatel'nykh domakh*, p. 52.
17. *Imperatorskii petrogradskii vospitatel'nyi dom, otchet za 1914 god*, p. 87.

TABLE 3. OCCUPATIONAL STATUS OF MOTHERS DELIVERING CHILDREN TO THE ST. PETERSBURG HOME, 1910–14

Occupation	1910		1911		1913		1914	
Servants	3,035	(48%)	2,482	(51%)	1,788	(44%)	1,434	(34%)
Unskilled day laborers	1,637	(26)	1,172	(24)	853[a]	(20)	1,063	(25)
Seamstresses	783	(12)	442	(9)	629	(15)	761	(18)
Agricultural workers	362	(6)	342	(7)	367	(9)	397	(9)
Factory workers	185	(3)	132	(3)	181	(4)	244	(6)
Other craft workers	199	(2)	132	(3)	129	(3)	186	(4)
Living at relatives' expense	80		55		44		28	
Unemployed	38		53		23		24	
Teachers and governesses	21		26		20		16	
Artisans	21		6		20		16	
Marketwomen	16		27		22		17	
Medical workers	8		9		8		2	
Students	5		1		7		3	
Professional beggars	2		—		2		1	
Prostitutes[b]	1		3		1		2	
Unknown[c]	315		?		275?		283	
Total (excluding unknown)	6,311		4,882		4,094		4,185	

N. B.: Percentages figured on total of those whose occupation is known.
[a]Not entered in published table; figured by subtracting other categories from the total.
[b]Prostitutes may have declared a more respectable occupation.
[c]Those admitted under a special provision for concealing the mother's identity.
SOURCE: *Imperatorskii S.-Peterburgskii vospitatel'nyi dom, otchet za 1910 god*, p. 44; *ibid.*, *Otchet za 1911 god*, p. 102; *ibid.*, *Otchet za 1913 god*; *ibid.*, *Otchet za 1914 god*, p. 87.

subsidies varied widely over the period, from 5.7 percent to 56 percent of all abandoning mothers, one may assume that the occupational breakdown reflected a strong bias in favor of settled urban women with families that could provide living space and help to care for the children. Hence the figures show a much higher proportion of factory and craft workers than would be found in the full reckoning given for the years 1910–14. Indeed, for the two years in which the records overlap, 1910 and 1911, domestic servants in the subsidy sample are understated by roughly 45 percent, while mothers engaged in craft work are overstated by 65 percent. Although the data are too variable to allow this discrepancy to be factored into the percentages noted for the limited subsidy sample covering the entire period 1891–1909, it is clear that domestic servants as a percentage of abandoning mothers in those years must have far exceeded the 48 percent level recorded

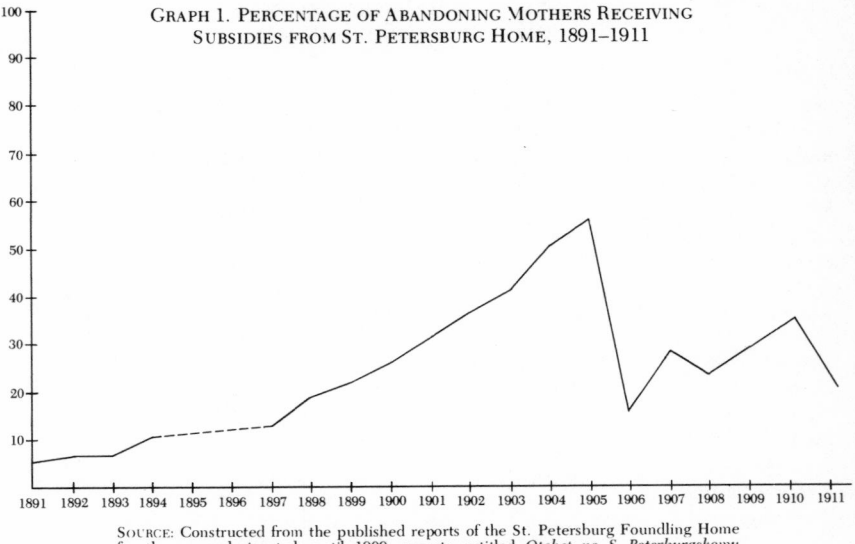

GRAPH 1. PERCENTAGE OF ABANDONING MOTHERS RECEIVING
SUBSIDIES FROM ST. PETERSBURG HOME, 1891–1911

SOURCE: Constructed from the published reports of the St. Petersburg Foundling Home
for the years designated; until 1909, reports entitled *Otchet po S.-Peterburgskomu
vospitatel'nomu domu za . . . god*, 1891–1907 compiled by V. A. Ban kovskii, 1907 compiled
by M. A. Korsakov, 1908–9 compiler not noted; 1910 and 1911 reports entitled *Imperatorskii
S.-Peterburgskii vospitatel'nyi dom, otchet za . . . god*, 1910 compiled by V. O. Gubert, 1911
compiled by S. K. Solov'ev.

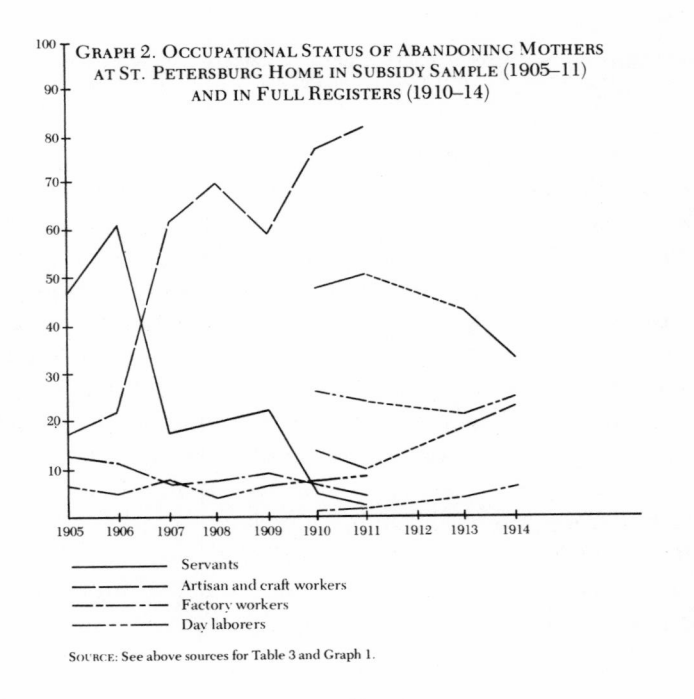

GRAPH 2. OCCUPATIONAL STATUS OF ABANDONING MOTHERS
AT ST. PETERSBURG HOME IN SUBSIDY SAMPLE (1905–11)
AND IN FULL REGISTERS (1910–14)

——— Servants
—·—·— Artisan and craft workers
- - - - - Factory workers
—· ·—· ·— Day laborers

SOURCE: See above sources for Table 3 and Graph 1.

198

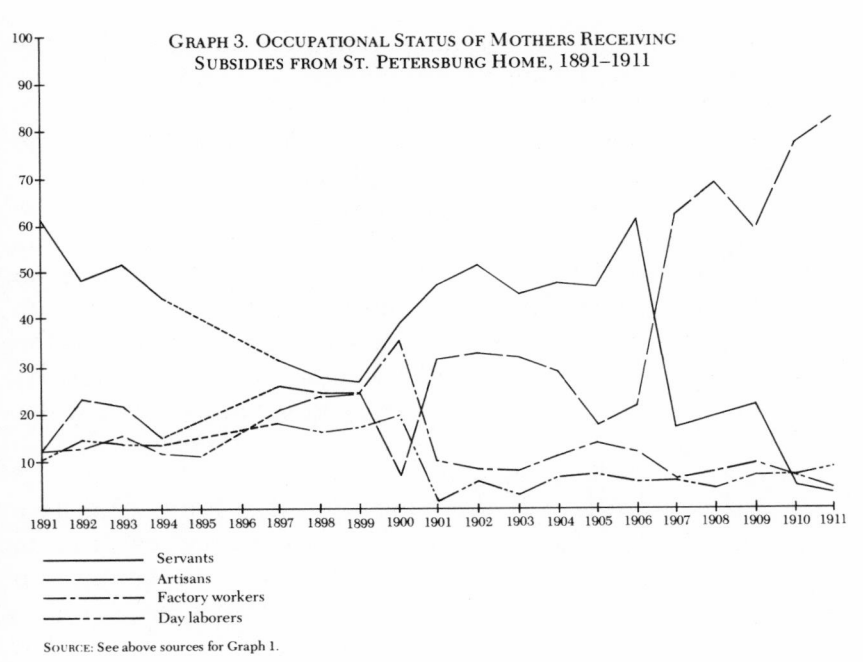

GRAPH 3. OCCUPATIONAL STATUS OF MOTHERS RECEIVING
SUBSIDIES FROM ST. PETERSBURG HOME, 1891–1911

———————— Servants
— — — — Artisans
—·—·—·— Factory workers
— - — - — Day laborers

SOURCE: See above sources for Graph 1.

for 1910 and may have run as high as 60–80 percent.[18] When one recalls that domestics constituted only 33 percent of the total female workforce in St. Petersburg during the same period, this over-representation eloquently testifies to their inability to defend themselves against economic and sexual exploitation. It also indicates their isolated position in the city, where they were without relatives and friends to help care for their children.

Finally, the question of motivation remains. Commentators usually framed this in terms of whether poverty or shame was the more important cause. As the retention of the *tour* until the 1890s

18. An independent check is provided by the limited data I have been able to obtain for the Moscow home. They give an occupational breakdown for all abandoning mothers during 1903 and 1904, with the exception of a rather sizable percentage (about 32%) who entered under the special provision for concealing the mother's identity. The following list includes only the largest occupational categories:

Occupation	1903	1904
Domestic servants	50 %	54 %
Agricultural workers	13.9	13.4
Artisans	13.6	12.9
Factory workers	12.6	11.2

SOURCE: *Otchet po moskovskomu vospitatel'nomu domu za 1903 god*, ed. D. B. Troitskii (Moscow, 1905), 16–17; *idem, za 1904 god* (Moscow, 1905), p. 20.

attested, officials long viewed the problem primarily as one of the shame of illegitimacy. But the issue was more complex than this framework implied. Several levels of shame have to be considered, especially in regard to the women not recorded in Table 3, i.e., the roughly one-third who would have placed their children in the homes under the secret reception but who failed to do so after the new rules were introduced. It is unlikely that this entire decline could be attributed to the fact that legitimate children were no longer accepted. There were, no doubt, also mothers of illegitimate children who preferred the shame of keeping their infants to the humiliation of publicly renouncing them at the home. Similarly, one must account for a marked increase in the rate of infanticides and abandonments in the street that accompanied the introduction of the new rules.[19] Were these the offspring of unwed mothers who preferred to run the risk of criminal penalties rather than face public humiliation? Or were the victims legitimate offspring of parents too poor to support them yet unable now to deliver them to the homes? In short, there are too many variables and too little information to allow evaluation of the motives of women excluded under the new rules.

For the women included in Table 3, poverty probably played a larger role than shame in their decision for abandonment. A provision in the new rules still allowed such a woman to conceal her identity if she could provide confirmation from a priest or trustworthy citizen that her child was illegitimate. Yet very few St. Petersburg women availed themselves of this opportunity (note the category "Unknown" in Table 3).[20] Although much more needs to be known about the stigma attached to illegitimacy in Russia,

19. Peshch-v, "Moskovskii vospitatel'nyi dom," pp. 68–69, gives a statistical rundown. Details of specific cases can be found in *Detskaia pomoshch'* (1891), no. 17, pp. 505–506.

20. Here one finds a striking contrast between the St. Petersburg and Moscow statistics. Between 1895 and 1905, the percentage of women who delivered children to the Moscow home under the special provision for concealing identity varied from 18 to 32, whereas the rate at the St. Petersburg home remained consistently low. The following table gives the years of greatest contrast.

Category "Unknown" (concealed identity) for years 1903–5

	1903	1904	1905
St. Petersburg	.06%	.03%	.02%
Moscow	32.5	32.3	29.8

Apart from the unlikely possibility that the statistics were cooked up, the discrepancy must have been a function of very different enforcement policies with respect to admitting children under the concealment provisions, or of very different attitudes with respect to the shame of illegitimacy and child abandonment. St. Petersburg was a more cosmopolitan city

available ethnographic material indicates that censure was far from universal and apparently varied considerably from region to region.[21] The move to the city likewise distanced the women from the moral strictures of the village; indeed, this was probably part of their problem. Their pregnancies may have been the result of traditional behavior (the desire to marry and establish a family) transplanted into a context where the social controls of village life no longer operated to provide them with a husband once a child was on the way.[22] The fact that most were working as domestic servants and day laborers again suggests poverty as the primary cause, for they could not retain their jobs while caring for infants. Faced with the decision of losing their means of subsistence or publicly renouncing their children, the choice was plain. They may have felt shame, but their economic situation was desperate enough to obscure the moral strictures impinging upon them.

WOMEN OF THE VILLAGE FOSTERAGE SYSTEM

The women at the other end of the traffic, the wet-nurse foster mothers who took the children from the foundling homes, were overwhelmingly peasants from the provinces surrounding the capital cities. In the Moscow system in the 1880s, at the height of the traffic, approximately 12,000 such women arrived annually to pick

and farther removed from peasant life and traditional values—circumstances that may have acted on both the women and the home administrators to discourage them from having recourse to the special concealment provisions. (For example, women may have been too far from their home village to be able to obtain the local priest's endorsement of illegitimacy or, alternatively, far enough away not to worry about exposure to shame.) Yet these factors in themselves do not seem adequate to cover the wide discrepancy in the figures. For a discussion of the policy implications of the St. Petersburg situation, see M. A. Oshanin, *O prizrenii pokinutykh detei* (Iaroslavl', 1912), pp. 36–37.

21. Note the following report from Vologda *guberniia:* "There are women and girls with families of illegitimate children who live on what is given in the name of 'Christ.' The people do not persecute or chase out these women, but laugh at them and say: 'Let them live as they wish. They also want to flirt and there are no husbands. They bear children?—so, there'll be an extra soldier.' To women who in the absence of their husbands have amorous liaisons they respond indifferently: 'The husband isn't living at home, and the woman, it's clear, must have a man.' " (*Arkhiv Muzeia Etnografii Narodov SSSR*, fond Tenisheva, Vologodskaia gub., Sol'vychegodskii u., Afanasyskaia volost', Puchuzhskii prikhod, 1899, soob. Vasil'evskii. I am indebted to A. N. Martynova for this and other references from the Tenishev archive.) See also field reports on attitudes in Siberia related by Shashkov, *Istoricheskie sud'by,* pp. 440–441, and the note in *Arkhiv sudebnoi meditsiny* (1870), no. 3, p. 10.

22. See the interesting hypothesis to this effect, advanced against Edward Shorter's sentiment thesis on increased illegitimate fertility in western Europe by Louise A. Tilly *et al.,* "Women's Work and European Fertility Patterns," *Journal of Interdisciplinary History* 6, no. 3 (Winter, 1976): 447–476.

up children. Under the normal procedures, each woman was required to undergo a physical examination to insure that she had an adequate supply of breast milk. Thereafter she served in the home for a short time before returning to the countryside with the child allotted to her. At the home she received a daily stipend plus upkeep; in the countryside she was paid a monthly subsidy, principally in cash, but also including clothing and linen for the child. Little need be said here about the social and occupational backgrounds of the wet nurses. Apart from the usual household and field duties of village women, their occupation was child care, or, in some cases, the transportation and sale of foundling children. This section, therefore, focuses not on the social and occupational status of the wet nurse, but on her material position, her motivation in taking a foundling, and the impact of the foundling traffic on her family and village.

As in the case of abandoning mothers, statistical information is sparse. One must rely chiefly on the observations of foundling home administrators, provincial physicians, and circuit overseers (okruzhnye nadzirateli); these last mentioned were officials appointed to supervise the okrugs, or territorial units, into which the homes divided the fosterage system. Some overseers were physicians, others simply low-level bureaucrats. The peasants, who carefully watched their comings and goings, styled them "orphan lords" (detskie bare).[23] Although these officials had the closest links to the village foster mothers, their view of foster case remained fairly limited. Posted in district capitals and burdened with paperwork, they normally visited the foster families only twice a year, and in some cases less often.[24]

Additional information on village fosterage can be gleaned from the complaints which were sometimes lodged against the foundling traffic. As early as 1804 an official involved in Empress Mariia Fedorovna's charitable work asked that the traffic be suspended because of its harmful effects on the children.[25] Evidence from the

23. The translation of barin as "lord" is used advisedly. A peasant would call anyone from the other culture barin, right down to a ragtag student passing through his village. The best rendering might be "massa" if it were not so culturally specific.

24. Materialy dlia istorii imperatorskogo moskovskogo vospitatel'nogo doma, ed. V. Drashusov (Moscow, 1863–68), I, 13 [hereafter MIMVD]; V. P. Obninskii, "Patronat nad pitomtsami Moskovskogo vospitatel'nogo doma," Trudy pervogo s"ezda russkikh deiatelei po obshchestvennomu i chastnomu prizreniiu (St. Petersburg 1910). p. 557.

25. A. I. Zabelin, Vekovye opyty nashikh vospitatel'nykh domov (St. Petersburg, 1891), pp. 23–29.

1830s reveals that some landlords were forbidding the delivery of foster children to their estates, on grounds that the practice caused mothers to neglect their own children and threatened to spread syphilis from the urban areas to the villages.[26] By the 1850s the governor-general of Finland was demanding a complete halt to the traffic in his jurisdiction. Like the landlords mentioned above, he cited neglect of village children and syphilis as reasons, and then added the further complaint that unmarried women were going so far as to prostitute themselves to become wet nurses and earn the attractive fees offered by the foundling home.[27] After 1864, complaints came mainly from *zemstvo* physicians who noticed the same problems, particularly the prevalence of syphilis and high mortality rates among the children in villages with a large number of fosterlings.

Of course, these sources contain a negative bias, and one must use care in evaluating their accuracy. (More will be said about this later, in the discussion of the traffic's impact on the families and villages of the foster mothers.) It can scarcely be denied, however, that the system had its share of problems. Immense difficulties accompanied the job of caring for tens of thousands of infants, attracting a sufficient number of qualified foster mothers, and checking on the treatment of the fosterlings. Matters were not helped by the fact that the peasants perceived and manipulated the system in ways that had little in common with the objectives of the foundling home administrators. Even under the most scrupulous management, the system was bound to lend itself to practices the urban officials regarded as abusive.

Some typical problems were found in one of the earliest published reports on foster care, the notes of Dr. A. I. Klementovskii, a Moscow Foundling Home director who made inspection tours in the Podol'skii and Vereiskii districts of Moscow province during the 1860s. On the positive side, he observed that most of the women had the basic qualifications for the work—they possessed sufficient

26. Complaints were referred to in government decrees of the period. For examples, see Termen, *Prizrenie neschastnorozhdennykh*, pp. 96–97, and A. I. Lebedev, "Ocherk deiatel'nosti Moskovskogo vospitatel'nogo doma (1764–1896 gg.)," *Izvestiia Moskovskoi gorodskoi dumy* (July-August, 1898), part 1, section 2, p. 44.

27. Cited in article on foundling homes in *Entsiklopedicheskii slovar'* (Brokgauz-Efron) (St. Petersburg, 1892), VII, 280. Further information on foundlings in these areas may be found in recent a Finnish study by Greta Karste-Liikkanen, *Pietari-suuntaus kannakselaisessa elämänketässä 1800-luvun loppupuolelta vuoteen 1918* (Helsinki, 1968), pp. 90–92 (with German summary).

breast milk to nourish a nursing infant. Either they had weaned their own infant after a reasonable interval—usually three fasts, counting only the Lenten and Assumption—or had lost their own or a foster child to death. As it happened, moreover, many of these women were from extended family households. Their absences during trips to the city to get foundlings did not place heavy burdens on their families, as their small children could be left temporarily in the care of other women of the household.[28] These were ideal conditions for the operation of the village fosterage system.

But Klementovskii also noted a less satisfactory situation: women who took children from the home with no intention of caring for them. In some cases, this was simply a matter of picking up a foundling for a friend or relative who could not get to the home on her own. Much more common, however, and of special concern to the foundling homes, was a category of women known as "peddlers" *(torgovki)*. As the name implied, these women were the equivalent of the *kommissionerki* on the intake side of the foundling traffic. They engaged in the business of fetching children from the metropolitan homes and selling them to women in the villages; the latter would then collect the regular monthly fees from the foundling home. Often agreements were made ahead of time, and the *torgovka* would use the passport of the buyer in her dealings with the foundling home. It frequently happened also that a *torgovka* picked up a child on her own account and then sought a buyer, sometimes simply selling the child on the road home or even at the gates of the city. Along with the child, the buyer received a pay booklet entitling her to the monthly stipend from the home. In all these transactions there was no guarantee that the eventual foster mother would have breast milk to feed the child; more often than not, the infant fell into the hands of a woman who fed it on the bottle or with hard food—practices that almost invariably brought an early death. Nevertheless, the buyer could continue to claim the monthly subsidy until the circuit overseer's infrequent rounds led him to the discovery that the child had died.[29]

28. "Izvlechenie iz donesenii Starshego Vracha doktora A. I. Klementovskogo," in *MIMVD*, II, 129–130.

29. In addition to Klementovskii's comments in *MIMVD*, II, 130–135, see those of Chief Doctor A. I. Blumental', *MIMVD*, II, 128, Lebedev, "Ocherk deiatel'nosti," p. 40; P. A. Peskov, *Opisanie Durykinskoi volosti moskovskogo uezda v sanitarnom otnoshenii*,

Within the fosterage system, *torgovki* formed a special category of poor, unattached women. Since their fees were not large—an initial stipend while at the foundling home, and a two- to four-ruble profit (in the 1860s) on the sale of a child—the work attracted only the neediest women who were unqualified for other jobs. Furthermore, they had to have breast milk to pass muster at the foundling home and yet be free of family responsibilities in order to travel to and fro, picking up children and seeking out customers. The *torgovki* were most often widows whose only infant had died, or unwed mothers and soldiers' wives who delivered their illegitimate children to the home and then returned to pick up a foundling before losing their breast milk. It was more unusual for a married woman to be a *torgovka,* although this too occurred, especially in families where the husband was absent for long periods as a migrant laborer. Here again the woman had either lost a child to death or abandoned her infant in order to be free to engage in the trade.[30]

The *torgovki* could usually escape detection at the foundling homes because of shifting staff assignments and the large number of women applying for children. It should be noted as well that the homes did not altogether discourage this practice. Desperately in need of wet nurses and aware that many qualified women were desirous of becoming foster mothers but unable, because of family obligations, to come to the home personally, officials were willing to avail themselves of the *torgovki*'s services in cases where they could obtain reasonable assurance of the ultimate foster mother's qualifications to nurse.[31] The increasing trend in some areas toward the breakup of extended family households created conditions favorable to the spread of the *torgovka* commerce. Women in nuclear families had fewer opportunities to go to the city to fetch children on their own, and the only means of reaching the foundling home was through a *torgovka.*[32] Still, since the *torgovki* worked the system to turn a quick profit, the abuses of this method of delivery no doubt far outweighed its positive contributions. One critic figured

vol. 1, part 3 of *Sbornik statisticheskikh svedenii po moskovskoi gubernii* (Moscow, 1879), p. 110; *Detskaia pomoshch'* (1890), no. 6, p. 200.

30. Klementovskii, *MIMVD,* II, 131–132.

31. Lebedev, "Ocherk deiatel'nosti," pp. 39–40.

32. Klementovskii, *MIMVD,* II, 133; V. Krasuskii, *Kratkii istoricheskii ocherk imp. moskovskogo vospitatel'nogo doma* (Moscow, 1878), pp. 151–153; A. Ia. Efimenko, *Issledovaniia narodnoi zhizni,* part 1, *obychnoe pravo* (Moscow, 1884), pp. 95–96.

that the survival rate for children placed in this manner was only 2 percent.[33] This was probably an exaggeration, but the mortality rate for the children delivered by *torgovki* was certainly higher than that for other foundlings.

Foster children were commonly exchanged among peasant families once they reached the village. Overseers and physicians found that, in almost every village, some children were not living with their assigned foster parents. They had either been farmed out to a relative or passed on to another woman in the same village, or even an entirely different village. Sometimes there was no record of a particular child ever having been in the village to which it was assigned, not even a registration of its death.[34] In these cases, it seems, the wet nurse had simply sold or buried the child along the road back from the foundling home. The apparent ease with which foster mothers passed children around again underscores the foundling's function, in the peasants' eyes, as an exchange commodity.

The sources evince little disagreement on the financial motivation for taking a foundling; nor were the villagers embarrassed to admit this directly. In a survey of the Moscow fosterage system, the responses of 500 families to the question of why they took a foundling echoed again and again: "Due to poverty" *(po bednosti)*.[35] Foster care was a typical commercial venture *(promysel)* like so many others the peasants engaged in to supplement their meager incomes. Just as the father hired himself out as a day laborer or went off to the woods to cut and haul timber, the mother would go off to the foundling home to, as they saying went, "hatch" a child.[36]

Most observers noted that the foundling traffic attracted families of slender means. This was further borne out by a number of

33. Peshch-v, "Moskovskii vospitatel'nyi dom," *Vestnik blagotvoritel'nosti* 3, no. 10 (1899):28–30.

34. Klementovskii, *MIMVD*, II, 136–137; Peskov, *Opisanie*, p. 110; Krasuskii, *Kratkii ocherk*, pp. 151–153. Termen, citing the 1865 Rosov report on foundlings, noted that in some cases the exchange of children had become sufficiently formalized to be regularly arbitrated by the village *skhod*. (*Prizrenie neschastnorozhdennykh*, p. 72.)

35. Discussion of this survey and the problems of carrying it out appear in A. G. Arkhangel'skaia, "Rezul'taty pervoi popytki po issledovaniiu vliianiia pitomnicheskogo promysla na zdorov'e naseleniia," *Trudy deviatogo gubernskogo s"ezda vrachei moskovskogo zemstva* (Moscow, 1888), pp. 270–281.

36. See opinion of 1865 Rosov report on the cash nexus discussed in Termen, *Prizrenie neschastnorozhdennykh*, p. 69, and Oshanin, *O prizrenii pokinutykh detei*, pp. 71–79.

TABLE 4. MATERIAL POSITION OF FOSTER FAMILIES IN THE MOSCOW SYSTEM

	1871–74	1880	1882	1890–94
Well off *(zazhitochnye)*	4.8%	5%	9%	11.1%
Middling *(srednye)*	82.9	72	63.6	57.9
Poor *(bednye)*	10.5 ⎫	23	24.2	27.5
Landless *(bobyli)*	1.8 ⎭		3	3.5

SOURCE: Lebedev, "Ocherk deiatel'nosti," p. 41; and *Sbornik svedenii po obshchestvennoi blagotvoritel'nosti*, VII (St. Petersburg, 1886), pp. 13, 31.

surveys taken for the Moscow system between the 1870s and 1890s. Although none too specific, the figures indicate an over-whelming proportion of poor and middling families. The criterion for distinguishing the latter was the possession of at least one cow. At its lower reaches this category, which formed the bulk of the foster families in all the surveys, must have included many very needy families. The steady relative decline of the middling group through the period was compensated for principally by a rise in the percentage of altogether poor and landless peasants, who by the 1890s represented roughly one-third of the foster families. Lebedev described their situation graphically in noting that these were families occupying *kurnye izby*, huts with neither stoves nor chimneys, warmed only by a fire in the middle of the floor and constantly filled with smoke—in other words, the poorest and most unhygienic conditions. Well-to-do families always represented a very small percentage; the slight increase in their numbers during the period can perhaps be explained by the regularly increasing payments for fosterage, which made the work marginally more attractive for some families in this category. A more favorable picture emerged from surveys of the Voronezh *zemstvo* foundling shelter, which estimated well-off families as 44 percent in 1904 and 23 percent in 1908. However, this shelter, with its relatively small number of children, had an easier task of placement and far sur-passed all other *zemstvo* shelters in the quality of its foster care.[37] Furthermore, the considerable discrepancy in the figures raises suspicions about both the internal consistency of the surveys and

37. M-T., "Zemstvo i bezprizornye deti-podkidyshi," *Trudovaia pomoshch'* (1905), nos. 4–5, p. 408; M. V. Ptukha, "Bespriiutnye deti-podkidyshi i nashe zemstvo," *Trudovaia pomoshch'* (1911), no. 7, pp. 138–141. On the situation in other shelters, see A. Amster-damskii, "Prizrenie pokinutykh detei v zemstve," *Zemskoe Delo* (1910), no. 5, pp. 397–403, and M. D. Van Puteren, *Istoricheskii obzor prizreniia vnebrachnykh detei i podkidyshei* (St. Petersburg, 1908).

David L. Ransel

their comparability with the Moscow data. In any case, even in this unusually successful system those families described as from very poor through middling constituted over half of the foster homes.

While the primary motivation for serving as a wet nurse was financial, the length of time a family engaged in this enterprise varied considerably. Many families apparently viewed the work as a means of temporarily supplementing income during a time of crisis. If their home burned down or their horse died, they would take a foundling and use the stipend to repair their losses. By the time the crisis was over, the child either would have died or, if still alive, could be returned to the home or passed on to another needy family in the village. In other cases, families worked at foster care as a steady job. As soon as one fosterling died, they returned for another or, if the mother's milk dried up, obtained one through a *torgovka*. Sometimes whole villages engaged in the traffic, either temporarily (after a bad harvest) or as a regular business stretching over many years.[38] These communities were usually located in areas with soil too poor to provide a living and where not enough large factories existed to afford well-paid alternative employment.

A look at Moscow province makes this distribution pattern clear. In the central and south-eastern districts, with their well developed factory bases, peasants were able to live comfortably without resorting to auxiliary trades. The foundling home did not succeed in placing many fosterlings with families in these areas, although the few youngsters to be found there were, as a rule, well cared for. The largest concentrations of foundlings appeared in the western and west-central districts—Vereiskii, Mozhaiskii, Ruzskii, and Zvenigorodskii—where industry was weakly developed and the soil was too poor to support the population. From these areas large numbers of men migrated to find work in the cities, or else families tried to make do with home handicraft, wood cutting and hauling, and other *promysly*, among which the foundling traffic (*pitomnicheskii promysel*) loomed large. In fact, as the factories in other districts gradually undermined the competitive position of small workshops and home handicrafts, some communities came to rely upon the foundling trade to the point of making the child care stipends a chief source of non-farm income.[39] The amount earned

38. Arkhangel'skaia, "Rezul'taty pervoi popytki," p. 277.

39. Krasuskii, *Kratkii ocherk*, pp. 155–171; Lebedev, "Ocherk deiatel'nosti," pp. 44–47; Peshch-v, "Moskovskii vospitatel'nyi dom," pp. 28–30; P. I. Zarin, "Bogorodskaia

by a single family was not large (fluctuating between one and four rubles per month in the late nineteenth century), but there were as many as a dozen villages with ninety or more fosterlings.[40] The aggregate transfer of wealth from the urban centers to these poor villages was far from insignificant: for the Moscow system in the 1880s, it reached as high as 650,000 rubles per year.[41]

Even so, the communities that opened their doors to the foundling trade could not be said to have made an especially good bargain. On the purely economic side, there were problems of distribution. Since many of the women could not travel to the district centers each month to collect their stipends and yet were in no position to wait for the circuit overseer to bring their pay while on his rounds, enterprising middlemen emerged to provide this service. Some women mortgaged their pay booklets to these brokers (*zakladchiki*) for up to six months in advance. The broker, usually a local retailer or innkeeper, then used the booklets to collect the stipends from the home, extracted an exorbitant delivery fee in addition to the customary 10–20 percent monthly interest, and passed the remainder on to the foster family. As a rule, this last payment was made not in cash but in comestibles from the *zakladchik*'s shop, figured at highly inflated prices and not always of the best quality. Certain entrepreneurs of this type held up to 200 pay booklets at a time and earned as much as 5,000 rubles a year on interest alone.[42] In such cases only a small proportion of the actual value of the stipends reached the foster families. A large part went directly from the homes to the middlemen, with a minimal amount trickling down to the working foster mothers and their villages. In his book on the systematization of Russian government, George Yaney has

volost' Vereiskogo uezda v sanitarno-statisticheskom otnoshenii," *Piatyi gubernskii s"ezd vrachei moskovskogo zemstva, protokoly zasedanii i trud* (Moscow, 1881), pp. 182–187.

40. Mikhailov, "K voprosu o vliianii," pp. 136–137. The saturation of some villages with foundlings occurred in the *zemstvo* systems as well. Dr. Gliko reported in 1911 that in two villages of the Kiev district (Verem'e and Vitachevo) almost every house had a fosterling and some contained two, three, and infrequently even five. A similar situation was reported in 1909 by the Saratov provincial administration. (Oshanin, *O prizrenii pokinutykh detei*, pp. 92–93.) On the high concentrations in Ruzskii district, Moscow Province, see S. P. Matveev, *Ocherk statistiki narodonaseleniia ruzskogo i mozhaiskogo uezdov* (Moscow, 1881), pp. 93–94.

41. Lebedev, "Ocherk deiatel'nosti," p. 47.

42. Obninskii, "Patronat," p. 558; N. B. Meder, "Obshchestvo popecheniia ob uluchshenii byta pitomtsev Imperatorskogo S.-Peterburgskogo vospitatel'nogo doma, vospityvaemykh v derevniakh Garbolovskogo okruga," *Vestnik blagotvoritel'nosti* 3, no. 7 (1899): 44–45, 49.

David L. Ransel

remarked on what he considered to be the foster mothers' "advanced" social behavior, in the sense that they were capable of exploiting an economic opportunity offered by the bureaucratized urban welfare institutions.[43] He may have had a point with regard to his main argument about peasant myth-making and its impact on village cohesion, yet a closer look at the actual economic mechanisms reveals that the most effective exploitation was occurring at the level of the middlemen.

Besides the unsatisfactory economic side of the bargain, the peasants involved in the foundling traffic may also have been exposing themselves to still worse consequences of a social and demographic nature. As indicated earlier, *zemstvo* physicians and local officials frequently voiced concern in this respect and argued that the women engaged in the traffic were subjecting their families and villages to serious health and safety risks. One issue that time and again provoked debate at medical congresses was the role of the fosterlings in the spread of syphilis. Although foundling home officials scoffed at this complaint and averred that syphilis was quite common in Russian villages, their opponents were able to score some important points. Researches by local physicians and *zemstvo* organizations turned up convincing evidence of higher rates of syphilis among foster mothers than among the female population as a whole, as well as appreciable jumps in the rate of syphilis in districts recently opened to the foundling traffic.[44] Researchers pinpointed the source of the disease by the appearance of chancres on the foster mothers' breasts and assembled detailed case-studies on the spread of the disease in this fashion. One study told of a forty-year-old wet nurse who contracted syphilis, in the form of a breast chancre, from a foundling. The child soon died, and in order not to lose her milk the woman began nursing three of her neighbors' children, all of whom subsequently contracted the disease. These children in turn infected their three mothers, giving them all breast chancres, and the mother of one child passed the scourge on to her husband. The investigation stopped at this point, although the chain of infection presumably did not. In another study of eight women who had worked at the St. Petersburg foundling home and

43. George Yaney, *The Systematization of Russian Government* (Urbana, Ill., 1973), p. 385.
44. Lebedev, "Ocherk deiatel'nosti," p. 45.

210

contracted syphilis, it was discovered that after returning to their villages they spread the disease among sixty additional persons.[45] These reports may have been somewhat exaggerated, as peasants were subject to many skin eruptions that could be mistaken for syphilis by an overzealous doctor eager to make his case against the foundling traffic. Nevertheless, the evidence was compelling enough to force the introduction of stringent controls on the release of foundlings with possible cases of congenital syphilis.[46] It should of course be pointed out that, despite the *zemstvo* physicians' implication of syphilis as an urban scourge inflicted on unblemished rustics, as many as 45 percent of the children at the foundling homes came from outside the cities, and so the rural populace too must have contributed its share of congenitally syphilitic infants.

If syphilis were not enough, the traffic was also blamed for harmful demographic effects occasioned by the foster mothers' neglect of their own children. Local officials regarded the eagerness of women to take a foundling as one of the chief causes of the high mortality rates which they observed among village children in areas with a heavy concentration of fosterlings. As one Moscow *zemstvo* doctor lamented, "The majority of new mothers from our area do not think merely of how it would be best to nurse their baby but how they might best draw advantage from their breast milk; this unfortunate phenomenon is expressed in two forms—either by becoming a [private] wet nurse or by taking a foundling, and sometimes not just one but several."[47] These criticisms could not, of course, be construed to mean that foster children took prece-

45. *MIMVD*, II, 126–128; Mikhailov, "K voprosu o vliianii," pp. 139, 145–147, and debates from same congress on this report, *Trudy vos'mogo gubernskogo s"ezda vrachei moskovskogo zemstva* (Moscow, 1886), pp. 13–15, 89–91; N. P. Domashnev, "Osmotry kormilits, kak predupreditel'naia mera po otnosheniiu k sifilisu," *Trudy obshchestva russkikh vrachei v Moskve za 1884 g.*, no. 1, pp. 88–100; A. Pospelov, "K diagnostike sifilisa kormilits," *Trudy obshchestva russkikh vrachei v Moskve za 1881 god*, no. 1, reports 1–5, accompanying discussion 70–75; K. K. Tolstoi, "O lechenii sifilisa," *Trudy piatogo gubernskogo s"ezda vrachei moskovskogo zemstva* (Moscow, 1881), pp. 175, 178–179; G. M. Gertsenshtein, "O zarazhenii kormilitsami detei sifilisom i obratno," *Meditsina* (St. Petersburg, 1891). See also Gertsenshtein's general work, *Sifilis v Rossii, materialy k meditsinskoi geografii i statistike Rossii* (St. Petersburg, 1885).

46. For the effect on the *zemstvo* system, see Amsterdamskii, "Prizrenie pokinutykh detei," p. 399.

47. V. N. Benzengr, "K voprosu o pitanii grudnykh detei i ob ukhode za nimi," *Trudy, chetvertyi gubernskii s"ezd vrachei moskovskogo zemstva* (Moscow, 1880), p. 139. See also a review of the literature on this issue in Oshanin, *O prizrenii pokinutykh detei*, p. 94; M-T., "Zemstvo i besprizornye," p. 404; and D. I. Orlov, "Ob uchastii zemstva v vospitanii detei," *Trudy piatogo gubernskogo s"ezda vrachei moskovskogo zemstva* (Moscow, 1881), p. 250.

David L. Ransel

dence over the village children. On balance, the fosterlings were clearly the losers in the competition, since their mortality was invariably greater than that of the local children.[48] While the traffic undoubtedly harmed the village children as well, the extent of their suffering is difficult to determine.

Demographic and sanitation studies commissioned by the Moscow Province *zemstvo* generally supported the view that the highest infant mortality among village children occurred in the areas with the largest concentration of foster children from the foundling home. But Peskov's detailed report on Durykinskaia *volost'* of Moscow District showed that, while this poor township had both a larger population of fosterlings and a higher mortality rate than other townships in the district, the mortality rate did not correlate as neatly with the foundling trade as it did with other purely sanitary factors such as hygiene and epidemic disease. Peskov could not deny that the traffic brought harm to the local populace; in fact, he was sure that it did. Quite apart from the question of neglect of village children, both the foundling traffic and the hauling trade (the other principal commerce of the area) served as transmission belts for disease, to which the people were particularly susceptible because of poverty and poor sanitation. Unable to isolate all the variables, Peskov preferred to identify the general cause of the high mortality as economic necessity, which likewise underlay the extensive development of the foundling traffic and hauling trade.[49]

One could also point to Kurkin's aggregate correlations for all of Moscow province between the number of foundlings and the rate of infant mortality in a particular district, presented here in Table 5. These figures are somewhat skewed, as they evidently include the mortality of the fosterlings along with that of the village children. Nevertheless, a similar result obtains in Zarin's study of Bogorodskaia *volost'* of Vereiskii District, which has the advantage of a village-by-village breakdown showing only the mortality of the native village children.[50] (See Table 6.) While both these tables

48. Zarin, "Bogorodskaia volost'," pp. 191–192; M. M. Ertel'-Arkhangel'skaia, "K voprosu ob ustroistve zemskogo sirotskogo priiuta," *Trudy desiatogo gubernskogo s"ezda vrachei moskovskogo zemstva* (Moscow, 1890), pp. 30–31.

49. Peskov, *Opisanie*, pp. 111–114, 151–156.

50. For St. Petersburg we have a report by a doctor Zachek, who found a childhood mortality rate among 534 women engaged in the foundling trade to be 59 percent. Among 546 women not participating in the trade, the corresponding mortality rate for their children was only 41 percent. Cited in Oshanin, *O prizrenii pokinutykh detei*, p. 94.

TABLE 5. FOSTER CHILDREN, BIRTHS, AND INFANT MORTALITY IN DISTRICTS
OF MOSCOW PROVINCE

Districts	Percent of foster children to 100 live births, 1885–95	Infant mortality, 1883–97
Ruzskii	30.6%	48.9%
Mozhaiskii	30.0	45.7
Vereiskii	22.3	42.4
Zvenigorodskii	12.9	36.2
Dmitrovskii	10.9	38.8
Volokolamskii	8.6	36.7
Klinskii	6.9	36.0
Serpukhovskii	6.2	31.2
Podol'skii	2.7	31.3
Bronnitskii	2.3	31.9
Kolomenskii	0.7	31.3
Moskovskii	—	35.9
Bogorodskii	—	33.7
Total for Moscow Province	10.3	36.3

SOURCE: P. I. Kurkin, *Detskaia smertnost' v moskovskoi gubernii i ee uezdakh 1883–1897 gg.*
(Moscow, 1902), p. 178.

TABLE 6. FOSTER CHILDREN IN RELATION TO MORTALITY OF NATIVE VILLAGE
CHILDREN BOGORODSKAIA VOLOST', 1870s

Village	Fosterlings per 100 native villagers	Percent of mortality of native children to 1 yr.
Zolot'kovo	3.5%	14.3%
Polchevo	8.6	36.3
Merchalovo	13.0	40.0
Denis'evo	26.0	44.4
Modenovo	43.0	87.5

SOURCE: Zarin, "Bogorodskaia volost'," p. 192.

yield suggestive correlations, the figures remain subject to question by virtue of the fact that the heaviest concentrations of foster children were in the poorest villages and townships, where one would expect to find high infant mortality rates. Moreover, if one compares the reduction of the foundling traffic to the reduction of infant mortaliy in the same areas over the period 1883–97, the picture that emerges is far from consistent. The figures are again Kurkin's on a district-by-district basis. (See Table 7.) Although they hold up in four districts (Vereiskii, Volokolamskii, Mozhaiskii, and Ruzskii) where the greatest reduction in infant mortality corre-

David L. Ransel

TABLE 7. REDUCTION IN INFANT MORTALITY RELATIVE TO DECLINE IN
FOUNDLING TRAFFIC, MOSCOW PROVINCE

District	Reduction in infant mortality, 1883-97	Decline in foundling traffic, 1885-95
Mozhaiskii	8.65%	33.1%
Ruzskii	7.93	47.5
Volokolamskii	4.39	16.9
Serpukhovskii	2.69	8.4
Vereiskii	2.10	20.7
Podol'skii	1.17	7.0
Zvenigorodskii	1.05	16.5
Moskovskii	1.03	—
Bronnitskii	0.59	4.0
Kolomenskii	0.55	1.2
Dmitrovskii	0.29	13.0
Bogorodskii	0.28	—
Klinskii	+0.75	6.2

SOURCE: Kurkin *Detskaia smertnost'*, pp. 179–180.

sponds to the greatest decline in the foundling trade, even in these cases the proportions are uneven. In other districts with a substantial decline in foundling population there was no significant drop in infant mortality, while Klinskii district actually showed a slight rise of infant mortality during a period when the influx of foster children declined from 10 to 4 percent. The inconclusiveness of these statistics forces us to suspend judgment on the degree of harm suffered by the local children as a result of the foundling traffic.[51] While the traffic would seem to have had a significant impact, there were obviously other powerful factors contributing to high infant mortality in Russian villages.

This raises the whole issue of infant care in pre-revolutionary Russia. Much has been written on this question by urbanized doctors and officials, who usually looked upon peasant child-care practices with a mixture of astonishment and revulsion.[52] Indeed, peasant care left much to be desired. This was fully evident from the

51. S. P. Matveev wrestled with this problem in his study of Ruzskii district and pointed up some of the problems with the data. *Ocherk statistiki narodonaseleniia*, p. 94.

52. For a vivid portrayal, see Arkhangel'skaia, "Rezul'taty pervoi popytki," 278–279; *Detskaia pomoshch'* (1886), no. 13, pp. 529–530; (1891), no. 18, p. 549; S. Khotovitskii, "O nekotorykh pogreshnostiakh i predrassudkakh kasatel'no soderzhaniia detei v pervoe vremia ikh zhizni," *Trudy sanktpeterburgskogo obshchestva russkikh vrachei* (1936), part 1, pp. 160–166; N. Aleksandrovskii, "Prizrenie pokinutykh detei v Kazanskoi gubernii," *Trudovaia pomoshch'* (1912), no. 6, pp. 50–51; Peskov, *Opisanie*, pp. 156–160; Oshanin, *O prizrenii pokinutykh detei*, p. 93.

infant mortality rates among Russians, which exceeded not only those of western Europe but even those of such "less developed" peoples of the Empire as the Tatars and Udmurts.[53] This is not the place to review the abundant ethnographic material on village sanitary conditions, nursing practices, the *soska*, the sometimes truly harmful methods of folk medicine, and the often noted indifference of peasants to the crushing mortality among their children.[54] These questions are treated elsewhere in this collection. Suffice it to say that the treatment of Russian children depended upon a particular family's economic position, cultural level, and access to modern medical facilities. As a rule, the sources emphasize the worst cases in efforts to capture the attention and sympathy of society and to engage it in the struggle to improve the conditions of infant care. Much of this literature quite naturally follows the trail of the foundling traffic to poor areas that, for want of alternative employment, had to resort to foster care on a large scale. It was scarcely surprising that in these areas child care practices were particularly unsatisfactory and the mortality of village children and foundlings alike inordinately high.

The foundling home reform of the 1890s, with its registration of abandoning mothers *(iavnyi priem)* and restriction of entry to illegitimate children or those found in the street, did much to improve the survival odds for foundlings.[55] Most important was the provision enabling mothers to nurse their own children through the dangerous early weeks before they were sent out to fosterage. This

53. *MIMVD*, I, 16; *Detskaia meditsina* (1901), no. 3, p. 257; D. E. Gorokhov, *Detskii organizm v bor'be s bolezniami i smert'iu* (Moscow, 1910), pp. 4–5, 8.

54. Criticism on the use of hard food for babies goes back at least to 1780 with the work by S. Zybelin, *Slovo o sposobe, kak predupredit' mozhno nemalovazhnuiu mezhdu prochimi medlennogo umnozheniia naroda prichinu, sostoiashchuiu v neprilichnoi pishche, mladentsam davaemoi v pervye mesiatsy ikh zhizni* (Moscow, 1780), esp. pp. 13–16. See also N. D. Sokolov, "Sanitarnyi ocherk s. Nikul'skogo-Karamysheva, Marfiskoi volosti, Moskovskogo uezda," *Piatyi gubernskii s"ezd vrachei moskovskogo zemstva* (Moscow, 1881), pp. 196–199; V. G. Bogoslovskii, "Zadachi vrachebno-sanitarnoi organizatsii v bor'be s letneiu detskoiu zabolevaemost'iu i smertnost'iu," *Trudy piatnadtsatogo gubernskogo s"ezda chlenov vrachebno-sanitarnykh organizatsii moskovskogo zemstva*, part 1, zhurnaly zasedanii, doklady sektsii (Moscow, 1903), pp. 213–223; V. O. Gubert, "Ob ustroistve gorodskoi stantsii dlia prigotovleniia i razdachi detskogo moloka bednym materiam," *Trudy obshchestva detskikh vrachei v S.-Peterburge* (St. Petersburg, 1904), p. 20. On folk medicine and child care, see two excellent works: V. T. Demich, "Pediatriia u russkogo naroda," *Vestnik obshchestvennoi gigieny*, 11, (1891), no. 2, 125–145; no. 3, 187–212; 12, (1892), no. 1, 66–76, no. 2, 111–123, no. 3, 169–185; and G. Popov, *Russkaia narodno-bytovaia meditsina* (St. Petersburg, 1903), esp. ch. 11.

55. For brief background on and a summary of reform, see Puteren, *Istoricheskii obzor*, pp. 79–81.

not only insured a more reliable supply of wet nurses at the homes, but also gave the infants the early breast milk appropriate to their needs instead of the "old milk" of women who had been lactating for some time.[56] The new regulations also reduced the number of entries into the homes; at the same time (although it is less clear why this happened) they diminished the proportion of children coming from outside the city.[57] The result was higher survival rates both at the homes and in the *okrugs*. This improvement was, however, bought at the cost of rejecting many children who would have come in under the old rules and hence produced a higher rate of infanticide and outright abandonment in the street, not to mention the unquantifiable social costs of the unwanted children who were kept by parents out of pure force of circumstance.[58]

Despite the reduction in the homes' foundling populations, which should have made placement in the *okrugs* easier, officials continued to have problems finding an adequate supply of qualified foster mothers. The difficulties were again a function of economic factors. As the growth of industry in and around the capital cities opened more opportunities to women, potential foster mothers gravitated to the more lucrative factory jobs. Competition came as well from a less obvious source, the expansion of other urban welfare services. To cite just one example, the St. Petersburg city government established its own system of farming out the mentally incompetent to foster care in the villages and provided (in addition to shoes, clothing, and linen) a stipend of over twice the amount paid by the local foundling home. It was not long before the peasants shifted their commerce in this direction.[59] By shrewdly responding to the relative advantages of one or another type of foster care work, the villagers were forcing urban institutions to act in accordance with aggregate supply and demand factors.

In summary, the system of village fosterage for foundlings pro-

56. Peshch-v, "Moskovskii vospitatel'nyi dom," (1898), p. 76; on the changing quality of breast milk, S. Ia. Erisman-Gasse, "K voprosu o vskarmlivanii detei v vospitatel'nykh domakh i priiutakh," *Trudy deviatogo gubernskogo s"ezda vrachei moskovskogo zemstva* (Moscow, 1888), p. 262.

57. Peshch-v, "Moskovskii vospitatel'nyi dom," pp. 70–71; Termen, *Prizrenie neschast-norozhdennykh*, pp. 91–92, 99; Iablokov, "Prizrenie detei," (June, 1901), pp. 12–13.

58. Termen, *Prizrenie neschastnorozhdennykh*, pp. 176–179.

59. A. N. Ustinov, "O smertnosti grudnykh detei v zavisimosti ot nedostatka grudnogo moloka po dannym Moskovskogo Vospitatel'nogo Doma," *Detskaia meditsina* (1899), no. 2, p. 146; *Imperatorskii petrogradskii vospitatel'nyi dom, otchet za 1914 god*, pp. 111–113.

duced an important economic and social nexus between the metropolitan homes and the villages in surrounding provinces. As was seen in the case of abandoning mothers, the link ran in both directions; a substantial number of village women joined their urban sisters in delivering children to the homes, sometimes with the specific intention of selling their milk as wet nurses or *torgovki* working the other side of the traffic. In the absence of an adequate statistical breakdown on the abandoning mothers, serious problems remain in identifying the motivations for abandonment. The shame of illegitimacy obviously played a part, but perhaps not to the extent that officials usually assumed. The likelihood that a large number of legitimate children were involved suggests that poverty was also a significant factor. Even in the case of the domestic servants and day laborers, who toward the end of the century comprised the bulk of abandoning mothers, the need to retain a precarious employment probably figured more significantly in their considerations than did shame.

As for the wet-nurse foster mothers, their involvement was a matter of exploiting an economic opportunity presented by urban welfare institutions. Predominantly from needy families in search of supplemental income, the women worked the fosterage system much as peasants worked other auxiliary trades *(promysly)*. They moved in and out of the trade in response to several factors: their own financial needs, the fluctuating pay levels within the system, and the relative wage differential between this work and alternative forms of employment. The children were viewed primarily as an exchange commodity to be passed around the village, sold, or returned to the foundling home as economic need dictated. The financial nexus provided a substantial outflow of urban capital to needy villages, even constituting a kind of permanent state subsidy to communities that engaged in the trade over a long period of time—although a considerable portion of this was siphoned off by middlemen quick to take advantage of the peasants' poverty and immobility. Questions remain as to whether the foster families were ultimately more harmed than benefited by the traffic, since their involvement exposed them to a variety of potentially hazardous social and demographic consequences.

SAMUEL C. RAMER

Childbirth and Culture:
Midwifery in the Nineteenth-Century
Russian Countryside

"We must see to it that children are born properly. This
is real revolution—of this I am quite sure."
— Issac Babel, "The Palace of Motherhood" (1918)

Almost half of the children born in rural Russia during the late
nineteenth century died before they were five years old.[1] The
Empire as a whole, with a population over four-fifths rural, had the
highest infant mortality rate in Europe. The reasons are to be found
primarily in Russia's economic and cultural backwardness. For
most of the rural population, diet was unbalanced and insufficient,
housing overcrowded, and clothing inadequate. The most elementary hygienic and sanitary measures were for the most part ignored,
and there was little popular understanding of their significance.
Disease flourished in such an environment, taking a disproportionately large toll among infants and young children. Medical care,
when it could be obtained at all, was often poor in quality, and in
many cases the limitations of contemporary medical knowledge
rendered even the best physicians powerless to do more than
supervise the inevitable.

Although childbirth itself was not the primary occasion for infant
death, it did involve considerable danger for mother and child

The present article is part of a larger study of *fel'dshers* and midwives in pre-revolutionary
Russia. I thank the Tulane Research Council, the National Endowment for the Humanities,
the International Research and Exchanges Board, and the Fulbright Faculty Fellowship
Program for their assistance in making the research for this paper possible.

1. The infant mortality rate varied significantly from province to province. For figures
and a discussion of regional variations, see V. I. Grebenshchikov and D. A. Sokolov,
Smertnost' v Rossii i bor'ba s neiu (St. Petersburg, 1901), pp. 20–24.

alike. The absence of adequate obstetric care made these dangers particularly acute during complicated deliveries and contributed to a high rate of infection during the post-natal period. In the middle of the nineteenth century there were virtually no rural midwives with any sort of modern medical training.[2] Peasant women usually gave birth either alone or with the assistance of a *povitukha,* an older peasant woman without formal medical education who was experienced in delivering babies. The infant and maternal deaths which resulted from the *povitukhi's* incompetence were especially intolerable to physicians and medical reformers because they seemed unnecessary. The reduction of such deaths through the improvement of obstetric care seemed a practical possibility which could gradually be realized, despite the expected persistence of Russia's more general backwardness. The task as reformers of the 1860s and 1870s envisioned it was to train a competent corps of rural midwives *(sel'skie povival'nye babki)* to replace the older *povitukhi.* If nothing else, it was argued, such trained midwives could reduce the instances of infection and eliminate the "barbaric" practices for which *povitukhi* were renowned in cases of difficult delivery. It was hoped that rural midwives, together with the physicians with whom they were expected to cooperate, would be able to provide modern obstetric care for the Russian peasantry.[3]

These arguments received a practical implementation. Whereas until the 1860s the only institutions in the Empire which trained a

2. For the Ministry of Internal Affairs' recognition of this, see *Tsentral'nyi Gosudarstvennyi Istoricheskii Arkhiv (TsGIA),* f. 1297, op. 142, d. 292, pp. 6–6 ob.

3. *Ibid.*, p. 6 ob. According to nineteenth-century Russian law there were three titles for obstetric personnel: *povival'nye babki, sel'skie* or rural *povival'nye babki,* and *povitukhi.* The first were distinguished by having completed training in an urban midwife institute. The second had graduated from a school for rural midwives, and were not entitled to practice in urban areas without passing a special examination. The third had no formal training at all, but were required to pass qualifying examinations. They were allowed to practice only when there were no trained midwives available. In practice, so many rural midwives qualified for urban practice that it is useful here to speak of midwives as a single group. Their skills varied enormously, but in the countryside the principle dichotomy was between the *povitukhi* and any midwife with training. Despite the law, many *povitukhi* had no license whatsoever and most practiced in competition with trained midwives. The term *akusherka* ("midwife," from the French *accoucheur*), while frequently used in general discussions, did not exist in Russian legislation except when appended to the term *fel'dsheritsa*—i.e., *fel'dsheritsa-akusherka (fel'dsher*-midwife). *Spisok statei Svoda Zakonov i pravitel'stvennykh rasporiazhenii o povival'nykh babkakh, sel'skikh povival'nykh babkakh i povitukakh* (St. Petersburg, 1885), pp. 2–3. In 1900 the titles of *povival'naia babka* and *sel'skaia povival'naia babka* were replaced by those of *povival'naia babka* of the first and second order, with no appreciable effect on the problem of obstetric care. *Sobranie uzakonenii i rasporiazhenii pravitel'stva* (St. Petersburg, 1900), p. 1160.

significant number of midwives had been the Imperial Foundling Homes in St. Petersburg and Moscow, by the late 1870s there were over twenty schools in provincial cities especially devoted to the training of such women.[4] By 1905 the total number of schools for midwives had grown to over fifty, with an enrollment of nearly 4,000. The majority, located in the larger cities and sponsored by either charitable organizations or city governments, had no particular commitment to the countryside and trained midwives legally qualified for urban practice. But a number of provincial governments *(zemstva)* and some private organizations continued to support over twenty provincial schools for midwives whose primary orientation was to the countryside.[5]

The same survey of 1905 records over 10,000 trained midwives already in practice, as contrasted to 15,000 physicians and 20,000 *fel'dshers,* or paramedics.[6] The numbers in all these cases are small, considering that the population was over 125 million, but significant progress had been made in the training of midwives. Nevertheless, available statistics indicate that as late as the turn of the century only 2 percent of rural births were attended by trained midwives.[7] The local governments' attempts to provide trained obstetric care for the peasantry would thus appear to have failed almost entirely. How can this be explained?

The central problem, predictably, was not simply a shortage but an uneven distribution of trained midwives. On the whole, these midwives tended to settle in urban areas, despite the fact that many of them had been recruited from the peasantry and trained with the peasantry in mind. This had a positive result in that by the turn of the century access to a trained midwife, and if necessary to a physician, was as readily available in the major cities of European Russia as it was in the capitals of western Europe. But this achieve-

4. *Otchet meditsinskogo departamenta ministerstva vnutrennykh del za 1876 god* (St. Petersburg, 1877), pp. 162–163. These first schools were established in Astrakhan, Vologda, Voronezh, Viatka, Kamenets-Podol'skii, Kishinev, Mitau, Mogilev, Moscow, Penza, Samara, Saratov, Simbirsk, Tambov, Tula, Khar'kov, Kherson, Chernigov and Iaroslavl'.

5. *Otchet o sostoianii narodnogo zdraviia i organizatsii vrachebnoi pomoshchi v Rossii za 1905 god* (St. Petersburg, 1907), pp. 176–187.

6. *Ibid.*

7. D. A. Paryshev, *Rodovspomozhenie v Rossii po dannym vserossiiskoi gigienicheskoi vystavki 1913 g. v S.-Peterburge* (St. Petersburg, 1914), p. 1. An absolutely accurate figure is impossible here, and the extent of effective obstetric care varied from province to province. Scattered checks of provincial physicians' reports tend to confirm the general statistic.

ment had come at the expense of the rural population, and as of the turn of the century no dramatic change in this urban concentration seemed imminent.

Trained midwives preferred the city to the countryside for obvious reasons. There were, in the first place, comparatively few salaried positions in the countryside. If local governments failed, it was less in the training than in the support of midwives for rural areas. In 1905, for example, the *zemstva*, which were the chief rural employers, provided only 2,200 positions for the more than 10,000 midwives in practice.[8] The situation in the non-*zemstvo* provinces was even worse.[9] There were a number of reasons why the *zemstva* and other local governments did not provide more salaried positions for midwives. Funds were limited, and the need for physicians and *fel'dshers* (who could be pressed into service as midwives)[10] seemed more compelling. Equally important was the fact that the rural population itself did not share the physicians' perception that trained midwives were needed, and those actually trained were only infrequently called upon. The cost per birth of providing trained midwives was thus relatively high, and the *zemstva* generally acquiesced in this peasant indifference. Local governments devoted little planning or funding to the organization of obstetric care per se until the 1890s.[11]

The majority of trained midwives (over 6,000 in 1905) were in private practice, and most of them worked in cities.[12] There was a demand for their services there, and the proximity of large numbers of reasonably affluent clients allowed at least some of them to support themselves by practicing—something almost impossible in the countryside, for a midwife without a salary, because of infrequent demand and peasant poverty. The competition among urban midwives was fierce, and many were in fact unemployed, but the

8. *Otchet o sostoianii narodnogo zdraviia*, p. 180.
9. For most of its history, the *zemstvo* existed only in the provinces of European Russia. The western borderlands, Siberia, Central Asia and the Caucasus continued to be governed through institutions of the central administration.
10. Those concerned with obstetric care were disturbed by the casual (and common) notion that a *fel'dsher*, or even a physician, was an adequate substitute for a trained obstetrician. Until late in the century *fel'dshers* were not given any obstetric training at all, and there is abundant testimony that a large proportion of physicians was incompetent in assisting at birth.
11. B. B. Veselovskii, *Istoriia zemstva za sorok let* (St. Petersburg, 1909–11), I, 412–413.
12. *Otchet o sostoianii narodnogo zdraviia*, p. 181.

possibilities for supplemental income either as hospital aides or in non-medical jobs were greater. However difficult life was in the city, private practice in the countryside did not appear as a practical alternative to most trained midwives.

For those able to maintain a practice, the city also provided more attractive working conditions. An urban midwife did not have to travel far to practice her trade, as her rural counterpart frequently did, and it was easier to call upon a physician in unusually difficult cases. While a rural midwife was supposed to refer all complicated deliveries (anything involving the active interference of the midwife) to a physician, and was in fact required by law to do so,[13] distances and poor communication in the countryside often rendered this a practical impossibility, placing upon the rural midwife's shoulders a medical responsibility which exceeded her training and skills.

The concentration of midwives (indeed, of all trained medical personnel) in cities was an old story, and the first sustained efforts to alter the balance coincide with the Great Reforms of the 1860s. During this era the Ministry of Internal Affairs, along with the local governments which it prodded, began for the first time to consider seriously how better obstetric care could be provided for the peasantry.[14] The solution advocated by the ministry involved establishing schools for rural midwives in conjunction with the maternity wards of provincial hospitals. These schools, at least ideally, would train girls in the hospital for one or two years before sending them to work in rural areas. In its circulars the ministry asked local physicians in its service to poll their peasant communities to determine the viability of such schools, and then to render their own opinions. Public awareness of the ministry's initiatives elicited a number of projects from physicians and concerned laymen on the question of how rural midwives should be trained and how their success as practitioners could be best assured.[15] The projects differed in many ways, but they shared a number of ideas which are of interest

13. *Spisok statei svoda zakonov i pravitel'stvennykh rasporiazhenii o povival'nykh babkakh, sel'skikh povival'nykh babkakh i povitukakh,* pp. 2–3.

14. The ministry's first circular "Ob uchrezhdenii pri bol'nitsakh Prikaza Povival'nykh uchilishch" is dated November 3, 1863. *TsGIA,* f. 1297, op. 142, d. 292, pp. 6–6 ob. For responses, see pp. 11–361.

15. Many of these projects are bound together with other answers to the Ministry's circular in *TsGIA,* f. 1297, op. 142, d. 292. See also the important project for the improvement of standards for midwives written in 1870 by N. I. Kozlov, N. F. Zdekauer, and A. Ia.

because they shed light not only on the problems involved in improving obstetric care, but also on the attitudes of contemporary physicians toward those problems.

The first (and most unequivocal) attitude was that rural midwives should be recruited from the peasantry and, insofar as possible, sent back to work in the areas from which they had come. (This emphasis on the importance of peasant origin should be noted, since by the turn of the century most medical professionals would cease to regard the social origin of medical personnel as a matter of primary importance.) The physicians of the 1860s recognized that peasant girls were not ideal students. Most were not literate when they began their studies, and their way of life in the village had not prepared them for study focused on the written word. Hence, most reformers recommended that schooling for rural midwives be practical, not theoretical, with emphasis on oral instruction and demonstration. Such training demanded an adequate supply of pregnant and parturient women who could be used as teaching material. Even in provincial hospitals it was difficult to maintain this supply at the low level considered sufficient (100 births per year) because of the novelty of maternity wards,[16] the understandable suspicion with which both urban dwellers and peasants viewed the hospital, and the very process of teaching, which violated the privacy in which most women preferred to give birth.

Almost all physicians consulted were in agreement that it was important not only to recruit peasant girls, but to structure life in the school so that they should remain peasants, culturally undifferentiated from the population they were to serve. Thus we find arguments for the maintenance of an austere regime, for the retention of peasant dress, for a ban on any luxuries which urban existence might provide, and for the use of students as service personnel in the hospital during non-school hours so that they "would not grow unused to being peasants."[17] The justification for these arguments was twofold. Reformers wanted to make sure girls returned to the countryside and feared that any pampering would cause them

Krassovskii, a project which quickly abandoned the exclusive consideration of midwives and in fact used the issue of midwifery as a means of opening up the discussion of women's medical education before the Medical Soviet. *TsGIA*, f. 1294, op. 6, d. 54, pp. 11–23 ob.

16. The estimate of the minimum number of births sufficient to support a midwifery school is that of Nikolai Mandel'shtam. *TsGIA*, f. 1297, op. 142, d. 292, p. 137.

17. *Ibid.*, p. 335 ob.

to reject their rural calling. Moreover, they argued that only women who had retained the outward manifestations of peasant culture could win the confidence of the people they would serve. To be effective with peasants, reformers insisted, midwives would have to be "their people" *(svoi liudi)*. Insofar as possible, they should be peasants from the local area who were familiar with its customs and known to its people. It was even more important that they not see themselves as superior to the peasantry, that they appear "neither as privileged persons nor as some kind of reformers."[18]

While arguments that students should retain a peasant way of life made sense on one level, they were incompatible with the other mission of midwifery schools—namely, to transform young peasant girls into capable representatives of modern medicine who would alter, rather than conform to, obstetric practices which prevailed in rural areas. The authors of the projects involved were to an extent aware of this contradiction but resolved it only weakly by implying that trained midwives in the countryside would essentially have to serve as cultural emissaries in disguise.[19] This resolution rested on the common assumption that medical authority among the peasantry was primarily personal in nature and that peasants, if not confronted with an open attack on their whole way of life, would ultimately believe in results. To suppose, however, that a significant number of peasant girls could maintain this sort of dual identity was clearly unrealistic, as experience would show.

If the physicians of the 1860s had no other solutions, it was partly because their imaginations were restrained by the funds available for rural obstetric care. The question of how midwifery schools should be financed was one to which they all directed their attention, and there was a considerable amount of agreement on several basic questions. Almost all the physicians polled by the Ministry of Internal Affairs in 1863 and 1864 agreed that no schools for rural midwives could succeed if the costs of training were put directly on the peasantry.[20] According to the physicians, the peasantry saw no need for such schools; given a choice, the local peasant community would refuse to pay tuition for one of its members to study, and the

18. *Ibid.*, p. 326 ob.
19. *Ibid.*, pp. 330–31.
20. *Ibid.*, *passim.*

community could not provide her with a salaried position after graduation. (Several physicians reported no volunteers for study in a midwifery school, even with the guarantee of tuition and room and board).[21] Because of this peasant indifference, most physicians recommended that provincial governments support students and hire trained midwives out of funds not specifically designated for midwifery.

There were some exceptions, the most noteworthy being that of Nikolai Mandel'shtam, the chief obstetrician in Mogilev Province. Ignoring the arguments of other provincial physicians, Mandel'shtam accepted the ministry's original recommendation that local communities (*sel'skie obshchestva* or *mirovye uchastki*) should select and support their own candidates as students and later provide jobs for them. Arguing on the basis of his own efforts in Mogilev, he emphasized both the feasibility of such an approach and the extent to which expense could be minimized by more thorough utilization of existing facilities.[22] The ministry ultimately accepted Mandel'shtam's project as a model for other provinces. It seemed more likely than others to achieve the desired goal, and it "did not demand any special expenditures."[23] The central government's decision to rely on peasant support of midwifery schools, a decision reached in the face of evidence that it would be disastrous for the schools, meant from the outset that the role of such schools would be limited.

The graduates of these early provincial schools did not fare well as rural midwives. Many went to the countryside for a year or two and then, unless supported by a fixed salary, either gave up their profession or retreated permanently to the city. By the turn of the century, according to one account, 90 percent of the graduates with the title of "trained village midwife" quickly passed examinations entitling them to an urban practice and moved to the city.[24] A year in school evidently did alter the expectations of graduates, and even peasant girls often experienced loneliness and social isolation upon returning to the countryside. The culture of the city—and, perhaps

21. *Ibid.*, p. 258.
22. *Ibid.*, pp. 136–136 ob.
23. *Ibid.*, pp. 239–239 ob.
24. Dmitrii Ott. *Proekt organizatsii akusherskoi pomoshchi sredi sel'skogo naseleniia (Doklad sektsii akusherstva i zhenskikh boleznei VII s"ezda russkikh vrachei v pamiat' N. I. Pirogova)* (St. Petersburg, 1899), p. 15.

more important, its higher material standard of living—were difficult to forget. As one inspector critical of Mandel'shtam's school in Mogilev reported, its graduates "no longer like to live in the countryside, and don't remove their city clothes. They go very unwillingly to visit peasants in their simple carts, and sometimes even refuse. They are so alienated from the peasants, and the latter from them, that the peasants almost never turn to them for help, continuing as before to use simple, untrained women."[25]

The problem was not only that peasant girls trained as rural midwives were attracted to the city because of their training or their difficult experiences. The fact was that, despite initial efforts to recruit midwives among the peasantry, an increasing proportion of the girls trained as rural midwives came from the city to begin with. At the Nadezhdin Obstetric Institute in St. Petersburg, all but three of the 419 girls in training as rural midwives in 1861 were peasants. In the same school during the decade 1881–90 peasants made up only 16.3 percent of all students. Of the others, 27.8 percent were from the nobility, 27.7 percent were children of townsmen *(meshchane)*, 15 percent were from clergy backgrounds, and 14 percent were from various lower ranks of society *(raznochintsy)*.[26] By virtue of its location in St. Petersburg, the Nadezhdin Institute cannot be regarded as typical of schools specializing in the training of rural midwives, but the trend is representative. Table 1 indicates the 1910 enrollments in centers of midwife training in the Empire.[27] Of all midwives in training, less than a quarter were of peasant origin. Even in the schools for rural midwives, students of peasant background constituted only 38 percent of the total. Thus by the eve of World War I (and, by all indications, much earlier) the city had become the main source of Russia's trained midwives, even of those preparing for rural practice. This was occasioned in part by the limited success that peasant midwives had achieved, which invalidated earlier claims made on their behalf. Furthermore, as we shall see, most Russian physicians had by then abandoned the almost exclusive earlier emphasis on social origin in favor of developing the best possible system of medical care.

25. *TsGIA*, f. 1297, op. 142, d. 292, pp. 427–427 ob.
26. V. Zhuk, "Shkola sel'skikh povival'nykh babok," *Zhurnal akusherstva i zhenskikh boleznei*, 4, nos. 7–8 (July–August, 1890): 507.
27. *TsGIA*, f. 1298, op. 1, d. 1754, pp. 3–9.

TABLE 1. ENROLLMENTS AT CENTERS OF MIDWIFE TRAINING, 1910, BY SOCIAL ORIGIN OF STUDENTS

	Peasants	Townsmen (*meshchane*)	Nobility	Children of bureaucrats, teachers, doctors	Clergy	Military	Merchant	Honored citizens	Foreign	Misc.
Women's schools for *fel'dshers* with midwife training	652	1,575	270	215	268	120	94	111	19	215
Schools for *fel'dshers* with midwife training (coed)[a]	209	604	92	67	37	15	29	26	—	57
Obstetric institutes (urban midwives)	185	569	108	73	36	27	15	23	12	15
Schools for rural midwives	735	948	137	56	53	25	22	32	2	44
Total	1,781	3,696	607	411	394	187	160	192	33	331
Percentage of total	22.8	47.4	7.7	5.2	0.5	2.3	0.2	2.4	0.4	4.2

[a] As of 1910 there were only 210 men studying to become *fel'dshers* with midwife training.

Perhaps more important in explaining the increasing dominance of the city is the general testimony that most of the girls who were eager to become midwives were urban, and were better prepared to enter a course of medical training than their rural contemporaries. It should be recalled that for many girls, rural as well as urban, training as a midwife was a way of escaping the confines of a traditional way of life. For Jews, and a highly disproportionate number of midwives were Jews (25 percent of those in training in 1910),[28] it meant freedom to live outside the Pale of Settlement. For peasant girls, however they happened to be chosen, midwifery meant emancipation from the patriarchal structure of the village. For the idealistic and politically committed among the educated youth, it offered a skill with which they could serve the people.[29] For all women it was a profession which offered at least the possibility of an autonomous life.

The urban preferences of most midwives, like the failure of efforts to provide trained midwives for the peasantry, cannot be understood without some reference to the peasants themselves. The fundamental and unpleasant fact facing physicians and medical reformers alike was the peasantry's reluctance to call upon the midwives who had been trained for them. The rural midwives themselves, of course, found this reluctance not only economically ruinous but also detrimental to their professional skills. How can the rural population's persistent preference for local *povitukhi* be explained?

In answering this question, it is necessary to consider the broader problem of childbirth in Russian peasant society. Customs differed from area to area, and no absolute rules can be offered; however, a number of generalizations seem both valid and germane. First, for the peasant woman parturition was a private, almost secret act surrounded with a great deal of custom and superstition.[30] Pregnancy itself was considered a particularly vulnerable time for a woman, and parturition even more so. One of the great fears was that a stranger would "give her the evil eye" (*sglazit' ee*), causing

28. *Ibid.*, p. 8 ob, 9.

29. For an excellent memoir recording the experiences of such a woman, see Anna A., "Na zemskoi sluzhbe. Iz zapisok fel'dsheritsy," *Vestnik Evropy*, 25, no. 12 (December, 1890): 549–593.

30. For a more detailed discussion of peasant attitudes toward childbirth, see Antonina Martynova's essay in this collection.

harm to her child. In many cases peasant women gave birth without any assistance at all. Birth could occur in a number of places, but ideally it did not take place inside the peasant house *(izba)* itself. The *bania* or peasant sauna was preferred, where one existed, and birth frequently took place in the cattle shed or grain storehouse. Since peasant women usually worked right up until delivery, childbirth in the fields was not unusual during the summer months.[31]

Most women gave birth with the help of a *povitukha*. This *povitukha* (or in some cases *znakharka,* or medicine woman) was generally an older peasant woman known in the local area. Often she was a widow, and in most cases she had borne children herself. For her, as for most peasants, birth was not simply a medical phenomenon but the beginning of a life, a mystical event to be accompanied and eased by the appropriate rituals, prayers, and sayings *(zagovory).* There seems little reason to doubt that such *povitukhi* were also capable assistants in cases where birth was normal. In addition to providing the practical and religious support just described, the *povitukha* generally took over household chores for the family for two or three days, allowing the mother to recuperate. This service was highly valued by the peasantry and was more important in accounting for the *povitukha*'s popularity than adherence to tradition, if we are to judge by physicians' reports. Someone had to continue the operation of the house—cutting wood, bringing water indoors, firing the stove, preparing meals, caring for other children, feeding and watering the livestock, milking the cow, and so on. The father or relatives might assume some of these tasks, but frequently their own work did not allow them to do everything. For the mother, the performance of arduous tasks immediately after giving birth, particularly in inclement weather, could bring great harm, causing post-natal complications which could maim and even kill.[32]

Because of the need to relieve the mother, the *povitukha* was often a necessity even in cases where a trained midwife was invited to assist at birth. To invite both was usually more expensive, so peasants contented themselves with the *povitukha*, resorting to trained midwives only in emergencies. In reform proposals, physi-

31. G. E. Rein, *O russkom narodnom akusherstve* (St. Petersburg, 1889).

32. Zhuk, *Shkola sel'skikh povival'nykh babok,* p. 511. See also A. G. Arkhangel'skaia, "K istorii razvitiia rodovspomozheniia v zemskikh guberniiakh," *Zhurnal akusherstva i zhenskikh boleznei,* 12 (April, 1898): 456.

cians repeatedly insisted that trained midwives should be willing to assume the chores which the *povitukhi* saw as an integral part of their work. In all likelihood the peasants themselves were not willing to accept the performance of chores by urban women, even those who did not see themselves as being above it. Lack of skills in rural tasks is another possible problem which should be kept in mind.

The cultural proximity of the *povitukhi*, the practical services they performed, and their relative cheapness were important reasons for their popularity among the peasantry, but there were other reasons as well. The *povitukhi* had the advantages of age, experience, and tradition over the younger, newly trained midwives of the 1860s and 1870s. It does not seem unreasonble, or even unenlightened, that the peasantry should have valued these traits. It is also clear that the *povitukhi* themselves were not disinterested bystanders, indifferent to the appearance of professional competitors. They ridiculed their rivals, sensing correctly that the midwives' youth (some were not mothers themselves) and their neglect of religious custom were serious disadvantages before a traditional audience. And there is no reason to doubt that they believed their own arguments.[33]

The most important single reason for the *povitukhi*'s sustained popularity is that midwives trained for the countryside were rarely able to demonstrate their purely medical superiority and win confidence through results. Doubtless the stories of the *povitukhi*'s barbaric, even grotesque, efforts in cases involving difficult births have some basis in fact. But the trained midwife, confronted with the same cases, could do no better. She could of course take no action at all, summoning a physician instead (a procedure which both her training and the law required). But the condition of the expectant mother and the remoteness of the nearest physician did not always make this alternative practical. Her efforts to proceed on her own might be no more successful than those of a *povitukha*, but her inability or refusal to act was, in the peasants' eyes, an admission of incompetence greater than the *povitukha*'s failure, and it controverted any claims she might have to superior knowledge. In cases where birth occurred without complications, the *povitukha* seems to have been as competent as a trained midwife.

33. For a good description of this conflict, see I. A. Larin, "Narodnaia meditsina Astrakhanskoi gubernii," *Russkii meditsinskii vestnik*, 6, no. 17 (September, 1904): 583–86.

The trained midwives' inability to demonstrate their medical superiority, and the peasantry's coincidental inability to perceive that superiority, was grounded in the fact that such superiority was marginal where it existed at all. Physicians' low assessments of rural midwives' abilities tend to confirm this. Surveying the state of midwife training in Russia in 1870, Dr. I. M. Tarnovskii reported to the Ministry of Internal Affairs that "midwives with their present education satisfy neither the demands of society nor those of physicians."[34] This view would be echoed throughout the rest of the century. The local and provincial governments' refusal to create more positions for trained midwives and to pay them better was directly connected with this generally shared view of their limited abilities. Such goverments found it more rational to invest what funds there were in the hiring of physicians, *fel'dshers*, and female *fel'dshers* with training as midwives.

When turn-of-the-century physicians contemplated the failure of efforts to provide modern obstetric care for the countryside,[35] several alternative solutions were offered. The first was the possibility of training the *povitukhi*, since these women already enjoyed popular confidence. Actually, this frequently occurred in an informal way, with either physicians or trained midwives giving *povitukhi* advice on techniques of delivery, and particularly on the need for antiseptic precautions.[36] There had also been at least one formal attempt to recruit *povitukhi* for a one-month crash course in modern obstetrics. The results of that training session, conducted in Saratov Province in 1888, had not been promising, although physicians there did not exclude the possibility of renewed attempts. Ironically, formal study tended to undermine rather than enhance the authority of the *povitukhi* who participated. The physician in charge, A. I. Sukhodeeva, reported that on their return to the village the population faulted them because, "having

34. Tarnovskii did go on to state that "in spite of the extremely limited nature of their knowledge and a very inadequate system of instruction there can still not be the slightest doubt that trained midwives render society a much greater service than rural *povitukhi* who have studied nothing." *TsGIA*, f. 1294, op. 6, d. 54, pp. 2–3.

35. The most significant meeting devoted to this subject was held at the ninth congress of the Pirogov Society in 1906. For papers delivered and discussion as well, see volume 6 of the *Trudy IX-go Pirogovskogo s"ezda* (St. Petersburg, 1906). This was also published separately by G. E. Rein as *Rodovspomozhenie v Rossii (Sbornik dokladov na IX Pirogovskom s"ezde)* (St. Petersburg, 1906).

36. Arkhangel'skaia, "K istorii razvitiia rodovspomozheniia," pp. 461–68.

studied a whole month, they still couldn't cure diseases, and tended to call for a physician at births more frequently than their untrained counterparts."[37]

Because of its author's prominence and the nature of the debate it generated, the most significant proposal was one made in 1899 by Professor Dmitrii Ott, the director of the Imperial Clinical Obstetric Institute in St. Petersburg.[38] Chairman of a special Pirogov Society committee charged with making recommendations on rural midwifery, Ott essentially reiterated the basic positions advocated by reformers during the 1860s. He urged a renewed effort to recruit peasant girls to study obstetrics for eight months in a provincial hospital, after which they would be returned to the countryside. He recognized that this suggestion was not new, but insisted that earlier attempts had failed not because they were wrong in principle, but because they had not been properly implemented.

Ott argued that the existing state of rural obstetric care in Russia demanded some departure from the medical ideals which he assumed all physicians shared. "At the present time," he wrote, "we have a choice. We can either leave things in the sad condition which obtains everywhere, making our peace with the horrible mortality rate among parturient women. Or, without rejecting the ideals we all have in our minds, we can seek through a temporary measure to decrease popular suffering."[39] The reaction of most physicians to Ott's project was negative, indicating that a change had taken place since the 1860s in their attitude toward the importance of recruiting rural midwives from among the peasantry. Most thought it impossible to train a competent midwife in only eight months, pointing to the unsatisfactory qualifications even of those who had been trained for two years.[40] To accept Ott's proposals, they argued, would only serve to legitimate and entrench dangerously incompetent personnel. Moved by these arguments, the Seventh

37. *Gubernskie s"ezdy i soveshchaniia zemskikh vrachei i predstavitelei zemskikh uprav Saratovskoi gubernii s 1876 po 1894 god. (Svod postanovlenii)*, ed. P. A. Kalinin and N. I. Teziakov (Saratov, 1894), p. 53.
38. Ott, *Proekt organizatsii*.
39. *Ibid.*, p. 6.
40. For a local response, see *Vrachebnaia khronika Khar'kovskoi gub.*, 3, no. 5 (Khar'kov, 1899): 315.

Congress of the Pirogov Society rejected Ott's proposal as "one which contradicts the basic tasks of *zemstvo* medical organization."[41] Underlying this rejection was not only a different estimate of the extent to which certain ideal standards would have to be placed temporarily in abeyance because of Russia's backwardness, but also a clear emphasis on expertise as the exclusive legitimate criterion in the choice of medical personnel. Not all physicians shared this view, of course, and the argument that only peasants would be able to penetrate the countryside was one that retained many proponents. Nevertheless, at the turn of the century the problem, as it was conceived by most physicians working in local governments, involved not the recruitment of peasant girls but the placement in the village of the increasing numbers of talented urban girls who were already studying midwifery. Their commitment to their profession and their overall intellectual superiority made a return to the programs of the 1860s an unacceptable solution for most physicians.

An increasing number of *zemstva* sought to place such urban women in the countryside by training them not only as midwives, but as *fel'dshers* as well, giving them the title of *fel'dsher*-midwife (*fel'dsheritsa-akusherka*).[42] The *fel'dsher* had a broader general preparation in medicine than the midwife, generally four years and sometimes five. Prior to their medical educations, all *fel'dshers* had completed at least four years of gymnasium or its equivalent. Female *fel'dshers* tended to have more general education than their male counterparts, and physicians considered them to be the best-trained auxiliary medical personnel in pre-revolutionary Russia.

Combining *fel'dsher* and midwife in one person had several practical advantages. For the rural employer, whether *zemstvo* or otherwise, hiring a *fel'dsher*-midwife served two purposes at the same time. Moreover, experience showed that the combination also tended to promote the obstetric practice of the female *fel'dsher*, thus making real inroads on the territory of the *povitukhi*. The midwife's limited obstetric practice had, in a sense, been

41. A. P. Artem'ev, "Kak trudno byt' sostavitelem proekta organizatsii akusherskoi pomoshchi v Rossii," *Zhurnal akusherstva i zhenskikh boleznei*, 14 (February, 1900): 1.

42. The Medical Soviet had recognized the superiority of schools which combined *fel'dsher* and midwife training as early as the 1880s. A combined course was allowed for the first time in 1879 in a school in Kishinev. I. V. Bertenson, "Vrachebno-professional'noe obrazovanie zhenshchin v Rossii," *Vestnik Evropy*, 25, no. 11 (November, 1890): 224–225.

self-reinforcing. Called only periodically to assist at peasant births (often to those which were already beyond any medical help), they had little opportunity to win popular confidence by exercising their trade. The female *fel'dsher*-midwife, in her first role, was able to ingratiate herself with the peasantry through the successful treatment of minor illnesses and injuries. Having established herself as a healer in a large number of cases, her reputation grew more rapidly, and the personal relationship and confidence important to peasants at childbirth were created. There were arguments against the growing emphasis on the training of *fel'dsher*-midwives, primarily that the all-consuming nature of the *fel'dsher*'s general medical practice would not allow her the time to function effectively as a midwife. These arguments were not validated by experience, however, and the growing tendency was to provide all medical personnel, male as well as female, with courses in obstetrics and gynecology. In critical cases, the peasantry understandably turned to whatever medical care was at hand, so most *fel'dshers*, whatever their training, assisted at births from time to time.

The problems which beset medical reformers interested in rural obstetric care were much the same as those in other areas of development. As in the more obvious fields of education, or even political reform, obstetric reform was but a chapter in the conflict between the rational and secular culture of the West, which had taken root in the city, and the more tradition-bound world of the Russian village. The central question of Russian development —that is, the extent to which Russia was different from the countries of western Europe, and the extent to which solutions adopted there were applicable to Russia—was mirrored in almost all discussions of rural obstetric care. It was posed exactly in Professor Ott's terms: To what extent should the highest possible medical standards be sacrificed temporarily in order to meet the peculiar and desperate needs of the Russian countryside?

There is no reason to expect a country's general approach to its medical problems (in this case, those of obstetric care) to differ radically from its attempts to solve other problems. In the case of medicine, of course, there is a body of specialized scientific knowledge which differentiates it from other areas of public life; however, the social and economic difficulties encountered in applying that knowledge are, not surprisingly, similar to those encountered by others interested in development. The interrelated character of such problems as education and health care suggests that any major change in one area would affect and be dependent upon changes in others. In the case of obstetric care, it was impossible to alter customs concerning something as intimate as childbirth until the cultural assumptions of the society being affected had themselves been changed. Physicians of the 1860s were aware of this, despite their understandable efforts to isolate the problem of obstetric care from the broader problems of cultural backwardness. As one of their number put it, "As long as the idea of having rural midwives is not a popular one, attempts to introduce them will be unsuccessful."[43] The midwife herself was not a passive observer in this drama, and if she was to be anything but a *povitukha*, she had to become a cultural missionary as well as a medical practitioner. The number of midwives who were able to perform such a role was small, and regular access to qualified obstetric care became a reality only well into the Soviet period.

43. *TsGIA*, f. 1297, op. 142, d. 292, p. 337.

NANCY M. FRIEDEN

Child Care: Medical Reform in a Traditionalist Culture

The threat of disease and death hovered over most infants and children in pre-revolutionary Russia. In 1900 Russia had the highest infant mortality rate in Europe: 275 of every 1,000 newborns died in their first year. Today the rate is only 25 per 1,000.[1] Although this achievement is, in part, the consequence of scientific advance and expanded health administration, medical and administrative skills alone could not have effected health reform. In the mid-nineteenth century Russian physicians began to combat illiteracy and cultural backwardness, the fundamental obstacles to medical progress. When they attempted to introduce new health concepts, they confronted timeless customs among the lower classes, who resisted unfamiliar health practices that challenged their way of life. Methods of infant and child care were especially intractable, undoubtedly because child-rearing is inextricably bound up with family structure and tradition. Only after the 1917 Revolution transformed Russian society could the reform of child care make rapid progress. Nevertheless, medical reformers of the pre-revolutionary

For research and travel support the author wishes to thank the National Library of Medicine (NIH Grant 1 RO1 LM 02590), the International Research and Exchanges Board, and the Ministry of higher and specialized education of the USSR. Special thanks for great courtesy and assistance are also due to the staffs of the Central State Historical Archives of the USSR in Leningrad and the Central State Medical-Scientific Library of the USSR in Moscow.

1. E. A. Osipov, I. A. Popov, and P. I. Kurkin, *Russkaia zemskaia meditsina* (Moscow, 1899), p. 29, and V. D. Markuzon, *Kak sokhranit' zdorov'e rebenka: ukhod i vskarmlivanie v grudnom vozraste*, 3rd ed. (Moscow, 1923), p. 161. Markuzon shows a graph (p. 164) with the following approximate statistics for deaths during the first year of life (termed "infant mortality") for 1900: Russia—275 per 1,000 live births, Austria—220, France—160, England—140, Sweden—90, Norway—80. *Historical Statistics of the United States: Colonial Times to 1970* (Washington, D.C., 1975), B181–192, gives the figure of 162.4 per 1,000 live births in the United States in 1900.

period contributed to that ultimate success. Their programs of hygiene education and nursery care, introduced in the years 1890–1905, laid the foundation for later accomplishments in the field of infant and child health.

Numerous statistical studies demonstrated the fragility of life during infancy and childhood in nineteenth-century Russia. A survey of an area of Moscow Province for the years 1864–79 showed that of 1,000 newborns, 519 died in their first year and 687 before the age of ten. In 1899 a respected authority reported that 426 of every 1,000 children born in European Russia died before the age of five.[2] The basic hazards, infectious diseases and extremely high mortality in the early months of life, reflected the general health conditions of the period. High infant mortality, a phenomenon that had not been satisfactorily explained, seemed to correlate with the abject living conditions of the lower classes.[3] Infectious disease accounted for 30–40 percent of the nation's total deaths and was considered a primary cause of child mortality. Medical science had developed few defenses against contagious disease in the nineteenth century, an era before the major bacteriological breakthroughs and the discovery of miracle drugs. Although Catherine the Great (1762–96) introduced smallpox inoculation in 1768, and in the nineteenth century the central government trained thousands of peasants to be vaccinators, in 1850 less than half the

2. P. A. Peskov, "Opisanie Durykinskoi volosti Moskovskogo uezda v sanitarnom otnoshenii," *Sbornik statisticheskikh svedenii po moskovskoi gubernii. Otdel sanitarnoi statistiki* (Moscow, 1879), vol. 1, no. 3, pp. 67–68; Osipov *et al., Russkaia zemskaia meditsina,* p. 28; O. A. Aleksandrov and Iu. P. Lisitsyn, *Sovetskoe zdravookhranenie* (Moscow, 1972), p. 137. G. I. Arkhangel'skii, "Zhizn' v Peterburge po statisticheskim dannym," *Arkhiv sudebnoi meditsiny i obshchestvennoi gigieny* 2 (1869), Section 3, p. 52, reported that mortality during the first year of life was 748 per 1,000 in St. Petersburg, compared to 267 in Brussels.

3. Medical administrators in the 1850s recognized the close relationship between living conditions and mortality: Tsentral'nyi gosudarstvennyi istoricheskii arkhiv-SSSR, f. 1297, op. 97, d. 68–69. "Otchety glavnogo medika ministerstva gosudarstvennykh imushchestv za 1852, 1853." At the turn of the century A. I. Shingarev's homestead study of health conditions as correlated with economic well-being provided concrete evidence for the empirical views. First published as "Selo Novozhivotinskoe i derevnia Mokhovatka v sanitarnom otnoshenii. Opyt sanitarno-ekonomicheskogo issledovaniia vymiraiushchei derevni," *Saratovskaia zemskaia nedelia,* 1901, nos. 38–41, it was republished with added political interpretations as *Vymiraiushchaia derevnia* (St. Petersburg, 1907). For the impact of infectious disease on infant and child mortality, see P. E. Zabludovskii, *Istoriia otechestvennoi meditsiny.* vol. 1: *Period do 1917 god* (Moscow, 1960), p. 349, and Aleksandrov and Lisitsyn, *Sovetskoe zdravookhranenie,* p. 137. The primary causes of infant mortality were undoubtedly impure water and milk supplies (the source of typhoid and other serious infectious diseases) and malnutrition.

population had been vaccinated.[4] No methods of immunization protected against the other numerous and often fatal childhood diseases. Some of Anton Chekhov's stories indicate the sudden, terrifying impact of diphtheria, typhus, and other highly contagious diseases; the statistics reveal how pervasive and devastating these illnesses actually were, and how little had been accomplished to limit their impact.[5]

Rampant epidemics and high infant mortality rates existed in western Europe also in the early nineteenth century. After mid-century, medical reformers in the West achieved considerable success with preventive measures such as improved sanitation and water supply, and hygiene education to train the public to take necessary precautions in times of crisis. Active interest in medical reform developed in Russia in the 1860s, reflecting the general upsurge of public activity with a particular emphasis on scientific advance. Physicians naturally looked to the West for guidelines, for some medical reformers had trained or traveled abroad, and the Russian medical press carefully reported foreign public health advances.[6] Unfortunately, Russia presented a special case, one that would not respond well to the mere importation of improved scientific methods. The prophylactic approach that worked well in the West required a number of preconditions, such as an adequate number of medical personnel, efficient medical administration, and a literate, cooperative populace. Russia lacked these fundamental elements. A scarcity of physicians and an inadequate public health administration presented major handicaps. But the most serious defect was Russia's cultural backwardness.

4. V. O. Gubert', *Ospa i ospivivanie* (St. Petersburg, 1898), pp. 255–290; N. M. Druzhinin, *Gosudarstvennye krest'iane i reforma P. D. Kiseleva* (Moscow, 1946, 1958), II, 267.
5. See, *e.g.*, Chekhov's "Typhus" and "Enemies"; the latter opens with a father mourning his six-year-old son, who has just died of diphtheria. *Vrach*, 1883, no. 11, p. 173, reported that in the years 1876–80 there were 343,007 cases of diphtheria resulting in 128,916 deaths. Cholera, a major killer in the nineteenth century, was known to be especially fatal to children.
6. I. V. Vengrova, *Iz istorii sotsial'noi gigieny v Anglii XIX veka* (Moscow, 1970), pp. 190–217, treats the awareness of English advances among Russian physicians. The rapidly developing medical press gave extensive coverage to western public health advances; see esp. *Meditsinskii vestnik*, *Moskovskaia meditsinskaia gazeta*, and *Arkhiv sudebnoi meditsiny i obshchestvennoi gigieny* in the 1860s. A. P. Zhuk, *Razvitie obshchestvenno-meditsinskoi mysli v Rossii v 60–70-e godakh XIX veka* (Moscow, 1963), reviews the medical thought of the 1860s and 1870s.

Illiteracy, compounded by ignorance, fatalism, distorted religiosity, and centuries of tradition reigned in the countryside. Russia's low rate of literacy—21.1 percent in 1897—greatly impeded the development of preventive medicine on the western model.[7] Most peasant women were completely unaware of the mechanism of contagion; they failed to realize that they practiced a lethal custom when they gave away, as "gifts in memory," the clothing of children who had died of virulent diseases. Peasants frequently hid sick children, fearing that they would be removed to dreaded isolation barracks, and thus a highly contagious case of diphtheria, scarlet fever, or measles could infect all the children of a village and even engulf an entire province. During the numerous epidemics in nineteenth-century Russia, physicians who tried to introduce preventive measures frequently clashed with traditional attitudes and practices. At times the consequences reached tragic dimensions. The uneducated lower classes often viewed a devastating epidemic as God's punishment for their sins and objected to interfering with His holy intent. Although many of the clergy cooperated with physicians, others refused to recognize official regulations that restricted funeral ceremonies to small groups; they conducted large services with the open coffin displayed, providing a source of infection for all who attended and who usually gave the corpse a parting kiss. The clergy also led ritualistic processions to supplicate divine deliverance from the disease; carrying church relics, people took part in day-long marches through their towns, visited all infected patients, and thereby helped to spread the epidemic.[8] Besides increasing the contagion, these practices provoked violent conflicts. Traditionally, during epidemics the police drew quarantine cordons around affected areas, forced patients into isolation barracks where the great majority died, dispersed all large gatherings, and then dealt brutally with the inevitable conse-

7. Arcadius Kahan, "Social Structure, Public Policy, and the Development of Education and the Economy in Czarist Russia," in *Education and Economic Development*, ed. C. Arnold Anderson and Mary Jean Bowman (Chicago, 1970), p. 368, table 4, gives the literacy rate for Russia in 1897 as 21.1; it was 29.3 for males and 13.1 for females.

8. See, *e.g.*, M. Lion, *Beseda vracha s krest'ianami ob ospe* (Kiev: Kievskoe Obshchestvo gramotnosti, no. 4, 1898); Pirogovskaia komissiia po rasprostraneniiu gigienicheskikh znanii v narode (hereafter, Pirogov Commission), leaflet no. 2, "O skarlatine," and pamphlet no. 5, A. E. Pombrak, *O zaraznykh ili prilipchivykh bolezniakh* (Moscow, 1903). For typical medical reports on the difficulties during cholera epidemics, see *Dnevnik obshchestva vrachei pri imperatorskom kazanskom universitete*, 1893, nos. 1–3.

quences of these tactics—the mass riots that welled up against the authorities.[9]

The improvement of both general and child health thus demanded concerted educational efforts to acquaint the lower classes with more modern methods of medical care. Hygiene education became an integral part of the medical profession's efforts in the field of public health. At mid-century responsible medical administrators tried to bring hygiene information to the peasantry by initiating the settlement of physicians in rural areas, a project that provided the model for later programs of rural health protection.[10] After the Great Reforms, physicians working in the countryside encouraged the local self-governments *(zemstvos)* to begin programs of health education. The renowned surgeon and educator N. I. Pirogov (1810–81) set the guidelines, calling upon the physician to "be not only a healer but also an educator."[11] Lethargy and indifference on the part of local governments, as well as bureaucratic interference, often hindered physicians' educational efforts. The situation changed in the 1890s, when a devastating cholera epidemic, compounded by massive popular riots, demonstrated the compelling need to educate the populace to take necessary precautions and to cooperate with medical personnel during epidemics. The Pirogov Society (the national medical society, founded in 1883) met in 1894 and reviewed the calamitous events of the recent cholera crisis. The society resolved to establish a Commission for the Spread of Hygiene Education among the Populace and received governmental approval for the venture.[12] Hundreds of physicians became involved in the Commission's educational work, convinced that they could effect a social and cultural

9. Roderick E. McGrew, *Russia and the Cholera, 1823–1832* (Madison, Wis., 1965), pp. 109–128, 153–158 *et passim;* D. N. Zhbankov, *Kholernye epidemii v Smolenskoi gubernii, 1832–1872 gg.* (Smolensk, 1893).

10. For an account of this project, see my "Roots of Russian *Zemstvo* Medicine," *Proceedings of the Twenty-fifth International Congress of the History of Medicine,* Quebec, August, 1976. See also TsGIA-SSSR, f. 1297. op. 97, dd. 68, 69, 70, "Otchety glavnogo medika ministerstva gosudarstvennykh imushchestv."

11. "Nikolai Ivanovich Pirogov: 1872," *Russkaia starina* 52, no. 11 (November, 1886): 505–507. An early program is described in TsGIA-SSSR, f. 1297, op 27. d. 1124: "Po khodataistvu kostromskogo uezdnogo zemskogo sobraniia o razreshenii zemskim vracham prochest' v narodnykh uchilishchakh uezda neskol'ko lektsii."

12. *Vrach,* 1894, no. 2, pp. 51–52, See also my "Russian Cholera Epidemic, 1892–93, and Medical Professionalization," *Journal of Social History,* 10, no. 4 (June, 1977).

transformation of the unschooled lower classes in the interest of their better health.

The Pirogov Commission assumed responsibility for evaluating and publishing hygiene literature; it reviewed pamphlets already in print, approving some for a mass audience and others for secondary schools and for teachers' libraries. It recognized the need for more skillful writing, however, and commissioned pamphlets to meet specific criteria: clarity of presentation, scientific accuracy and terminology, attractive style devoid of condescension, and the use of diagrams to explain the functioning of the human body, the microscope, and bacteria. The Pirogov Commission approved for publication a series of pamphlets of about sixty pages that explained various diseases, their causes, prevention, and treatment; it also published, for mass distribution, one-page leaflets based on the longer pamphlets.[13]

The Pirogov Commission did not design its literature solely for a reading audience. The hygiene education program served a vital additional function, for it facilitated physicians' efforts to present health lectures to the uneducated lower classes. The Ministry of the Interior regarded educational work among the illiterate as a most suspicious activity. Whenever physicians wished to provide health information in a group setting, they could do so only with the permission of various local authorities, who required precise evidence of the contents of their proposed lectures. The Pirogov Commission's pamphlets helped to surmount this obstacle, for instead of merely submitting a general topic that they intended to discuss, physicians could now cite the pamphlets as the substance of their lectures and more easily receive approval.[14] Thus hygiene literature reached beyond the reading public, providing the core of health lectures in factories, schools, rural clinics, workers' clubs,

13. The extent of the Commission's work can be gauged from the 116-page listing of the hygiene literature it had reviewed and commissioned by 1904: Pirogovskaia Komissiia po shkol'noi gigiene i rasprostraneniiu gigienicheskikh znanii, *Spravochnik meditsinskikh narodnykh chtenii* (Moscow, 1904).

14. TsGIA-SSSR, f. 1284, op. 188–1902 g., d. 272, "O razreshenii Saratovskomu sanitarnomu obshchestvu uchredit' pri obshchestve voskresnuiu shkolu," indicates the rigid controls. V. V. Khizhniakov, *Spravochnaia knizhka dlia ustroistva populiarnykh meditsinskikh chtenii v S. Peterburgskoi gubernii* (St. Petersburg: 1901), provides a list of permitted publications and also advice to physicians on methods to obtain official permission for lectures.

and tea rooms. As the program grew, the Pirogov Commission provided slides to be projected with the lectures to demonstrate scientific aspects, and after the lectures members of the audience frequently received leaflets with a résumé of the oral presentation.[15]

In addition to workers and peasants, the audience for hygiene literature included *fel'dshers* (paramedics), teachers, and other members of the local intelligentsia. These *intelligenty*, many of whom had but recently emerged from the lower orders of society, needed guidance when they cooperated in such work as the improvement of sanitary conditions in schools, vaccination programs, medical statistical surveys, epidemic control, and the supervision of summer nurseries. Before the 1917 Revolution, the program had reached 10–20 million people in a nation of over 125 million.[16]

Analysis of the hygiene literature provides a dual image of Russian society—the living conditions of the lower classes, filtered through the perceptions of an educated, scientifically oriented group. An excellent source for information on popular health customs, child-rearing, and family relationships, this literature also reveals the authors' attitudes. Physicians had a distinct prejudice against popular customs. They battled ignorance, superstition, and pervasive unsanitary habits; when describing the evils of lower class life, they severely judged the conditions they observed. The introduction of preventive medicine had as its counterpart the destruction of the harmful past: the victory of medical expertise over superstition, of the educated physician over the witch doctor, of the wise patient who respected medical science over the foolish one who did not. The intended recipients of medical enlightenment might well resent and resist efforts to change their customary health practices.

15. *Zhurnal obshchestva russkikh vrachei v pamiat' N. I. Pirogova*, 45, nos. 1–4 (February-May, 1905): 41–44, 142–147, 269–277. Minutes of meetings of the editorial board and of lecture groups active in the city of Moscow in 1905, give a good picture of this work. This publication also carried an annual supplement reporting on the Commission's work.

16. In the pre-revoluntionary period, the Pirogov Commission published thirty-five different titles, with a press run of over eight million copies, according to Zabludovskii, *Istoriia otechestvennoi meditsiny*, I, 362. Between January, 1902, and October, 1903, the Commission printed 550,000 short leaflets and distributed all but 100,000, according to "Otchety o deiatel'nosti grupp," *Zhurnal obshchestva vrachei v pamiat' N. I. Pirogova*, 44, nos. 1–2 (January-March, 1904): supplement, p. 4.

All hygiene literature shared the assumption that modern methods must be substituted for traditional ways. This genre of literature can, however, be divided into two general categories, roughly corresponding to the degree of scientific knowledge about the problems addressed. After the advances in microscopy in the 1880s, scientists rapidly gained expertise on contagious diseases. By the end of the nineteenth century, medical science had discovered the etiology of and devised preventive measures for many epidemic diseases, such as smallpox, diphtheria, cholera, and malaria. Although the mechanisms of other contagious diseases remained obscure, physicians recognized the need for isolation, water purification, and other modes of prevention. Hygiene literature used this scientific information to counteract popular remedies and resistance to rational medical care.[17] Another body of literature dealt with problems lacking medical explanations. Many aspects of infant and child care fell within this category, for physicians had little besides empirical evidence on which to base advice to mothers. They focused primarily on nurturing and methods to improve the home environment, contending that cultural patterns of child-rearing and the unsanitary living conditions of the lower classes accounted for the high infant mortality rates.[18]

Hygiene literature concerning contagious diseases attacked prevalent superstitions and fears. The schismatic Old Believers, for example, refused to have their children vaccinated because it left what they termed the "mark of Anti-Christ." To overcome such resistance, a pamphlet on vaccination cited the high incidence of smallpox among Old Believers and described their villages, where one could see cripples, motherless families, ugliness, blindness, and needless suffering; the pamphlet then explained how the disease could be safely averted.[19] Popular practices also hindered the treatment of trachoma, a highly contagious eye disease prevalent in crowded conditions such as army barracks, factory housing, and

---

17. E. E. Eikhval'd, *Chto delat' v ozhidanii kholery i pri pervom eia poiavlenii?* (St. Petersburg, 1886); Pirogov Commission, leaflet no. 12, "O kholere." A similar approach is taken in Pirogov Commission leaflets nos. 1, 2, 3, 7, 8, 14, 15, on smallpox, scarlatina, syphilis, malaria, diphtheria, plague, and typhoid fever.

18. Pirogov Commission, leaflets nos. 4, 5, 17. "O rodakh," "O vskarmlivanii grudnykh detei, " "O shkol'nom privarke." For a full bibliography, see the *Spravochnik* listed above, n. 13, and *Spravochnik po sanitarnomu prosveshcheniiu. Muzeino-vystavochnoe delo,* ed. A. V. Mol'kov (Moscow, 1925).

19. Pirogov Commission, leaflet no. 1, "Kak uberech'sebia ot ospy."

schools. A leaflet urging reliance on trained medical personnel explained the dangers of folk remedies: witch doctors consulted for blindness often "treated" patients by licking their eyes—a dangerous procedure, the leaflet warned, for many witch doctors had syphilis and could transmit it in this manner.[20]

Superstitions about malaria abounded. In a pamphlet describing the need to eradicate swamps that bred the anopheles mosquito and emphasizing the value of quinine in treating malaria, the author first attacked popular beliefs about the source of the disease. He described an encounter with a coachman who complained of symptoms of *likhomanka,* a name derived from the belief that twelve sisters (*likhomanki,* or fever maidens), each with her own form of fever, travelled the roadways and infected whomever they met. To combat the fever maidens, witch doctors used such "cures" as "herbs mixed with vodka or spread on a cross . . . or as fumigation for patients"; or they advised the patient to lie on a board at night in a bathhouse until the fever maiden appeared, or to ride a slow horse beyond the fields until the fever fell. Realizing that the coachman had malaria, the author deplored the fact that "he had suffered for three weeks, listened to absurd stories of twelve *likhomanki* and performed foolish practices, when long since he could have been cured if he had consulted a physician. . . . The people [*narod*] know not whence come illnesses and therefore believe the witch doctors and the crones." Convinced that ignorance lay at the root of the problem, he argued that "there would be less sickness if people knew the causes of and how to prevent illnesses."[21]

In addition to ignorance and superstition, physicians confronted profoundly fatalistic attitudes. To arouse people from their passive acceptance of disease and death, physicians appealed to elemental emotions. "All know how dear is sight and what sadness there is without it," read a pamphlet on trachoma. "The blind person is helpless and defenseless as a child . . . lives as a burden to himself and to his near ones. For him there is no happiness in life, eternal night surrounds him."[22] Other pamphlets described villages decimated by diphtheria or scarlatina, the suffering of families when malaria-infected parents could not work, the heartbreak as well as

20. *Idem,* leaflet no. 11, "O bolezni glaz nazyvaimoi trakhomoiu."

21. *Idem,* pamphlet no. 7, N. A. Vigdorchik, *O bolotnoi likhoradke: Beseda* (Moscow, 1904), p. 5.

22. *Idem,* leaflet no. 11, "O bolezni glaz."

economic loss when all the children of a family succumbed to a contagious disease. With the audience's emotions thus aroused, pamphlets would then reveal the astounding fact that such great loss through illness did not exist in other parts of the world. Other governments had instituted malaria controls, eliminating areas of stagnant water that bred the anopheles mosquito, and distributing adequate amounts of quinine as both a preventative and a cure.[23] "Now in other lands," remarked a leaflet on smallpox, "few children are not vaccinated; for the past thirty years the German government has re-vaccinated every ten years and smallpox rarely occurs there." In contrast to these advances in the West, Russia had a deplorable record: "Unfortunately in Russia people do not provide the same protection for their children."[24] A leaflet on trachoma openly criticized the government for its neglect: "In no country in Europe is there such an enormous number of blind people as among us in Russia, where two out of every thousand are blind."[25] These comparisons obviously implied that Russia must take positive action to prevent needless illness and loss of life.

Many hygiene pamphlets stressed great progress in the conquest of disease as evidence that medical science could radically change health conditions. The contrast between current methods and the past, when little could be done to prevent disease, was a frequent theme: "In ancient times in all the world no disease ruined or disfigured as many people as did smallpox. Few were untouched by it. . . . Only a hundred years ago one of every fifteen people had smallpox, and three of every ten of those died, the rest becoming blind and weak. People knew not how to protect themselves against this dreadful sickness."[26] Dramatically the pamphlet on smallpox described Jenner's work, encouraging respect for progress and for the physicians who devoted their lives to the improvement of the general good. Similarly, a pamphlet on malaria explained recent discoveries about the disease; using pictures (or slides for a lecture based on the pamphlet), it showed the breeding of the anopheles mosquito and the transmission of the malaria parasite to humans.

23. *Idem*, pamphlet no. 7, *O bolotnoi likhoradke*, p. 63.
24. *Idem*, leaflet no. 1, "Kak uberech'sebia ot ospy."
25. *Idem*, leaflet no. 11, "O bolezni glaz," and the longer pamphlet on which is based, V. V. Khizhniakov, *O bolezni glaz nazyvaemoi trakhomoiu. Kak uberech' ot trakhomy svoi glaza i ne peredat' ee drugim. Sovety zdorovym i bol'nym* (Moscow, 1901).
26. Pirogov Commission, leaflet no. 1, "Kak uberech' sebia ot ospy."

Although serious and scientific, this pamphlet is a model of clarity, well designed for a non-scientific and even illiterate audience. The author obviously assumed that, after learning the facts, the audience would "laugh at the myth of the fever maidens" and seek proper medical advice for malaria.[27]

In contrast to educational efforts concerning diseases with a known etiology or therapy, guidance for the proper care of infants and children usually spoke to a different problem and in non-technical language. Instructions for mothers rarely included sophisticated information on modern science, microbes, or microscopes, but instead stressed the dangers of an unsanitary environment and of popular customs. Viewing the cultural and social conditions of homes in villages and factory towns as the primary causes of childhood illnesses, physicians stressed the need for rudimentary knowledge of cleanliness and nurturing. Usually they appealed to mothers' common sense, giving logical, clear arguments. But, in addition, they almost invariably had one specific axe to grind: the problem of the backwardness of the average Russian mother. To improve family health, physicians argued or implied, they must effect a drastic re-education of the women.

By the late nineteenth century, physicians had developed a generalized view of the average uneducated woman as an untrustworthy guardian of her family's health. In a society with gross illiteracy, where women as a group had the lowest literacy rate,[28] the peasant woman became a symbol of ignorance and superstition. Physicians' memoirs, reports on work during epidemics, and studies of village and factory conditions frequently described women whose attitudes seemed callous and negligent. Many medical workers responded with shock and despair when they confronted the peasantry's fatalism about their offspring. Treating a sick child, a physician might have to argue with a mother who insisted that it was God's will that the child die. Regarding infant mortality as some kind of divinely ordered means of population control, the peasant might say in resignation, "Many mouths—little bread," or "If the children do not die what will we do then? . . .

27. *Idem*, pamphlet no. 7, *O bolotnoi likhoradke*, p. 63.
28. Arcadius Kahan, "The 'Hereditary Workers' Hypothesis and the Development of a Factory Labor Force in Eighteenth- and Nineteenth-Century Russia," tables 1, 2, and 6, and "Social Structure, Public Policy, and the Development of Education," tables 2 and 4, in *Education and Economic Development*.

Soon there will be no place to stand in the house *(izba).*"[29] It was primarily the women as negligent mothers, witch doctors, untrained midwives, and bearers of old wives' tales whom the medical profession perceived as its major adversaries in the battle for health reform. Literature on child care combatted the unschooled woman's backward ways, her seeming lack of maternal instincts, and the various harmful practices born of ignorance and the conditions of her impoverished life.[30]

The conflict between popular child-care practices and the medical profession's opposing conceptions of infant and child care is evident in a hundred-page manual, *The Care of Young Children*, published in 1903.[31] The author, E. A. Pokrovskii, chief doctor at the Moscow Children's Hospital and an authority on popular health customs, sought to enlighten the average mother by giving basic advice in an easy, conversational manner, using logical arguments that presumed a modicum of natural good sense. He began by recalling a visit to a friend, a village priest. Pokrovskii found the priest overwhelmed with grief; he had just finished the funeral rites for five children, a devastating loss in a village of only one thousand. "Among my parishioners children die like flies," the priest lamented, and then vigorously protested the prevalent opinion that peasants considered children a burden and neglected them. Having worked for ten years among the peasantry, he insisted that they loved their children and made great sacrifices for them. Mothers exhausted from fieldwork spent sleepless nights caring for their infants, and they would travel far to seek help for a sick child. "We raise them," they would say to him, "so that little children will comfort us, when grown they will help us in our work, and after death remember us."[32] Pokrovskii acknowledged that infant mortality was exceedingly high in Russia: half of all children died before the age of fifteen, whereas in other lands the figure was only one-fourth or one-fifth. If Russia could reduce these losses, half a

---

29. D. I-va, "Iz zapisok zemskogo vracha," *Russkaia mysl'*, 5, no. 12 (December, 1884): 75; A. I. Shingarev, *Vymiraiushchaia derevnia*, p. 139; V. A. Posse, *Moi zhiznennyi put': Dorevoliutsionnyi period* (1864–1917gg.) (Moscow-Leningrad, 1929), pp. 91–97.
30. Lev Tolstoi based his play "The Power of Darkness" (1886) on an actual case of infanticide, according to David Magarshak, *The Storm and other Russian Plays* (New York, 1960), p. xi. Tolstoi portrays the women as the incarnation of evil, but also takes into account their poverty and ignorance.
31. E. A. Pokrovskii, *Ob ukhode za malymi det'mi* (Moscow, 1903).
32. *Ibid.*, p. 3.

million children would be saved each year. The major cause of sickness, blindness, crippling, and death, he asserted, was the average mother's faulty knowledge of how to feed and care for her children. At the priest's urgent request, Pokrovskii continued, he agreed to write a book to instruct the "dark people" *(temnye liudi)* on correct methods of child care.[33]

Care of Young Children discussed marriage, maternal health care, and childbirth, as well as infant and child care. Despite an underlying, implied judgment on the average peasant's coarse milieu, the manual adopted an optimistic attitude toward the potential for change. The book's cover set the tone, picturing a loving peasant household with a mother leaning over an infant's cradle, another child playing near the stove, and a third bouncing happily on the knee of a bearded, jovial father. The first section presents a major prerequisite for healthy children: a marriage between parents who are physically and psychologically healthy. Obviously referring to venereal disease, Pokrovskii noted that in 900 B.C. the law of ancient Persia prohibited the marriage of a diseased person, but that Russian law did not impose such restrictions. Nevertheless, he warned that those with "serious illness" who marry must realize that their disease will be transferred to their children, that "it is sinful and shameful to enter marriage if not cured, for they will not bring happiness to a family but sorrow and burdensome grief." A good marriage also required psychological harmony, mutual understanding, and a peaceful relationship. A husband's tyranny *(samodurstvo)* or a shrewish wife would create "inextinguishable hell for the spouses and a bitter existence for their children."[34] Moreover, a husband's sexual demands must be moderate and legal (that is, only when conception was possible, and not during pregnancy and nursing), and when intoxicated he must not commit the sin of forcing himself on his wife. Few other pamphlets used the fire-and-brimstone approach to defend peasant women against their menfolk, but many did suggest the difficulties of the peasant woman's life. One leaflet on childbirth explained the need for a modified workload before and after giving birth, and the importance of using a trained midwife. The arguments were neither ethical nor religious, but highly practical, based on the value to the

33. *Ibid.*, pp. 4–7.
34. *Ibid.*, p. 12.

family of the woman's work: "It is not easy for a woman to give birth and there is much danger to her before and afterwards. . . . Misfortune can befall her if she does not receive proper care. From an unsatisfactory birth a woman can contract many diseases and become a cripple for life, having no happiness, becoming a burden to her husband, and no longer a useful worker for the family."[35]

Pokrovskii dealt at length with childbirth customs that posed serious hazards to mother and child. For reasons of modesty, or "fear of being seen by the evil eye," some women preferred to give birth in bathhouses, barns, and other secluded places. While recognizing the virtue of modesty, Pokrovskii warned of the unhealthy consequences of such practices and described how to prepare a section of the peasant's cottage for childbirth. He also ridiculed the custom of dressing the newborn in the father's shirt and trousers "so that the father would love the child more and the child would have greater respect for the father."[36] This practice might cause great harm, for the clothes were harsh, abrasive, and probably germ-laden. Instead, infants needed soft, clean, loosely fitting clothes. They should not be swaddled, for tight binding could stunt a child's growth, cripple him, interfere with the breathing or blood supply, and even cause death.[37]

According to Pokrovskii, the key to infant health was breast feeding, and he relied on emotional, religious warnings to drive home his argument. Domestic animals nursing their young exemplified natural, God-given law; this law applied to humans as well, and it was "forbidden to go against the natural law of God." Contrary to common practice, the infant should be nursed soon after birth, without waiting several days for the priest's blessing or until the regular milk appeared. When fed anything other than the mother's milk, the infant became weak, sick, and usually died. It was, therefore, the mother's duty to breast feed, instead of "abandoning her child like an orphan to the arbitrary will of fate." She should know that if she failed to nurse her infant she could be guilty of her child's death, "the greatest sin a woman can commit against the law of God."[38] Pokrovskii also vigorously attacked the Russian version of a pacifier, the *soska*, a rag covering crumbled bread or

35. Pirogov Commission, leaflet no. 4: "O rodakh."
36. Pokrovskii, *Ob ukhode za malymi det'mi*, pp. 13–20.
37. *Ibid.*, pp. 15, 63.
38. *Ibid.*, pp. 21–29.

rolls, wet dough, or milk kasha—a device ripe with bacteria, especially when combined with milk, or, as was the custom, prechewed by an adult. Pokrovskii asserted that in England and Sweden, all mothers breast fed their offspring and never used pacifiers, and that consequently only 9–12 percent died in their first year, whereas in Russia 30–60 percent died. "And why? for no other reason than that foolish custom of using pacifiers."[39] Pokrovskii departed from his usual moderate approach when venting his wrath on this issue. He argued that one must respect the gains of human intelligence and disregard relatives who give dangerous advice: their claim that ancient habit constituted wisdom was ridiculous, for "if this were so, then we would still eat people as our forebears did."[40] Selecting the good and rejecting the harmful, mothers must heed scientific evidence, nurse their infants, and abandon the pacifier, the "cause of more deaths than plague, cholera and all other diseases in Russia."[41]

Turning to another aspect of the peasant's world, Pokrovskii assailed the use of corporal punishment. Beginning with a discussion of children's games, he stressed the healthy effects of happy play to "aid the child's growth as the sun does the flowers." Punishment, on the other hand, harms body and soul, as the peasants well knew, judging from their many proverbs against harsh discipline. Quoting sayings such as "Is the back guilty if the spirit decides?" "Force is death to the mind," and "Gentleness, not a rod on the back, breeds courage," he encouraged the peasantry to follow their own natural wisdom."[42]

Pokrovskii's book was highly representative of hygiene literature that attempted to counteract harmful customs and attitudes on family health by re-educating the women. These publications do have an aura of prejudice against women of the lower classes, whom physicians (both male and female) perceived as uninformed and sometimes negligent. Physicians knew that customs which discouraged a mother from nursing a newborn for its first few days of life could act as a screen for willful neglect, and that pacifiers posed dangers beyond the bacteria they carried, for they could quiet an unwanted, starving child. To combat the underlying fatalistic at-

39. *Ibid.*, pp. 41–44.
40. *Ibid.*, p. 45.
41. *Ibid.*, p. 46.
42. *Ibid.*, pp. 87–89.

titude toward child mortality, physicians persistently reiterated arguments on children's right to life, their value to their parents for work and care, and the sinfulness of child neglect.

It was not easy to extricate peasant women or female factory workers from age-old customs and socio-economic conditions that endangered their children. Lectures, pamphlets, and medical advice given in a busy local clinic could not overcome centuries of superstition or the average mother's exhaustion. It would be superficial and incorrect, however, to view the clash between modern medicine and popular child-rearing mores as merely one of science versus superstition. These mores were imbedded in the basic structure of the village household and received their vitality and continuity from that matrix. In areas where the peasant joint family existed, the mother of a first child was usually in her early twenties or younger, and lived in a complex household with other women kinfolk.[43] The older women could offer experienced advice on rearing children, and, more important, could provide actual assistance in caring for the newborn. Especially in the difficult early weeks after childbirth, the young mother received moral and psychological as well as physical support. During this period, so often marked by fatigue and feelings of inadequacy, it is unlikely that a peasant woman would reject such aid. If a new mother received conflicting advice from medical personnel, she would have difficulty implementing it when it contradicted the methods of her kin. The physician who tried to change ingrained practices waged a losing battle. He confronted a firmly entrenched mechanism of female interdependence and support.

Medical reformers confronted with durable and resilient popular traditions of health care eventually found a means to counteract the pattern of resistance. An innovation of the late nineteenth century, summer nurseries *(iasli-priiuty)* presented an unusual opportunity to circumvent and even overcome customary practices. Originally introduced to curb the steep rise in infant mortality during periods of intense fieldwork, the nurseries responded to a specific, critical need. Their long-range impact, however, was an essential shift in the structure and direction of medical education and reform.

By the turn of the century the need for and potential significance

43. Peter Czap, Jr., "Marriage and the Peasant Joint Family in the Era of Serfdom," in the present volume.

of the nurseries were evident. "Every year in villages throughout the land," began one pamphlet, "one can see the all-too-familiar sight of parents following tiny coffins to the cemetery," for in Russia hundreds of thousands of children "become ill and die like flies in autumn."[44] Medical statistics had pinpointed the fact that child mortality rose precipitously in the summer, and analyses of the contributing factors revealed that the period coincided with the time when many mothers worked long hours in the fields and either took their infants with them or left them poorly supervised or even completely unattended. If a nursing mother took her infant with her, she had little time to feed it; moreover, the hard work, heat, and lack of fluids cut her milk supply. More often children were left at home. A physician tried to persuade the *zemstvo* of Tver' Province to open summer nurseries; he used as an epigraph to his report a poem by Nekrasov, describing the typical, tragic village scene:

> The village suffering in the heat of the night. . .
> The neighbor's tiny son cries out—
> Fixing her kerchief the babushka goes out—
> The infant must be rocked.[45]

Rocking the cradle and using the germ-ridden pacifier hardly replaced breast feeding in the mother's absence. Moreover, substituting cereals and raw cow's milk for the very young caused illnesses, particularly the perennial, severe problems of diarrhea and dysentery. Underfed and left untreated, infants with diarrhea became dehydrated and did indeed "die like flies." Older children also suffered from neglect. Malnourished and unsupervised, they were prey to numerous hazards, especially the frequent fires caused by the inexperienced five- and six-year-old "nannies" left in charge of the household.[46] The Tver' physician argued in 1900 that Russia's high infant mortality rate was the consequence of this pattern of neglect. According to his figures, in Russia 305.3 of every 1000 born died in their first year, compared to England's rate of 14.5 percent.[47]

44. Pirogov Commission, pamphlet no. 4: A. I. Shingarev, *Iasli-priiuty dlia detei v derevniakh vo vremia letnei rabochei pory* (Moscow, 1904), p. 15.

45. P. F. Kudriavtsev, "O detskoi smertnosti v naselenii Tverskoi gubernii i bor'ba s nei pri pomoshchi iaslei-priiutov," *Trudy XIV-ogo s"ezda vrachei Tverskoi gubernii* (Tver', 1900), p. 98.

46. Shingarev, *Iasli-priiuty*, pp. 1–15.

47. Kudriavtsev, "O detskoi smertnosti," p. 100, presents the following comparative

Several *zemstvos* inaugurated summer nurseries to counteract child mortality during periods of intensive agricultural work. *Zemstvo* representatives argued for the financial as well as the health advantages of the nurseries. The *zemstvos* supported costly fire insurance for the peasantry; frequent fires in the summer, some believed, were often caused by children who had been left alone. The nurseries might help to remove this cause of fires, reduce the need for insurance, and also improve child care. In 1898 the Voronezh provincial *zemstvo* pioneered in the nursery movement by allocating funds for child care centers throughout the province. The nurseries provided meals, supervision, and the services of the local physician; all participating children received a medical examination and, if sick, were treated and cured before admission to the nursery.[48] The local physician thus gained a convenient opportunity to screen for congenital syphilis, trachoma, malaria, and other endemic diseases. The nursery day began about six o'clock when mothers brought their children on their way to work. Children were washed, combed, dressed in clean clothes, and fed; they remained there until the mothers' return, usually the same evening but sometimes after several days. Simple meals provided the infants pasteurized milk and the older children typical peasant fare, but with the precaution of eliminating the coarse grains that produced intestinal disturbances. Activities included games, listening to stories, and "learning to pray." The older children swam, and girls learned to sew and knit.[49]

At first the nurseries encountered resistance among the peasants, who wondered why strangers would want to care for their "habitually dirty and unruly children," and ugly rumors circulated about the evil intentions of the nurseries' directors. The policy of admitting the neediest children caused some peasants to "feel shame before their neighbors." Fathers in particular objected and

---

data on deaths per 1,000 born:

	Before one year old	Between first and second year	Total
England	145.19	57.05	202.26
Germany	235.07	64.28	299.35
Russia	305.25	110.90	416.15

48. N. I. Teziakov, "Obshchii obzor deiatel'nosti iaslei-priiutov," *Derevenskie letnie iasli-priiuty v Voronezhskoi gubernii letom 1899 goda* (Voronezh, 1900), pp. 1–15.
49. *Ibid.*, pp. 16–28.

sometimes insisted that the mothers bring the children home.[50] After the first year or two, however, the nurseries' popularity grew, and even in villages of Old Believers they gained support. After surveying the nurseries in Kostroma Province in 1904, a *zemstvo* physician reported that grateful parents thanked the directors for giving food and warm shelter to their hungry, unprotected children. "With tears in their eyes, crossing themselves, they say, 'Dai Bog! Good health to the *zemstvo* and to all of you!'"[51]

An unanticipated benefit accompanied the development of nurseries. Initially designed to counteract summer epidemics and infant mortality during the harvest, and to prevent summer fires, the nurseries quickly acquired the additional function of educational institutions. According to one report, "Mothers bringing their children see for the first time in their unhappy lives a place that graphically teaches good, sensible habits. . . . Where nurseries are well developed they are highly valued as a most welcome, perhaps sole educational and sanitary effort in the villages. They provide a preparatory stage for school and benefit from the close cooperation of the local teachers."[52] Dr. Teziakov of Voronezh considered the nurseries' educational impact one of their most significant contributions. "When the children enter the nursery," he wrote, "they seem so unsociable [*neliudimye*], but with their ensuing visits they become quite different from the savages [*dikari*] they were during their first days there."[53]

Regarding the nurseries' original purpose of health improvement, physicians perceived only limited gains, for after the brief period of nursery care the children returned to their disease-laden environment. At the beginning of the twentieth century, infant mortality had reached 1.5 million each year; nurseries might protect a few thousand children from death, but they could hardly solve the vast general problem. Instead, their major contribution continued to be educational, providing a means to spread among peasant women and growing girls "the correct views on the care and feeding of infants and children."[54] Instituted initially

50. *Ibid.*, pp. 32–34.
51. "Otchet sanitarnogo vracha 4-go okruga Kostromskoi gubernii P. A. Loshilova," *O khode meditsinskogo dela v Varnavinskom uezde, Kostromskoi gubernii v 1903–04 gg.* (Kostroma, 1905), pp. 17–18.
52. *Ibid.*
53. Teziakov, "Obshchii obzor," p. 29.
54. A. V. Solov'ev, "Ob ustroistve iasli-priiutov v letnee vremia," *Trudy 11-ogo*

to control illnesses during harvest time, nurseries evolved into important centers for demonstrating and propagating modern child-rearing techniques.

The Pirogov Commission for Hygiene Education published a pamphlet to encourage the peasantry to use the summer nurseries and to organize their own if such facilities had not been instituted in their region.[55] The pamphlet is attractively presented; its cover shows a baby in a sling, swinging from the slim branch of a tree while the mother works in a nearby field. The first pages explained the hazards of taking infants into the fields and of leaving children unattended. The author explained that for many years in foreign lands, and more recently in Russian factories, nurseries helped working mothers who could not be employed without such assistance. "Now in the countryside," he continued, "*zemstvos*, the clergy, teachers, landlords, charitable institutions and individuals, and even the peasants themselves" have begun to open nurseries during the time of hard field work. "What is their use?" he asked, and answered with an accounting of the many tragedies that befell children left alone. In the nurseries, however, "the milk is fresh, the clothes are clean, the baby remains well and satisfied, and if he should become sick the doctor is nearby to treat him. The parents can have peace of mind." The author then waged an emotional attack on the peasantry's fatalism about infant death: "Some say, 'Let them go to God . . . let them die, for we need the room,' but this is a great loss of the mother's efforts and her strength. Every child born deserves his life; . . . if he dies he will not be able to feed and care for his parents."[56] The Pirogov Commission's pamphlet explained how peasants could open their own nurseries; they should ask the district *zemstvo* board or local physician, who would help them find a supervisor, explain what was needed, arrange for the medical examinations, and locate a proper building. This task might be too difficult for a few people to undertake, but fortunately the peasantry had the advantage of the cooperative organization of the commune. Quoting the proverb, "The commune is an enormous person," the pamphlet suggested that the combined efforts of commune members, with each contributing only a few kopeks,

sobraniia chlenov i predstavitelei zemskogo uchrezhdeniia po vrachebno-sanitarnomu delu Vladimirskoi guberniu, May 27-June 5, 1905 (Vladimir, 1905), pp. 95–99.

55. Shingarev, *Iasli-priiuty*.
56. *Ibid.*, p. 16.

could create a nursery. Another proverb, "With threads the commune can make a shirt for the poor," suggested that the commune could make a "shirt" (the nursery) for the protection of small children.[57]

The medical profession's keen support of summer nurseries indicated changed attitudes toward health reform, based on the positive educational results achieved in these institutions.[58] In the 1890s physicians believed they could influence "the impenetrably dark realm of the popular masses" by reading and circulating hygiene literature, but they gradually became aware that such an approach, although helpful, could not change a problem as immense as Russia's cultural backwardness. Where women lived in abject poverty and unfathomable ignorance that crushed their maternal instincts, where the demands of work took precedence over child care, lectures could not produce a healthy populace. However, physicians knew that, to improve family health, they must change the traditional attitudes of women. Nurseries provided a shortcut. In these community institutions the local intelligentsia could teach children the rudiments of personal hygiene and encourage mothers to follow the nursery's routine and to discard such practices as swaddling and the use of the pacifier. So effective were the nurseries that some physicians sought to keep them open all year to maintain a line of communication between the educated members of rural society and those in need of informed advice. Where modern medicine vied with ingrained practices of an un-

57. *Ibid.*, p. 22.
58. A. I. Belozerov, *Iasli-priiuty v Voronezhkoi gubernii v 1905 g.* (Voronezh, 1905), p. 2, shows the growth of summer nurseries in Voronezh Province:

Year	Number of nurseries	Children served
1899	24	2,119
1900	36	3,019
1901	45	4,682
1902	98	12,266
1903	45	4,094
1905	52	8,054

B. B. Veselovski, *Istoriia zemstva za sorok let* (St. Petersburg, 1909), I, 320, presents a table showing that nineteen *zemstvo* provinces had summer nurseries between 1889 and 1905. In 1902 approximately 400 nurseries functioned, serving from 40,000 to 80,000 children. See also D. N. Zhabankov, *O deiatel'nosti sanitarnykh biuro i obshchestvenno-sanitarnykh uchrezhdenii v zemskoi Rossii* (Moscow, 1910), pp. 52–54, for an evaluation of the very limited effect of these institutions. He notes (p. 54, n. 1) that to be effective in Moscow province, 4,000 nurseries were needed, costing 250 rubles each, for a total cost of about one million rubles.

educated populace, these community institutions gave critical support to health reform.

The improvement of child care in pre-revolutionary Russia demanded confrontation with a tradition-bound people. Having diagnosed the basic ailment as cultural backwardness, physicians recommended education as the cure. The doctor's black bag carried not only medications, but also a strange mélange of leaflets on childbirth, baby care, and infectious diseases; given the primitive stage of medical therapy, the educational materials may have been the most useful of their medical wares. But publishing, distributing, and explaining these prescriptive materials were merely preliminary efforts. A fearful and suspicious public had to be convinced. In the village, moreover, a mechanism of mutual support among female family members perpetuated age-old methods of healing and of infant and child care. Summer nurseries provided an alternative means to overcome harmful popular customs. Indeed, they became a model for the future, when community organizations would become the focal points of hygiene education and child welfare activities. After 1905, with the rapid development of rural education, local schools appropriated new health responsibilities.[59] By the time of the 1917 Revolution, medical reformers routinely used these community institutions to gain greater control over the health and welfare of Russia's youngsters.

The Soviet government continued and measurably strengthened earlier programs of health protection and child welfare services. Soviet ideology, Lenin's particular interest in public health, and the eradication of illiteracy undoubtedly influenced this development.[60] General advances in medical science also contributed to improved health. However, the blueprints for Soviet public health programs were drawn long before 1917, and the element of continuity is especially evident in programs to improve child care. In the mid-1920s the Ministry of Health reactivated the Pirogov Commission for the Hygiene Education of the Populace,

59. Robert H. Dodge, "Zemstvo Health Surveys of School-Age Children and a Strategy for Health, 1910–1914," Eighth National Convention of the American Association for the Advancement of Slavic Studies, October 7, 1976, St. Louis.

60. M. N. Barsukov, *Velikaia oktiabr'skaia sotsialisticheskaia revoliutsiia i organizatsiia sovetskogo zdravookhraneniia (Oktiabr' 1917 g.—iiul' 1918 g.)* (Moscow, 1951); *Ocherki istorii zdravookhraneniia SSSR (1917–1956 gg.),* ed. M. I. Barsukov (Moscow, 1957).

appointing as its president the man who had served in that post from 1901 to 1919.[61] A new publication entitled "Sanitary Enlightenment" clearly expressed the medical reformers' persistent concern about conditions in the villages, where lack of hygiene education and modern medicine continued to endanger public welfare. The publication's first issue lauded nineteenth-century physicians for their service in the countryside and careful attention to educational needs. It also reiterated physicians' earlier prejudices against uneducated women. "Sanitary Enlightenment" quoted approvingly a pre-revolutionary physician's counsel that "whoever subjugates the peasant woman to culture also subjugates the village and opens wide the door to successful sanitary activity."[62] The Soviet physician, like his pre-revolutionary colleague, reasoned that medical reform must undermine the deleterious effects of popular custom, especially the influences of uneducated, tradition-bound women. Community organizations would continue to serve this function, but the difference lay in the state's greatly increased support for such institutions. The policy of drawing women out of the home into employment, and children into crèche and kindergarten, loosened the family controls that had obstructed modern child care practices.

Traditional ways succumbed to the modern, antiseptic world as the state successfully introduced an extensive network of nurseries, schools, and health clinics. These changes undoubtedly weakened the bonds among women kinfolk, affected age-old patterns of child care, and eroded some wholesome aspects of traditional family life. Martynova has demonstrated the contemporaneous decline of traditional lullabies,[63] a change that indicates the cultural costs of modernization. Most Russian children no longer experience the intimate family structure with multiple mothering; on the other hand, they no longer "die like flies in autumn."[64] The records of

61. A. V. Mol'kov (1870–1947) served as president of the Pirogov Commission before and after the 1917 Revolution. *Sanitarnoe Prosveshchenie: Sbornik I*, ed. I. D. Strashun and A. O. Edel'shtein, (Moscow, 1925), pp. 3–15, includes a welcoming address to Mol'kov on resuming his post, "Zavety proshlogo i zadachi dnia," his response, "V redaktsiiu 'Sanitarnogo Prosveshcheniia'," and a review article, L. Kanevskii, "K tridtsatiletiiu Pirogovskoi komissii." The Mol'kov archive is held by the Muzei instituta organizatsii zdravookhraneniia i istorii meditsiny im. N. A. Semashko, Moscow, f. 1 (1920–44).

62. *Sanitarnoe Prosveshchenie* (1925), p. 4.

63. Antonina Martynova, "Life of the Pre-revoluntionary Village as Reflected in Popular Lullabies," in the present volume.

64. Aleksandrov and Lisitsyn, *Sovetskoe zdravookhranenie*, p. 140, states that infant

infant and child health in pre-revolutionary Russia reveal few charms of an idealized, pre-industrial world. Progress in child health depended directly on the passing of traditional methods of child care.

---

mortality in 1970 was 25 per 1,000. *The Statesman's Year Book: Statistical and Historical Annual of the States of the World for the Year 1976–1977*, ed. John Paxton (New York, 1976) p. 1392, gives the infant death rate of 27.9 per 1,000 live births in Russia in 1974. *Statistical Abstract of the United States, 1975* (Washington, D. C., 1975), p. 51, gives the U.S. rate of 16.5 of 1000 in that year.

Section Five

Family Correlates of the
Urban Workforce

ROBERT EUGENE JOHNSON

Family Relations and the Rural-Urban Nexus: Patterns in the Hinterland of Moscow, 1880–1900

The connection between industrialization and patterns of family life has recently come under close scrutiny from historians and sociologists. As noted by David Ransel in the introduction to this volume, many cherished notions have been called into question, among them the "classical [extended] family of Western nostalgia"[1]—the idea that extended, multi-generational family units were characteristic of the pre-industrial past, but were superseded by the nuclear family, a unit better suited to the needs of modern society. Recent studies have suggested, on the contrary, that the nuclear family has been predominant in western society for many hundreds of years, and that the modern industrial system, rather than promoting this pattern, may in some instances have led to its modification.[2] Most researchers would still agree that there is a basic congruity between the small family unit and the modern industrial system, but would also emphasize the two-way nature of the relationship: family forms may be influenced by the course of industrial development, but they may themselves help to determine that course. Family and economic variables may both be affected by other factors such as ideology and tradition, and as a result societies which are developing in the same general direction may exhibit opposite trends in such areas as divorce, age at marriage, or illegitimacy.[3]

1. William Goode, *World Revolution and Family Patterns* (New York, 1970), p. 7.
2. Peter Laslett, "Mean Household Size in England since the Sixteenth Century," and Michael Anderson, "Household Structure and the Industrial Revolution: Mid-Nineteenth-Century Preston in Comparative Perspective," in *Household and Family in Past Time*, ed. Peter Laslett and Richard Wall (Cambridge, England, 1972), pp. 139, 156–158, 229ff.
3. Goode, *World Revolution*, pp. 10–25.

The experience of pre-revolutionary Russia is especially relevant to these investigations, standing in contrast to western nations' development in the pace and direction of industrial growth, as well as in the socio-political background against which growth occurred. One obvious difference, underscored in Peter Czap's contribution to the present volume, is that historically the small nuclear family was something of a rarity in Russia. Perhaps more fundamental is the fact that Russia, much more than England, France, or Germany, industrialized *as a peasant society*. This is not to suggest that other industrializing nations had no peasantry, or that their agrarian populations were sealed off from the industrial sector. Rather, the constant *interaction* between town and country, village and factory, constituted a peculiarly Russian pattern. In England and some other western nations, early generations of factory workers included many agriculturists who had been forced off the land. In Russia, from the time of Peter I to at least 1906, the growth of extractive and manufacturing industries was keyed to the institutions of peasant life—serfdom and the manorial economy in the eighteenth and early nineteenth centuries, and the village commune well into the twentieth century. For reasons which were traditional and juridical, ideological and pragmatic, the Russian worker often retained significant ties to the peasant village.

This aspect of Russian society has long been familiar to historians and economists, many of whom have tried to explain the distinctive features of Russia's economic and political history by referring to the "half-peasant" nature of the Russian worker.[4] Nevertheless, the effects of rural-urban ties upon family life have not been systematically explored. Available evidence makes it clear that, in an industrial area such as Moscow at the end of the nineteenth century, the population of towns and factories was effectively limited to persons of working age. Almost all workers were peasant migrants *(otkhodniki)* recruited from the countryside, and their living and working conditions were such that they could not maintain families in the towns. Bound to their native villages through taxation, land-redemption obligations, and the passport system, peasant workers nevertheless could and frequently did maintain wives and children

---

4. A well-known example is Alexander Gerschenkron's classic essay, "Economic Backwardness in Historical Perspective," in *The Progress of Underdeveloped Countries*, ed. B. Hoselitz (Chicago, 1952), pp. 7ff.

in the country. This practice was reinforced by a continuing pattern of two-way migration and short-term visiting.[5] Year-round workers still managed to return to the villages at Easter; wives, if they were unable to join in the factory work, could at least make occasional visits to their migrant husbands.[6] Grandmothers and other kin in the countryside provided the child care which factories lacked, enabling some mothers to join their spouses.[7]

This paper explores some implications of this novel pattern of family life, especially the demographic consequences in respect to age at marriage, fertility, and household size. While the limited data thus far uncovered do not yield definitive statements on these issues, it is possible to present some suggestions and tentative conclusions that will serve as guides for future study.

Moscow city and its surrounding provinces were chosen as a focus, by virtue of their importance as an industrial region and their long tradition of manufacturing and migrant labor (*otkhodni-chestvo*). Industrialization was more firmly established in Moscow than in most other localities; hence, its social dimensions should be easier to trace. Moreover, the Moscow region was the ethnographic as well as geographic heartland of Russia, inhabited by a largely homogeneous Great Russian population. Chance ethnic factors and variations were therefore less likely to have affected its family patterns.

One of the most convenient ways to examine family patterns is through statistics on marriage. Comparative studies have found a sharp contrast between "European" and "non-European" marital patterns in the modern era.[8] In general, the nations of northern and western Europe have shown a pattern of later marriage and a higher proportion of bachelors and spinsters than most other parts of the world. In this respect Russia and eastern Europe have generally exhibited a "non-European" pattern, in which marriage is early and almost universal.

5. R. E. Johnson, "Peasant Migration and the Russian Working Class: Moscow at the End of the Nineteenth Century," *Slavic Review* 35, no. 4 (December, 1976): 652–664.

6. Permission for such family visits was occasionally an issue in strikes and other labor disturbances. One such case was the June, 1894, strike at the Tsindel' cotton mill in Moscow city.

7. R. E. Johnson, "The Nature of the Russian Working Class: Social Characteristics of the Moscow Industrial Region" (Ph. D. dissertation, Cornell University, 1975), pp. 115ff.

8. J. Hajnal, "European Marriage Patterns in Perspective," in *Population in History*, ed. D. V. Glass and D. E. C. Eversley (London, 1965), pp. 101–106.

TABLE 1. AGE AND MARITAL STATUS (Single population as percentage of total population in selected age groups)

	Men			Women		
	20–24	25–29	45–49	20–24	25–29	45–49
Sweden (1900)	92	61	13	80	52	19
Moscow city-born[a] (1902)	84	54	23[b]	52	35	22[b]
Russia (1897)		41	4[b]		23	5.1[b]
Serbia (1900)	50	18	3	16	2	1

[a]Refers to persons born in the city and residing there at the time of the municipal census.
[b]Statistics include ages 40–49 instead of 45–49.
SOURCES: Sweden and Serbia: J. Hajnal, "European Marriage Patterns in Perspective," in D. V. Glass and D. E. C. Eversley, eds., *Population in History* (London: Edward Arnold Ltd., 1965), p. 101; Russia, 1897: Ministerstvo Vnutrennykh Del, *Pervaia vseobshchaia perepis' naseleniia rossiiskoi imperii, Obshchii svod dannykh perepisi 1897 g. po Imperii* (St. Petersburg, 1905), part 1, table 5, pp. 78–79; *Perepis' Moskvy 1902 g.* (Moscow, 1904–6), part 1, no. 1, section 1, table 4, pp. 9–10.

Table 1 presents comparative data on age and marital status in European Russia as a whole, in Sweden, in Serbia, and in the city-born population of Moscow city. The two non-Russian cases represent extreme examples of the "European" and "non-European" patterns. In general, the Russian figures seem much closer to the Serbian ones, and the Moscow city-born population closer to the Swedish pattern. (Rates of marriage among Moscow-born women are even lower than in Sweden.) Since the Russian national statistics pertain to a population overwhelmingly peasant in composition, it would be logical to picture the city and countryside as two opposite poles, analogous to the differences between Sweden and Serbia. At one extreme we find a society which is modern, technologically sophisticated, industrialized, and cosmopolitan; at the other, peasant backwardness. One could then adduce various factors in "modern" societies which should discourage or prevent marriage: increased labor mobility; low wages and lack of economic security; increased number of years devoted to education and specialized job training; overcrowding in unsanitary conditions; and a work situation in which, in contrast to agrarian society, a spouse and children are more a liability than an asset.

The foregoing analysis seems quite plausible; yet if it is taken a few steps further, problems and anomalies emerge. The apparently modern marital patterns found in Moscow city and Sweden, for example, seem to have occurred in some western nations as early as the fifteenth century.[9] Can they then be attributed to moderniza-

9. Laslett and Wall, eds., *Household and Family in Past Time*, p. 75.

tion? A more general problem is that the data in Table 1 refer to only one historical moment, from which long-term societal *trends* cannot readily be inferred. The observed differences between the Moscow statistics and those for Russia as a whole may reflect static urban-rural differences having little to do with education, technological advance, or industrialization. To determine whether (and how) marital patterns were changing over time, we need data from several different historical moments. Unfortunately, we have only one satisfactory national census for the entire pre-revolutionary history of Russia.

One way out of this dilemma is to look more closely at sub-groups within the city's population. Here factory workers and peasant migrants become especially interesting.[10] Born in the countryside, they spent much of their adult lives in cities, towns, and factories, and were exposed to most of the same "modernizing" pressures as the native urban population. If the argument outlined above is sound, we would expect these groups to occupy an intermediate position between the extremes of city-born and peasant marital patterns.

Table 2 presents age-specific rates of marriage for three major sub-groups: persons born in Moscow, migrants, and factory workers. "Migrants" include persons of all occupations and social estates, but the majority (roughly 75 percent) came from the peasantry. The category of factory workers, on the other hand, overlaps with the other two; over 90 percent of all workers were migrants, recruited almost exclusively from the peasantry, but the rest were city-born.[11] The peasant element was thus slightly more prominent among factory workers than in the total migrant population.

Looking first at males, we find that the proportion married was lowest among the city-born: at all ages, migrants and factory workers showed a greater tendency to marry. Male factory workers show slightly higher rates of marriage than other migrants, probably because of the higher proportion of non-peasants in the latter group.

10. Of all migrants of both sexes living in Moscow city, 10–15 percent were factory workers. Approximately the same number worked as artisans in smaller workshops, while the remainder were employed in domestic service, transport, and various small-scale service occupations. Over 90 percent of male migrants in Moscow were gainfully employed, and over 50 percent of females. *Perepis' Moskvy 1902 g.*, (Moscow, 1904), part 1, no. 2, table 2, pp. 8–10.

11. *Ibid.*, part 1, no. 1, section 1, table 5, p. 11; part 1, no. 2, table 2, p. 10.

TABLE 2. AGE AND MARITAL STATUS OF CITY-BORN, MIGRANTS, AND FACTORY WORKERS IN MOSCOW CITY (1902), COMPARED TO RUSSIA AS A WHOLE (1897)

Age	Percent Males Married	Percent Females Married
15–19:		
city-born	.5	8.7
migrant	3.6	12.5
factory	4.1	13.3
Russia	4.4	15.4
20–29:		
city-born	29.5	52.7
migrant	54.3	55.6
factory	63.4	59.7
Russia	58	76
30–39:		
city-born	65	61
migrant	83	61
factory	89	60
Russia	90	88
40–49:		
city-born	71	48
migrant	86	52
factory	90	50
Russia	92	81
50–59:		
city-born	70	30
migrant	80	35
factory	83	33
Russia	87	66

SOURCE: *Perepis' Moskvy 1902 g.*, part 1, no. 1, section 1, table IV, pp. 9–10; *ibid.*, part 1, no. 2, table III, pp. 12–15. For Russia, 1897, *Pervaia vseobshchaia perepis' naseleniia rossiiskoi imperii*, part 1, table 5, pp. 78–79.

When the statistics for workers and migrants are compared to those for all of Russia, they turn out to be almost indistinguishable. Instead of occupying an intermediate position between the "city" and "peasant" marital patterns, male workers and migrants seem to have married at least as readily as the peasant majority. Indeed, factory workers appear to have married even earlier than the national average—63.4 percent of workers in the age group 20–29 were married, as compared to 58 percent of males throughout Russia. (Female workers and migrants, on the other hand, show significantly lower rates, and will be discussed separately below.)

These figures cannot readily be explained by reference to a "peasantry in transition," whose members were progressing step by step from the backward village to the modern city. On the contrary, employment away from the native village seems to have reinforced or exaggerated the pre-existing marital pattern of peasant men. The apparent paradox can be explained by re-examining the concept of rural-urban interaction. Given the possibility of maintaining families in the countryside, peasant-workers may have encountered fewer obstacles to marriage than did "pure" peasants or city-born workers. Unlike other workers, they were not inhibited by the lack of housing or the high cost of living in the city; unlike other peasants, they were receiving a relatively reliable money income independent of their meagre land allotments.[12] From the available statistics, we cannot determine whether the wage-earning peasant youths were defying their fathers by contracting early marriages, or whether the migrant's wages, by enhancing the prosperity of the parental household, encouraged the parents to seek a daughter-in-law. In either case, the logic of the rural-urban nexus seems to have encouraged young men to marry early.

Indirect support for this hypothesis can be found in marriage statistics for the whole of Moscow Province. In the years 1883–97, the number of marriages per annum per 1,000 population varied directly with the state of the job market, especially in the more industrial sections.[13] Elsewhere in Russia, nuptiality was strongly influenced by the state of the agrarian economy. Provinces which were net exporters of grain exhibited above-average rates of marriage, while those which were net consumers generally had lower rates. In Moscow, however, industrial employment was a better determinant of economic security. The rate of marriage dropped

---

12. A recent study of marital patterns in rural England in the seventeeth and eighteenth centuries reached a similar conclusion: "Since marriage was conditioned upon economic independence, the stagnancy of the preindustrial economy created conditions which led to late marriage. This customary restraint on population growth was broken down by a series of economic changes which transformed peasants and artisans into agricultural and industrial proletarians. . . . When employment became available to all who were willing to sell their labour, it was no longer possible to maintain the equilibrating mechanism of postponed marriage because . . . there was no longer any reason to defer marriage." David Levine, "The Demographic Implications of Rural Industrialization: A Family Reconstitution Study of Shepshed, Leicestershire, 1600–1850," *Social History*, 2 (May, 1976): 191–192.

13. I. I. Kurkin, "Statistika dvizheniia naseleniia v moskovskoi gubernii v 1883–1897 gg.," *Sbornik statisticheskikh svedenii po moskovskoi gubernii*, Otdel sanitarnoi statistiki, 6, no. 6 (Moscow, 1902), pp. 32ff.

as low as 7.45 per 1,000 during the depression years around 1885 and 1891, and went as high as 8.7 in such "boom" years as 1888 or 1897.[14]

Moscow's municipal census of 1902 provides further evidence of the connection between nuptiality and out-migration in its statistics on the marital patterns of separate occupational groups. Table 3 compares male factory workers with two other categories: non-factory extractive and manufacturing *(dobyvaiushchii, obrabaty-vaiushchii)* workers, and those in transport. The former group, which included such occupations as carpenter, painter, blacksmith, or tailor, showed rates of marriage slightly higher than those of factory workers in the 15–to–19 year-old bracket, though slightly lower in the older brackets. The transport workers, on the other hand, had a rate more than twice as great as any in Table 2 for ages 15–19, and significantly higher than other occupations for ages 20–24 and 25–29. All three categories of workers were recruited predominantly from the peasantry (only 5 percent of transport workers and 7 percent of each other group had been born in Moscow), and the range of wages was approximately the same for all. The non-factory and transport workers, however, had more opportunity to travel back and forth between Moscow and the countryside; railway workers enjoyed the right of free travel, while

TABLE 3. AGE AND MARITAL STATUS OF MALES IN SELECTED OCCUPATIONAL CATEGORIES, MOSCOW, 1902

Age and occupation	Percent married
15–19:	
factory	4.1
other extractive and manufacturing	5.4
transport	9.8
20–24	
factory	48.8
other extractive and manufacturing	47.8
transport	54.1
25–29	
factory	77.9
other extractive and manufacturing	73.7
transport	78.5

SOURCE: *Perepis' Moskvy 1902 g.*, part 1, no. 2, table III, pp. 12–13 (my calculation).

14. *Ibid.*, pp. 31, 33.

carpenters and other artisans often hired themselves out as artels to work in the city on a seasonal basis. This mobility seems to have reinforced the effects of rural-urban ties, with the result that these workers married even earlier than their brethren at the factories.

Among women, *otkhodnichestvo* seems to have had the opposite effect. Instead of maintaining the "peasant" pattern of early marriages, female migrants and factory workers adapted themselves to the urban pattern. Their rates of marriage for all ages were lower than the rates for Russia as a whole; for all ages over twenty-five they are virtually indistinguishable from those of city-born women. The reasons for this phenomenon are not hard to find, especially in light of our previous discussion. Male migrants married earlier because they could leave their families in the countryside. To the extent that they did so, their wives were excluded from the population of the cities and factories—not all wives, certainly, but enough to have a serious impact on the census statistics. Although data are not immediately available, we can assume that wives who were pregnant, as well as those with very young children, would be the most likely to stay in the countryside.

There were several other reasons for the city to have attracted unmarried women from the countryside. One was the pattern of factory labor itself, while another was rooted in the very structure of post-Emancipation village life. At the factories, the last decades of the nineteenth century were ones of technological advance, in which, as in other industrializing societies, increasing numbers of jobs could be performed by persons who lacked special skills or physical strength. This situation in itself would have increased the number of women at the factories, but its effects were enhanced by the tsarist government's efforts to regulate the conditions of factory life. Laws of 1882, 1884, and 1885 prohibited the employment of children under the age of twelve, and imposed a number of limits on the hiring of adolescents. Deprived of the very cheapest labor pool, employers tended to substitute the next cheapest. As a result, the proportion of women rose significantly over the following decades. An extreme example was the cotton industry, in which the proportion of female workers rose from around 40 percent in the early 1880s to 64 percent in 1908.[15]

Employers understandably preferred to hire single women and

15. Johnson, "The Nature of the Russian Working Class," p. 94.

were often loath to make concessions to the exigencies of child-rearing. In 1883 the Moscow factory inspector Ianzhul noted that only 4 out of 174 factories he had visited provided facilities for child care. Nursing mothers might even be denied permission to attend to their children at four-hour intervals.[16] Nurseries or living accommodations for families were costly, as were interruptions in the factory's work schedule. Rather than allow expensive machinery to stand idle while mothers nursed their babies, employers hired childless women.

In the older, more primitive factories these considerations counted for less, and family life was more common. In the bast-matting industry, workers customarily slept on the floor under their handpowered looms, and children entered the workforce as early as age five. The growth of mechanization and the regulation of the factory system's worst abuses may thus have led to a reduction in the number of families, a circumstance which helps to account for the low proportion of married women in the factory population.[17]

The village commune also helped to account for the low proportion of married women among migrants and factory workers. Membership in this venerable institution was almost inescapable for peasants prior to 1906. Exception was made, however, for one important category: women without husbands. Because these women were often regarded (probably wrongly) as less able to support themselves on a land allotment, they were sometimes allowed to depart permanently from the village.[18] As a result, a constant stream of spinsters and widows flowed into Moscow. Many were rather old to begin factory work, and most went instead into service work, especially domestic service. Nonetheless, some entered the factory labor force as late as age forty. In a sample of Moscow textile workers in 1881, only 2.1 percent of males over the age of forty had less than three years' factory experience; for women, the comparable figure was 17 percent.[19]

16. I. I. Ianzhul, "Zhenshchiny-materi na fabrikakh," *Ocherki i issledovaniia* (Moscow, 1884), I, 391.

17. On employers' preference for hiring unmarried girls or older women, see *Sbornik statisticheskikh svedenii po moskovskoi gubernii*, Otdel sanitarnoi statistiki, 4, no. 1, pp. 268–271. A study of workers in St. Petersburg in the years 1905–14 found that there, too, the proportion of married women was higher in more backward industries and factories: E. E. Kruze, *Peterburgskie rabochie v 1912–1914 gg.* (Leningrad, 1961), p. 84.

18. Peasant customary law varied from region to region in the rights it accorded to widows and spinsters. The presence or absence of minor children was sometimes decisive. Teodor Shanin, *The Awkward Class* (Oxford, 1972), pp. 222–223.

19. P. A. Peskov, *Sanitarnoe issledovanie fabrik po obrabotke voloknistykh veshchestv v*

The foregoing discussion suggests that the city and factory did not so much prevent marriage as attract or reject different groups from the female population. Marriage itself was alive and well in the countryside. This in turn raises a whole new series of questions about patterns of family life in rural areas. Here the data are less complete, but a few observations may still be in order.

If migrant males were marrying earlier, enjoying slightly greater material security, and maintaining families in the countryside, the net result might well be an increase in average family size.[20] Such a tendency would likely be promoted by other features of the Moscow region's pattern of labor migration which may have discouraged or retarded the break-up of large peasant households. Would an absent male be as likely to insist on separating from his father's household and receiving his own land? Would not a wife with young children be better provided for if she remained in the household of her in-laws?[21] In many cases the bifurcated peasant-worker household had to take on additional members, such as seasonal agricultural laborers, in order to remain viable as an agricultural unit.[22] Grandmothers or other kin might be brought in to care for the children of absent mothers, or children below a certain age might be attached to the households of their grandparents or other relatives.

All of these forces could have produced a peasant-worker household which was larger, more complex, included more outsiders (non-kin), and contained more children than other peasant households. These possibilities can be tested by examining household and marriage patterns in specific areas of Moscow's hinterland. One

gorode Moskve (Moscow, 1882) I, 103–113. Another study of factories throughout Moscow province reached the same conclusion: 20 percent of all women questioned had begun factory work after age 25, but only 8 percent of males had begun at such an age. *Sbornik statisticheskikh svedenii*, 4, no. 1, pp. 285–286.

20. Workers at the Tsindel' cotton mill reported an average family size of 7.3—significantly higher than the national average of 6. The source of this statistic does not, however, indicate whether all these dependents were residing in a single household, or precisely how they were related to the factory workers. P. M. Shestakov, *Rabochie na manufakture "Emil' Tsindel'" v Moskve* (Moscow, 1900), p. 36.

21. D. N. Zhbankov, *Bab'ia storona* (Kostroma, 1891), noted such a tendency in Kostroma province: males whose household did not include a grandmother or some comparable person were sometimes obliged to remain in the village until their children were grown. As an alternative, wives took up residence with in-laws, but personal frictions often led them to insist on a separate household (pp. 68–69).

22. At the Tsindel' mill, 7.3 percent of male workers reported that they hired laborers to work their land. (Shestakov, *Rabochie na manufakture "Emil' Tsindel'*," p. 38.) In Kostroma Province, a "majority" of migrants' households was said to employ outsiders. (Zhbankov, *Bab'ia storona*, p 51.)

test, comparing regions of high and low out-migration within a single province, is described in the following pages.

The province chosen was Riazan', whose northern districts *(uezdy)* had a highly developed pattern of out-migration.[23] According to Moscow's municipal census of 1902, four districts (Mikhailovskii, Zaraiskii, Riazanskii, and Pronskii) sent a total of 56,000 migrants to the city, a figure equal to roughly 10 percent of their total population as recorded in the national census of 1897.[24] The remaining eight districts of the province, with a population of 1.2 million, sent 38,000 migrants to Moscow, roughly 3 percent of their population. If out-migration affected family patterns, this should be reflected in statistics on marriage and household composition. The computations discussed below were derived from the 1897 census.[25] The census distinguished between rural and urban sections of each district, and only the former have been used.

Three computations were performed which revealed clear differences between districts of high and low out-migration. First, the dependency ratio (defined as the sum of children and elderly persons, divided by the total adult population of ages 15–64) in the four districts was .900, and in the rest of the province .792. This suggests that more adults were departing from the four districts, leaving behind a greater proportion of old people and children. Second, the sex ratio for the age group 15–64 was 73.5 males per 100 females in the four districts, but 80.1 in the rest of the province. This suggests a pattern of differential out-migration, with males departing and females remaining behind. Third, the proportion of women married between the ages of seventeen and twenty-nine was 77.1 percent in the four districts and 70.6 percent in the remainder of the province. This pattern seems to be the reverse of that exhibited in Table 2 and is precisely what one would expect if

23. The comparison was restricted to a single province in order to limit the effects of other variables which might influence family life, *e. g.*, prosperity, patterns of land use, local traditions. Nonetheless, a province is still a large unit with much internal variation; Riazan's northern and southern districts differed not only in their levels of out-migration, but in several other important respects. Quality of soil was higher in the south, but average land allotments were smaller; southerners also engaged in labor migration, but preferred to seek work in agricultural regions further south.

24. *Perepis' Moskvy 1902 g.*, part 1, no. 2, table 5, p. 45.

25. *Pervaia vseobshchaia perepis' naseleniia rossiiskoi imperii*, 1897 g., vol. 35 (Riazanskaia guberniia) (St. Petersburg, 1903), tables 1, 2, 3b, 5, pp. 4–5, 6–9, 14–25, 28–35.

early-marrying migrants left their wives behind in the village. (For males residing in Riazan', there were no clear-cut differences between the four districts and the rest of the province. Evidently males who did not migrate to the city married at approximately the same age as their counterparts elsewhere in the province.)

Other computations did not reveal clear-cut differences between the two regions. Contrary to expectations, the mean household size was smaller in the four northern districts—6.1 persons, as compared to 6.5 in the whole of the province. The proportion of households with six or more members, however, was marginally higher in the four districts.[26] In the north, 47.9 percent of all households had fewer than six members; in the south, 48.7 percent. These figures imply that while out-migration did not produce larger households, members of larger households were more likely to migrate out.

In the northern districts the proportion of infants under one year of age was 42.1 per 1,000 population, while in the province as a whole it was 42.2. The four northern districts did have a larger proportion of "outsiders" *(prishlye)* living within their borders—54 per 1,000 population, as compared to 40.8 per 1,000 in the rest of the province. This would support the suggestion that hired hands were replacing absent migrants. When figures on outsiders *(postoronnye)* in actual households are compared, however, the differences between the four districts and the rest of the province seem minuscule.

The relatively small differences between north and south provide indirect support for the hypotheses outlined earlier. Roughly one-tenth of the inhabitants of the four northern districts had departed for Moscow, and the dependency ratio and sex ratio seem to reflect their absence. If those who stayed behind were *not* compensating for the migrants' absence—if they were not maintaining extended households or hiring outsiders—then the northern households should have been significantly smaller than they appear in the census. The migrants, in other words, should have left more empty

26. The explanation for this paradox is that, even though there were more "large" households in the northern districts, their average size was smaller. The northern districts had 42,900 households with six or more inhabitants; these households had 357,000 inhabitants, an average of 8.31. In the south there were 83,200 "large" households with 787,000 inhabitants—an average of 9.45. (My calculations from *ibid.*, table 2, pp. 6–9.)

spaces in the northern population. The fact that they did not suggests that compensatory measures of one sort or another were being taken.

In considering the number of outsiders in northern households, we must also remember that the census was taken in January. Since wage laborers in agriculture were normally hired seasonally, they were unlikely to be present in the middle of winter. By the same token, migrants who departed from southern districts to work in agriculture were most likely to be counted at home in January, while northerners who worked in city occupations were more likely to be absent. Households in the south would therefore be at their largest in the winter months, while those in the north would be at their smallest. Once again, the apparent absence of north-south differences may be deceptive.

A comparison of the northern and southern districts of Riazan' provides only an indirect indication of migration's effects. Migrants still represented a relatively small proportion of the total population (roughly 20 percent of the adult population of the four districts), and any distinctive features of their family and household patterns may have been understated or buried in overall totals. The southern districts, moreover, were also sending a certain number of migrants to cities and industrial centers, which would tend to reduce the contrast between north and south. Unfortunately, the general census figures cannot identify specific households which did or did not send members off in search of work. When differences appear between northern and southern districts, we cannot be sure that they were caused by labor migration. Thus, however reasonable the suggestion that southerners (including migrant agricultural laborers) married later or had smaller families than urban migrants, any firm conclusions will ultimately depend on devising some means to compare specific households.

Further testing will be necessary before these hypotheses can be accepted or rejected. Nevertheless, the evidence presented above is suggestive enough to warrant further investigation. A few words about its possible implications may also be in order.

If, as suggested, earlier marriage and larger households were associated with industrial out-migration, this phenomenon may have had serious consequences for Russia's social and economic development. Russian workers and their families followed a pattern exhibited in much of the Third World today. Able-bodied young adults went off to the city, leaving agriculture to the very old and the very young. This system could affect the course of agricultural and industrial development, as well as the stability of the social order.

In agriculture, the overall effect would be to intensify overcrowding and inefficiency. As H. J. Habbakuk noted some years ago, a system of equipartitional inheritance tends to retard accumulation of capital and introduction of technological innovations in agriculture.[27] By guaranteeing each offspring a piece of land, the inheritance system fragments holdings and perpetuates small-scale production. Assured of a share of land, children have little incentive to delay marriage or control fertility. This was especially true in those regions of Russia where communal repartition was practiced. Labor migration, as practiced in the Moscow region, served to accentuate this pattern, for each new offspring was also a potential source of wages. In contrast to western countries, a migrant was unlikely to sever all ties with the parental or familial household. Even if the security of rural bonds lost appeal, the village commune and the passport system could forcibly remind the migrant of his obligations.

To the extent that the migrant's wages were not swallowed up by taxes and land redemption payments, they might have been used to strengthen his household's economic position, e.g., by renting or purchasing additional land or equipment. His absence may have delayed the breakup of the parental household for a time, thereby encouraging a more efficient use of labor and capital. Yet, as the data presented above suggest, outside wages also encouraged less "rational" expenditures (e.g., those associated with marriage), increased the ratio of consumers to producers, and ultimately led to greater fragmentation of land and movable capital. (If migrants had more offspring, households would eventually be divided into a greater number of units.) Labor migration could thus reinforce what Teodor Shanin has called the cyclical mobility of peasant households. Wealth was unstable, and households rich at one point were likely to be poor a few years later.[28] The net effect was to discourage innovation.

27. H. J. Habbakuk, "Family Structure and Economic Change in Nineteenth-Century Europe," *Journal of Economic History*, 15, no. 1 (1955): 1–12.
28. Shanin, *The Awkward Class*, pp. 73–76ff.

This suggestion is borne out by the predominant agricultural patterns of the Moscow region. Despite the greater profitability of other crops, in 1916 74 percent of the sown area was under cereals—a figure close to the national average of 81 percent.[29] Soviet historians have pointed to a trend toward rational or capitalistic systems of land rent in the southern and Volga steppe provinces around the turn of the century, contrasting this to the provinces close to Moscow. At the center, "semi-feudal" practices continued to be prominent, as illustrated by the persistence of labor-rent and share-cropping arrangements. The rental price of land was set not by the profitability of working it, but by the magnitude of peasant demand. Small-scale land rental was usually for a single season, precluding efficient and rational cultivation.[30] The regions of heaviest labor out-migration, then, showed little progress on the agrarian front.

In industry, this pattern meant that members of each new generation of workers, even those whose fathers and grandfathers had worked in the factory, would spend their formative years in the countryside. The habits and routines of city life would be less familiar to them, and their efficiency as workers might be lower than if they had been reared in the city. This problem of "generational succession" (or its absence) would be intensified by the pattern of female labor outlined earlier. Women who were childless or who had cut their ties to the village would not be passing on their skills and experience to sons or daughters. If women moved to the factory at a more advanced age, the habits of the countryside would be more deeply ingrained in them.

As for the effects of these patterns on social unrest, one would like to know more about the nature of the peasant "community" that existed at factories of the Moscow region. Evidence suggests that rural-urban networks helped newly arrived migrants to find work in the cities and factories, and that migrants from particular regions tended to remain together for many years. Their peculiarities of dress and speech, together with the "closed-door" policies of many employers, often served to segregate peasants from outside or cosmopolitan influences. Yet the factories closest to the coun-

29. George Pavlovsky, *Agricultural Russia on the Eve of the Revolution* (London, 1930), pp. 39, 328.

30. A. M. Anfimov, *Zemel'naia arenda v Rossii v nachale XX veka* (Moscow, 1961), pp. 191–192.

tryside, either physically or spiritually, were often the scene of the largest and best organized labor-management confrontations. Some of the landmarks of Russian labor history, such as the Morozov strike in Orekhovo-Zuevo in 1885 or the formation of the first Soviet of Workers Deputies in Ivanovo in 1905, took place far from the major urban centers. The famous Petersburg textile strike of May-June, 1896, unprecedented in its duration and in the coordination and self-discipline of the workers, occurred among the least urbanized elements of the working class, while the more "proletarian" metalworkers remained on the sidelines. It seems reasonable to assume that these events were in some way connected with peasant traditions, or that rural-urban ties contributed in some fashion to the cohesion displayed by these workers. While this notion will obviously have to await further study,[31] it bears on the issues of the present paper. If rural-urban ties were indeed a contributing factor in social unrest, the instability owed something to the familial patterns described here, which helped to perpetuate those ties.

31. A preliminary assessment of evidence is offered in my "Strikes in Moscow, 1880–1900: Rural-Urban Ties as a Factor in Social Unrest," *Russian History*, 5, no. 1 (Spring, 1978).

DIANE KOENKER

Urban Families, Working-Class
Youth Groups, and the 1917 Revolution
in Moscow

The emergence of youth as a forceful agent for social change has been one of the phenomena closely associated with the transformation of the modern world. In the nineteenth century, movements calling themselves "Young Russia," "Young Italy," and "Young Turkey" attempted to rejuvenate their societies on the basis of the energy and idealism of youth. In our own century, such generational groups as the Hitler Youth, Maoist Red Guards, or American student radicals have continued this tradition. Explanations of the youth phenomenon are manifold: the demographic revolution resulted in an increasing segment of young people in a society which was not able to expand sufficiently the opportunities for youth; young people in such societies became frustrated and rebellious.[1] Or, traditional institutions which once absorbed the natural energies of youth disappeared with the shift of the family away from the village to the city.[2]

The Bolshevik Revolution, too, was in some respects a "youth revolution," although this aspect of the party's appeal is usually overshadowed by other social and political factors. As early as 1905, the party was more attractive to youth than were the rival Men-

In addition to the discussion at the Illinois symposium, this paper has benefited from the careful criticisms of Terry Parssinen, Richard Eiter, and colleagues at the Temple University history department seminar on modernization.

1. Herbert Moller, "Youth as a Force in the Modern World," *Comparative Studies in Society and History*, 10 (1968): 237–260.

2. See the excellent essay by Alan B. Spitzer, "The Historical Problem of Generations," *American Historical Review*, 78, no. 5 (December, 1973): 1353–85, also S. N. Eisenstadt, "Archetypal Patterns of Youth," in *Youth: Change and Challenge*, ed. Erik H. Erikson (New York, 1963), pp. 31–32.

sheviks, and the few existing age studies of Russian revolutionary parties indicate the Bolsheviks tended to be younger than the rest.[3] Within the party, the youngest members were often most radical. The militant Bukharinites in the Moscow regional organization were young; Red Guards—the Bolshevik military arm in October—were also especially attractive to youth.[4]

But to say that the Bolshevik party appealed to youth and that this appeal may have helped the party succeed in 1917 is not to explain the reasons for this attraction or the characteristics of those attracted. Why, for instance, did the populists—the Socialist Revolutionaries in 1917—not retain their young followers? Why did the youth and the Bolshevik party not combine to create a revolutionary situation earlier, say in 1902, when there was already a substantial pool of young workers in Russian cities? The answers to these questions lie partly in a consideration of the political moment of 1917, but also in the nature of Russian urban society in the early twentieth century. The Russian working class was undergoing an important transformation during this period, and the role of youth in politics (indeed, in the timing of the revolution) must be seen against the backdrop of this transformation.

I shall consider the role of youth in the revolution by focusing on the emergence of working-class youth groups in Moscow in 1917. While these groups were the vehicle through which many young workers were drawn to the Bolshevik party, they must be evaluated not simply as an outlet for revolutionary fervor but first and foremost as a response by youth to the exigencies of their urban environment. The Russian Revolution was a social revolution, and it is the task of social historians to explore the intricate links be-

3. Solomon M. Schwartz, *The Russian Revolution of 1905: The Workers' Movement and the Formation of Bolshevism and Menshevism*, trans. Gertrude Vakar (Chicago, 1967), p. 30; David Lane, *The Roots of Russian Communism* (London, 1975), pp. 34–39; Maureen Perrie, "The Social Composition and Structure of the Socialist Revolutionary Party before 1917," *Soviet Studies*, 24, no. 2 (October, 1972): 223–250; Richard Eiter, "Rank and File Membership of the Socialist Revolutionary Party in Russia, 1905–1907," paper presented at the Midwest Slavic Conference, Chicago, 1976; Tsuyoshi Hasegawa, "The Petrograd Bolsheviks in 1917: A Profile," paper presented at the Duquesne History Forum, Pittsburgh, 1975. In Moscow, the Bolshevik candidates to the city duma in 1917 were significantly younger than Menshevik or SR nominees, even though the party explicitly recruited its most experienced members for candidacy. A. N. Ul'ianov, *Pervye demokraticheskie vybory v Moskovskuiu dumu* (Moscow, 1917), p. 16.

4. Stephen F. Cohen, *Bukharin and the Bolshevik Revolution* (New York, 1973), pp. 49–51; G. P. Georgievskii, *Ocherki po istorii krasnoi gvardii* (Moscow, 1919), p. 88; G. A. Tsypkin, *Krasnaia gvardiia v bor'be za vlast' sovetov* (Moscow, 1967), p. 108.

tween the social units in Russian life—families, villages, communities, workplaces—and the political structures they helped to shape. The nature of the life of urban youth must first be considered in order to understand the political choices made by young workers in 1917.

What was life in Moscow like for young workers in 1917? Were there particular reasons why some youths, and not others, joined first youth groups and then the Bolshevik party? My conjecture, which will be demonstrated below, is that the youth groups appealed to the most urbanized youth in Moscow, who found in them and in the revolution a community of peers. The need for such a community was both created by and unfulfilled by the urban environment in which they and their families lived. While the crucial aspects of this environment will be documented below, it might be helpful to outline the general theme in advance. Family life, due to the peculiarities of Russian urban and industrial development, was often limited to an elite stratum of city workers, and thus opportunities for city youths to create adult family lives of their own were limited. Especially during the World War, adolescents found themselves in the position of doing adult work but without adults' social possibilities (marriage and family), and a "youth culture" was aborning. This culture, too, was shaped by the city environment: there was little privacy at home, and too few recreational opportunities. When the revolution suddenly thrust itself into the lives of these young urban workers, they readily embraced its opportunities to enrich their social as well as their political lives, and thus began the organized youth movement. The social features of this movement and the transition from youth-oriented social groups to more active participation in revolutionary life will be the focus of the second part of this essay, but to understand this transition, we must begin with the urban environment itself.

From the outset, we must consider the peculiar nature of the development of the Russian working class. The process of urbanizaton in nineteenth-century Russia was not identical to the process of industrialization, and the differences between the two processes created a peculiarly hybrid urban working class. Especially surrounding Moscow, the countryside industrialized alongside the city, and factories in both locations were supplied primarily by peasant labor with strong legal and social ties to the land. This phenomenon contributed to a very transient working class, whose members kept one foot in each of two worlds—industrial and agricultural. In the cities especially, the migrant workers, who brought with them rural customs and values and who adjusted slowly to urban life, constituted the great majority of the proletariat. On the other hand, the direction of the evolving Russian working class was toward a permanent labor force of workers born into working-class families, sharing urban traditions, with minimal ties to their rural past.[5] The number of these native urban proletarians was certainly small even in 1917, but it was by no means negligible.

There exist, then, two models of the Russian urban proletarian: the peasant-migrant who retained his ties with the countryside (as Robert Johnson has demonstrated in his paper), and the native urban proletarian, with little ambivalence about his identity or cultural loyalty. The image of a bi-polar working class is convenient in understanding the nature of the social evolution of the working class, but it must be stressed that these worker-types are only paradigms. Many workers moved back and forth across these artificial limits. Children born to working-class parents were not always reared in the city; quite often they were sent to live with rural relatives until they reached school or working age. Few urban workers, however long their urban residence, had completely abandoned all rural ties. Conversely, some rural-born children might be just as familiar with urban ways as their city-born cousins. A woodworker at a big Moscow textile factory had been born in a village outside the city, for example, but lived in the city with his widowed mother, served an apprenticeship in Moscow, and eventually returned permanently to the city to work, far more accustomed to the urban environment than his place of birth might at first glance suggest.[6]

Despite the imperfections of the bi-polar view of an urban working class at once peasant and urban, the statistical evidence shows that Moscow's workforce in the early twentieth century was developing along this rural-urban continuum, with the relative share

5. A valuable Soviet treatment of this problem is L. M. Ivanov, "Preemstvennost' fabrichno-zavodskogo truda i formirovanie proletariata v Rossii," in *Rabochii klass i rabochee dvizhenie v Rossii (1861–1917)* ed. L. M. Ivanov (Moscow, 1966). The whole volume is an excellent compendium of recent Soviet studies in Russian working-class history.

6. E. O. Kabo, *Ocherki rabochego byta. Opyt monograficheskogo issledovaniia domashnego rabochego byta* (Moscow, 1928), I, 48.

of permanent, so-called hereditary proletarians continually growing. One characteristic of the peasant-migrant end of the continuum was that the workforce was predominantly male. In 1902, there were in Moscow only 75 women for every 100 men in the working-class districts surrounding the city center.[7] The implications of this imbalance for family life are suggested by Johnson: male migrants married at home and left their wives and children in native villages, where living was cheaper. The "typical" youth entering the Moscow workforce at the beginning of the century, even if he was a worker's son, was likely to be unfamiliar with city life and would adapt slowly and painfully, if at all, to the urban milieu.[8]

But the situation was beginning to change. The reforms of the Stolypin government after 1905 enabled many peasants to divest themselves of their village landholdings and to move with their households to the city.[9] Indeed, by 1912 the female-male ratio had improved slightly, to 82 women for every 100 men.[10] Available statistical evidence makes further direct comparisons between the census years 1902 and 1912 problematic, but there are signs that the permanent workforce was indeed growing. For example, among metalworkers in Moscow province who entered the workforce before 1905, 41 percent owned some land. Only 35 percent entering between 1906 and 1913 were landholders, and by 1918 only 22 percent said they had owned land prior to the revolution.[11] In a study of Moscow workers' parentage by age group, the younger the worker, the more likely he was to have come from a worker family himself.[12]

The ultimate outcome of this transition was a full-time native

7. *Perepis' Moskvy 1902 goda* (Moscow, 1904).
8. One such youth was the future activist Semen Kanatchikov, whose memoirs indeed tell a story of a difficult transition from country to city. See Reginald E. Zelnik, "Russian Bebels: An Introduction to the Memoirs of Semen Kanatchikov and Matvei Fisher," *Russian Review*, 35, nos. 3 and 4 (July and October, 1976).
9. On the impact of the Stolypin reforms in Moscow Province, see S. I. Antonova, *Vliianie stolypinskoi agrarnoi reformy na izmeneniia v sostave rabochego klassa (po materialam moskovskoi gubernii 1906–1913 gg.)* (Moscow, 1951).
10. *Statisticheskii ezhegodnik goroda Moskvy i moskovskoi gubernii,* (Moscow, 1927), part 2, p. 14.
11. A. G. Rashin, *Formirovanie rabochego klassa Rossii,* 2nd ed. (Moscow, 1958), p. 576; Tsentral'noe statisticheskoe upravlenie, *Trudy,* 26, part 2 (Moscow, 1926): 120–121. The comparisons are not exact: the 1918 data are for all Russian metalworkers. It can be assumed from other sources that the share of landowning metalworkers in Moscow was somewhat higher.
12. I. M. Koz'minykh-Lanin, *Ukhod na polevye raboty fabrichno-zavodskikh rabochikh Moskovskoi gubernii* (Moscow, 1911), table 6.

urban proletariat. However, even in 1912 this outcome was far in the future, if indeed cities ever become self-sustaining. Only 9 percent of male and 11 percent of female factory workers had been born in the city by that year, but the family situation of these workers vis-à-vis that of migrants is instructive. For the 15,600 native-born workers, there were 42,000 dependents, a dependent-worker ratio of almost 3:1. But for the 150,000 migrant factory workers, the situation was reversed; these migrants claimed only 35,000 dependents. The migrants must either have been overwhelmingly single, or (as was the case earlier in the century) they were married but kept their families down on the farm.[13] When we speak of urbanized youth, we mean first of all the city-born children of the permanent urban residents. The 35,000 migrants' dependents represent a transitional group, born in the country but reared in the city. The young people in this category would likely be closer in values to native urban workers than to rural youths who first came to the city as teenagers seeking their fortunes.

Once established in the city, all youths faced the same problems: poor housing, minimal social opportunities, long work hours. The characteristics of life which shall be called "urban" affected youths of all backgrounds; it was the response to these characteristics that changed according to urban acculturation. Consider, for example, the impact of city residence on family life. It appears that marriage took place relatively late for Moscow's workers, in comparison both with rural peasants and with rural factory workers. In 1897, only 6 percent of Moscow city males (workers and non-workers—the sources preclude a more precise analysis) in the 17–19 age group were married, as opposed to 13 percent in the predominantly rural Ruzskii District *(uezd)* of Moscow Province. Furthermore, just over half of urban residents in their twenties were married; in contrast, in Ruzskii *uezd* 68 percent of males and 82 percent of females in that age group were married.[14]

These data describe the entire urban population, not simply the

13. *Statisticheskii ezhegodnik,* p. 70. See also Robert Eugene Johnson's paper in the present volume.
14. *Pervaia vseobshchaia perepis' naseleniia rossiiskoi imperii 1897 goda,* 24 (St. Petersburg, 1904). For urban and rural women, however, the proportion was about the same: 18 percent of the seventeen- to nineteen-year-old age group were married in both city and country.

working-class segment. Johnson has demonstrated that factory workers on the whole married younger than city residents—partly because they were able to support families back home. But as more and more workers abandoned their ties with the land after 1905, it seems logical that early marriage would become less common. Much housing for workers was barracks-style, and married workers were liable to lose their jobs if they tried to bring their brides into factory housing.[15] If the young couple had no country relations, they were forced to wait until they could afford to rent private lodgings, which created a pattern of delayed marriage much closer to the western European model. By 1914 in Moscow, the median age of marriage, in both working-class and non-working-class districts, was well above twenty years old. Half the women married that year were at least twenty-three; the median age for grooms was twenty-six.[16]

An important implication of late marriage for youths growing up in the city was that their youthful period lasted longer. They had more time to develop and participate in their own generational culture, whether in the form of delinquent gangs, self-education societies, or political shock-troops: all were characteristic of modernizing societies in the West at similar stages of development, and were present in Moscow as well.[17] But Moscow's urban workforce was much newer than its western counterpart. Because accelerated growth of a full-time labor force occurred only after 1905, this generational subculture might have become defined only shortly before the Revolution.

The factors which shaped this new urban youth culture were both negative and positive, for urban life imposed hardships as well as compensations. A serious drawback was the deplorable state of housing in Moscow at the turn of the century. With adequate housing at a premium, few workers had the means to support families in the city. Although some enlightened factory owners built barracks-style housing for their workers, and even for workers'

15. *V Oktiabr'skie dni. Iz vospominanii uchastnikov oktiabr'skoi revoliutsii 1917 goda v Shcherbakovskom raione goroda Moskvy* (Moscow, 1957), p. 21.

16. *Spisok fabrik i zavodov goroda Moskvy* (Moscow, 1916): *Ezhemesiachnyi statisticheskii biulleten' goroda Moskvy*, no. 7 (July, 1915), p. 29. These figures describe the aggregate urban population, but there are no significant differences in marital ages between working-class and middle-class areas of the city.

17. See John R. Gillis, *Youth and History: Tradition and Change in European Age Relations 1770–Present* (New York, 1974).

families, most Moscow workers lived in private accommodations ranging from a cot (*koika*) in the corner of a room to an entire, although small, suburban cottage. Subleasing was common: a family renting an entire apartment (which meant one or more rooms plus a kitchen) would rent rooms or corners of rooms to lodgers in order to bring in extra income. Among printers in 1905, only 5 percent could afford to rent apartments without taking in lodgers.[18] Whatever the circumstances, living space was small. Even married workers in the "model barracks" at the Trekhgornaia textile mill lived four couples to a room only thirteen feet square. In 1912, the average apartment in the working-class outskirts housed nine persons; privacy for most urban residents, including the young, was practically non-existent.[19] Poor housing also helped cause small working-class families: by 1923 the median worker's household included just one child.[20] Adolescents had to seek companionship of peers outside the family circle, another new feature of urban life.

With both parents working to afford to stay together at all, working-class children grew up with little adult supervision. Since factory and private housing provided no indoor space for children to play, they roamed the corridors or courtyards of their lodgings. "Kitchen mothers" received a ruble or two a month to look after neighbors' children; other families hired nannies—often young country cousins—in exchange for room and board.[21] Nurseries were few before the Revolution, despite the high proportion of women in the labor force, and adequate child-care facilities would be a major demand of organized women in 1917.[22]

Their own working lives began soon enough for these children. Workers' children received some instruction from their parents

18. A. Svavitskii and V. Sher, *Ocherk polozheniia rabochikh pechatnogo dela v Moskve* (St. Petersburg, 1909), pp. 34–35.

19. *Usloviia byta rabochikh v dorevoliutsionnoi Rossii (po dannym biudzhetnykh obsledovanii)* (Moscow, 1958), p. 116; *Trudy statisticheskogo otdela Moskovskoi gorodskoi upravy* (Moscow, 1913), part 1, pp. 31–32; D. L. Kasitskaia and E. P. Popova, "Polozhenie i byt rabochikh Prokhorovskoi Trekhgornoi manufaktury," *Trudy Gosudarstvennogo istoricheskogo muzeia*, part 23: *Istoriko-bytovye ekspeditsii 1949–50* (Moscow, 1953), p. 178.

20. Kabo, *Ocherki rabochego byta*, p. 24.

21. M. Davydovich, "Khoziaistvennoe znachenie zhenshchiny v rabochei sem'e," *Poznanie Rossii*, 3 (1909); Kasitskaia and Popova, "Polozhenie i byt rabochikh Prokhorovskoi Trekhgornoi manufaktury," p. 180.

22. *Vek nyneshnii i vek minuvshii. Rasskazy rabochikh sukonnoi fabriki imeni Petra Alekseeva* (Moscow, 1937), p. 133. Both the Menshevik and Bolshevik parties included nurseries in their election platforms in 1917. The Socialist Revolutionaries, who directed their appeals toward recently-migrated peasants, did not.

—sewing and knitting for girls, the father's trade for boys. Formal apprenticeships began at age twelve.[23] In the printing industry, where a four-year apprenticeship was standard, two-thirds of workers surveyed in 1907 had entered the trade before they were fifteen.[24] Thus the urban youth generation reached social and economic independence at a comparatively early age. Their lives were not completely centered on the family or home, since parents were likely to be at work and "home" was a kitchen-mother down the hall.

On the other hand, despite crowded living conditions and early entry into the labor force, urban youths enjoyed many advantages not available to their rural counterparts. Chief among these in Moscow was the city's educational system. In 1910 the municipal government made four years of schooling compulsory for city children, compared with three years offered on a voluntary basis by rural *zemstvo* schools. By 1912 Moscow primary schools enrolled about 56,000 children, or 62 percent of the school-age population.[25] Even more important for working-class youth was the city's system of vocational training. Boys could attend commercial, tailoring, or artisan schools, and for girls twelve handcraft schools taught sewing and design, along with general subjects.

A primary education was a prerequisite for many jobs in the city. Apprentices in the gold and silver trade were required to be literate, for example, and the vocational schools accepted only candidates who had completed primary school. This requirement was an especially strong incentive for equal educational opportunties: in Moscow provincial villages, for example, only 30 percent of the pupils were girls, but in Moscow city they made up 47 percent of the primary school population.[26] Judging by workers surveyed in 1924, it was the vocational offerings of Moscow public schools which overcame parents' traditional reluctance to educate their daughters. The son of a textile worker was preparing to study literature at the university, but the father grudgingly sent his

23. V. Iu. Krupianskaia, "Evoliutsiia semeino-bytovogo uklada rabochikh," in *Rossiiskii proletariat: oblik, bor'ba, gegemoniia*, ed. L. M. Ivanov (Moscow, 1970), p. 279.

24. Svavitskii and Sher, *Ocherk polozheniia rabochikh pechatnogo dela v Moskve*, pp. 14–16.

25. *Sovremennoe khoziaistvo goroda Moskvy* (Moscow, 1913), p. 34, and *Statisticheskii ezhegodnik*, p. 15.

26. *Pervyi obshchezemskii s"ezd po narodnomu obrazovaniiu 1911 goda* (Moscow, 1912), p. 247.

daughter to school only because her sewing classes required literacy. "Young girls, what's the use of them?" he asked the interviewer. "They go and get married and that's that." But nonetheless, the daughter, by virtue of living in the city, was able to attend a school.[27]

Education provided the foundation for the creation of a specifically urban youth culture in Moscow. The Prechistenskii school —an educational cooperative with night courses—attracted the most intellectual young workers, both those seeking only to qualify for better jobs and those attracted by the political and social themes of the courses and the similar interests of fellow students.[28] These evening courses brought together young workers from all trades and all parts of the city, and they helped to create new social networks as well as to provide workers with new skills. Familiarity with arts and literature became an important symbol of status for the most advanced young workers, who could be distinguished by the writing desks and portraits of authors with which they furnished their rooms.[29] Such symbols of culture would characterize the revolutionary youth groups in 1917 as well.

Dramatic circles were extraordinarily popular among urban youth. Leo Tolstoi himself took personal interest in one such circle at the Trekhgornaia textile mill.[30] In the fast-growing working-class suburb of Preobrazhenskoe in the northeast of Moscow, municipal leaders opened a People's House to serve as a cultural center for the entire local population. The chief patrons of the center's library, reading, choral, and dramatic circles turned out to be youths between the ages of fifteen and twenty.[31] The popularity of such groups testifies to young workers' great demand for social activities outside the family and the workplace; it also suggests the predilection of at least one segment of working youth for a culture with intellectual content. (No doubt there were young people whose activities tended more toward hooliganism and pranksterism, just as there were in the rapidly growing cities of England, Europe,

27. Kabo, *Ocherki rabochego byta*, p. 58.
28. M. Dergachev, "Iz proshlogo (1915–1917 gg.)," in *Nashe rozhdenie*, ed. A. Atsarkin (Moscow, 1931), p. 25.
29. Krupianskaia, "Evoliutsiia semeino-bytovogo uklada rabochikh," p. 283.
30. *Materialy k istorii Prokhorovskoi Trekhgornoi manufaktury* (Moscow, 1915), p. 410; Sh. Ibragimov, "O Lefortovskom raione (s 1915 g. do nachala 1917 g.)," *Put' k oktiabriu*, 5 (Moscow, 1923): 160.
31. *Izvestiia moskovskoi gorodskoi dumy*, no. 2 (1917).

and America, but of this aspect of Moscow youth culture there is unfortunately little record.[32])

If we can identify a culture shared by urban youth after they left their families' strict tutelage and before they started family life themselves, can this culture be characterized as distinctly urban? Surely village residents had their traditional youth-specific activities, akin to the charivaris and rough music depicted by historians of early modern Europe.[33] Promenading was a form of courtship which, in England, survived the transition from village to city. It was also a favorite pastime for Moscow youth, who chose forested areas on the outskirts of town (perhaps because here they felt closest to the rural setting of their past?) for their courtship rituals.[34]

However, in many areas of life, urban youth culture did assume a distinct flavor. Dress was an important indicator of a youth's assimilation into the urban milieu. On holidays, the well-dressed urban youth wore a "troika"—trousers, vest, and jacket, with a starched shirt and tie on very special occasions. It was a mark of culture for the young worker to be indistinguishable from those in the educated upper classes. One of the leaders of a Moscow youth group, despite good-natured teasing from her peers for dressing like a "gymnasium student," insisted upon wearing fashionable clothes during non-working hours.[35] On the other hand, the least assimilated urban youths continued to dress as they had in their villages. An early social democratic activist, Ivan Babushkin, recalled his astonishment at finding that a group of youths at a Petersburg factory reminded him of "a respectable village of some province or other. The girls arrested my attention by the brightness of their outfits, completely alien to the urban style. . . ."[36]

The effect of urban values upon youth can also be seen in the

32. The Preobrazhenskoe People's House (above) was created by city authorities partly to reduce petty juvenile crime in the area.

33. See Natalie Zemon Davis, "The Reasons of Misrule: Youth Groups and Charivaris in Sixteenth-Century France," *Past and Present*, 50 (February, 1971); 41–75, and E. P. Thompson, " 'Rough Music': Le charivaris anglais," *Annales Économies Sociétés Civilisations*, 27, no. 2 (March-April, 1972): 285–312.

34. Gillis, *Youth and History*, p. 62; Krupianskaia, "Evoliutsiia semeino-bytovogo uklada rabochikh," p. 283; *The Village of Viriatino* ed. Sula Benet (Garden City, N. Y., 1970), pp. 136–139.

35. Krupianskaia, "Evoliutsiia semeino-bytovogo uklada rabochikh," p. 281; Anna Litveiko, "V semnadtsatom," *Iunost*, 3, no. 3 (1957): 13–18.

36. I. V. Babushkin, *Vospominaniia 1893–1900* (Moscow, 1951), p. 39.

transformation of working-class marriage customs. Religion in the cities was far less important than in the villages; in fact, after the Soviet government legalized civil marriage in 1918, the annual marriage rate in Moscow more than doubled, suggesting that many couples had preferred common law marriages to the ritual of a church wedding.[37] In cities the marriage ritual itself was much simplified. Whereas in the countryside the wedding ceremony was almost incidental to the elaborate series of rituals preceding and following it, in cities the actual nuptials were more central. Instead of the rural matchmaking, dowry, bed-selling, and other standard rituals, the participation of the bridal couple's peers in the city was limited to a post-ceremony celebratory *"bal"* which resembled those given by urban middle classes more than anything from the village.[38]

Finally, urban youth culture was characterized by the breakdown of the traditional patriarchal authority of the village order. The participation of all family members in wage-earning, suggested a contemporary observer, created a sense of equality among family members at the expense of filial obedience.[39] The small worker families were probably manageable social units, and order did not depend on the strict imposition of patriarchal authority. Young people chose their own marriage partners in the city; the institution of the matchmaker survived, but in a purely ritual way. Such a breakdown in the traditional vertical order perhaps freed young people to seek more extensive horizontal, or peer-group ties.[40] Thus the transition to the urban milieu provided both the incentive and the opportunity to create a particularly urban generational culture, and it was within this culture that seeds of political radicalism flourished in 1917.

Moscow's working class, and its youth, were gradually abandoning peasant traditions and were developing a distinctively urban

37. *Statisticheskii ezhegodnik*, p. 88.
38. G. V. Zhirnova, "Russkii gorodskoi svadebnyi obriad kontsa XIX—nachala XX veka," *Sovetskaia etnografiia*, no. 1 (1969): 48–58.
39. Davydovich, "Khoziaistvennoe znachenie zhenshchiny v rabochei sem'e," pp. 120–121.
40. This process is suggested by S. N. Eisenstadt: "Youth groups tend to develop in all societies in which such a division of labor exists. Youth's tendency to coalesce in such groups is rooted in the fact that participation in the family became insufficient for developing full identity or full social maturity, and that the roles learned in the family did not constitute an adequate basis for developing such identity and participation" ("Archetypal Patterns of Youth," pp. 31–32).

Diane Koenker

culture. The outbreak of war in 1914 temporarily halted this process and created serious disruptions in the urban social fabric. One-fourth of Moscow's labor force was mobilized into the tsarist army, including many skilled and city-wise workers between the ages of eighteen and forty.[41] Eventually, the most skilled workmen were reassigned to military production work, where they were far more valuable than in the trenches, so some urban cadres came marching home again. In the meantime, their places, and the extra jobs created by the demand for military goods, were filled by workers ineligible for military service, especially children under twelve, youths, and adult women. In 1914, according to health insurance society figures, 15 percent of working-class members were under seventeen years old, and 25 percent were adult women. By 1917, the youth component had risen to 26 percent, and women to 38 percent.[42]

Where did these new industrial recruits come from, and how did their influx affect the developing urban culture outlined above? Some of the women may have been former workers, lured back to the factories through patriotism or for high war wages. Others were wives of departed soldiers; since the government did not grant military supplements to soldiers' common-law wives, these women had to support themselves and their families.[43] Young people abandoned their schooling to work for the war; the future writer Konstantin Paustovskii, then a Moscow university student, took leave to become a tram conductor.[44] But non-urban peasant migrants also accounted for an important share of the new wartime working class. Among young people aged fifteen to nineteen in 1917, for example, *at least half* had not resided in the city five years before.[45] The newcomers—of whom there were 123,000 just in this age group—were not all peasant migrants, of course. The evacuation of technologically advanced plants from the Baltic provinces brought over 100,000 highly skilled and urbanized

41. See my dissertation "Moscow Workers in 1917" (University of Michigan, 1976), pp. 117–123, for a discussion of these figures.
42. M. Romanov, "Rabochii sostav i ego dvizhenie v promyshlennykh predpriiatiiakh goroda Moskvy v period voiny," *Statistika truda*, 6–7 (1918): 4–5.
43. *Soldat-Grazhdanin*, May 27, 1917.
44. Konstantin Paustovsky, *The Story of a Life*, trans. Joseph Barnes (New York, 1967), pp. 276–290.
45. *Statisticheskii ezhegodnik*, p. 15.

workers to Moscow. In addition, the educated and mobile youth of skilled workers' families in smaller industrial towns around Moscow were attracted by the city's expanding opportunities and left home to seek jobs in the capital.[46] But although there are no precise figures for the rural-born share of the Moscow proletariat after 1912, migrant peasants must have accounted for much of the increase in the number of new young residents during the war.

This influx of peasants, particularly among youths under seventeen or young men seeking occupational military deferments, created a curious schism in the social fabric of the city's younger generation. Native youths, who perhaps had been schoolchildren or apprentices before the war, now found themselves in line for the best jobs in the city since, compared to the newly arriving peasants, their skills were the best available. To their developing youth culture, these young workers could now add the independence and mobility created by important jobs and relatively good wages.

By contrast, the new peasants had few skills to bring to the workplace and were relatively less familiar with urban life. Like new migrants in less volatile times, they retained much of their village culture as a buffer against the strange ways of the city. Young people in this group probably had little contact with their city-wise coevals.[47]

Thus, on the eve of the 1917 Revolution, Moscow employed two distinct groups of young workers: one urbanized, experienced, relatively well paid; the other newly arrived and unfamiliar with urban ways. Both groups faced the same urban environment: work-oriented, with little time and less opportunity for private social life. But the urban youth had had more chance to develop ways to cope with this environment; evening schools and dramatic circles were open to all, but it was not likely that a new peasant arrival would immediately seek such opportunities. When the March revolution added to this environment the new ingredient of freedom of association (and more free time, as well—the eight-hour

46. O. N. Chaadaeva, "Vooruzhenie proletariata v 1917 godu," *Istoriia proletariata SSSR*, 11 (1932): 48.

47. On village communities in the city, see Robert Eugene Johnson, "Peasant Migration and the Russian Working Class: Moscow at the End of the Nineteenth Century," *Slavic Review*, 35, no. 4 (December, 1976): 652–664.

working day was soon declared by the workers' soviet), we would expect once again that the urbanized youth would most quickly take advantage of the new opportunities offered by the revolution.

Indeed, the first achievement of the revolution was that workers, young or old, urban or migrant, were suddenly free to organize, to plan for the future, to participate fully in public life. "Day and night, across the whole country, a continuous disorderly meeting went on from February until autumn in 1917," recalled Paustovskii.[48] Workers in factories and workshops, groups of friends in dramatic circles and evening schools, veterans of once-legal trade unions instinctively realized that they must organize in order to secure the triumphs of the revolution. Card printers and rubber stamp manufacturers enjoyed a booming business as interest groups all over Moscow sought to formalize their newfound freedom of association, and in this rush to organize, young workers were no exception. In addition to participation in factory committees, local councils (soviets), and trade unions, Moscow working-class youth formed their own generational organizations of circles, youth unions, and youth clubs. Herein lies the crux of the present investigation: What was the relationship of these revolutionary organizations to the facts of urban life already discussed? The answer lies in the nature and function of the youth organizations in the special context of 1917.

Youth groups, like other revolutionary associations, originated in a variety of ways. Some grew spontaneously out of existing youth circles based at neighborhood people's houses or at individual factories. Others were instigated by energetic individuals, some representing party organizations and some only the idea of organization. In the district of Khamovniki, in southwest Moscow, for example, a youth organization was initiated by one A. Viatich, who in 1912 at age fifteen had joined a literary-musical circle, and later attended evening classes at the Prechistenskii school. In 1917, he and his friends from work and from these other activities decided to form a youth organization. Other groups formed in similar ways. One began under the auspices of the local Bolshevik committee; others formed in separate factories. Only in August did the youth of Khamovniki officially unite as a "Third International Union of Youth."[49]

48. Paustovsky, *The Story of a Life*, p. 481.
49. A. Viatich (Berezhnykh), "Khamovnicheskii molodniak," in *Nashe rozhdenie*, pp. 130–132.

The activities of this union varied with the constituencies. At the Vtorov explosives plant, which employed both highly skilled chemical workers and untrained, illiterate women, a clubroom was set aside where advanced workers could read and discuss newspapers; for the women, there were evening classes to learn the rudiments of reading. The differences between native and migrant working youth are evident in the nature of these activities. At the Shchenkov textile factory, which employed only recently migrated village girls, the union also organized literacy classes, taught here by the student members of the group.[50]

Youth groups in the neighboring Zamoskvorech'e district developed somewhat differently. Here at least three distinct youth organizations sprang up, separate and mistrustful of one another. The first group, known as the Third International Union of Youth (but not affiliated with others of the same name in other parts of the city), originated as a faction of young workers at the Mikhel'son metal plant. At first, interested young people met in the evening in the vacant room of the factory committee. They all agreed on the need for a six-hour day for youths and on the importance of further education, but they could not agree on politics. Therefore the nascent union declared it would be "above parties," a common solution to the vexing problem of party conflict at that time.[51] In April the Mikhel'son youth group decided to expand into other factories, ordered 2,000 membership cards printed (which their leader ended up stealing from the printer because the group had no funds to pay for them), and moved into the student cafeteria of the Moscow Commercial Institute, located in the center of their district.[52]

This Zamoskvorech'e union led a double life. Many of its leaders were Bolshevik party members, and one founder recalled that the group's only activities consisted of carrying out Bolshevik agitation, including tearing down opposition posters and breaking up meetings when they failed to win their points by more orderly proce-

50. N. Pen'kov, "1917 god v Khamovnikakh," *ibid.*, pp. 125–126; L. Fedorov, "Khamovnicheskii soiuz rabochei molodezhi," in *Oktiabr' v Khamovnikakh* (Moscow, 1927), pp. 73–75.
51. S. Rigosik, "Pervye komsomoltsy. Vospominaniia," *Molodaia gvardiia*, 12, no. 5 (1933): 121.
52. E. Karmanova and A. Kolpakova, "Soiuz rabochei molodezhi 'III Internatsional' v Zamoskvorech'e," in *Oktiabr' v Zamoskvorech'e* (Moscow, 1957), and Rigosik, "Pervye komsomoltsy," p. 123.

dures. Yet these same Bolshevik leaders refused to make party membership a prerequisite for union membership. In fact, this position caused their exclusion from a conference with an all-Bolshevik youth union late in the year.[53] Such an ambivalent attitude toward party politics was typical of many groups in Moscow, where organizational behavior had more to do with personal loyalties and associations than with ideology. During much of 1917, differences among parties were simply not clear enough to warrant factional battles within organizations as homogeneous as the youth groups.

The Third International youth group had two major rivals for the allegiance of Zamoskvorech'e youth. The first was the Union of Youth of the Moscow Bolshevik Committee, begun in the Tsindel factory by a young worker who had brought the idea from Petrograd. Youths in this factory organized first to represent their interests before the local factory committee, and then expanded to provide social and cultural activities for other area youths. There were sewing and bookbinding lessons for girls and boys, political and literary discussion groups, and, most popular of all, a dramatic group. Membership in the union was limited to party members, but the group sought to expand its political influence by opening a club for non-party youth.[54]

The third Zamoskvorech'e youth group has received the most abuse in subsequent Soviet histories of the Revolution. The Union of Socialist Youth was not limited to workers; sponsored by the Zamoskvorech'e district workers' soviet, the group had two incarnations. At first it was the district's official youth group, attracting "mensheviks, anarchists, and SRs," as well as students who welcomed the revolution because "examinations would not be held" and "they could smoke cigarettes as much as they wanted."[55] This union lost its Bolshevik contingent in April over a theoretical dispute on whether the patriotic socialist Plekhanov would be welcomed as an honorary member. With this defection, the soviet group faltered in midsummer, and was reconstituted in July as the "above-party" socialist union of working youth, with a peak

53. Rigosik, "Pervye komsomoltsy," p. 126.
54. S. Kravchuk, "Nemnogo iz togo, chto zapomnilos'," and P. Deliusin, "Na shturm," in *Oktiabr' v Zamoskvorech'e*, pp. 212–213, 226–230; N., "Odno vospominanie o kollektive," in *Nashe rozhdenie*, pp. 97–98.
55. Deliusin, "Na shturm," pp. 229–30.

membership of four or five hundred. Political difficulties notwithstanding, the union promoted a variety of activities similar to
those offered by other groups: a club, lectures, discussions, and
a library. With at least four hundred members, this group appears to have been one of the largest youth organizations in the
city in 1917.[56]

Even this brief catalog of activities indicates that such youth
groups were only tangentially related to revolutionary politics:
education and culture appear to have been far more important. In
fact, the rather formal and party-minded recollections of youth
activists in Zamoskvorech'e and Khamovniki tend to obscure
another essential function of urban youth groups in 1917, which I
believe provides a key to their popularity. Self-improvement and
politics were an important part of the revolutionary climate, of
course, but the groups also expanded the social opportunities for
Moscow's young workers. This was the chief attraction of the
Bolshevik-sponsored youth group in the Presnia district. The group
was deliberately non-partisan: the young Bolshevik leaders attempted to win converts to the party through the union, rather than
simply to organize youth sections within party cells.[57] The union
was therefore advertised as a new club for youth, rather than as a
political organization.

The leaders, three young Bolsheviks, created the group in May
1917. They were soon joined by two young women friends who
worked at an electrical parts plant. From this nucleus the group
began to solicit members among fellow workers. One of the
women, the well-dressed, city-born Anna Litveiko, found (to her
chagrin) that the biggest attraction of the union among her young
co-workers was that they would be able to meet young men from
other factories at the group's activities. Two of the founders tried to
lead discussion groups on Karl Marx, but Marxism was difficult to
understand, and the youths instead tried to relate the theoretical
concepts to more immediate concerns about their place in the
future society. On Sundays they would go on outings to the countryside, recalled Litveiko, and muse about what life would be like
under communism, which they expected to take its utopian form

56. N. Maslov, "Soiuz sotsialisticheskoi molodezhi v Moskve v 1917–1918 godakh," and
A. N. Atsarkin, "SSRM," in *Nashe rozhdenie*, pp. 102, 79–83.
57. M. Dugachev, "Komsomol krasnoi presni," *Krasnaia Presnia 1905–1917 godov*
(Moscow, 1930), pp. 455–457.

immediately after the inauguration of Soviet power.[58] Would money disappear, they wondered, and what should be the appropriate dress for the model communist? This last was a barb at workers like Litveiko, garbed in "troikas" or matching skirts and tailored jackets.

Also important to the Presnia youth were the relations between male and female members of the group, which tended to overshadow programmatic political differences. Litveiko's sister had fallen in love with a Socialist Revolutionary, and now she was full of the slogans of "land and freedom." Anna's best friend had fallen in love with Fedia Shenogin, an "older man" of thirty, who commanded the local people's militia. When Fedia dropped out of revolutionary activity late in 1917, so did his girl, a charter member of the youth organization. There were even "backward types" who went so far as to marry, but they felt such shame that they kept the union a secret. (Revolutionaries did not have the right to rear a family before the final victory of the revolution, insisted the youth.) But even Litveiko felt the pressure to pair up. She resisted by remaining true to her boyfriend Donat, a student then serving in the army. In short, she acknowledged, "We were all a little in love that summer," and the youth group served as the revolution's romantic instrument.[59]

Finally, it was not only the rank-and-file factory youth who strove to organize in 1917. Even the young members of Moscow's criminal population were inspired by the prospects for radical social change. Leontii Kotomka, the Bolsheviks' indefatigable youth organizer, recalled a visit from two "unusual-looking" youths who, after a moment of embarrassed silence, said they were "representatives of criminal youth." These two wanted to organize a group of their brothers and to give up the life of crime. Kotomka went so far as to attend a meeting of other young thieves and pickpockets in the notorious Khitrovo market, but apparently nothing further came of this attempt at self-rehabilitation.[60]

Although available evidence permits only a selective view of the functions which many youth groups served for their members, even in the intensely political year of 1917, much of the activity was

58. Litveiko, "V semnadtsatom," pp. 3–18.
59. *Ibid.*, p. 9.
60. Leontii Kotomka, "Rozhdenie revoliutsii," *Molodoi Kommunist*, 19, no. 8 (1957): 109–110.

clearly non-political. Dramatic circles, including an entire school of dramatic arts, appear from newspaper reports to have been the most popular activity, but the press also reported evening parties, songfests, excursions, and lectures on assorted non-political themes. Nonetheless, politics could hardly be ignored in these turbulent times. The drama school was justified because workers could develop consciousness through art. [61] Courses were offered in political economy and political "literacy" *(grammotnost')*, and surely gatherings of young people could not avoid discussing the latest political crises. On the eve of the allegedly counter-revolutionary State Conference in August, the constituent meeting of a local youth group sent greetings to the Bolshevik newspaper *Sotsial-Demokrat*, hailing it as the defender of the proletariat. [62] Another group published a resolution demanding that eighteen and nineteen year olds be entitled to vote in local elections, with the familiar argument that if eighteen was considered old enough to fulfill military obligations, it was old enough to fulfill civic obligations, too. [63] Such resolutions give evidence of a growing political consciousness in these youth groups. When the scattered local groups finally combined to form a single youth organization, it was under the banner of proletarian internationalism, in solidarity with the peace-loving workers of the world.

The youth movement reached its peak on October 15. Ten days before the ten that shook the world, an estimated 7,000 to 10,000 young people, including the 2,500 members of the consolidated Third International Union of Youth, took to the streets to demonstrate their presence and their political views. They demanded an end to the war, suffrage for eighteen and nineteen year olds, better protection for young factory labor, and all power to the Soviets. [64] (To be sure, the demonstrators represented only a small fraction of young Moscow workers, of whom there were probably well over 100,000. The demonstration received little public notice; only the self-congratulatory items contributed by the organizer Kotomka appeared in the press the next day.)

When the Bolshevik party seized power in the name of the Soviets, the Red Guard units which formed to defend the seizure

61. *Izvestiia Moskovskogo Soveta Rabochikh Deputatov*, September 17–30, 1917.
62. *Sotsial-Demokrat*, August 10–23, 1917.
63. *Ibid.*, August 20–September 2, 1917.
64. *Nashe rozhdenie*, p. 210.

were composed disproportionately of youth, and many recruits were veterans of the youth movement. Of Red Guards, 43 percent were under twenty-five, compared to only 24 percent of the Moscow male population.[65] This imbalance can be explained in part because the party's Military Organization discouraged the enlistment of married workers, who tended to be older; however, it is also a reflection of the great desire of young partisans to be involved in the fighting. Even the so-called middle-class youth groups, whose members were certainly not Bolshevik supporters, volunteered to serve in the Red Guard medical brigades.[66] One local party branch prohibited its youth section from participating in the fighting, with the secretary going so far as to sit on a box of rifles to keep them out of the hands of young hotheads. But the youthful Bolsheviks forced her from her post and set off to join the street skirmishing.[67] A partial list of the Red Guard casualties in those days confirms the degree of youth participation. At least thirteen of the thirty-five Red Guard victims were twenty-two or younger, boys such as Pavlik Andreev, a fourteen-year-old apprentice at the metal factory where his father was foreman; Aleksei Savkov, an eighteen-year-old railway depot locksmith; and Nikolai Khodiakov, a youth group member and at eighteen already a foreman in a musical instruments workshop.[68]

Although the radicalization of Moscow's youth cohort merely paralleled the leftward shift of the Moscow working class,[69] this examination of the youth organizations suggests some additional reasons why the young, and especially the members of youth groups, were such ardent supporters of the October Revolution and readily risked their lives in its defense. One explanation emerges when we consider which youths were most active in organized

65. Tsypkin, *Krasnaia gvardiia*, p. 108.
66. *Nashe rozhdenie*, p. 83.
67. *Desiat' let* (Moscow, 1927), p. 85.
68. Bolshevik casualties from the October street fighting were estimated to have been 238, according to the official party newspaper. (M. Akhun and V. Petrov, *1917 god v Moskve. Khronika sobytii* [Moscow, 1934], p. 199.) The list of thirty-five is from *Oktiabr'skie dni v Moskve i raionakh* (Moscow, 1922).
69. For a detailed consideration of political shifts in the proletariat at large in Moscow, see Diane Koenker, "The Evolution of Party Consciousness in 1917: The Case of the Moscow Workers," *Soviet Studies*, 30, no. 1 (January, 1978). For Petrograd, see Alexander Rabinowitch, *The Bolsheviks Come to Power* (New York, 1976). See also William G. Rosenberg, "The Russian Municipal Duma Elections of 1917: A Preliminary Computation of Returns," *Soviet Studies*, 21, no. 2 (October, 1969): 131–163.

activities. Did youth groups appeal randomly to Moscow working-class youth, or can certain patterns of involvement be explained by what we know about urban working-class life? Biographical information on youth group activists is scarce and not at all systematic, yet it is possible, using circumstantial evidence and extrapolation from data for older generations of workers, to advance a tentative composite portrait of the active youths.

I have compiled a list of about eighty youths reported in memoirs to have been leaders of these organizations.[70] Most of the few activists whose backgrounds are known tended to be city-born and reared, either in Moscow or Petrograd, and only two of eighty-one were clearly of rural origin. Of the remaining activists, the predominant occupations were printing and metalwork, with textiles and all artisan crafts conspicuously absent. The printing workers in general were the most urbanized in Moscow in 1912. Since entry into the trade was facilitated by prior connections, it is likely that young printers were also of urban stock five years later. The metal industry, while less urbanized than printing, also employed a relatively large number of urbanized workers. Even though the industry expanded as the result of the war, and many young peasants went to the city in search of work, I suspect that the metal industry first hired urban youths away from other industries. Those youths, who, by virtue of their urban residence, knew where to find the best jobs, may then have been replaced by peasants in their old jobs. Such a hypothesis conforms to the picture of urban youth outlined above: city youth had higher educational levels and were better able to adapt to the requirements of the relatively highly skilled metal industry. In any case, it can be established that there was a great deal of inter-factory and inter-industry mobility during the war years,[71] and it is reasonable to assume that the educated and knowledgeable urban youths were able to take advantage of the great demand for skilled metalworkers.

It is dangerous to inch out on this web of prosopographical assumptions, but I propose that the youth groups active in Moscow in 1917 were composed primarily of urban-born or reared young

70. These names come from the collections of memoirs of participants in working-class and youth group activities cited throughout this paper. Additional biographical information was taken from *Geroi Oktiabria* (Moscow, 1957), but the information is so sparse that these conclusions are purely impressionistic.

71. Romanov, "Rabochii sostav i ego dvizhenie." p. 4.

people. In this composition can be found part of the appeal of these groups. Far from feeling alienated and uprooted from familiar surroundings, rural youths who migrated to the city usually entered immediately into communities of fellow villagers who had made the journey before, much as immigrants to the United States today tend to settle with friends and relatives not only of the same ethnic stock, but from the same villages. Rather, it was the urban youth who may have felt alienated: their families were no longer part of this transplanted rural community, and young people had to look elsewhere for a community to which they could belong. For some workers, evening classes and dramatic circles filled this need before the revolution, and in 1917 a major attraction of the youth unions and clubs must have been to provide the kind of community they had missed in the long wartime factory shifts and crowded conditions of city life.

The youth groups alone put young urban workers in the path of political ideas, but their existence does not explain why youth leaned so strongly toward the Bolshevik position by October. Here again a number of factors come into play. Young people generally find themselves in an age of transition, writes Erik Erikson. They are searching for something to believe in and have not yet committed themselves to the existing value structure. [72] The Bolsheviks, more ideologically separate than other more conciliatory parties in 1917, were outsiders, like youth; further, their vision of a radically new social structure was rivaled only by that of the anarchists, who were inherently unable to organize. Others characterize youth as a generation particularly susceptible to extremist "psychopathological" behavior. [73] Again, the Bolshevik party, with its extreme program of Soviet power and its disdain for parliamentary niceties, appealed to this characteristic of youth. With no family responsibilities, few material possessions, and a low stock of human capital (time invested in learning and seniority) youths were freer to take risks with their futures, such as by supporting the Bolshevik gamble for power in October. Finally, the urban character of youth group activists provides another clue to the Bolshevik appeal. Analysis of election results shows that only the Bolshevik party drew its support exclusively from the working class. Socialist

72. Erik H. Erikson, "Youth: Fidelity and Diversity," in *Youth*, p. 3.
73. Moller, "Youth as a Force," citing studies by psychiatrists, p. 258.

Revolutionaries appealed to many peasants and middle-class urbanites as well as to workers, and the Mensheviks also drew substantial support from other groups. [74] Urban youth may have chosen to identify with the party that symbolized urbanism, the party of the urban proletariat.

Credit must also go to the Bolsheviks' handling of the problem of youths' political affiliation. Although some party members wished to subordinate all youth groups to the party hierarchy, the majority of the party's youth organizers recognized that youth, although inherently tending toward radicalism, was too independent to tolerate political subordination. [75] Citing the radicalism of German socialist youth ten years earlier, and how regimentation destroyed these groups' revolutionary potential, Bolshevik organizers propounded a "Little Bo-Peep" strategy: leave youth alone, and they will come home—and in bigger numbers than could ever be expected if they were forced to affiliate with the party in order to join youth organizations. [76] The party's Sixth Congress in August duly adopted this position and continued to support the organization of youth outside of closed party ranks, with results that have been described above. Judging by their newspapers, none of the other socialist parties showed any special interest in the youth groups' potential.

After October the urban youth, mobilized in no small part by their experience in the youth organizations and Red Guard, volunteered for the Red Army. They spent the next three years in active combat with the counter-revolution. Anna Litveiko, for example, broke off with her student friend Donat and joined Kamo's army on the Caucasian front. The 1918 Russian industrial census shows a sharp drop in almost every occupation for males in the 20–25 age group:[77] young workers, many of them veterans of youth groups and Red Guards, committed themselves to defense of the revolu-

74. The composition of voting patterns in 1917 is considered in some detail in Koenker, "Evolution of Party Consciousness."

75. Kenneth Keniston has characterized this attitude as the typical ambivalence of youth toward adult society. The result is a youthful counterculture which wishes not always to oppose society, but merely to keep its distance. (*Youth and Dissent: The Rise of a New Opposition* [New York, 1971], p. 11.)

76. *Shestoi s"ezd RSDRP (bol'shevikov), avgust 1917 goda, Protokoly* (Moscow, 1958), pp. 181–191. On German socialist youth, see Carl E. Schorske, *German Social Democracy 1905–1917* (New York, 1972), pp. 97–108.

77. Tsentral'noe statisticheskoe upravlenie, *Trudy*, vol. 26, tables 3–4.

tion. Judging from the capsule biographies of youth group leaders, many of them were struck down by disease or by White Army bullets and did not return to the city. These youths were the offspring of the new urban working-class family, true "leading proletarians" who had outgrown the values of peasant society. They were skilled, urbanized, educated, and could have provided the new Soviet state with a generation of trained and experienced leaders. Instead, in their zeal they suffered disproportionate casualties during the civil war years. Of those that survived, a substantial number seem to have died in the purge years of 1937 and 1938. Undoubtedly countless other youth activists from 1917, as yet unrehabilitated, were also found guilty of excessive devotion to party principles during this time. Their devotion may have been implanted by the decisive experiences of their youth, and perhaps those experiences permanently transformed the values of this cohort of the population.[78] One of the great tragedies of the Civil War and of the subsequent purges was certainly that some of the country's most able potential leaders perished while serving the cause in which they came to believe in 1917.

78. Social scientists, after Mannheim, call this the "generational effect." Some generational differences are not due to the particular character of youth, but represent the values acquired during the critical years of youth and preserved thereafter. Spitzer, "The Historical Problem of Generations," p. 1385.

Annotated Bibliography

Family history, as a relatively new, interdisciplinary area of study, has no ready starting points for the beginning student or researcher. While western scholars are producing a growing body of literature on aspects of family history of western Europe and the United States, as yet very few studies of Russian family history have appeared, despite a vast corpus of published sources for study in the field, much of it readily available in North American libraries. As is evident from the papers in this volume, a wide variety of sources can and have been used to throw light on the Russian family and its history. These sources range from demographic and medical data (both published and archival) to memoirs, biographies, folk literature and folklore, legal materials, and descriptive and historical studies of various aspects of Russian life. A complete listing of such materials would require a separate volume. We have, therefore, limited the scope of the present bibliography to a small sample of basic works in the several disciplines most relevant to family history (for example, demography, ethnography, the women's emancipation movement) as an introduction to these disciplines and as background for further reading and research. We also list the major monographs by western writers on family history published since the early 1960s, although these works deal almost exclusively with general or theoretical issues or with the history of the family in the western world. A number of the most important bibliographies have been included as an aid to further research, and many of the monographs chosen for inclusion contain useful bibliographies and indications of sources.

One of the principal problems facing anyone doing research on Russian topics is the lack of thorough bibliographic control of Russian books, particularly acute for nineteenth-century publications, and the absence of detailed indexes to material contained in collections, periodicals, and government publications. These gaps in bibliographic coverage make searching for material by subject especially difficult. For this reason we

have included, in the general reference section, some of the most important general guides to and bibliographies of Russian publications, as an aid
to those desiring a systematic guide to materials available in a particular
discipline. We have also included several standard catalogs that provide subject access to materials held by U.S. libraries with large
Russian collections.

The compilers have personally examined all items included in this
bibliography, either at the University of Illinois Library or the Library of
Congress; most items will undoubtedly be available also at other libraries
with substantial Slavic holdings. While our insistence on *de visu* examination of items to be included may exclude some important items, it insures
that students and scholars will have ready access to all titles listed, by
means of interlibrary loan, photocopying or microfilming services, or
personal visits to libraries. We have used standard Library of Congress
romanization for Cyrillic throughout and, in most cases, the Library of
Congress's form of main entry, as an aid to the easy location of items in
library catalogs.

I.   WESTERN WORKS ON FAMILY HISTORY, 1960–

Ariès, Philippe. *Centuries of Childhood: A Social History of Family Life.*
Trans. Robert Baldick. New York: Alfred A. Knopf, 1962. 447 pp.
>   Translation of Ariès's *L'Enfant et la vie familiale sous l'ancien
>   régime*, first published in 1960, the work generally considered as the
>   first serious scholarly study of family history. Ariès gives a detailed
>   description and analysis of important aspects of upbringing and edu-
>   cation of children, and of the evolution of an awareness of childhood
>   as a distinct state in the human life cycle.

Berkner, L. "Recent Research on the History of the Family in Western
Europe." *Journal of Marriage and the Family*, 35 (1973): 395–405.
>   A critical and bibliographic essay examining 131 books and period-
>   ical articles in the field of family history published between 1960 and
>   1972. An excellent bibliographic introduction to the major published
>   works treating western European family history.

Bronfenbrenner, Urie. *Two Worlds of Childhood: U.S. and U.S.S.R.*
New York: Russell Sage Foundation, 1970. viii, 190 pp.
>   A cross-cultural study of childhood, based on the author's extensive
>   observations of Soviet child-rearing and early education, with em-
>   phasis on the roles of the family and various "collective settings."
>   There is a long discussion of the psychological and sociological impli-
>   cations of Soviet methods.

Communal families in the Balkans: The Zadruga. Essays by Philip E.

Moseley and essays in his honor. Ed. Robert F Byrnes. Introduction by Margaret Mead. Notre Dame, Ind.: University of Notre Dame Press, 1976. xxvii, 285 pp.

An excellent compendium on early and recent research on the Balkan complex family forms, with eleven essays on Yugoslav, Albanian, and Romanian peasant families. The volume also includes Moseley's essay "The Russian Family: Old Style and New" (pp. 70–84).

Conze, Werner, ed. *Sozialgeschichte der Familie in der Neuzeit Europas.* Stuttgart: E. Klett Verlag, 1976. 401 pp. (Industrielle Welt: Schriftenreihe des Arbeitskreises für moderne Sozialgeschichte)

A collection of fifteen papers (of which three are in English) on family history, including case studies of German-speaking Europe. The volume contains A. Plakans's paper "Familial Structure in the Russian Baltic Provinces: The Nineteenth Century." There is a useful bibliography.

DeMause, Lloyd, ed. *The History of Childhood.* New York: Psychohistory Press, 1974. 450 pp.

Ten essays covering childhood history from the Roman period through the nineteenth century. DeMause's essay on the periodization of modes of parent-child relations presents a general background for the other papers which deal mainly with childhood in particular cultures and historical periods. Patrick Dunn's essay, "That Enemy Is the Baby," examines the treatment of children and the evolution of ideas on childhood in eighteenth- and nineteenth-century Russia.

Dollar, Charles M., and Richard J. Jensen. *Historian's Guide to Statistics: Quantitative Analysis and Historical Research.* New York: Holt, Rinehart and Winston, 1971. viii, 332 pp.

Introduction to the use of quantitative methods in historical research, including elementary statistics and fundamental data processing. Includes an extensive annotated guide to "resources of value in quantitative historical research" (pp. 236–297).

Family and Inheritance: Rural Society in Western Europe, 1200–1800. Ed. Jack Goody, Joan Thirsk, E. P. Thompson. Cambridge: Cambridge University Press, 1976. vi, 421 pp.

Ten essays on the relationships between familial change and inheritance patterns in western Europe. Fundamental for coverage of recent research.

Family and Society: Selections from Annales: économies, sociétés, civilisations. Ed. Robert Forster and Orest Ranum. Trans. Elborg Forster and Patricia M. Ranum. Baltimore: Johns Hopkins University Press, 1976. x, 261 pp.

Eleven studies in family history from the twelfth through the eighteenth centuries, centering primarily on western Europe, but with an article each on Poland and the Turko-Mongolian cultural area. The articles were originally published in the July-October, 1972, issue of *Annales: économies, sociétés, civilisations.*

The Family in History: Interdisciplinary Essays. Ed. Theodore K. Rabb and Robert I. Rotberg. New York: Harper & Row, 1973. 240 pp. (Harper Torchbooks)

Fifteen articles on various aspects of family history from issues of the *Journal of Interdisciplinary History.* The articles focus on the history of the family in western Europe and the United States, and on theoretical and methodological issues. Includes a bibliographic essay by C. J. Somerville, "Toward a History of Childhood and Youth" (pp. 227–235).

The Family in History. Ed. Charles E. Rosenberg. Philadelphia: University of Pennsylvania Press, 1975. 207 pp. (Haney Foundation series, no. 17)

Seven studies in family history of several areas and periods, including England, Italy, China, and the United States. All the papers have extensive bibliographical references.

Fortes, Meyer. *Kinship and the Social Order: The Legacy of Lewis Henry Morgan.* Chicago: Aldine, 1969. ix, 347 pp. (Lewis Henry Morgan Lectures, 1963)

A study of the development of anthropological theories of kinship and descent, and of Lewis Henry Morgan's pioneering work in this field. Based primarily on data and observations from non-western, traditional societies, the work provides a theoretical framework for the concepts of kinship and social organization.

Geiger H. Kent. *The Family in Soviet Russia.* Cambridge, Mass.: Harvard University Press, 1968. xii, 381 pp. (Russian Research Center Studies, no. 56)

Although primarily oriented toward the Soviet family, this work contains much information that applies to the pre-revolutionary period as well. Topics covered include the Marxist theory of the family; the Soviet regime's attitude and policies toward the family in the early period of Soviet rule; Soviet marriage patterns and types; and parents and children. Contains a useful bibliography and extensive notes on sources.

Glass, D. V., and D. E. C. Eversley, eds. *Population in History: Essays in Historical Demography.* Chicago: Aldine, 1965. ix, 692 pp.

A collection of twenty-seven essays on selected topics in historical demography, with six on general and theoretical aspects, ten dealing with Great Britain, and eleven treating continental Europe and the United States. While not specifically oriented toward family history as such, the contributions include extensive treatment of the historical consequences of family and marriage patterns. The papers have extensive bibliographical data and information on sources.

Goode, William J. *World Revolution and Family Patterns.* New York: Free Press, 1963. xii, 432 pp.

A detailed discussion of traditional family patterns in several major world cultures (sub-Saharan Africa; India; Arabic Islam; China; Japan; the West) and how they have changed in the face of industrialization and urbanization.

Hareven, Tamara K. "Modernization and Family History: Perspectives on Social Change." *Signs: Journal of Women in Culture and Society*, 2, no. 1 (Autumn, 1976): 190–206.

Hareven discusses general concepts and models of modernization, household structures and kinship organization, changing family functions and values, and examines the "usefulness of modernization as a concept for understanding changes in family behavior in American society."

Historical population studies. Special issue of *Daedalus: Journal of the American Academy of Arts and Sciences*, 97, no. 2 (Spring, 1968).

Eighteen papers on historical demography, including several general and theoretical articles and essays on specific areas and times. Countries covered are France, Britain, Spain, Netherlands, and Austria-Hungary.

Hunt, David. *Parents and Children in History: The Psychology of Family Life in Early Modern France.* New York: Basic Books, 1970. xiv, 226 pp.

A study of the childhood of Louis XIII and a discussion of childhood in seventeenth-century France, based on a number of contemporary sources. Hunt summarizes the ideas and works of Erik Erikson and Philippe Ariès and discusses their implications for a general theory of family history and psychology.

Laslett, Peter. *Family Life and Illicit Love in Earlier Generations: Essays in Historical Sociology.* Cambridge: Cambridge University Press, 1977. vii, 270 pp.

A collection of seven essays on various aspects of historical sociology, based on Laslett's research on the history of the family in Western Europe. Also included is a chapter on household and family on slave plantations in the United States. Laslett's introduction discusses the "necessity of a historical sociology," and the first essay gives an overview of the historical characteristics of the Western family. There is a bibliography which includes a number of important recent contributions to family history.

————. *The World We Have Lost*. New York: Scribner's, 1965, xvi, 280 pp.

Laslett describes pre-industrial English social structure, with emphasis on the village community, birth, marriage, and death, and discusses general questions of social change and revolution in the traditional world.

————, ed. *Household and Family in Past Time*. Edited, with an analytic introduction on the history of the family, by Peter Laslett, with the assistance of Richard Wall. Cambridge: Cambridge University Press, 1972. xii, 623 pp. (A publication of the Cambridge Group for the History of Population and Social Structure)

"Comparative studies in the size and structure of the domestic group over the last three centuries in England, France, Serbia, Japan and colonial North America, with further materials from Western Europe." Laslett's introduction (pp. 1–90) provides a general overview of issues and methods in the study of the history of the family. Three articles on Serbian family history are included, one of them on the distinctively Balkan *zadruga*.

Pinchbeck, Ivy, and Margaret Hewitt. *Children in English Society*. London: Routledge and Kegan Paul, 1969–1973. 2 volumes.

Covering the period from Tudor times to the mid-twentieth century, this work examines "social attitudes toward children and the resulting influence on social policy and legislation." Contains an extensive bibliography of childhood studies.

Rosaldo, Michelle Zimbalist, and Louise Lamphere, eds. *Woman, Culture and Society*. Stanford: Stanford University Press, 1974. xi, 352 pp.

Sixteen essays dealing primarily with non-western cultures. The volume includes several cross-cultural, theoretical studies, including Rosaldo's "Woman, Culture, and Society: A Theoretical Overview" (pp. 17–42) and N. Chodorow's "Family Structure and Feminine Personality" (pp. 43–66).

Shorter, Edward. *The Making of the Modern Family*. New York: Basic Books, 1975. xiv, 369 pp.

Shorter traces the evolution of the family and attempts to describe how the processes of modernization affect the family. He discusses household, community, and family relations in traditional society; sexual revolutions; mothers and infants; and the rise of the nuclear family. There is a good annotated bibliography and indication of sources, primarily for the family in western Europe and the United States.

Wrigley, E. A., ed. *Identifying People in the Past*. London: Edward Arnold, 1973. 159 pp.

Six essays dealing with the problems and methods of record linkage of historical records, such as names found in parish registers, early census returns, etc., and of the reconstruction of family histories by these means. Includes a "select bibliography of record linkage" (pp. 151–154).

————. *An Introduction to English Historical Demography, from the Sixteenth to the Nineteenth Century*. New York: Basic Books, 1966. xii, 283 pp.

Six papers in the areas of historical demography, population history and local history, the use of parish registers, family reconstruction, and the use and reliability of early census returns. The collection has a useful annotated bibliography of books and journal articles related to the topics of the papers.

————. *Nineteenth-Century Society: Essays in the Use of Quantitative Methods for the Study of Social Data*. Cambridge: Cambridge University Press, 1972. 448 pp.

A collection of studies on several topics in historical demography and statistical methods in historiography, applied to nineteenth-century Britain. Topics include family structure, utilization of census data, sampling techniques in historical research, criminal statistics and their use, and sources for educational statistics. Includes a bibliography of books, articles, and sources relating to the British Isles.

————. *Population and History*. New York: World University Library, 1969. 255 pp.

An introduction to historical demography, with many examples from British and French population data.

————. "Reflections on the History of the Family." *Daedalus: Journal of the American Academy of Arts and Sciences*, 106, no. 2 (Spring, 1977): pp. 71–85.

The most recent, and probably the best, concise statement of the current state, goals, and importance of family history. Wrigley examines the chief results of research obtained so far (since the early 1960s) on the western European family and mentions a number of areas and issues in need of further investigation. The footnotes serve as a good guide to the best and most important literature in the field.

JOURNALS

The following are among the journals most active in publishing recent research in the area of family history.

Annales: économies, sociétés, civilisations. 1946–. Paris: A Colin. Bimonthly.

Comparative Studies in Society and History. 1958–. Cambridge: Cambridge University Press. Quarterly.
Geschichte und Gesellschaft: Zeitschrift für historische Sozialwissenschaft. 1975–. Göttingen: Vandoeck & Ruprecht. Quarterly.
Journal of Family History: Studies in Family, Kinship and Demography. 1976–. Minneapolis: National Council on Family Relations. Semiannual.
Journal of Interdisciplinary History. 1970–. Cambridge, Mass.: M.I.T. School of Humanities and Social Science. Quarterly.
Journal of Marriage and the Family. 1939–. Minneapolis: National Council on Family Relations. Quarterly.
Journal of Psychohistory: A Quarterly Journal of Childhood and Psychohistory. 1973–. New York: Association for Psychohistory. Quarterly. (Vols. 1–3, 1973–76, had title *History of Childhood Quarterly.*)
Journal of Social History. 1967–. Pittsburgh: Carnegie-Mellon University Press. Quarterly.
Past and Present: A Journal of Historical Studies. 1952–. Oxford: Past and Present Society. Quarterly.
Social History. 1976–. Hull: Department of Economic and Social History, University of Hull. Irregular.

II. PRIMARY REFERENCE SOURCES

GENERAL GUIDES, HISTORICAL BIBLIOGRAPHIES
Horecky, Paul L., ed. *Basic Russian Publications: An Annotated Bibliography on Russia and the Soviet Union.* Chicago: University of Chicago Press, 1962. xxv, 313 pp.

Basic guide to Russian-language publications in social science and humanities fields, including bibliographies, reference sources, important monographs, and periodical titles. Most items are annotated, many in great detail. Relevant sections for an introduction to the literature relating to family history include "Demography" (pp. 58–65), "History" (pp. 66–83), "Women, Marriage, Family" (pp. 150–154), "Youth" (pp. 154–156), "Health Services" (pp. 157–159), "Folklore" (pp. 212–215). The volume is indexed by authors and titles of publications.

———. *Russia and the Soviet Union: A Bibliographic Guide to Western-Language Publications.* Chicago: University of Chicago Press, 1965. xxiv, 473 pp.

A companion volume to Horecky's *Basic Russian Publications,* listing western-language reference sources, monographs, and periodical titles on Russia and the USSR. Emphasis is on publications on the

Soviet period, but literature on pre-revolutionary topics is also included.

Istoriia SSSR: annotirovannyĭ perechen' russkikh bibliografii, izdannykh do 1965 g. Ed. Z. L. Fradkina. 2nd ed. Moskva: Kniga, 1966. 426 pp.

One of the most complete bibliographies of bibliographies on Russian history from the earliest times, with 1,000 listings. In addition to separately published bibliographies, this work includes bibliographies published in monographs, periodicals, and *sborniki*. Additional access to the works listed is provided by personal and geographic name indexes.

Rubakin, N. A. *Sredi knig: opyt obzora russkikh knizhnykh bogatstv v sviazi s istoriei nauchno-filosofskikh i literaturno-obshchestvennykh idei.* 2nd ed. Moskva: Nauka, 1911–15. 3 volumes.

An invaluable basic recommendatory bibliography of pre-revolutionary Russian publications (including translations from western languages), originally meant for libraries and bookstores. The prefatory material is almost 200 pages in length and includes a bibliographic essay on the value of books and their study. Self-education, the theory of bibliographic selection, and classification schemes are discussed. Topics in volume 1 include the study of languages, literature, art, public affairs, and ethics. Volume 2 includes history, religion and the church, the family and its history, public education, political and judicial systems, economic and social systems, systems of material culture, statistics and demography and sociology. Volume 3 covers man and his relationship with nature, and includes the fields of geography, ethnography, and anthropology, and a section on the nationality question in Russia and abroad. Each section is preceded by a bibliographic essay discussing major books in the subject area.

Spravochnik po istorii dorevoliutsionnoi Rossii: bibliografiia. Ed. P. A. Zaĭonchkovskiĭ. Moskva: Kniga, 1971. 514 pp.

A list of almost 4,000 reference aids for research in all aspects of Russian history. Types of materials include encyclopedias, bibliographies, biographical sources, dictionaries, legal materials, archival guides, directories and registers, statistical sources, government publications, and materials on each *guberniia* and many other major cities.

ENCYCLOPEDIAS

Entsiklopedicheskiĭ slovar'. Ed. I. E. Andreevskiĭ. S.-Peterburg: Brokhaus i Efron, 1890–1907. 82 volumes plus 4 supplementary volumes.

The most comprehensive pre-revolutionary Russian encyclopedia, with a wealth of biographical, bibliographical, and geographical data, in addition to articles on individual subjects by prominent Russian scholars. Volumes 54 and 55 are devoted to "Rossiia" and contain much statistical information and many detailed maps.

Entsiklopedicheskiĭ slovar' T-va br. A. i Granat. 7th ed. Moskva: T-vo br. A. i I. Granat, 1910–48. 57 volumes.

The "Granat" encyclopedia went through a number of revisions and reprintings and remains one of the best sources for information on pre-revolutionary Russia and the early Soviet period. Articles are signed and usually give further bibliographic information.

Bol'shaia sovetskaia ėntsiklopediia. Ed. O. Iu. Shmidt. Moskva: Sovetskaia entsiklopediia, 1926–47. 66 volumes.

———. 2nd ed. Ed. S. I. Vavilov. Moskva: Bol'shaia sovetskaia ėntsiklopediia, 1950–57. 51 volumes plus 2-volume index.

———. 3rd ed. Ed. A. M. Prokhorov. Moskva: Sovetskaia ėntsiklopediia, 1970–

The standard Soviet encyclopedias, the third edition of which is now in process of publication. If available, the first edition is preferable, as it has much more information on pre-revolutionary Russian topics than the second or third editions. Contains many longer review articles in addition to short, factual information, and a number of useful bibliographies.

PERIODICAL BIBLIOGRAPHIES

Lisovskiĭ, N. M. *Russkaia periodicheskaia pechat', 1703–1900 gg.: bibliografiia i graficheskiia tablistsy.* Petrograd: Tip. Shumakhera i Brukera, 1915. xiv, 267 pp.

A listing, with bibliographical details, of all periodicals published in Russia before 1900. The volume contains a subject index (pp. 225–252) which identifies periodicals in broad subject areas; for example, children's magazines, education, medicine, ethnography.

Beliaeva, L. N.; M. K. Zinov'eva; and M. M. Nikiforov. *Bibliografiia periodicheskikh izdaniĭ Rossii, 1901–1916.* Leningrad: Gos. publichnaia biblioteka im. M. E. Saltykova-Shchedrina, 1958–61. 4 volumes.

A listing of over 9,500 periodicals published in Russia from 1901 through 1916. Descriptive information for each title includes starting date, exact number of issues published each year, editor, supplements, and availability of indexing. A subject index provides access by specific subject (*e.g.*, "Zhenskiĭ vopros," "Gigiena"), and other indexes give access by city of publication, issuing organization, and editor.

U.S. LIBRARY CATALOGS

New York Public Library. *Dictionary Catalog of the Slavonic Collection.* 2nd ed., rev. and enl. Boston: G. K. Hall, 1974. 44 volumes.

Reproduction of the card catalog (including all subject-heading cards) of one of the richest collections of Russian materials, especially strong for the pre-revolutionary period. Subject access is by specific subject heading; *e.g.*, "Family—Russia," "Children—Russia" or "Russia—Social conditions." The first edition of the catalog (1959; 26 volumes) is also useful for earlier, pre-Soviet materials.

U.S. Library of Congress. *Cyrillic Union Catalog of the Library of Congress. Microprint Edition.* New York: Readex Microprint Corp., 1963.

Divided into three separate sections (authors and added entries, titles, subjects), this catalog represents holdings of Cyrillic alphabet material published in 1956 or before in major North American libraries and reflects the holdings of these libraries as of early 1956. While the catalog does not reflect acquisitions of American libraries since the early 1960s, it does provide virtually the only subject access to older Russian publications in these libraries. Library of Congress subject headings are used.

———. *Library of Congress Catalog. Books: Subjects, 1950–1954.* Ann Arbor: J. W. Edwards, 1955. 20 volumes.

———. *Library of Congress Catalog. Books: Subjects, 1955–1959.* Paterson, N. J.: Pageant Books, 1960. 22 volumes.

———. *Library of Congress Catalog. Books: Subjects, 1960–64.* Ann Arbor: J. W. Edwards, 1965. 25 volumes.

———. *Library of Congress Catalog. Books: Subjects, 1965–69.* Ann Arbor: J. W. Edwards, 1970. 42 volumes.

These four five-year cumulations represent book and journal titles cataloged by the Library of Congress from 1950 through 1969, and provide subject access by the Library's subject headings. The catalog is currently issued quarterly (the title is now *Library of Congress Catalogs: Subject Catalog*) with annual and quinquennial cumulations. The quarterly issues and annual cumulations provide good access to recent material in all languages on specific subjects.

ARCHIVE GUIDES

Grimstead, Patricia Kennedy. *Archives and Manuscript Repositories in the USSR: Moscow and Leningrad.* Princeton, N.J.: Princeton University Press, 1972. 436 pp.

A basic guide to the extensive archival and manuscript holdings in Moscow and Leningrad, intended, among other things, as a starting point for those planning research in the Soviet Union. There is an introductory historical survey on the Soviet archival system and its development, with some explanations of basic procedures involved in using this system. The list itself begins with a general bibliography of comprehensive materials, followed by sections on individual institutions, special archives, and manuscript divisions of libraries and museums. All citations are annotated, and there are indexes and a glossary of archival terms.

III.   DEMOGRAPHY; FAMILY; USE OF QUANTITATIVE METHODS IN HISTORICAL RESEARCH

Darskii, L. E. *Formirovanie sem'i; demografo-statisticheskoe issledovanie.* Moskva: Statistika, 1972. 206 pp.

A general, theoretical treatment of the demography of the family, including detailed discussion of marriage and divorce rates, fertility, and age of first marriage, with examples from recent Soviet statistics. Darskii presents a mathematical model of fertility as a function of a woman's age and the number of previously born children, and examines the influence of massive war losses on demographic processes. A good background in statistics is required to follow some of the analyses. The book has an extensive bibliography of both Soviet and western works on the family and population statistics.

Gozulov, A. I. *Ocherki istorii otechestvennoi statistiki. Moskva: Statistika,* 1972. 312 pp.

A thorough examination of the development and accomplishments of pre-revolutionary Russian statistics. In the absence of a detailed bibliography of pre-1917 Russian statistical sources, this and similar works help to indicate exactly what statistical coverage was maintained and published. Gozulov pays special attention to the roles of the national government, the *zemstva*, and learned societies in gathering and publishing statistical data on Russia. This study includes detailed description of population statistics, primarily those included in the official publications of the Tsentral'nyi statisticheskii komitet such as *Vremennik* and *Statistika Rossiiskoi imperii.* A bibliography of studies on the history of Russian statistics is included.

Gromyko, M. M., and Minenko, N. A. *Iz istorii sem'i i byta sibirskogo krest'ianstva v XVII-nachale XX v.: sbornik nauchnykh trudov.* Novosibirsk: Novosibirskii gosudarstvennyi universitet, 1975. 158 pp.

A collection of six papers on the history of the Siberian peasant family, including an important analysis by N. A. Minenko on the structure of the peasant family in Western Siberia in the early nineteenth century based on archival household census data. Other papers treat folk medicine and the folk religion of the Siberian peasant population, chiefly in the last half of the nineteenth century.

Gurevich, I. B. *Roditeli i dieti. S prilozheniem postanovovlenii dieistvuiushchago zakonodatel'stva, opredieliaiushchikh vzaimnyia otnosheniia roditelei i dietei.* S.-Peterburg: Izdanie Ia. Kantorovich, 1896. 211 pp. (Iuridicheskaia biblioteka, no. 10)

Beginning with a historical essay on the relationship of parents and children, and drawing on both Russian and western sources, the author goes on to discuss many of the legal aspects involved in this relationship—the limitations and cessation of parental authority, the protection of children, responsibilities toward upbringing and education, and adoption and trusteeship. There are bibliographic notes. The supplement consists of a collection of Russian legislation regarding parents and children.

Istochnikovedenie: teoreticheskie i metodicheskie problemy. Ed. S. O. Shmidt *et al.* Moskva: Nauka, 1969.

Eighteen recent essays on a number of general and practical issues dealing with historical sources and their interpretation. Includes a paper by I. D. Koval'chenko on the use of mathematical and statistical methods in historical studies (pp. 115–133) and an essay by A. Ia. Gurevich on the nature of historical sources for the study of social psychology and social history (pp. 384–426). All contributions are extensively documented.

Kabuzan, V. M. *Izmeneniia v razmeshchenii naseleniia Rossii v XVIII— pervoi polovine XIX v., po materialam revizii.* Moskva: Nauka, 1971. 188 pp.

An example of recent research by a Soviet historian on population characteristics of eighteenth- and nineteenth-century Russia, based on archival statistical sources. Kabuzan presents all the statistical data upon which he bases his conclusions and provides extensive bibliographic notes about published and archival sources for the study of Russian population of the period.

Leontovich, F. I. *Istoriia russkago prava.* Varshava: Tip. Varshavskago uchebnago okruga, 1902.

Volume 1, entitled "Literatura istorii russkago prava," is an extensive bibliography on the history of Russian law. All areas of law are covered, and there is access to the many citations on the family, family law, marriage, parents and children, guardianship, adoption, and kinship through the civil law section of the subject index. Other sections of this index include citations on foundling hospitals and orphanages, and there is a section devoted to the legal history of the clergy. An author index is also included.

Matematicheskie metody v issledovaniiakh po sotsial'no-ekonomicheskoi istorii. Ed. by I. D. Koval'chenko. Moskva: Nauka, 1975. 318 pp.

A representative collection of fourteen essays by Soviet historians presenting the results of their research using mathematical and statistical methods. Papers include a general treatment of the use of quantitative analysis in social history and several studies devoted to pre-revolutionary Russia, although none is concerned primarily with the family.

Matematicheskie metody v istoricheskikh issledovaniiakh: sbornik statei. Ed. I. D. Koval'chenko. Moskva: Nauka, Glavnaia redaktsiia vostochnoi literatury, 1972. 234 pp.

Eleven studies devoted to general or specific topics in the use and results of quantitative historical methods. Among the contributions are several on pre-1917 Russian history, including one by N. B. Selunskaia on the problems of using cadastres of Russian estates (pp. 105–124), and two useful review articles: one by Iu. L. Bessmertnyi on some of the main issues of quantitative research in the works of Soviet historians (pp. 3–14), and a bibliographical essay by E. D. Grazhdannikov on historico-statistical research in Russian pre- and post-revolutionary historiography (pp. 208–215).

Mironov, B. N., and Z. V. Stepanov. *Istorik i matematika: matematicheskie metody v istoricheskom issledovanii.* Leningrad: Nauka, Leningradskoe otdelenie, 1975. 183 pp. (Seriia "Sovremennye tendentsii razvitiia nauki")

A general introduction to and discussion of current issues in quantitative historical research, with a number of examples of specific analyses based on eighteenth- and nineteenth-century Russian data. The authors present what they consider to be the most "accepted" mathematical methods in historiography and discuss the historical interpretation of data and problems inherent in using statistical sources of varying reliability. A short bibliography presents essential Soviet works in quantitative historical research.

Palli, H., and R. Pullat. *Eesti ajaloolise demograafia bibliograafia.* Tallinn: Eesti NSV Teaduste Akadeemia, Ajaloo Instituut, 1969. 131 pp. (Töid ajaloolise demograafia alalt)

An exhaustive bibliography of demographic materials relating to general historical demography and to the population development of Estonia in particular, with 559 items listed. The introduction and table of contents are given also in English and Russian.

Problemy byta, braka i sem'i. Comp. N. Solov'ev *et al.* Ed. N. Solov'ev.
Vilnius: Mintis, 1970. 246 pp.

Twenty-six papers on the family, marriage, and family life in general, originally presented at the First Inter-Republic Symposium on the Family and Marriage held in Vilnius in 1967 and sponsored by the Committee for Family Studies of the Soviet Sociological Association. The conference brought together a number of scholars in different disciplines, including medicine, ethnography, education, history, law, and economics. These published papers reflect the interdisciplinary nature of the Symposium, although none of them treats pre-revolutionary Russia. Topics covered include statistical methods and their use in the study of marriage and the family; the family role of working women; divorce; health problems of working women; the influence of education on women's role in the family; the family's influence on domestic architecture.

Problemy demografii: voprosy teorii i praktiki. Ed. D. L. Broner and I. G.
Venetskii. Moskva: Statistika, 1971. 212 pp.

Nineteen papers representing recent Soviet thought and trends in demography, including the economic aspects of population, mathematical and statistical methods in demography, the influence of demography on government policy, as well as general articles summarizing the current state of demographic research in the Soviet Union. Includes a good bibliographical essay on demographic literature (pp. 193–206).

Rashin, A. G. *Naselenie Rossii za 100 let, 1811–1913 gg.; statisticheskie ocherki.* Moskva: Gos. statisticheskoe izd-vo, 1956.

Rashin presents a wide variety of Russian demographic data in summary form (with indication of the source of his data) on a variety of topics relevant to the historian, such as fertility, marriage, morbidity and mortality rates, population movements, urbanization, literacy, class structure, and occupation. While somewhat difficult to use because it lacks an index and table of contents, the bibliographic footnotes provide rich data for further sources of Russian demographic statistics.

Rozhdaemost': problemy izucheniia. Ed. L. E. Darskii. Moskva: Statistika, 1976. 140 pp.

A collection of articles by researchers at the Demography Section of the Research Institute of the USSR Central Statistical Agency, dealing with fertility rates and their implications in various aspects of Soviet life. While oriented toward the Soviet period, the papers represent the most recent Soviet trends in the theory and methodology of this important aspect of demographic research.

Studia historica in honorem Hans Kruus. Ed. J. Kahk and A. Vassar. Tallinn: Eesti NSV Teaduste Akadeemia, Ajaloo Instituut, 1971. 415 pp.

Nineteen essays, some by Estonian historical demographers, in Russian, German, English, and Estonian, including H. Palli's "Historical Demography of Estonia in the Seventeenth-Eighteenth Centuries and Computers" (pp. 205–222; in English).

Ustinov, V. A., and A. F. Felinger. *Istoriko-sotsial'nye issledovaniia, EVM i matematika.* Moskva: Mysl', 1973. 324 pp.

Basic treatment of the uses of mathematical, statistical, and computer approaches to historical and social research, based on Ustinov's pioneering *Primenenie vychislitel'nykh mashin v istoricheskoi nauke* (Moskva: Mysl', 1964).

Vasil'eva, E. K. *Sem'ia i ee funktsiia; demografo-statisticheskii analiz.* Moskva: Statistika, 1975. 179 pp.

A study focusing on the urban Soviet family, detailing the influences of the family on contemporary "social" factors such as education and labor. Includes a good review of the history of family study in the Soviet Union (with some material on pre-revolutionary Russian studies) and copious bibliographical notes.

Vladimirskii-Budanov, M. F. *Obzor istorii russkago prava.* 6th ed. S.-Peterburg: Izdanie knigoprodavtsa N. Ia. Ogloblina, 1909. 699 pp.

One of the basic histories of Russian law, with a section devoted to the history of Russian family law. From a judicial standpoint, the family is viewed in two ways—the husband and wife, and parents and children, with the rights and responsibilities of each being discussed. Particular emphasis is given to all the legal aspects of marriage. There are footnotes and a lengthy bibliography, with its own section on the history of family law.

IV.   ETHNOGRAPHY; FOLKLORE; FOLK ART

Afanas'ev, A. N., comp. *Narodnye russkie skazki.* Ed. M. K. Azadovskii, N. P. Andreev and Iu. M. Sokolov. Moskva: Academia, 1936–40. 5th ed. 3 volumes.

One of the most famous collections of Russian folktales, with an introductory essay on the life and work of Afanas'ev. Notes and bibliographies.

Azadovskii, M. K. *Istoriia russkoi fol'kloristiki.* Moskva: Gos. uchpedgiz., 1958–63. 2 volumes.

A basic text in Russian folklore historiography, this work traces the development and problems of Russian folklore studies in the context of the social, literary, and political environment of Russia from the eighteenth century to the Soviet period. Individuals important to folklore scholarship are discussed in some detail, as is the relationship between folklore studies and other emerging fields such as ethnography. Extensive bibliographic notes.

Balashov, D. M., comp. *Narodnye ballady.* Ed. A. M. Astakhova. Moskva: Sovetskii pisatel', 1963. 2nd ed. 446 pp.

Collection of folk ballads, with an introductory essay by the compiler. Bibliography and source notes.

Binkevich, E. R., comp. *Ustnoe tvorchestvo narodov SSSR; bibliograficheskii ukazatel'.* Moskva: Gos. biblioteka SSSR im. V. I. Lenina, 1940. 95 pp.

This bibliography on the oral tradition of the Soviet peoples is divided first geographically, then by genre, with the section on Russian folklore being the largest. Brief annotations for most items.

Bunakova, O. V., and R. V. Kamenetskaia, comps. *Bibliografiia trudov instituta etnografii im. N. M. Miklukho-Maklaia, 1900–1962.* Leningrad: Nauka, 1967. 281 pp.

A bibliography of over 5,000 items, all publications of the Soviet Academy of Sciences' Institute of Ethnography and its Museum of Anthropology and Ethnography. The five major divisions include general works, general and theoretical works on ethnography, the ethnography of the peoples of the Soviet Union, the ethnography of foreign peoples, and a final section on anthropology. Of particular interest are the sections devoted to social structure, the family and marriage, and systems of kinship.

Dal', V. I. *Poslovitsy russkago naroda; sbornik.* Moskva: Goslitizdat, 1957. 990 pp.

A collection of Russian proverbs, sayings, riddles, etc., reprinted from the 1862 edition. There is an introduction to the reprint edition by V. Chicherov, as well as the original introductory essay by Dal'.

Dunn, Stephen P., and Ethel Dunn, eds. *Introduction to Soviet Ethnography.* Berkeley: Highgate Road Social Science Research Station, 1974. 2 volumes.

A selection of representative articles translated into English to acquaint the reader with the Soviet tradition in ethnographic studies, with articles chosen specifically to elucidate those aspects which most differ from western scholarship in this field. There is a long introductory essay discussing these differences, and a bibliography of selected readings in English.

Oinas, Felix J., and Stephen Soudakoff, eds. *The Study of Russian Folk-*

lore. The Hague: Mouton, 1975. 341 pp. (Slavistic Printings and Reprintings, Textbook Series, no. 4. Indiana University Folklore Institute, Monograph Series, no. 25)

Translated selections from Russian monographs and journals by prominent Soviet folklorists, chosen with the aim of acquainting western folklorists and students with representative trends in Soviet research. Included are a glossary of special Slavic folklore terms and a selected bibliography of Russian, other Slavic, and western language works.

Pronin, Alexander, and Barbara Pronin. *Russian Folk Arts.* South Brunswick and New York: A. S. Barnes, 1975. 192 pp.

Areas covered include the icon, the *lubok* (broadside), lacquers, bonecarving, woodcarving, ceramics, tiles, toys, metalwork, embroidery, weaving and prints, and carpets. A brief history of each art form is given, with mention made of the major Russian texts and scholars in that area. There are definitions of Russian terms throughout, many illustrations, a selective bibliography and a detailed index.

Propp, V. Ia., comp. *Narodnye liricheskie pesni.* Leningrad: Sovetskii pisatel', 1961. 2nd ed. 609 pp.

A collection of lyric folksongs by a prominent Russian folklorist. There is a long introductory essay on the genre, a bibliography, and source notes.

Pypin, A. N. *Istoriia russkoi etnografii.* S. Peterburg: Tip. M. M. Stasiulevicha, 1809–92. 4 volumes.

An important work in ethnographic historiography, with a strong emphasis on the development of ethnography as a science. Very broad in scope, it discusses not only important individuals and trends, but also the societies and institutions related to the study of ethnography. Important journals and individuals are also discussed in detail, as well as expeditions and new research. The first two volumes are devoted to Great Russia, while volume 3 examines developments in Little Russia (Ukraine) and Poland; the last volume is concerned with White Russia and Siberia. There are extensive footnotes, but no bibliography.

Russkie. Istoriko-etnograficheskii atlas. Zemledelie. Krest'ianskoe zhilishche. Krest'ianskaia odezhda. (Seredina XIX–nachalo XX veka.) Ed. V. A. Aleksandrov *et al.* Moskva: Nauka, 1967. 356 pp.

―――. *Karty.* Moskva: Nauka, 1967. 40 sheets.

Valuable reference source combining a general description of the material culture of the Russian people, along with an elaborate series of ethnographic maps. There are many illustrations and typological tables, with detailed information on sources, including some bibliographic notes.

Russkii fol'klor. Ed. A. M. Astakhova *et al.* Moskva: Akademiia nauk SSSR, 1956–72. 13 volumes.

Each volume consists of a selection of articles generally devoted to one aspect of folklore scholarship, as well as containing previously unpublished material, proceedings of meetings, etc. Each also includes a section consisting of bibliographic essays, bibliographies on various genres or individual folklorists, and on dissertations in the field. Volume 10 includes a subject index of the articles in the first ten volumes of the series.

Russkii fol'klor; bibliograficheskii ukazatel', 1917–1944. Comp. M. Ia. Mel'ts. Ed. A. M. Astakhova and S. P. Luppov. Leningrad: Biblioteka Akademii Nauk, 1966. 682 pp.

Russkii fol'klor; bibliograficheskii ukazatel', 1945–1959. Comp. M. Ia. Mel'ts. Ed. A. M. Astakhova and S. P. Luppov. Leningrad: Biblioteka Akademii Nauk, 1961. 401 pp.

Russkii fol'klor; bibliograficheskii ukazatel', 1960–1965. Comp. M. Ia. Mel'ts. Ed. A. M. Astakhova and S. P. Luppov. Leningrad: Biblioteka Akademii Nauk, 1967. 538 pp.

A series of comprehensive bibliographies listing all folklore literature published in the Soviet Union between 1917 and 1965. Each volume begins with a bibliographic essay on the state of Soviet folklore research. In addition to monographs and newspaper and journal articles, the bibliography also includes special collections, research papers, and musical and literary adaptations. First listed are texts, divided by genre, followed by a section of works about folklore, and a final section on pedagogical and methodological materials, as well as bibliographic surveys.

Semenov-Tian'-Shanskii, Veniamin P., ed. *Rossiia; polnoe geograficheskoe opisanie nashego otechestva. Nastol'naia i dorozhnaia kniga dlia russkikh liudei.* S. Peterburg: Izdanie A. F. Devriena, 1899–1913. 11 volumes.

Each volume in this basic reference work is devoted to a different area of the Russian Empire. Each has three major divisions, the first being Nature, and describing in some detail the area's geology, climate, flora, and fauna. For basic ethnographic information, the second division on Population is the most directly useful. A short history of the region is followed by a section on population distribution, the region's ethnic composition, and the life and culture of its people. Family life, morality and religion, language, dress, and habitat are all discussed. Other sections deal with trade, business, and agriculture. In the final major division the region's major cities and places of interest are described. There is a great deal of statistical information, and many maps and illustrations. Each volume has a bibliography of Russian and western language sources.

Sokolov, Iu. M. *Russkii fol'klor*. Moskva: Uchpedgiz, 1941. 559 pp. Trans. Catherine R. Smith as *Russian Folklore*. Introduction and bibliography by Felix J. Oinas. Hatboro, Penn.: Folklore Associates, 1966. 760 pp.

This university textbook (reprinted from the 1938 ed.) is very comprehensive, covering all aspects of Russian folklore from earliest times, but with its major emphasis on the nineteenth and twentieth centuries. All of the various genres (except ballads) are discussed, and the book ends with a general review of non-Russian Soviet folklore. There is a long chapter giving a basic review of folklore scholarship. Each chapter has a selective bibliography. The English translation includes a brief introductory essay discussing Sokolov and his work. There is an additional bibliography of basic western language works.

Tereshchenko, A. V. *Byt russkago naroda*. S. Peterburg: Tip. Ministerstva vnutrennikh diel, 1848. 7 volumes.

A detailed description of customs, traditions, and lifestyles of the Russian peasantry, based primarily on the author's personal observations. There is a great deal of material on customs and ceremonies surrounding birth, marriage, family life, and death.

Tokarev, S. A. *Etnografiia narodov SSSR; istoricheskie osnovy byta i kul'tury*. Moskva: Izd-vo Moskovskogo universiteta, 1958. 615 pp.

Based on the author's university lectures, this survey begins with a brief introduction on the methodology of ethnography. A short history of each major Soviet nationality group is then given, followed by descriptions of its material culture (agriculture and industry, crafts, architecture, etc.) and the various aspects of its social and cultural life, such as the family, marriage, religion, folklore, folk art, and music. A bibliography corresponds to the divisions of the text.

Zelinin, D. K. *Bibliograficheskii ukazatel' russkoi etnograficheskoi literatury o vnieshnem bytie narodov Rossii, 1700–1910 g.g. (Zhilishche. Odezhda. Muzyka. Iskusstvo. Khoziaistvennyi byt.)* S.-Peterburg: Tip. A. V. Orlova, 1913. 731 pp. (Zapiski Imp. Russkago geograficheskago obshchestva po otdieleniiu etnografii, t. 40, vyp. 1. Trudy Komissii po sostavleniiu etnograficheskikh kart Rossii, 1)

An extensive bibliography on the literature of Russian ethnography, divided into six major categories. The first, dealing with general works, lists ethnographic maps, books, and articles dealing with the lifestyles of individual and related peoples of the Russian Empire. Section two deals with habitats, three with dress, four with music, and five with folk art. Section six, the largest, deals with the economic and agricultural life of the various nationalities.

V. MEDICAL AND PUBLIC HEALTH ASPECTS

Bol'shaia meditsinskaia entsiklopediia. Ed. N. A. Semashko. Moskva: Sovetskaia entsiklopediia, 1928–1936. 35 volumes.

————. 2nd ed. Ed. A. N. Bakulev. Moskva: Sovetskaia entsiklopediia, 1956–65. 36 volumes.

Detailed, extensive treatment of medical topics, including public health and medical history. The first edition is preferable, as it contains much more information on pre-revolutionary Russian medicine and public health, including bibliographic and biographic data.

Griaznov, Pavel. *Opyt sravnitel'nago izucheniia gigienicheskikh uslovii krest'ianskago byta i mediko-topografiia Cherepovetskago uiezda.* S.-Peterburg, 1880.

Ethnographic and statistical study of a peasant district in the Novgorod *guberniia*, aimed at showing the medical and public health conditions of the area. Griaznov presents much of the statistical data on which he bases his description and conclusions, including detailed data on infant mortality, fertility, and morbidity. An example of a number of "medical topographies" published in the latter part of the nineteenth century.

Levit, M. M. *Stanovlenie obshchestvennoi meditsiny v Rossii.* Moskva: Meditsina, 1974. 230 pp.

A history of the early years of the public health movement in Russia in the 1850s and 1860s. Detailed consideration of factors leading to increased awareness of rural and urban health conditions, and of the roles of individuals and organizations in gathering information on health conditions and planning systematic public health services. Contains an extensive bibliography on the history of the public health movement.

————. *Meditsinskaia periodicheskaia pechat' Rossii i SSSR, 1792–1962.* Moskva: Gos. izd-vo meditsinskoi literatury, 1963. 242 pp.

A history of the medical press and a complete, annotated bibliography of medical journals published in Russia, this guide is especially useful in identifying those journals which published material on "social medicine" and public health. The bibliography is arranged alphabetically by title of the journal and contains a subject index and a bibliography of works about Russian medical periodicals

Lotova, E. I. *Russkaia intelligentsiia i voprosy obshchestvennoi gigieny: pervoe gigienicheskoe obshchestvo v Rossii.* Moskva: Gos. izd-vo meditsinskoi literatury, 1962. 196 pp.

A history of the *Obshchestvo okhraneniia narodnogo zdrav'ia,* founded in 1877, and of the society's efforts and campaigns in the public health movement. Many of the society's publications contain valuable source material for the study of Russian health conditions, and this work gives a full bibliography of the society's journals, conference proceedings, annual reports, etc.

Merkova, A. M., ed. *Ocherki istorii otechestvennoi sanitarnoi statistiki.* Moskva: Meditsina, 1966. 286 pp.

Five papers, four of them treating the pre-revolutionary period, on the history of Russian medical and public health statistics and on the public health movement in general. Belgorodskaia's essay, "Istoki sanitarnoi statistiki v Rossii," is a historical and bibliographical essay outlining the development of medicine and public health statistics in Russia from the mid-eighteenth to the mid-nineteenth centuries. Other papers discuss the history of public health statistics in the latter nineteenth century, the role of provincial physicians in the development of public health statistical coverage, and problems of urban health statistics. All the papers contain a wealth of bibliographic data.

Petrov, B. D. *Ocherki istorii otechestvennoi meditsiny.* Moskva: Gos. izd-vo meditsinskoi literatury, 1962. 301 pp.

A collection of several articles on various aspects of Russian medical history, including the public health movement, public health legislation, medical societies, and individuals prominent in the development of Russian medicine.

Popov, G. I. *Russkaia narodno-bytovaia meditsina, po materialam Etnograficheskago biuro kniazia V. N. Tenisheva.* S.-Peterburg: Tip. A. S. Suvorina, 1903. viii, 404 pp.

A detailed ethnographic study of the folk medicine of the Great Russian peasantry, including folklore regarding physical and mental illness.

Rossiiskii, D. M. *Istoriia vseobshchei i otechestvennoi meditsiny i zdravookhraneniia: bibliografiia, 996–1954 gg.* Moskva: Gos. izd-vo meditsinskoi literatury, 1956. 935 pp.

An extensive bibliography of works on the history of medicine and public health. The long section on the history of pre-revolutionary Russian medicine (pp. 239–715) has separate sections on Russian medicine in the eighteenth century, the public health movement, and folk medicine.

Zabludovskii, P. E. *Istoriia otechestvennoi meditsiny. chast 1: Period do 1917 goda.* Moskva: Tsentral'nyi institut usovershenstvovaniia vrachei, 1960. 398 pp.

A history of Russian medicine from the Kievan period through 1917, with emphasis on the eighteenth and nineteenth centuries. Contains detailed history of the public health movement, including discussion of *zemstvo* medicine, Pirogov societies, urban medical care, and medical societies and congresses.

PERIODICALS

Much information on Russian medical and public health conditions is available in the periodical literature of the latter nineteenth and early twentieth centuries. The most important titles are listed below.

Arkhiv sudebnoi meditsiny i obshchestvennoi gigieny. 1865–71. S.-Peterburg. (Continued by *Sbornik sochinenii po sudebnoi meditsiny, subebnoi psikhiatrii, meditsinskoi politsii, obshchestvennoi gigienie.*)

Gigiena i sanitarnoe dielo. 1914–17. Petrograd. (Continues *Zhurnal Russkago obshchestva okhraneniia narodnago zdraviia.*)

Obshchestvennyi vrach. 1909, 1911–19, 1922. (Continues *Zhurnal Obshchestva russkikh vrachei v pamiat' N. I. Pirogova.*)

Russkii vrach. 1902–17. S. Peterburg. (Continues *Vrach.*)

Sbornik sochinenii po sudebnoi meditsiny, sudebnoi psikhiatrii, meditsinskoi politsii, obshchestvennoi gigienie. 1872–81. S.-Peterburg. (Continues *Arkhiv sudebnoi meditsiny i obshchestvennoi gigieny;* continued by *Viestnik sudebnoi meditsiny i obshchestvennoi gigieny.*)

Viestnik obshchestvennoi gigieny, sudebnoi i prakticheskoi meditsiny. 1889–1917. Petrograd. (Continues *Viestnik sudebnoi meditsiny i obshchestvennoi gigieny.*)

Viestnik sudebnoi meditsiny i obshchestvennoi gigieny. 1882–88. S.-Peterburg. (Continues *Sbornik sochinenii po sudebnoi meditsiny, sudebnoi psikhiatrii, meditsinskoi politsii, obshchestvennoi gigienie;* continued by *Viestnik obshchestvennoi gigieny, sudebnoi i prakticheskoi meditsiny.*)

Zhurnal akusherstva i zhenskikh boleznei. 1887–1917. S.-Peterburg.

Zhurnal Russkago obshchestva okhraneniia narodnago zdraviia. 1891–1913. S.-Peterburg. (Continued by *Gigiena i sanitarnoe dielo.*)

Zhurnal Obshchestva russkikh vrachei v pamiat' N. I. Pirogova. 1895–1908. S.-Peterburg. (Continued by *Obshchestvennyi vrach.*)

VI. WOMEN

Amfiteatrov, A. *Zhenshchina v obshchestvennykh dvizheniiakh Rossii.*
Zheneva: Tip. Bunda, 1905. 56 pp.

A reprint of a lecture given at the High Russian School of Social
Sciences in Paris in 1905, the work discusses in a general way the role
of women in the literary and social context of eighteenth and
nineteenth-century Russia.

D'iakonova, E. A. *Dnevnik Elizavety D'iakonovoi, 1886–1902 g.*
Literaturnye etiudy, stikhotvoreniia, stat'i, pis'ma. Moskva: Izdanie
V. M. Sablina, 1912. 4th ed. 837 pp.

Three previously published diaries of a young Russian student of
the 1890s (*Dnevnik odnoi iz mnogikh; Dnevnik na Vyshikh Zhenskikh Kursakh; Dnevnik russkoi zhenshchiny*). Well received by literary critics of the day, these diaries were praised as both a historical
and a biographical document, revealing characteristics of contemporary intellectual trends and attitudes. Although the diaries are very
personal in nature, their value was felt to be that they were "typical,"
reflecting a great many young, intelligent, literate girls of the period.
Biographical and critical information is given in the prefatory material. Also included is a small selection of D'iakonova's verse
and articles.

Engel, Barbara Alpern, and Clifford N. Rosenthal, eds. *Five Sisters:
Women Against the Tsar.* Foreword by Alix Kates Shulman. New
York: Knopf, 1975. 249 pp.

The translated memoirs of five female revolutionaries: Vera
Figner, Vera Zasulich, Praskovia Ivanovskaia, Olga Liubatovich, and
Elizaveta Kovalskaia. Their writings give an intimate portrait of
women of various backgrounds of the last half of the nineteenth
century. There is a selected bibliography, including the sources of
the translated material.

Kechedzhi-Shapovalov, M. V. *Zhenskoe dvizhenie v Rossii i zagranitsei.*
S.-Peterburg: Tip. E. Evdokimova, 1902. 210 pp.

A brief survey of the women's emancipation movement in Russia,
Europe, America, and Japan, with the section on Russia being the
most comprehensive. Broad in scope, such aspects of the movement
as education, employment, women's societies, women in the professions, and self-help organizations are covered. Also discussed are
philosophical and theoretical aspects of the movement—the right of
women to serve in various professions, and women's involvement in
world affairs. There are some notes and a bibliography.

Likhacheva, E. O. *Materialy dlia istorii zhenskago obrazovaniia v Rossii.*

S.-Peterburg: Tip. M. M. Stasiulevicha, 1899–1901. 2 volumes.

Broad in scope, this history, encompassing the eleventh to the late nineteenth centuries, examines both private and public attitudes about women's education, efforts toward reform and reorganization, and the establishment of various kinds of institutions specifically for women. Theoretical questions concerning free schools, education for peasant women, and professional training for women are also discussed. A valuable work because it goes beyond the history of education and touches on many aspects of women's changing role in Russian society. There are extensive footnotes, but no bibliography.

Rubakin, N. A. "Stroi semeinyi i ego istoriia," in his *Sredi knig. Opyt obzora russkikh knizhnykh bogatstv v sviazi s istoriei nauchno-filosofskikh i literaturno-obshchestvennykh idei.* Moskva: Nauka, 1913. Vol. 2, pp. 340–361.

A large portion of this section of Rubakin's bibliography deals specifically with women and covers books, chapters, and articles on motherhood, marriage, the woman question, women's position in society, the right to equal education and career opportunities, the problems of prostitution and crime, and the problems of the emancipation movement. Although many of the items cited deal with these topics in a general way or with reference to other countries, a substantial number deal specifically with women in Russia. There is a lengthy introductory essay which discusses each topic in its turn.

Satina, S. *Obrazovanie zhenshchin v dorevoliutsionnoi Rossii.* N'iu Iork, 1966. 152 pp. Trans. Alexandra F. Poustchine as *Education of Women in Pre-Revolutionary Russia.* New York, 1966. 153 pp.

A general survey of elementary, secondary, and higher education for women, with the major emphasis on 1850–1900. Public and private institutions of all kinds are discussed. Particularly interesting are the personal recollections of the author, who was a graduate of the Russian School of Higher Education for Women (Bestuzhev Courses). A popular treatment of the subject. There are tables and charts and a selective bibliography.

Shashkov, S. S. *Istoricheskiia sud'by zhenshchiny, dietoubiistvo i prostitutsiia.* S.-Peterburg: N. A. Shigin, 1871. 623 pp.

Claiming that previous historians have been against the emancipation of women, the author attempts to present a history of women. His basic premise is that the emancipation movement is not a new occurrence, but the result of a gradual progression over a long period of time. He presents extensive material on the history of women in Russia and western Europe. Each section begins with a selected bibliography.

Shchapov, A. P. *Sochineniia*. S.-Peterburg: Izdanie M. V. Pirozhkova, 1906–8. 3 volumes.

A collection of essays by a historian and writer of the 1860s who discussed the various movements within society in a natural history context. Several of the essays deal specifically with women in Russian society and are interpretive rather than strictly descriptive.

Stites, Richard. *The Women's Liberation Movement in Russia. Feminism, Nihilism, and Bolshevism, 1860–1930*. Princeton, N.J.: Princeton University Press, 1978. 465 pp.

A thorough examination of the philosophical and historical developments which resulted in "the communist variety of women's liberation in Russia." In the first two sections the author discusses developments up to 1881, including Russian feminism, nihilism and radicalism, while in the final two sections, which comprise the major portion of the book, he discusses the suffrage struggle of the early years of the twentieth century, and the status of women during and after the Bolshevik Revolution. The only comprehensive study in English, this is a valuable source of information, which includes extensive notes and a lengthy bibliography.

Trudy 1-go Vserosiiskago zhenskago s"ezda pri Russkom Zhenskom Obshchestvie v S.-Peterburgie, 10–16 dekabria 1908 goda. S.-Peterburg: Tip. S.-Peterburgskoi Odinochnoi tiur'my, 1909. 927 pp.

This conference addressed itself to all aspects of woman's position in society and in the family, discussing her economic, political, and legal status, as well as the state of education for women. Topics of the many papers presented are wide-ranging, examining such issues as woman's role as artist, worker, and mother, the problems of alcoholism and prostitution, as well as many papers devoted to the history of the woman question in Russia and abroad. Bibliographic notes, but no bibliography.

"Ukazatel' literatury zhenskago voprosa na russkom iazykie." *Sievernyi viestnik*, vols. 7–8(1887): 1–55.

A comprehensive bibliography of over 1,700 citations, including original Russian works and numerous translations from western language sources. Citations cover material about women throughout the world, from ancient to modern times, but a sizable number pertain specifically to women in Russia. Topics include the history of women, their contemporary position in society, female literary types, the woman question (marriage, love, childbearing, prostitution, crime, etc.), education, and women in the professions, the arts, labor, and agriculture.

PERIODICALS

Drug zhenshchin; literaturno-nauchnyi zhurnal. 1882–84. Moskva.

In addition to stories, poems, and essays, the journal includes articles on women's education, employment, the woman question in general, and the upbringing of children.

Zhenskii viestnik; ezhemesiachnyi obshchestvenno-nauchno-literaturnyi zhurnal, posviashchennyi zhenskomu voprosu. 1904–17. S.-Peterburg.

Includes articles and essays on the social and economic life of women in Russia and abroad. There are sections on *belles lettres,* legislation about women, and critical articles and bibliographies.

Zhenskoe dielo; ezhenediel'nyi illiustrirovannyi zhurnal. 1910–16. Moskva.

As well as articles on the woman question and the position of women in society, art, and science, the journal includes biographies of contemporary women, articles on the history of emancipation, legislative developments, and also a section on fashion and the household. Articles are generally more popular in nature than those in *Zhenskii viestnik.*

Zhenskoe obrazovanie; pedagogicheskii listok dlia roditelei, nastavnits i nastavnikov izdavaemyi pri S.-Peterburgskikh zhenskikh gimnaziiakh. S.-Peterburg, 1876–91.

Divided into an official section concerned with curriculum and new programs and an unofficial section of articles on women and children's education, as well as historical and methodological articles.

VII. CHILDREN; YOUTH; CHARITABLE INSTITUTIONS

Alpatov, N. I. *Uchebno-vospitatel'naia rabota v dorevoliutsionnoĭ shkole internatnogo tipa: iz opyta kadetskikh korpusov i voennykh gimnaziĭ v Rossii.* Moskva: Gos. uch.-ped. izd-vo RSFSR, 1958. 243 pp.

A recent Soviet study of the education of orphans in military schools in Russia from the mid-eighteenth century through 1917. Alpatov examines the development of these institutions, the type of upbringing and education they provided, and indicates sources for further study of the question.

Bozherianov, I. N. *Dietstvo, vospitanie i lieta iunosti russkikh imperatorov.* S.-Peterburg: Obshchestvo popecheniia o bezpriiutnykh dietiakh, 1914. iv, 128 pp.

A popular work on the childhood and youth of the Russian emperors from Peter the Great to Alexander III, including discussion of their early education and upbringing. Includes many reproductions of portraits of the czars as children.

Bozhovich, L. I. *Lichnost' i ee formirovanie v detskom vozraste: psikhologicheskoe issledovanie.* Moskva: Prosveshchenie, 1968. 463 pp.

    A modern Soviet study of children and youth from a psychological point of view. Topics covered include child-rearing and its psychological and social effects, the development of personality, and a general theory of child development. The study includes a 237-item bibliography of Russian and western works on children.

Materialy dlia istorii Imperatorskago Moskovskago vospitatel'nago doma. Moskva: Tip. Semena, 1863–68. 2 volumes.

    Published on the occasion of the hundredth anniversary of the Moscow Foundling Home, the volume presents, in addition to the history and sources for the study of the home, a wealth of statistical material on children, including statistics on morbidity and mortality.

Obshchestvennoe i chastnoe prizrienie v Rossii. S.-Peterburg: Glavnoe upravlenie po dielam miestnago khoziaĭstva Ministerstva vnutrennikh diel, 1907. 296 pp.

    A general work on the development of charitable institutions in Russia, prepared for the Fourth International Congress on Public and Private Charities. A long introductory essay by E. D. Maksimov on the development of charities in Russia (pp. 1–68) includes a bibliography on the topic. A special section on charitable institutions and homes for children (pp. 185–296) contains six articles on various aspects of the subject, including a detailed study of child mortality in the years 1895–99 in fifty *gubernias* of European Russia (pp. 261–296).

Schil'der, N. K. *Imperator Nikolaĭ Pervyĭ, ego zhizn' i tsarstvovanie.* S.-Peterburg: A. S. Suvorin, 1903. 2 volumes.

    A detailed biography of Nicholas I, with much information on his childhood and youth. Schil'der reproduces many original documents and source materials, and there are many illustrations. Schil'der wrote similarly detailed works on Paul I (*Imperator Pavel Pervyĭ: istoriko-biograficheskiĭ ocherk;* S.-Peterburg: Suvorin, 1901) and Alexander I (*Imperator Aleksandr Pervyĭ, ego zhizn' i tsarstvovanie;* S.-Peterburg: Suvorin, 1897–98, 4 volumes).

Szeftel, Marc. "Le Statut juridique de l'enfant en Russi e avant Pierre le Grand." *Recueils de la Société Jean Bodin pour l'histoire comparative des institutions,* vol. 36, pp. 635–656. Bruxelles: Editions de la Librarie encyclopédique, 1976.

    A paper on the legal position of children in Russian families, based on Old Russian sources from the Kievan and Muscovite periods. All the papers in this volume deal with the legal position of children; there are contributions on Hungary, Romania, and Poland, as well as for the western European countries.

Zenzinov, Vladimir. *Bezprizornye.* Paris: Sovremennyia zapiski, 1929. 318 pp. Trans. Agnes Platt as *Deserted: The Story of the Children Abandoned in Soviet Russia.* Westport, Conn.: Hyperion Press, 1975. viii, 216 pp:

A study of the causes and effects of child and adolescent abandonment and delinquency during the revolution and civil war years, based primarily on the author's personal observations. Includes a short bibliography.

PERIODICALS

Bratskaia pomoshch': zhurnal blagotvoritel'nosti, tiur'moviedieniia, i narodnago zdraviia. 1888–1903. Saratov. Weekly.

Obshchestvennaia i chastnaia blagotvoritel'nost' v Rossii. 1912, nos. 1–11. S.-Peterburg. (Continued by *Prizrienie i blagotvoritel'nost' v Rossii.*)

Prizrienie i blagotvoritel'nost' v Rossii. 1913–17. S.-Peterburg: Vserossiĭskiĭ soiuz uchrezhdeniĭ, obshchestv i dieiateleĭ po obshchestvennomu i chastnomu prizrieniiu. Monthly.

Trudovaia pomoshch'. 1897–1917. S.-Peterburg: Komitet popechitel'stva o domakh trudoliubiia i rabotnykh domakh. Monthly.

Viestnik blagotvoritel'nosti. 1897–1902. S.-Peterburg: Tsentral'noe upravlenie dietskikh priiutov Viedomstva Imp. Marii. Monthly.

VIII.   WORKING CLASS; WORKING-CLASS FAMILY

A. M. Gor'kiĭ i sozdanie istorii fabrik i zavodov: sbornik dokumentov i materialov v pomoshch' rabotaiushchim nad istorieĭ fabrik i zavodov SSSR. Comp. L. M. Zak, S. S. Zimina. Moskva: Izd-vo sotsial'no-ekonomicheskoi literatury, 1959. 362 pp.

A detailed guide to archival materials on factories and factory workers, primarily from the Soviet period, but including prerevolutionary Russia as well.

Istoriia sovetskogo obshchestva v vospominaniiakh sovremennikov, 1917–1957: annotirovannyi ukazatel' memuarnoi literatury. Moskva: Kniga, 1958–67. 2 volumes in 3.

An exhaustive guide to workers' published memoirs from one of the richest memoir periods. Volume 1 includes separately published books and articles in *sborniki*, 1917–57; volume 2, part 1, contains memoirs published as periodical articles from 1917 to 1927, and volume 2, part 2, lists the periodical literature from 1928 to 1957.

Harold M. Leich and June Pachuta

Krupianskaia, V. Iu, and N. S. Polishchuk. *Kul'tura i byt rabochikh gornozavodskogo Urala, konets XIX— nachalo XX veka.* Moskva: Nauka, 1971. 288 pp.

A detailed ethnographic study of working-class life in the industrializing countryside of the Nizhnii Tagil region.

Kruze, E. E. *Peterburgskie rabochie v 1912–1914 godakh.* Moskva: Izd-vo Akademii nauk SSSR, 1961. 343 pp.

A study of the social and economic aspects of workers' life in St. Petersburg, with many references to published and archival sources.

Rabochiĭ klass i rabochee dvizhenie v Rossii, 1861–1917. Ed. L. M. Ivanov. Moskva: Nauka, 1966. 409 pp.

Sixteen papers on various aspects of the working class from 1850 to the Revolution, originally presented at the All-Union Conference on the History of the Russian Proletariat in Rostov-on-Don, 1963. The papers provide a good orientation to a number of issues in the area of the working class, including periodization, published and archival sources, and the relations between workers and bourgeoisie and the government. An article by L. M. Ivanov, "Preemstvennost' fabrichnozavodskogo truda i formirovanie proletariata v Rossii" (pp. 58–140), studies the characteristics of working-class life, including family life.

Rashin, A. G. *Formirovanie rabochego klassa Rossii: istoriko-ekonomicheskie ocherki.* Moskva: Izd-vo sotsial'no-ekonomicheskoi literatury, 1958. 622 pp.

A comprehensive work on the formation, history, and conditions of the Russian working class, with many valuable statistical tables and references to statistical sources for the study of the working class. Contains a chapter and several statistical tables on child labor in pre-revolutionary Russia.

Zelnik, Reginald E. *Labor and Society in Tsarist Russia; The Factory Workers of St. Petersburg, 1855–1870.* Stanford: Stanford University Press, 1971.

Among the best comprehensive views of the urban working class, treating its origins, living conditions, efforts at education of workers, and early labor organization.

IX. CLERGY

"Dukhovenstvo." *Entsiklopedicheskii slovar'.* S.-Peterburg: Izd. F. A. Brokgauz, I. A. Efron, 1893. Vol. 11, pp. 253–267.

A basic article on the history of the Orthodox clergy in Russia, discussing the various ranks of clergy, their administration, and the reforms of the clerical estate. Separate sections discuss the clergy in Little Russia (Ukraine), the contemporary clergy, the "black" clergy, and the clergy of other Slavic Christians in Russia. Most sections are signed by the contributing author. There are selective bibliographies.

Freeze, Gregory L. "The Disintegration of Traditional Communities: The Parish in Eighteenth-Century Russia." *Journal of Modern History*, 48, no. 1 (1976): 32–50.

Examines the disintegration of the traditional parish community, discussing the economic, social, and cultural functions of the parish and its forced reorganization. There are extensive bibliographic notes.

————. "Social Mobility and the Russian Parish Clergy in the Eighteenth Century." *Slavic Review*, 33, no. 4 (1974): 641–662.

Traces the development of the clerical estate from one of upward and open mobility in the seventeenth century to a gradual restriction in mobility by the end of the eighteenth century. The changing status of the clergy and the position of its children are discussed. Extensive notes are particularly valuable to the beginning student in this area for their definitions.

Papkov, A. *Tserkovno-obshchestvennye voprosy v epokhu tsaria-osvobo-ditelia, 1855–1870.* S.-Peterburg: Tip. A. P. Lopukhina, 1902. 184 pp. (Reprinted with an introduction by G. Florovsky. Farmborough: Gregg International Publishers, 1972.)

A history of the Russian Orthodox parish in the broader context of the social history of Russia during the reign of Alexander II, with particular emphasis on parish structure and its reorganization. Improvement of the material life of the clergy, the reform of church schools, and the social status of the clergy and its civil rights are also examined. There are extensive bibliographic notes.

Znamenskii, I. *Polozhenie dukhovenstva v tsarstvovanie Ekateriny II i Pavla I; sochinenie.* Moskva: Tip. M. N. Lavrova, 1880. 184 pp.

Examines the rise of the Russian Orthodox clergy, the conflict between church and governmental powers, reforms, and the rights and privileges granted to the clergy in the eighteenth century. Notes.

Znamenskii, P. V. *Prikhodskoe dukhovenstvo v Rossii so vremeni reformy Petra.* Kazan': Univ. tip., 1873. 850 pp.

One of the few comprehensive studies of the clergy, ranging from the time of Peter through the reign of Alexander II. Using mainly legal sources, the author examines both the ordained clergy and lay churchmen, the civil rights of the clergy, its methods of support, and its administration. Bibliographic notes.

Contributors

PETER CZAP, JR., Professor of History, Amherst College

STEPHEN P. DUNN, Director of Research, Highgate Road Social Science Research Station

BARBARA ALPERN ENGEL, Assistant Professor of History, University of Colorado

GREGORY L. FREEZE, Associate Professor of History, Brandeis University

NANCY M. FRIEDEN, Assistant Professor of History, Mount Holyoke College

ROBERT EUGENE JOHNSON, Assistant Professor of History, University of Toronto

DIANE KOENKER, Assistant Professor of History, Temple University

HAROLD M. LEICH, Assistant Professor of Library Administration and Slavic Acquisitions Librarian, University of Illinois at Urbana-Champaign

ANTONINA MARTYNOVA, Research Associate, Folklore Section, Institute of Russian Literature (Pushkinskii Dom), Leningrad

ANDREJS PLAKANS, Associate Professor of History, Iowa State University

JUNE PACHUTA, Assistant Professor of Library Administration and Slavic Bibliographer, University of Illinois at Urbana-Champaign

SAMUEL C. RAMER, Assistant Professor of History, Tulane University

DAVID L. RANSEL, Associate Professor of History, University of Illinois at Urbana-Champaign

JESSICA TOVROV, Graduate Student, University of Chicago

RICHARD WORTMAN, Professor of History, Princeton University

Index

339